Educational leadership and learning

Educational leadership and learning

Practice, policy and research

Sue Law and Derek Glover

Open University Press
Buckingham · Philadelphia

Open University Press
Celtic Court
22 Ballmoor
Buckingham
MK18 1XW

email: enquiries@openup.co.uk
world wide web: www.openup.co.uk

and

325 Chestnut Street
Philadelphia, PA 19106, USA

First Published 2000
Reprinted 2001, 2003

Copyright © Sue Law and Derek Glover, 2000

A catalogue record of this book is available from the British Library

ISBN 0 335 19752 3 (pb) 0 335 19753 1 (hb)

Library of Congress Cataloging-in-Publication Data
Law, Sue.
    Educational leadership and learning: practice, policy, and
research / Sue Law and Derek Glover.
        p. cm.
    Includes bibliographical references (p.) and index.
    ISBN 0–335–19753–1 (hard). – ISBN 0–335–19752–3 (pbk.)
    1. Educational leadership–Great Britain. 2. School management
and organization–Great Britain. 3. School administrators–Great
Britain. I. Glover, Derek. II. Title.
LB2900.5.L39 1999
371.2'00941–dc21   99–15326
                                                          CIP

Typeset by Graphicraft Ltd, Hong Kong
Printed and bound in Great Britain by Biddles Ltd, www.biddles.co.uk

List of abbreviations

ACSET	Advisory Committee on the Supply and Education of Teachers
AST	Advanced Skills Teacher
BECTA	British Educational Communications and Technology Agency
C&IT	communications and information technology
CPD	continuing professional development
CTC	City Technology College
DES	Department of Education and Science
DfE	Department for Education
DfEE	Department for Education and Employment
ERA	Education Reform Act 1988
ESM	Effective Schools Movement
FEFC	Further Education Funding Council
GCE	General Certificate of Education
GCSE	General Certificate of Secondary Education
GM	grant-maintained
GMC	General Medical Council
GMS	grant-maintained school(s)
GNVQ	General National Vocational Qualification
GRIDS	Guidelines for Review and Internal Development in Schools
GTC	General Teaching Council
HEADLAMP	Headteacher Leadership and Management Programme
HEI	higher education institution (universities and colleges)
HMCI	Her Majesty's Chief Inspector (of schools)
HMI	Her Majesty's Inspectorate
HRM	human resource management
ICT	information and communications technology
IIP	Investors in People
INSET	in-service education and training
IT	information technology
ITE	initial teacher education
ITT	initial teacher training
LEA	local education authority

LFM	local financial management
LMS	local management of schools
LPC	least prefered co-worker
LPSH	Leadership Programme for Serving Headteachers
MA	Master of Arts
MBA	Master of Business Administration
MIS	management information systems
NC	National Curriculum
NCITT	National Curriculum for Initial Teacher Training
NGfL	National Grid for Learning
NPM	New Public Management
NPQH	National Professional Qualification for Headteachers
NQT	newly qualified teacher
Ofsted	Office for Standards in Education
PD	professional development
PDC	professional development coordinator
PRP	performance-related pay
PSE	personal and social education
QA	quality assurance
RoA	Records of Achievement
SATs	Standard Assessment Tasks
SDP	strategic development plan
SEN	special educational needs
SMART	strategic, measurable, achievable, realistic, time-related
SMTF	School Management Task Force
TA	transactional analysis
TEC	Training and Enterprise Councils
TQM	total quality management
TTA	Teacher Training Agency
TVEI	Technical and Vocational Education Initiative

Contents

Acknowledgements

We have endeavoured to root this book in our own professional learning, personal experience and occupational practices as teachers and managers in a wide variety of educational organizations – schools, colleges and universities. We have learnt much about the nature of leadership and management in our day-to-day work with colleagues, but also owe a considerable debt to the course members with whom we have worked on various Master of Business Administration (MBA) and Master of Arts (MA) education management programmes. The professional commitment and rigour shown by these colleagues has not only challenged our views and helped us explore educational leadership and management issues, but has shown us that effective educational leaders *can* make a difference. For us, the biggest difference they make is to create a structure of support for others – whether students or staff – in all sorts of predictable and unpredictable ways. In addition to these colleagues, we are also grateful to our Open University Press commissioning editor, Shona Mullen, for her patience and tolerance, and to Jackie Pedley for her secretarial support with the bibliography. Lastly, this book could not have been written without the longstanding commitment and support of our respective families – both offspring and partners – who have unselfishly encouraged us in the face of very many other distractions and demands. Needless to say, all errors of both fact and judgement remain ours alone.

Sue Law and Derek Glover

Part I

Leading and managing

1 The context for educational leadership

Leaders learn by leading and they learn best by leading in the face of obstacles.
As weather shapes mountains, so problems make leaders.

(Bennis 1989: 37)

Exploring the context

A group of retired headteachers (all male and all of whom had taken up their first headship some two decades ago) were reminiscing about their appointments. One recalled that he had been appointed after touring the school, being given copies of two previous governors' reports, and 'sitting in on a very polite forty-minute interview'. Another recalled sitting in the secretary's office (which served as both waiting room and candidates' reception), only to hear her say on the phone to County Hall, 'yes . . . he's arrived and I think he's just what we are looking for', while a third recalled the interview panel asking him if he 'knew much about girls' (this being a mixed school) and 'could he cope with them?' Clearly, some things have changed over the past twenty years!

While such 'traditional' practices undoubtedly remain in certain areas, the marketization of education over the past decade has ensured that candidates for senior education posts now often face very different challenges. Nowadays, aspiring organizational leaders need to demonstrate the professional competences deemed necessary to lead and manage complex organizations in a quasi-market educational environment (Le Grand and Bartlett 1993), as well as articulate a clear philosophy as educational professionals. More problematically perhaps, they need to convince their appointing panel that they can reconcile the concepts of 'professionalism' and 'managerialism' – by integrating or at least harmonizing a 'leading professional' focus with the 'chief executive' role (Hughes 1972, 1988; Ribbins 1995). Overlying all of this, they need to show how they can *live their rhetoric* during increasingly rigorous and sophisticated selection procedures.

England, among other industrialized Western countries, is in the midst of 'a phase of deep transition' (Ranson 1994), where incrementalism and the predictable gradualism of change – what Galbraith (1992) has described as 'the culture of contentment' – has been replaced by 'discontinuous change' (Handy 1989). The notion that Western society is moving into a postmodern age has become increasingly influential in the growing international literature on public service management in general (see, for example, Osborne and Gaebler 1992; Burrows and Loader 1994; Dunleavy and Hood 1994), and educational literature in particular (e.g. Beare and Lowe Boyd 1993; Smyth 1993; Whitty *et al.* 1998). The seeming predictabilities of the postwar education settlement in England, which had stressed stability, hierarchy and specialized functions, are now being superseded by tensions, pressures and uncertainties emanating largely from the economic and social crises of the 1970s and 1980s. Educational development over the past decade has, therefore, been framed by a socio-political context characterized by:

- growing consumerism, client-power and customer-orientation;
- a developing 'knowledge revolution', 'information age' and 'learning society' characterized by an 'information explosion' and emphasis on 'lifelong learning';
- the dramatic impact of new information and communications technology on organizational structures, strategies and relationships;
- growing short-termist, profit-focused practices;
- increasingly globalized and intensified competition;
- increasingly global economic turbulence arising through, for example, takeovers, currency realignments, financial deregulation;
- the growing use of regulatory power as a frame for business practice.

These shifts are nevertheless articulated in a language redolent with a combination of both the earlier predictabilities and current uncertainties ('*post*-modernist', '*post*-Fordist' and '*post*-industrialist'), reflecting, perhaps, the difficulties we now face in articulating the sheer pace of change. Within this context, there is evidence that a significant number of, but by no means all, school leaders and teachers have cautiously welcomed many of the post-1988 reforms and the opportunities brought by delegated management (Caldwell and Spinks 1992, 1998; Levačić 1995; Hall 1996). The difficulties created by the new market environment are, however, also highlighted, both in terms of the fundamental philosophies underpinning change and the practicalities involved in its introduction (Ranson 1994; Grace 1995; Whitty *et al.* 1998). For example, education is criticized for turning too readily for answers to 'business' practices, theories and research. Indeed, despite demands for more integrated and 'home grown' education management theory in education, it has become largely reliant and dependent on business for its management theories and frameworks (Davies 1990; Bottery 1992; Grace 1995).

While we need to recognize that a number of 'commercial' concepts may be applicable to education scenarios as it becomes more market-driven, it is clear that there are no ready-made or universally applicable theories we can simply 'pull off the shelf'. As Bottery (1992: 127) has argued, if we are going to develop education management both in practice and theory, we must acknowledge the centrality of professionalism, reject 'the quick prescription' and accept that management concepts 'are not the kind of things which can be taken down ready-made from the shelf and bolted onto the educational organization. *They must be moulded, adapted, re-invented almost*' (our italics). Although the relatively limited development of 'homegrown' education management theories may be partially explained by the fact that, until the late 1980s, demonstrable 'business acumen' was not required of headteachers, this ignores the fact that educational leaders have needed to demonstrate people management skills as a key aspect of their *primus inter pares* role for many years. Indeed, it may be that it is precisely these 'people' strengths that, over the past decade, have enabled headteachers to temper the worst excesses of market-driven managerialism in their schools and colleges.

Leading professionals and chief executives?

Despite assertions that the reorientation of education is 'deskilling', 'depro-fessionalizing' and 'proletarianizing' teachers (Lawn and Ozga 1988), re-creating them as skilled technicians rather than reflexive professionals (A. Hargreaves 1994; Codd 1996), a strong and important emphasis on teacher *professionalism* remains in education (Elliot 1990; Hoyle and John 1995; Thompson 1997), reflecting the longstanding commitment to and existence of 'extended' rather than 'restricted' notions of professionality (Hoyle 1974). While some educa-tionists have attracted a mixture of both criticism and praise for articulating a 'desire for teachers to be seen as technologists rather than as philosopher kings' (Reynolds 1998), it is essential that we consider whether an emphasis on a foundation of skilled technical expertise can actually *support* rather than *inhibit* concepts of teacher professionalism. In our view, educational leaders (and teachers) can and should readily embody an *integration* of technical, pedagogic, professional and managerial skills – characterizing, perhaps, what Hughes (1988) has described as the 'professional-as-administrator', albeit a role underpinned by a clearer focus on technical competence.

Hughes (1972) characterizes the 'professional-as-administrator' as encom-passing both 'chief executive' and 'leading professional' roles: 'the simul-taneous activation of two sub-roles which deeply inter-penetrate each other', incorporating 'internal and external aspects to both role conceptions' (Hughes 1988: 14). Importantly, Hughes's research found that 'significantly. . . elements of the two sub-roles were related to each other so that, as suspected, the notional separation into distinct sub-roles proves to be no more than a convenient heuristic device' (p. 14). Indeed, 'It seems that the professional-as-administrator does not act in some matters as a leading professional and in others as a chief executive. Professional knowledge, skills and attitudes are likely to have a profound effect on the whole range of tasks undertaken by the head of a professional organization' (Hughes 1988: 15). Building on Hughes's conception of educational leadership, we offer our own picture of the *duality* of roles in Figure 1.1. While this book acknowledges the com-plexities and difficulties inherent in combining both leading professional and chief executive roles, its argument is that effective educational leaders are capable of (and frequently do) combine *both* aspects. Rather than being mutually exclusive, they can be mutually reinforcing and complementary – helping to create a vital professional synergy.

The heightened profile of the 'chief executive' role in educational leader-ship in the post-1988 era has led some to call for a formal disagregation of 'professional' and 'executive' roles (D. H. Hargreaves 1994). However, the implications of such a role division raise significant questions about the underlying nature of professionalism and its relationship with leadership and management: it is arguable that, within the current policy milieu, really effective headteachers are those able to create synergy out of both 'leading

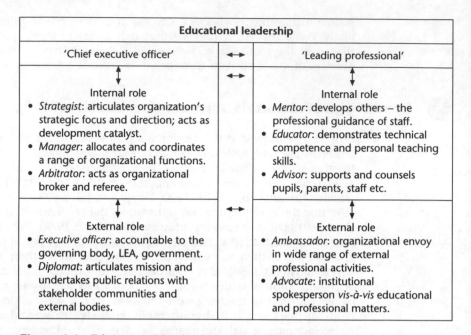

Figure 1.1 Educational leadership: the duality of roles.

professional' roles and 'chief executive' responsibilities (Ribbins 1995; Hall 1996; Law 1999).

The language of reform has undoubtedly reframed educational management around business-related concepts: we now speak of 'competences' rather than 'knowledge', of teacher 'training' rather than 'education' and of 'curriculum delivery' rather than pedagogy. The overt threat to teacher professionalism that this represents might be countered by the fact that much that is central to day-to-day classroom practice remains within the ambit of teachers' professional judgements – despite the growth of teacher accountability. Despite the best efforts of educational policy makers and Office for Standards in Education (Ofsted) inspectors, classrooms remain the teachers' professional domain.

The nature of the tension between professionalism and managerialism also highlights the centrality of '*appropriate* leadership in promoting an ethos of professional and organizational well-being – echoing Brighouse's (1986) ideal of the '*perceptive professional developer*' as educational leader, supported by '*critical friends*' rather than 'hostile witnesses' or 'uncritical lovers' (Brighouse and Woods 1999).

REFLECTION

How far, in your view, is teaching becoming 'deskilled' and/or 'deprofessionalized', with teachers as little more than 'technicians'? How far does your own principal or headteacher exemplify the synergy of both 'chief executive' and 'leading professional' roles?

The gender agenda: change yet . . . no change?

Although the managerialist agenda now framing educational policy making has impacted in substantial ways on the working practices, traditions and philosophies of schools and colleges, some aspects of education remain relatively unchanged. Despite the dramatic impact and growth of information and communications technology (ICT) in society at large, many classrooms, staffrooms, schools and colleges still look like and operate in remarkably similar ways to those of two decades ago and more. Moreover, while the rhetoric of site management may have a high profile, some aspects of educational management practice have seen only limited change: for example, the recruitment of women to senior education management positions remains slow (Al Khalifa 1992; Ouston 1993; Dunlap and Schmuck 1995; Coleman 1997), as does the recruitment of ethnic minority groups (Mortimore and Mortimore 1991). Even though the 'new managerialist' agenda driving education and framing teachers' work has encouraged a re-evaluation of educational leadership, its impact in these areas remains barely perceptible.

Despite the so-called 'feminization' of education management, gender issues have, for example, only relatively recently gained any serious research attention (e.g. Evetts 1990, 1994; Ouston 1993; Hall 1996) – having, in Hall's colourful imagery, 'hovered in the wings like a wallflower at a party'. There has been no 'shattering of the glass ceiling' (Davidson 1992) and no smashing of the so-called 'concrete ceiling' which confronts many would-be women managers from the ethnic minorities (Davidson 1997), even though there are some recently claimed sightings of 'small cracks' in educational ceilings (Howson 1998). In addition, studies of women heads who seem to have 'danced on the ceiling' are now appearing (Evetts 1994; Hall 1996). Nevertheless, in the early 1990s, women comprised 80 per cent of primary teachers but only 50 per cent of primary heads (DES 1991). More recently, while women now comprise 76 per cent of primary teachers, the number of female primary heads is little changed. In secondary schools, while 52 per cent of teachers are women, they comprised only 24 per cent of secondary heads in 1996 (2 per cent higher than in 1992) (Howson 1998).

People and systems

Achieving and maintaining a balance between 'management as systems' and 'management as people' undoubtedly becomes difficult in a constrained financial environment. Nevertheless, while systems are necessary, they are not sufficient for effective management: ultimately, organizational systems can only be as good as the people 'operating' them. Even in our increasingly technologically sophisticated world, systems are not yet (and arguably may never be) flexible or creative enough to second guess professional judgement. In future, creative and successful managers in education are likely to maximize and combine the potential which arises from the 'predictability' of organizational systems with the 'chaos' of human ingenuity and spontaneity. It is the ambition of this book to support and encourage that creative balance.

Because we consider that both *people* and *systems* are crucial for organizational and personal success, this book emphasizes several key notions:

1 People are crucial: they are often dynamic, but can also be unpredictable.
2 Systems are important: they are essentially predictable, but tend to become undynamic.
3 Management is complex: balancing dynamism and predictability is difficult because changing contexts strongly influence outcomes.
4 Reflection and reflexivity is essential: evaluating what we do engenders supportive, creative and effective development for both individuals and their organizations.

On this basis, effective educational institutions need organizational frameworks which are acknowledged as dynamic: providing scope for imagination and ingenuity but offering a relatively rational framework for development. To rely too heavily on 'the system' or to place too much emphasis on 'people skills' is to risk organizational incoherence. The headteacher who is 'brilliant with parents and a very good front man' but 'is no good at dealing with the budget . . . he tends to dish out money on an *ad hoc* basis, depending who's just bent his ear', is, in fact, neither maximizing the school's effectiveness nor supporting his colleagues and pupils as well as he might.

Strategies and styles

The book emphasizes the value of leadership *strategies* rather than implicitly fixed leadership *styles*. Rather than seeing management in terms of autocratic or democratic styles (with managers moving from one to another), we focus on management strategies rooted in a professional rather than managerial ethos. Effective managers draw upon a wide range of personalized management 'strategies', whether in classrooms or the wider school context. They know how and when to utilize professional judgement, when to 'push', when to 'support' and when to give others opportunities to lead. In fast-changing educational settings, both teachers and managers need the synergy deriving from an interplay of skills, knowledge and judgement to determine how students and staff might maximize their potential.

In our view, the roots of effective educational management lie within its professional ethos: if management practice operates without a clear ethical dimension, it becomes rootless, managerialist and potentially destructive. This is crucial, for example, when decisions which emphasize 'cost-effectiveness' and 'value for money' are not necessarily educationally desirable. We need to understand both the costs and the value of management decisions and actions: educational organizations driven largely by cost imperatives, where values issues become subsumed, are likely to alienate their own internal communities of staff and students, and become separated from their wider communities.

Who is the book for?

This book aims to encourage readers to take an active and creative approach to their personal and professional development. While it may be of most interest to those in middle or senior education management, it is also designed to help teachers, governors and those in organizations allied with education. If management theory is to be genuinely valuable it will speak to teachers as well as managers; it will also be beneficial to pupils and students and will be a force for greater institutional democracy. Individual leaders, like individual teachers, will become powerful catalysts for change if their management strategies support others' responsibilities, enhance organization effectiveness and improve each individual's personal professional skills.

In our view, effective leaders are those who, often in the most basic of ways, create opportunities and galvanize commitment, encouraging colleagues into action so that collaborative effort becomes rewarding and important. The book may be of value to those endeavouring to match the Teacher Training Agency's (TTA) National Standards for Headteachers (TTA 1998a) and Subject Leaders (TTA 1998b) since its focus is on practitioner improvement – the development of leadership capability and the enhancement of professional knowledge and understanding – encouraging a reflective focus on experience and skills development. As such, we have tried to ensure that the book's structure and layout demonstrates the value of reflection and review through the integration of practice-based learning and theoretical frameworks. For example, most chapters offer 'stimulus points', based on:

- *Cameos*: 'issue' scenarios based on actual experience; designed to provoke questions and possible learning points by encouraging you to think how you might respond in similar circumstances.
- *Reflections*: designed to pursue theoretical points made in the text; asking you to relate issues to your own particular experiences.
- *Actions*: practical activities which you might wish to pursue within your own professional context in order to test ideas against evidence.

In essence, this book endeavours to:

- combine evidence with analysis, providing an integrated approach to theory, practice and research;
- explore issues in coherent ways, using accessible language;
- present current and relevant research findings in ways which are pertinent for those managing in education.

The book is loosely divided into three parts, although each chapter is also constructed in such a way as will allow readers to 'dip' into them separately.

Part I: Leading and managing

This part provides a framework for the rest of the book and examines the variety of relationships between individuals, groups and the organization as a whole. While Chapter 1 offers an overview and briefly delineates the social, political and educational context within which management now takes place, Chapter 2 explores the concepts framing management tasks and responsibilities in educational organizations. The nature of individual responsibilities and roles and self-management concerns are considered in Chapter 3. We then move on, in Chapter 4, to examine the concept of motivation in detail. Chapter 5 then assesses the value of teamwork and how individuals, groups and teams work within the changing organizational context of education.

Part II: Changing and learning

Recognizing that the process of management can often be strongly influenced by concerns and issues beyond our control, this part of the book begins, in Chapter 6, by exploring the importance of effective communication. Chapter 7 then examines the concept of organizational culture and its centrality to effective institutional development, while Chapter 8 reviews different strategies for managing change and how far they can stimulate innovation and creativity at both individual and organizational levels. While Chapter 9 examines how far the current focus on educational effectiveness and school improvement is supported by a prescriptive inspection regime, the last chapter in this part, Chapter 10, explores how far the notion of the 'learning organization' is becoming a reality in educational institutions.

Part III: Tasks and responsibilities

This section acknowledges the importance of reflecting on particular management roles and responsibilities in order to maintain organizational processes and practices, both internally as supportive and healthy organizations, and externally as responsive and accountable organizations. If management is to be fully creative and innovative, then productive and high quality staff management becomes crucial – an issue we explore in Chapter 11. We assess, in Chapter 12, how far resource and financial management strategies can be utilized productively to maximize the benefits for organizations and those who work in them. Chapter 13 assesses the changing nature of stakeholder partnerships and relationships and examines power balances across the education system as a whole. Chapter 14 then examines the nature and implications of professional development, exploring how far it represents a realistic springboard for future personal, professional and organizational success.

The focus of the book

At a time of endemic change, when professional autonomy and public accountability are key issues, this book endeavours to provide a supportive but not uncritical structure for those committed to personal–professional learning in pursuing management responsibilities, whether as middle or senior education managers, while acknowledging the policy context within which they operate. While a variety of perspectives abound regarding the value and impact of what is variously called 'New Public Management' (NPM) (Pollitt 1993),

'new managerialism' and 'the new education management' (Whitty *et al.*
1998), it is our view that those undertaking educational leadership roles in
the twenty-first century will need a complex skills mix, a secure knowledge
base and a reflexivity which enables them to work through the demands and
tensions between 'managerialism' and 'professionalism'.

Despite the plethora of books over the past decade which seemingly 'sell
the secrets of education management success', educational management is
not simply about magic or quick fixes: if only it was that simple! Notions of
'management by ringbinder' (Halpin 1990), the growth of 'how to' management books and the popularity of 'management biographies' written by
'successful leaders' with a 'guru touch' can threaten the seriousness with which
those in education approach their management responsibilities, whether at
classroom, departmental or whole-school levels. Management learning is not
simply a question of following ready-made 'management maps'. While it
may adopt 'discovery' approaches, this is often because we are provoked to
ask hard questions of ourselves and others. The changing nature of these
questions has been investigated by Caldwell and Spinks (1998), who look
towards the management demands on teachers and educational leaders in a
new millennium.

There is growing acknowledgement that while education managers need
to offer high quality leadership for organizational effectiveness, management
development is an iterative process (Bolam 1997). Ultimately, leaders and
managers achieve little on their own, whether on the basis of 'charisma' or
hard work: effective managers and leaders are those surrounded by effective
followers and collaborators. As Barth (1990) has observed, the principal needs
to be seen as 'the head learner'. It is this process of professional learning and
'becoming effective' which is crucial – for followers as well as leaders – and
which we are concerned with in this book. We provide neither ready-made
'route maps' nor 'magic potions', since management is about effectiveness
within a given *context* as much as about having all-encompassing *skills* and
knowledge. It is about asking the right questions more than offering the
'correct' answers. It enables us to appreciate and extend the scope and
parameters of both individual and group opportunities – a vital focus if we
want to affect the future – for ourselves, our colleagues, our students and the
communities in which we work and live.

This books focuses on practical purposes and has benefited from our work
with very many energetic and thoughtful colleagues from schools, colleges
and universities as they have pursued MBA and MA programmes in education management or have worked with us on a variety of school-focused
professional development projects. They have helped us to examine and
assess the many perspectives and many complexities which now frame
educational management and its development. As a new millennium dawns,
we are confident that, judging by our experience, the vast majority of those
leading and managing in education will maintain and enhance the highest
standards of professionalism, while showing they are both competent and
considerate in their approach to their management responsibilities.

The most reliable way to anticipate the future is by understanding the
present.

(Naisbett 1984: 37)

● Suggestions for further reading

Bottery, M. (1992) *The Ethics of Educational Management*. London: Cassell.

Hargreaves, A. and Evans, R. (eds) (1997) *Beyond Educational Reform: Bringing Teachers Back In*. Buckingham: Open University Press.

Richards, C. and Taylor, P. (eds) (1998) *How Shall We School our Children? The Future of Primary Education*. Lewes: Falmer Press.

Strain, M., Dennison, B., Ouston, J. and Hall, V. (eds) (1998) *Policy, Leadership and Professional Knowledge in Education*. London: Paul Chapman Publishing.

Tomlinson, S. (ed.) (1994) *Educational Reform and Its Consequences*. London: IPPR/ Rivers Oram Press.

Whitty, G., Power, S. and Halpin, D. (1998) *Devolution and Choice in Education: the School, the State and the Market*. Buckingham: Open University Press.

② Developing leadership and management effectiveness

Culture and structure, leadership and management: all are necessary if an organization is to become highly effective.

(Schein 1985: 171)

● Leadership and management

Although there has been much debate over the differences between *leadership* and *management*, the terms tend to be used interchangeably: agreement over definition – or even the nuances of distinction – is not easily reached. Leadership is frequently seen as an aspect of management, with 'real leaders' often characterized as charismatic individuals with visionary flair and the ability to motivate and enthuse others – even if they lack the managerial or administrative skills to plan, organize effectively or control resources. On this basis, it is often argued that managers simply need to be good at everything that leaders are not!

Kotter (1989) argues that leadership and management functions can be separated out fairly clearly according to context: for him, strategic development is a key function of leadership for change, while day-to-day problem-solving is clearly a management function. He sees 'institutionalizing a leadership-centred culture' as essential because it motivates and empowers people. Leadership is also seen as a cohesive force by Armstrong (1994: 165), because even simple management tasks are complex and involve a combination of elements: 'All managers are by definition leaders in that they can only do what they have to do with the support of their team, who must be inspired or persuaded to follow them.' Effective leadership, then, presupposes effective teamwork.

Bennis and Nanus's (1985) research has identified that a 'range of talents' is central to highly successful leadership, and this includes fostering a culture of trust, developing an openness to learning, encouraging and stimulating staff learning and communicating organizational aims/vision with clarity. Where leaders were successful, they argued, staff acknowledged their responsibilities and accountabilities. In his assessment of the prospects for educational change, Fullan (1991: 157) argues that while *leadership* 'relates to mission, direction, inspiration', *management* 'involves designing and carrying out plans, getting things done, working effectively with people' (p. 158).

Table 2.1   Distinctions between leadership and management

Management	Leadership
'Building and maintaining an organizational structure' (Schein 1985)	'Building and maintaining an organizational culture' (Schein 1985)
'Path-following' (Hodgson 1987)	'Path-finding' (Hodgson 1987)
'Doing things right' (Bennis and Nanus 1985)	'Doing the right things' (Bennis and Nanus 1985)
'The manager maintains . . . relies on control' (Bennis 1989)	'The leader develops . . . inspires trust' (Bennis 1989)
'A preoccupation with the here-and-now of goal attainment' (Bryman 1986)	'Focused on the creation of a vision about a desired future state' (Bryman 1986)
'Managers maintain a low level of emotional involvement' (Zaleznik 1977)	'Leaders have empathy with other people and give attention to what events and actions mean' (Zaleznik 1977)
'Designing and carry out plans, getting things done, working effectively with people' (Louis and Miles 1992)	'Establishing a mission . . . giving a sense of direction' (Louis and Miles 1992)
'Being taught by the organization' (Hodgson 1987)	'Learning from the organization' (Hodgson 1987)

These views are reinforced by some of the typical distinctions which are drawn between leadership and management in the management literature (see Table 2.1).

In reality, the distinctions between *management* and *leadership* are not so clearly defined. As high profile educational leaders are increasingly pressurized to use both human and material resources more creatively, the integration of these roles for those charged with leading, managing and even administering policy decision making has produced greater pressures. In our view, each of these functions – leadership, management or administration – requires different, but *overlapping*, skills, knowledge and abilities. For example, the minutiae of budget details are definitely not normally a central leadership concern, since the focus is on determining overall areas of expenditure to achieve institutional aims. While some budgetary detail is important for managers allocating specific resources to support policy, the minutiae are absolutely crucial for those actually administering and tracking resources and expenditure. The extent to which we are all involved as leaders, managers and administrators is suggested in Table 2.2: it needs to be emphasized that the presentation is schematic and does not try to incorporate all organizational roles or staff. It may, however, help us to reflect on the nature of leadership, management and administration across various institutional roles.

'Teaching' educational leadership

Aside from questions about the differences between leadership, management and administration and a review of what precisely leaders and managers do, we need to consider briefly the extent to which leadership and management can be 'taught' and 'learnt'. This has major policy and professional implications, especially since the government and TTA in England has recently

Table 2.2 Leadership, management and administration in educational organizations: a possible outline

	Principal/headteacher	Subject leader/coordinator	Class teacher/course leader
Focus	Whole school/college	Subject department	Curriculum delivery
Through	Institutional development plan	Departmental development plan	Schemes of work
Leadership	Vision	Departmental aims	Classroom tone
	Aims and objectives	Targets	Subject mission
	Strategy	Resource bidding	Teaching and learning
	Team formation	Team cohesion	style
	Organizational policies	Subject policies	
Management	Overall control of resource base	Resource allocation	Materials development
		Subject staff development	
	Overall development of staff	Curriculum organization	Resource use
		Monitoring and evaluation	Curriculum tracking
		Student progress	Student assessment
Administration	Responsible, but not active	Staff records	Student records
		Resource tracking	Teaching and learning
		Lists, lists, lists!	records

invested substantial resources on the assumption that education managers can be trained to be more effective leaders largely on the basis of competence assessment and skills development (DfEE 1997a; TTA 1997).

The growth of emphasis on training means that the 'teaching' of educational management and leadership – what Grace (1995) calls 'education management studies' (which, he argues, is accompanied by its own language, assumptions and ideology) – has thus become a major growth area in both education and educational publishing post-1988. (No doubt this book will also be seen as serving such a market!) The TTA is currently either introducing or revamping several major leadership and management programmes, e.g. for aspiring heads (the National Professional Qualification for Headteachers, NPQH), for newly appointed heads (the Headteacher Leadership and Management Programme, HEADLAMP) and for serving heads (the Leadership Programme for Serving Headteachers, LPSH). Each programme is seen by policy makers as central to the development of educational improvement and effectiveness, since, it is argued, 'The quality of leadership makes the difference between the success and failure of a school' (Millett 1998: 3).

The TTA's control of the funds for teachers' professional development ensures that providers working in the new market economy of education have to take seriously the need to develop programmes which match TTA's new training imperatives – provider survival requires that they develop cost-effective and adaptable ways of 'teaching' and 'developing' education leaders and managers (Grace 1995). During the past decade this imperative has, for example, stimulated a particular growth in self-supported learning through open, flexible and distance-taught education management programmes (Law 1997a).

The TTA's perspective, echoed by developments in the USA, Australia and elsewhere (Whitty *et al.* 1998), requires that those aspiring to or already in leadership positions demonstrate their ability to meet TTA National Standards: the initial list required individuals to be proficient in 23 task areas, 14 skills and abilities and eight areas of knowledge and understanding. The extent to which using the Standards as a framework for development will actually improve school leadership remains to be seen: while such an initiative may offer guidance, scope and space for genuine professional learning, it is clear that continuing professional development (CPD) is also determined by our prior experience, the professional context we work in and our personal theoretical and philosophical standpoint. Moreover, the task of 'measuring' a headteacher's post-training impact on schools, pupils and teachers provides a major research challenge for the TTA and others, offering an exciting, if problematic, prospect for the future. As one way of engaging with the debate about effective leadership and management, we now consider some commonly used concepts.

What do managers do?

Each manager . . . needs a pocket theory of management. It is seldom formal, to be sure, but more likely an implicit list of 'ten things I really believe' . . . So each reader-practitioner has a theory.

(Peters 1987: 38–9)

While we may find Tom Peters's notion of the manager's 'list' overly simplistic, his acknowledgement of the need for a theoretical framework for management activity and the importance of *integrating* theory with practice is important. Taking this up, we explore five perspectives on management: functional management; rational management; scientific management; human relations management; and systems or data processing management.

Functional management

Fayol's (1916) functional perspective emphasizes, first, that the manager's role is to achieve the task, and second, that managing organizations – regardless of size, nature or mission – follows certain basic functions, i.e. to determine and decide objectives, to forecast, to plan, to organize, to direct, to coordinate, to control and communicate. He conceded, however, that the weighting of functions varied according to hierarchical levels and functional specialisms. Fayol's eight basic functions have been subsumed under several more commonly used headings:

- *Managers plan*: setting objectives, forecasting, analysing problems and making decisions – in other words, formulating policy.
- *Managers organize*: determining what activities are required to meet objectives, classifying work, dividing it up and assigning it.
- *Managers coordinate*: inspiring staff to contribute both individually and as a group to the organization's purposes, being loyal to its aims.
- *Managers control*: checking performance against plans.

Drucker (1988a, 1990a), a well known American management 'guru', prefers the term 'measure' to Fayol's 'control', which in his view emphasizes 'giving orders'. Drucker also added a vital fifth element:

- *Managers develop people*: ensuring that people maximize their potential to achieve agreed outcomes – 'someone who is directly responsible for getting work done through and by other people'.

Rational management

During the early twentieth century, managerial work was also examined from a sociological perspective, which emphasized that organizational design ensured managerial control and worker compliance, incorporating certain elements vital for organizational survival, e.g. hierarchy, role authority and office. The sociologist Max Weber (1924, 1947) defined the framework of authority as 'a bureaucracy' based on legitimate authority. The manager's task was viewed as working within a predictable, hierarchical system, with the basic concept being that once organizational objectives are set, authority structures ensure rational processes operate. This viewpoint appears to underpin current 'rational' processes within which schools and colleges are encouraged to operate.

Scientific management

'Scientific management' emphasizes work measurement and economic reward ('a fair day's pay for a fair day's work') rather than the organization itself, and has led to both task-oriented analyses of processes and the application of concepts of efficiency. Frederick Taylor (1947) argued that 'economic man' was motivated by the need to earn and that maximum output could be achieved if jobs were broken down into their component parts, which would enable the most efficient method of working on tasks to be identified.

Taylor and his colleagues, who were largely instrumental in developing scientific methods of job design, argued that a manager's prime organizational function is to control and design tasks to enable work to be done in the most efficient manner. Although Taylor's views are often now seen as largely outmoded, recent government publications on benchmarking and target setting (DfEE 1995a, 1996, 1997a), together with the criteria for success implicit in Education Development Plans (DfEE 1998a), suggest that elements remain, and, if anything, are being re-emphasized.

Human relations management

While Taylor's views of 'economic man' focused on separating the individual off from the group, the human relations approach emphasizes the group and, as part of it, individual contributions. Elton Mayo's research studies (1933, 1949) (carried out at the Hawthorne Plant of the Western Electric Company) argued that improved performance resulted when workers felt valued, were part of a group and found meaning in their roles. Moreover, he argued, where spontaneous cooperation occurred, output increased and production problems were readily resolved. Although the basis of his research is sometimes contested, Mayo's views have held significant sway over management development, moving the focus away from rational, quantitatively driven management approaches towards emphasizing more behaviourally aware, understanding and caring individual managers – exemplified in much of the current management development literature (e.g. Bush and Middlewood 1997; Day *et al.* 1998).

Systems or data processing management

The theme of communication runs through all the studies of managers as rational individuals. Because organizational operations are so complex, communicating information becomes a key management responsibility: the growth of ICT and ease of information storage and retrieval has given it even greater centrality as managers become information processors, collectors, collators and maintainers.

This perspective emphasizes that effective management decision making demands reliable and quantifiable information and may push the notion that decisions should be rational rather than intuitive. However, many see this viewpoint as supplementing rather than replacing other perspectives: elements of this approach can be seen in the way some schools utilize information systems, e.g. for measuring value-addedness and supporting benchmarking.

ACTION

Does one management perspective appear to reflect your own approach to management, or does each perspective have relevance at different times? Try to find out how others might interpret *your* management perspective.

Personal perceptions

The activity above may demonstrate the various kinds of discrepancy we may experience between our own perspective of our approach and the way others see us. The Johari window offers one way of exploring these differences in perspective (see, for example, Mullins 1993). As Figure 2.1 shows, this simple framework for exploring self-concept can be helpful, by classify-

	Behaviour known to ourselves	Behaviour unknown to ourselves
Behaviour known to others	**Public self** (is common knowledge to both ourselves and others)	**Blind self** (is seen/known by others but unknown by ourselves)
Behaviour unknown to others	**Hidden self** (is known to ourselves but hidden from others)	**Unknown self** (is unknown to both ourselves and others)

Figure 2.1 The Johari window.

ing behaviour according to what is known/unknown to ourselves (i.e. how others see us) and what is known/unknown to others (i.e. how we see ourselves).

A central emphasis in the personal use of this framework is a reduction of our 'hidden self' behaviour through self-disclosure and a reduction of our 'blind self' behaviour through feedback, these being based on trust and openness. How we perceive the organizations in which we work is extremely complex. Indeed, organizational roles may imply the presence of various perspectives: for example, a principal's perception of the way his or her college is being successfully restructured to meet newly agreed aims may differ widely from a variety of staff views about what some call the 'unnecessary instability' being created.

Internal differences of perspective often remain part of the 'private' territory of organizations and are not usually revealed to wider 'public' perceptions, unless someone breaks rank and exposes the discontinuities. The importance of the intersection between public and personal perceptions and the reality of the outcomes is a key issue for managers and leaders – and a key concern of ours in writing this book. While management complexities may not readily be resolved, in our view even where 'tasks' may need to predominate – as in responding to yet another government directive – it is essential that we understand the 'people perspective' if we are to make the systems work effectively.

Put simply, management is not simply a matter of systems, but is first a matter of people and relationships focused around clear organizational aims. Hargreaves and Hopkins (1991), who emphasize this human dimension in developing the concept of an *empowered* school, have identified three key management dimensions: frameworks (i.e. institutional aims, policies and systems); roles and responsibilities (needed to carry through frameworks); and working together. In our view, it is the *synergy* between these aspects which is vital, even if the balance of people–systems relationships actually differs between organizations. The value of synergy is reinforced in Mintzberg's (1990) identification of ten management roles within three sets of behaviour (see Table 2.3), since it is noteworthy that a high proportion of the roles are people centred.

Table 2.3 Mintzberg's ten management roles

Interpersonal behaviour	Informational behaviour	Decisional behaviour
Figurehead	Monitoring	Entrepreneurialism
Leadership	Dissemination	Disturbance handling
Liaison	Spokesperson	Resource allocation
		Negotiation

Source: after Mintzberg (1990).

Arguing for an approach to management that is essentially personal, non-rational and assumptive, Mintzberg dismisses Fayol's classic management functions because they fail to capture its intuitive and chaotic nature. He emphasizes instead that informal authority is as important as formal authority, with management being a holistic activity. Bennett (1997) summarizes this divergence of management perspectives as being between a traditional rational/cerebral model and what he describes as a non-rational/insightful approach (see Table 2.4).

Table 2.4 Rational and non-rational approaches to management

	Rational/cerebral approaches	Non-rational/insightful approaches
Management relationships	Control-focused	Delegation-focused
Global and organizational perspectives	World view = focus on 'portfolio' approaches, with disaggregation and segmentation of elements. Linear and rational emphasis through 'one best way' approach	World view = focus on integrated and holistic approaches. Emphasis on multiple realities and competing perspectives, with limited rationality
Emphasis and language	Language of rationality; numerical emphasis and focus on calculation	Language of management integrity, personal values and emphasis on professional commitment

Source: after Bennett (1997).

REFLECTION

How far does your own organization reflect the different approaches outlined by Bennett and how far do Mintzberg's sets of behaviours characterize your own perceptions of your 'management roles'?

What do leaders do?

Clearly, unidimensional distinctions between leadership and management are unhelpful when unravelling the complex interplay of skills, knowledge and abilities required nowadays. Since educational leadership occupies an increasingly high profile in government policy making (both nationally and internationally), we need to ask: what constitutes effective leadership? Adair (1983) has identified five distinguishing leadership characteristics:

- *Gives direction*, e.g. finding ways forward, generating a clear sense of movement/direction; identifying new goals, services and structures.
- *Offers inspiration*, e.g. having ideas and articulating thoughts that are strong motivators for others.
- *Builds teamwork*, e.g. seeing teams as the natural, most effective form of management, spending their time building and encouraging collaborative effort.
- *Sets an example*, e.g. showing that 'leadership is example': it is not only what leaders *do* that affects others in the organization, but *how* they do it.

- *Gains acceptance*, e.g. while managers may be designated by title, they are not *de facto* leaders until their appointment is ratified by their followers' consent.

A key aspect for Adair is that *real* leadership is that which is acknowledged and effectively 'granted' by others. However, this focus is not always emphasized in the literature. Brown and Rutherford's (1998) assessment of middle management in schools, for example, identifies five leadership 'images':

- *Servant leader*: stresses empowerment through working with people.
- *Organizational architect*: initiates and orchestrates change.
- *Leading professional*: shows awareness of work contexts.
- *Moral educator*: demonstrates transmissible values to guide relationships.
- *Social architect*: shows awareness of social and development issues.

While we might question exactly what terms like 'empowerment' mean in this context, individual leaders may appear – superficially at least – to match some descriptors more readily than others. For example, leaders impatient to 'get things done' may less readily fit the 'servant leader' role, if only because it is more time consuming. Nevertheless, they may also feel pressured to demonstrate 'the range of talents' in order to be 'fully realized' leaders.

Stoll and Fink's (1996) examination of the relationship between educational leadership and effective schooling distinguishes 'technocratic' and managerialist systems approaches from 'humanist' and facilitative ones, emphasizing another potential leadership/management distinction. While the language of recent inspection and audit reports concerning schools and further and higher education institutions often implies that *leadership* is about vision, mission and strategic direction, while *management* involves developing and implementing policies to achieve these ends, there is a danger that the rhetoric gets interpreted overly mechanistically by those receiving the feedback. In educational terms, Barth (1990) sees the leader as 'head learner', while MacGilchrist *et al.* (1997) argue that the real challenge leaders face is to establish and maintain inclusivity, a view supported by Bolam *et al.* (1993), who see the facilitation of good quality professional relationships as of key importance. So, what makes good leaders? How do they help to motivate, inspire and persuade others? Handy (1993) outlines three 'theories' of leadership (trait, style and contingency) – although he effectively uses the term 'theory' as a descriptor for 'various forms of leadership behaviour':

Trait theories

Trait theories attempt to describe key leadership features exemplified by successful leaders in the past, reflected in the way the 'great headteachers' (i.e. male headteachers) of the nineteenth century, e.g. Arnold of Rugby, were revered. Trait theories focus on identifying the key success characteristics of leadership, with most concentrating on, for example, the 'gifts' of intelligence, initiative and self-assurance (traits apparently almost exclusively demonstrated by men!), suggesting that leaders are 'born and not made'. Despite attempts to show the contrary, as in Green's (1991) competency analysis, these theories suggest that leadership cannot be 'taught'. Furthermore, so the argument goes, the qualities which create good leaders may not be sustainable in a variety of organizational contexts. It is interesting to consider where this perspective leaves women managers!

REFLECTION

Review your own perceptions of several leaders with whom you have worked, listing those traits you think have made them effective (or ineffective). How far does your evidence point to limitations in 'trait' theories?

Murgatroyd and Gray (1984: 45) have argued that there is 'no necessary connection between formal position and leadership', concluding, in line with trait theorists, that leadership is not necessarily related to role. For them, 'Leadership is a term used to describe a particular combination of personal qualities (ways of being) which both encourage and enable others to follow' (p. 47). This conception is enormously important in education, where collaborative activity is traditionally part of the professional culture, where individuals in a department are able to influence colleagues' work or where a particularly inspiring primary school teacher, who is also a curriculum co-ordinator, actually leads by example and inspiration.

Style theories

These theories attempt to show how the way in which leaders approach their roles in given situations fosters success or failure. This focus is reflected in the way, for example, that headteachers have been drafted in to 'turn round' failing schools (or those on the verge of failing), often because the previous head's 'style' is seen as inappropriate.

Although it may not readily clarify leadership and management distinctions, Likert's (1967) analysis of the 'power sharing' management style of supervisors and clerks in both the more and less productive parts of an American insurance company is an example of 'style theory' in operation. Likert argued that those who were successful supported others in a general rather than specific way, recognizing the need to be *employee-focused* rather than *production-oriented* – a style theory which separates leadership and management by implication. Likert's scheme suggests four approaches to leadership:

- *Exploitative and authoritarian*, e.g. an approach seen as having contributed to post-incorporation staffing problems in further education colleges.
- *Benevolent and authoritarian*, e.g. often considered characteristic of independent schools and the 'old' grammar school ethos.
- *Consultative*, e.g. often characterized as typical of effective leadership in secondary departments, which value both individual and group views.
- *Participative*, e.g. traditionally seen as at the heart of effective primary school cultures, with a strong emphasis on group-focus.

While we may all know colleagues whose general approach to leadership can be categorized in these ways, Likert's categorization is, once again, based on an assumption that such ways of working are somehow immutably fixed and that leaders and managers have one 'style'. Although staff in four large secondary schools researched by Glover *et al.* (1998) wished to see consistent leadership, leaders used a variety of 'approaches' as part of their 'vocabulary' of 'management in action'. Duignan (1989) also notes the tendency to develop a 'vocabulary of leadership strategies' in response to different situations, while Pocklington and Weindling (1996) suggest practical guidelines on the way reflection can be organized, emphasizing particularly the mentoring and facilitating role. Reflection is most effective if it is articulated: especially if having reflected on our experiences (context, process, relationships and action) we then build a repertoire of useful guides for future action. Used in this sense, our leadership and management approaches – rather than any single 'style' – become intelligent responses to complex problems which inevitably arise through working with others.

Clearly, the various leadership approaches we adopt are significant in advancing or inhibiting the cause of change and organizational effectiveness. Hersey and Blanchard's (1977) 'situational leadership' is one of the better known approaches. In distinguishing between the 'task' to be achieved and the 'relationship' with members of the working team, they identified four leadership 'styles'. These are described in Table 2.5, with the management implications shown in Figure 2.2.

Table 2.5   Situational leadership: task and relationship focused characteristics

Delegating	Low relationship and low task focus Leader 'authorizes': passes responsibility for a role or function to a member of staff and holds him or her accountable
Supporting	High relationship and low task focus Leader 'shares': maintains a strong link with the member of staff, offering support as necessary but does not become involved in the actual work
Coaching	High task and high relationship focus Leader 'sells': allocates tasks while supporting the member of staff and offering constant attention to the work in hand
Directing	High task and low relationship focus Leader 'tells': insists on the achievement of targets whatever the impact on the person undertaking the work

Source: after Hersey and Blanchard (1977).

Hersey and Blanchard also identified the 'maturity' level of followers as the key factor to be taken into account by leaders when determining the specific tasks or functions they want to achieve in working with and through others. The *relative maturity* of each follower influences the degree of emphasis which the leader needs to place on task or relationship behaviour at any given moment. They define maturity as the 'capacity to set high but attainable goals, willingness and ability to take responsibility, and education and/or experience of an individual or a group', arguing that such variables should only be considered in relation to specific goals or tasks.

Task-focused

		High direction	Low direction
Relationship-focused	High support	High task direction and high support **Coaching** ('selling')	Low task direction and high support **Supporting** ('sharing')
	Low support	High task direction and low support **Directing** ('telling')	Low task direction and low support **Delegating** ('authorizing')

Figure 2.2 Situational leadership: the management implications (adapted from Hersey and Blanchard 1977).

In applying this theory, Blanchard and Zigarmi (1991) offer a highly personalized approach to leadership, arguing that followers' maturity levels may, of course, be highly variable, both between individuals in an organization and within individuals themselves, relating to the different tasks they are asked to perform. In addition (and most importantly), maturity levels can change year-on-year as colleagues develop greater personal and professional maturity. This model may be used to accommodate the degree of development of any given follower (see Table 2.6).

Table 2.6 Leadership styles indicating competence and commitment

Development level of follower	Appropriate leadership style
Low competence High commitment	**Directing** Structure, control, supervise
Some competence Low commitment	**Coaching** Direct, support
High competence Variable commitment	**Supporting** Praise, listen, facilitate
High competence High commitment	**Delegating** Give responsibility for day-to-day decision making

Source: after Blanchard and Zigarmi (1991).

ACTION

Reflect on a new or recent responsibility you have taken on and consider how (a) your commitment and (b) your competence was identified by the person asking you to undertake it. Did the 'leader' act appropriately to gain your support and what influential factors were involved?

Contingency theory

Our examination of Hersey and Blanchard's concept of 'situational leadership' highlights the importance of *contextual* factors, e.g. when you are asked to do something because no one else is available or because the role would 'be good for your personal development'. However, as Fiedler (1978) has noted, leadership behaviour which is appropriate in one context may not be effective in another. In his view, organizational leaders need the ability to 'diagnose' the human and organizational context if they are to determine the best-fit behaviour for a given situation. Contingency theory attempts to analyse interrelationships between leaders and potential 'followers', and the nature of relationship between them. Contingency theory approaches are often evident in analyses and narratives about 'successful schools', where change has been achieved through developing an understanding of the complexity of this relationship.

Fiedler's 'contingency theory' (where successful leadership is contingent upon the situation as well as upon the people involved) endeavours to assess a leader's basic approach to managing people – what Fiedler called the leader's 'least preferred co-worker' (LPC) score. According to Fiedler, three factors influence leadership effectiveness:

- *The task*: the extent to which the task in hand is structured (i.e. has clear goals, few correct/satisfactory solutions).
- *The leader*: the leader's position power.
- *The relationship*: the nature of the relationship between the leader and followers.

Fiedler's assessment of leadership situations across several organizations found that a 'structuring' style was especially effective where the situation either strongly favoured or was clearly unfavourable to the leader; when only moderately favourable, 'supportive' styles worked best. Although Handy (1993: 105) sees Fiedler's approach as useful, 'not least because it reminds us that there are occasions when it pays to be distant and tasked centred, rather than democratic', contingency theory has also been criticized. First, Fiedler's three key variables (task structure, leadership power and relationships) are difficult to assess in practice and, in the end, judgements may be largely intuitive. Second, Fiedler's framework fails to account for the needs of those being led. Third, because the need for leaders to be technically competent is ignored. Fiedler's contingency theory has, nevertheless, also been praised for helping to identify the importance of contextual factors in determining leadership behaviour and for providing a systematic framework for developing managers' self-awareness.

REFLECTION

Consider how far your own experience of appraisal, for example, has confirmed or refuted the contingency view of leadership development.

Handy (1993) extends Fiedler's 'best fit' approach by arguing that there are four sets of influencing factors in leadership situations. The first three,

- the leader's preferred operating style and personal characteristics;
- the followers' (or 'subordinates' as Handy calls them) preferred style of leadership in the light of circumstances;
- the task, the job, its objectives and its technology;

depend to some degree on the fourth influencing factor,

- the environment: the organizational setting of the leader, his group and the importance of the task.

Handy's best fit approach argues that there is no such thing as a correct 'style' of leadership. Instead, fit can be measured on a 'tight–flexible' scale. For Handy, leaders need to shape their environment as well as being shaped by it: in effect, leadership is about being interactive. The centrality of leadership in promoting interactive and integrated approaches to school effectiveness and pupil achievement was identified first by Rutter *et al.*'s (1979) 'fifteen thousand hours' research and later by Mortimore *et al.*'s (1988) 'school matters' work in this area. Among others, Myers (1995) has stressed the role of a professional leadership which integrates three key characteristics: being firm and purposeful; adopting a participative approach; and operating as a leading professional. In order to match these characteristics, trait, style and contingency approaches may all be required: the cameo opposite may be illustrative in this respect.

● An alternative view

A summative stance which brings together trait and style approaches has been offered by McGregor Burns (1978), whose analysis of leadership has distinguished between *transactional leadership* (getting things done) and *transforming leadership* (being inspirational, visionary). McGregor Burns argued that most leaders use transactional management – what Leithwood (1992a: 9) calls 'an exchange of services', a simple negotiation of one thing for another and 'a trade-off'. This approach focuses primarily on managing structure, emphasizing organizational purpose, development planning and task completion, while transformational leadership also attempts to satisfy immediate needs, assess motives and satisfy higher needs through 'engaging the full person of the follower'. Mitchell and Tucker (1992: 32) indicate that transformational leadership occurs 'when leaders are more concerned about gaining overall co-operation and energetic participation', and that it is 'an approach that transforms the feelings, attitudes and beliefs of their followers'. Being people-oriented, they build relationships and help followers develop goals and identify strategies, rather than emphasize tasks and performance.

Transactional and transformational leadership styles fit well with well recognized models of 'task' and 'maintenance' management roles – for example, like that delineated by Adair's (1983) concept of 'action-centred

> ### Cameo   The boss has lost his marbles!
>
> George Jones had been a member of staff of Millpond Community
> College for eighteen years. He was originally appointed as head of
> geography and managed a large and successful department for four
> years. During this time he developed a reputation as a firm disciplinarian
> who would brook no nonsense from students or colleagues but who
> would listen to reasoned argument and act with determination and good
> sense. He was then appointed deputy head and 'hatchet man' for the
> head, who was frequently absent on professional business for the local
> education authority (LEA), successfully working with staff in negotiating
> working relationships during the union action of the mid-1980s.
>
> During George's third year as deputy, the head died suddenly and after
> six months as acting head George's post was made substantive. Staff
> expected a continuation of the 'firm, tight ship, and a determination to
> make us the best by telling us what to do'. While this policy held for the
> first three years of headship, George realized that he 'was doing it all for
> them', and as the work piled up he considered 'we needed to develop
> our corporate managerial and leadership skills'.
>
> After a weekend sharing thoughts and six weeks of debating issues with
> his deputy heads, George decided to hand over much of the executive
> power within the organization, becoming 'strategic planner, team
> member and facilitator'. However, within a term he was being criticized
> for having 'lost his drive', and for being too consultative: 'He's lost his
> marbles, and we're now left wondering just what on earth he's up to!'
>
> Trait, style, contingency or . . . ?

leadership' (see Figure 2.3). He sees three elements as vital (task, team and the individual), with leaders analysing and managing the relationships between each of the needs in order to achieve successful outcomes.

Despite extensive levels of research interest in the nature of transactional and transformational leadership, its value is also questioned: Stoll and Fink (1996) argue that the 'reality in schools is significantly different', while Southworth (1994: 18) comments that in the context of primary school leadership, 'these categories . . . do not capture the character and nature of leadership in action. They are too abstract and omit the vigorous quality of headteachers at work.'

By relating task to relationship through their 'managerial grid' (see Figure 2.4), Blake and Mouton (1978) argued that leaders could tend towards various combinations of both. For example, where a leader demonstrates only low levels of concern for task achievement but has high levels of concern for those involved, the danger arises that 'we have a cheerful crew, but we haven't repaired many engines'. Blake and Mouton identified four major tendencies (admittedly representing extremes) plus a midpoint profile:

- *Impoverished management*: low concern for task and low concern for people.
- *Authority-compliance management*: high concern for task, low concern for people.
- *Middle-of-the-road management*: moderate concern for task, moderate concern for people.
- *'Country club' management*: low concern for task, high concern for people.
- *Team management*: high concern for outcomes, high concern for people.

Figure 2.3 Action-centred leadership: interlocking task, team and individual concerns.

	Low		High
High	'Country club' management (A 'good place to be', but little is achieved: complacent)		'Team-driven' management (People are valued, outcomes encouraged)
Concern for people		Management as a 'dampened pendulum' (Little or no real drive: 'somewhere to work')	
Low	'Impoverished' management (Apathy rules OK!)		'Task-driven' management (Results are achieved but at what cost to relationships?)

Concern for outcomes/task

Figure 2.4 The managerial grid (after Blake and Mouton 1978).

Although this approach may now seem overly simplistic, it can provide a framework which helps to show how leadership and patterns of behaviour may impact on organizational progress. Rather than presenting management as a dichotomy – an 'either/or' – Blake and Mouton claim their grid illustrates that leaders can maximize the benefits of both task and people concerns: in other words, the team management approach is worth working towards.

Tannenbaum and Schmidt's (1973) 'continuum' of leadership styles examined the freedom experienced by 'followers' in relation to leadership authority and identifies a range of possible combinations and outcomes. While their continuum can be criticized for characterizing complex issues in somewhat simplistic, unidimensional terms, it is indicative of the kind of balance available between the various elements in management relationships (see Figure 2.5). The complexity of relationships was more overtly acknowledged by Tannenbaum and Schmidt when they produced a 'retrospective commentary' with the second version of the continuum, which recognized the relative powers and interdependency of forces between managers and those whom Tannenbaum and Schmidt called their 'subordinates', plus the context within which they worked. While some decisions need whole group participation if they are to be effectively implemented, others do not, and while leaders may often delegate specific decisions to competent and mature group members, this is often most effectively achieved within clearly defined limits. As Handy and Aitken (1986) have argued, those who are most effective are those able to combine both the elements of freedom and authority.

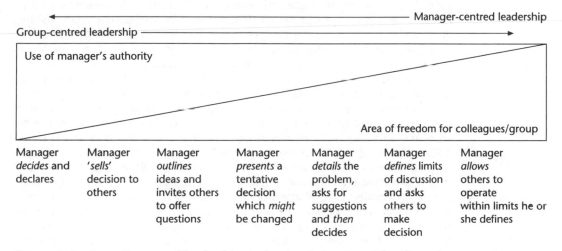

Manager-centred leadership

Group-centred leadership

Use of manager's authority

Area of freedom for colleagues/group

| Manager *decides* and declares | Manager *'sells'* decision to others | Manager *outlines* ideas and invites others to offer questions | Manager *presents* a tentative decision which *might* be changed | Manager *details* the problem, asks for suggestions and *then* decides | Manager *defines* limits of discussion and asks others to make decision | Manager *allows* others to operate within limits he or she defines |

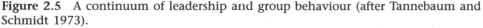

Figure 2.5 A continuum of leadership and group behaviour (after Tannebaum and Schmidt 1973).

Although much of the literature on management and leadership style is researched and written from an industrial/commercial perspective, there is an increasing body of writing on the impact of leadership and management in education, focusing particularly on headteachers (e.g. Fullan and Hargreaves 1991, 1992; Grace 1995; Leithwood *et al.* 1999). Everard and Morris (1996) use the concept of 'dominant' and 'back-up' educational leadership styles, and emphasize that leaders must be situationally sensitive – using the most appropriate approach for given circumstances. Reddin (1971) has described this facet of effective leadership as 'style-flexibility', while Gronn's (1996) recent review of educational leadership theory development indicates that a developmental emphasis in education tends to emphasize transformational leadership as a support for new visions and greater effectiveness. Gronn also argues, however, that aspects of transactional management are essential for policy implementation – effectively another plea for flexibility of approach!

Gender and educational leadership

The concept of flexibility is particularly emphasized with respect to gender issues in educational leadership and management – a growing area of focus and research for both policy makers and practitioners. Historically, however, it has often been assumed that women managers were inclined 'naturally' towards people, relationships and transformational management approaches, while men would adopt more task-oriented transactional approaches. However, this emphasis might also be perceived as masking traditional perspectives that women are simply 'deficit' versions of male leadership models (Schmuck 1986) and need training to achieve the 'norm' of male behaviour.

Coleman's research evidence (1994, 1996) reinforces Gray's (1993) view that gender similarities are greater than their differences, with both genders able to display 'masculine' and 'feminine' characteristics in leading and managing, often depending on the specific work context. As Coleman asserts, factors like experience and the particular nature of staff–leader relationships are likely to have greater significance than stereotypical gender models. However, age, too, is important: there is evidence that women often experience the 'double whammy' of gender and age discrimination (Acker, 1994).

It is sometimes argued that women may be advantaged by the 'new managerialist' context and the development of site-based education management, since more flexible organizational structures have created opportunities for collaborative and non-hierarchical leadership – traditional characteristics of women's approaches to management (see, for example, Shakeshaft 1987, 1993). However, while women's representation at senior school management levels may have increased slightly (Howson 1998), it remains too early to link any positive response to 'New Public Management' with it. The past decade has brought no 'shattering of the glass ceiling' and women still predominate at lower organizational levels (DfEE 1995b). Their reluctance to undertake training for senior management posts (e.g. the TTA's NPQH initiative) often stems from concerns over the scale of demands imposed by both the new training initiatives and the role itself – issues increasingly acknowledged by those charged with implementing policy (Millett 1998).

Despite these issues, the 'feminization' of management means that women's apparently more consensual and people-oriented management approaches are, according to Caldwell and Spinks (1992), likely to make them better educational leaders. In addition, Hall's (1996) study of women headteachers argues that women may more readily resist a managerialist stance than male colleagues because they are particularly concerned 'to preserve the integrity of the educational enterprise and its ultimate goal: young people's learning and development'. She adds:

> the integrity of their leadership styles would appear to have given them the strength to transform (through working with rather than against) New Right educational reforms . . . They demonstrated the possibility of playing the game but according to their rules which were not always the same as the other players.
>
> (Hall 1996: 192–3)

Perceptions about the interplay between gender and the new managerialist agenda are, however, highly contested. For example, some consider that education management has, in the new policy climate, become more 'macho' and less consensual (Gewirtz *et al.* 1995), while others stress the dangers of 'remasculinization' (Blackmore 1996). Writing from an Australian context, for example, Blackmore argues that men are now 'recolonizing' senior professional roles and areas which women had recently begun to occupy, and that this has resulted in women becoming relatively marginalized from headships in 'resource-rich' schools, leaving them with the challenge of leadership in the relatively 'resource-poor' schools.

Leadership and 'effectiveness'

Busher and Saran (1994) review the ways in which different leadership elements (i.e. task, relationships and context) relate to each other by identifying five models:

- *Structural-functional model*: emphasizes rationality, role and success based on 'fit'.
- *Open systems model*: focuses on the ways people interrelate to achieve organizational aims.
- *Cultural pluralism model*: recognizes that in a professional situation leadership needs to maximize the differing potential of individuals as members of a group.
- *Interpersonal models*: rely on the management of individuals as individuals working from differing viewpoints.
- *Political model*: characterized by a manipulation of power systems to achieve required ends as determined by the leader.

While their typology may help us to classify examples from our own experience, these models also need to be judged against the considerable evidence that leaders and led frequently offer very different perceptions of the same event: although headteachers may see their actions as fair and reasonable, the recipients may experience events very differently!

We explore the concept of 'effective' educational institutions in more detail later (e.g. in relation to 'corporate cultures'), but consider 'effectiveness' here briefly in relation to leadership. Brighouse's (1986) exploration of 'effective schools' asserts that three kinds of school leader may be identified:

- *Perceptive professional developers*: those who empower staff to carry the organization and themselves forward through joint planning and involvement.
- *System maintainers*: those who follow a more rigid and mechanistic approach, offering a framework for all but with little flexibility.
- *Inadequate, security-conscious others*: those who follow inconsistent approaches and act according to prevailing pressures (n.b. this is not the same as 'contingency').

REFLECTION

Does your experience chime with Brighouse's perspective that 'many leaders are instinctively system maintainers. They are too distrustful of change.' How might such leaders be transformed?

While links can be detected between the Brighouse models and Busher and Saran's systems, it remains the case that leaders have, in theory at least, a wide variety of models or approaches available to them: in 'stakeholder' terms, much depends on the way leaders interrelate and interact with others, something which is frequently connected most closely to the ways in which power is exercised.

● Organizational power and influence

So far we have focused on management and leadership roles. In reality, however, leaders do not act in isolation regardless of organizational setting. Since leadership requires a recognition of the dynamics of relationships, it is possible to see that people operate at three possible organizational levels:

- *As individuals*: with a personal agenda, perceptions and aspirations.
- *As group/team members*: contributing to a collective view of what needs to be achieved, or as part of a complex web of relationships with power ambitions.
- *As leaders*: 'reading' the messages which individuals and groups give in working within the organization.

From an individual's point of view, the most important concept is that of 'role', which stimulates questions like:

- What am I doing in this organization?
- Where do I stand in relation to my colleagues?
- What is my status and value within the organization?

Table 2.7   Kinds of organizational power

Resource power	Based on the perception that leaders have resources to reward others; used as an inducement by leaders; sometimes known as 'reward' power
Physical power	Based on fear and the perception that leaders can punish in various ways those who are non-compliant; sometimes known as 'coercive' power
Position power	Based on the perception that leaders have the right to exercise influence because of their position/role: comparable to 'authority' and sometimes known as 'legitimate' or 'legal' power
Expert power	Based on the perception that leaders are competent and have special knowledge, skills or expertise valued by others
Personal power	Based on a sense of identification with leaders who display personal 'charisma' and the leadership qualities which others wish to copy; often known as 'person', 'referent' or 'charisma' power

Source: after French and Raven (1959); Handy (1993).

Within the context of organizational leadership, we need to understand how individuals gain and develop power in order to sustain (or alter) their roles. We have implied that leadership is a social process because it is only when followers are prepared to act *with* leaders that effective and sustainable progress is made. However, as Handy (1993: 123) notes, power and influence 'make up the fine grain of organizations, and indeed of all interactions. Influence is the process whereby A seeks to modify the attitudes or behaviour of B, while power is that which enables him to do it.' In discussing power, however, Handy reminds us we need to consider issues of:

- *Relativity*: if your power is of no importance to me in a given situation, then it is ineffective. Power which intimidates *you* may have little consequence for *me*.
- *Balance*: most power/influence situations and relationships represent a power equation. Power is seldom one-sided, e.g. we all have access to 'negative power', the ability to disrupt or inhibit.
- *Domain*: few sources of power are universally valid in all situations. Ultimately, the legitimacy of everyone's power domain is limited.

REFLECTION

Try to recall a relatively recent policy change within your own working unit and consider how identifiable influence, power and authority were in the process.

Handy's analysis is built on French and Raven's (1959) research which identified the way five kinds of power are influential over organizational function (see Table 2.7).

It is not easy to differentiate between all these sources at any one time because power and leadership are *perceived* qualities: leader and led may see things very differently! As Handy stresses, power is only really effective if the relationship between leader and follower is mutually understood. Handy suggested that, depending on the roles and personal skills of participants, power struggles get resolved through an interplay of the various kinds of power identified above.

Recent research into the impact of 'power' on the combination of delegation, support and commitment – summarized as the 'empowerment' of teachers – concludes that the use, by headteachers, of expert and personal power is more likely to lead to an empowering culture for all staff (Johnson and Short 1998). Obviously, however, we may not necessarily be aware of the sources of power or ways it is being used – perhaps because many of our actions and reactions are relatively intuitive. Nevertheless if, as leaders, we are better able to identify how power is conferred and how it is being used – by us and others – then our ability to manage situations and give a lead is likely to improve.

ACTION

How far have relativity, balance and domain affected the development of one aspect of the National Curriculum (NC) or NVQs, or a similar curricular requirement within your own organization?

Whereas power implies some degree of force, influence is altogether far more subtle. The nature of professional cultures, especially in education, is such that persuasion is generally acknowledged as the way in which ideas and practices are best exchanged. As Handy suggests, however, sources of power are linked with both overt (i.e. obvious) and unseen (i.e. implied) methods of influence, as Table 2.8 indicates.

Understanding sources of power and influence can be helpful in 'playing' or dealing with the so-called 'organizational power game'. Moreover, an awareness of the relationship between environment and the application of tactics is important. As Handy (1993) notes, when attempting to influence others we need to be aware of:

- The choice of method available to us in a given situation.
- The kind of individual responses we are likely to get from those on the receiving end, which is affected by the likelihood that the individual: (a) will *comply* with our request/ideas; (b) will *identify* with our views/beliefs; and/or (c) will *internalize* our ideas/proposals.

Case studies documented by Glover *et al.* (1996) reveal the ways in which individuals within groups influence other participants to the point where discernible pressures may affect decision making. These pressures may be influenced by the nature of the organization or the roles adopted by participants; they may evolve as a result of interactions in group situations; or they may emerge through tactical power games. Ball (1987) defines the last as the 'micropolitics' of school life and examines the ways groups interact with

Table 2.8 Organizational power and influence

Methods of influence	Power source
1 *Overt/open strategies*	
Force and/or coercion	The crudest of influence methods; derives from physical power or occasionally, resource power
Rules and procedures	Used directly or indirectly; derives largely from position power, usually backed by resource power; often used in 'playing politics'; an efficient but possibly damaging way of getting results
Exchange/bargaining	Goes from friendship to negotiating to cajoling; can derive from any power source, but most often resource and position power; can be self-cancelling, like incentive or motivation theories
Persuasion	Least value-laden and often most preferred method; often influenced by other methods; derives from personal and/or expert power
2 *Unseen/hidden strategies*	
Organizational 'ecology' or environment	Sets the conditions for behaviour, can be used positively or negatively; derives largely from hidden aspects of position power and resource power, the right to access, information etc.
Magnetism/'invisible' power	Generally the application of personal and sometimes expert power; open to abuse

Source: after Handy (1993).

each other and their leaders. While he argues that the fundamental nature of conflict or consensus is related to power over people, resources, organizational development and knowledge, he acknowledges that educational institutions are different from most other employing organizations, 'in that the leader will almost inevitably have risen from the ranks' (1987: 120). Heads have what Ball describes as the 'Janus face of power' problem: on the one hand, 'they must achieve and maintain control (the problem of domination) and, on the other hand, encourage and ensure social order and commitment (the problem of integration)' (1987: 120).

REFLECTION

How far do you think the management of power and interest groups in educationally focused organizations is within the leader's control?

While there may be similarities between Ball's comments and Handy's analysis of the power framework, it is often the case that power is used most openly and overtly in the resolution of conflict – either because there is resistance to change or because, in relatively static situations, role preservation is believed to be important for the maintenance of power – a theme we return to later.

Power and organizational groups

Groups can often become strongly influential over the motivation, participation and acceptance of norms of individual members. Within educational environments, for example, pressures on individuals to conform may become more evident because of the dominance of group ethos, professionalism and 'way of life', where a strong emphasis is placed on shared values. Group existence and influence may be formal (e.g. through structure) or informal (e.g. through association).

Southworth (1988) has argued that the concept of 'collegiality' and collaborative activity in departments or schools can become a somewhat formal, perhaps idealistic, arrangement for bringing groups together. While collegiality helps to develop group participation and cohesion, and encourages the 'valuing' of individuals, he also sees it as a problematic concept. Developing collegiality is time consuming and may make leadership difficult in situations of apparent equality. This, in turn, implies the use of more covert influences of power (like 'persuasion' power), where arguments get framed in particular ways or where environmental improvement is offered as a spur to 'feeling good about the place'. Clearly, this reminds us that we need to assess how far groups in educational organizations differ from those in business organizations – where much current management theory has been developed.

Curriculum is about processes as well as outcomes. It is clear that, despite the introduction of appraisal, individual teachers retain considerable personal power within classrooms. In an era of increasing accountability and emphasis on continuous improvement, leaders need to find ways of influencing (as a leading professional as well as chief executive) what goes on 'behind closed doors' – especially in classrooms – while acknowledging the value of professional autonomy. This is a difficult path to tread but is by no means a new issue for senior managers. At one level it is now simply a more overt and formal responsibility: good headteachers have always tried to influence for good what has gone on in classrooms.

An analysis of Ofsted reports indicates that a productive balance between accountability and autonomy can often be achieved in more effective schools through the power of persuasion and debate and through the establishment of common aims, enabling leaders to begin to influence the tone of classroom life (Law and Glover, forthcoming). Perhaps the greatest potential for influencing curriculum delivery in classrooms lies with middle managers, heads of department and subjects coordinators – a role increasingly acknowledged by the TTA in its establishment of national standards. Terrell et al.'s (1996) questionnaire, for example, stressed the following criteria for middle management effectiveness: reflection; critical enquiry and evaluation; development planning; curriculum planning; concern for people; and staff development.

When all these are achieved it is possible that what O'Sullivan (1996) has called 'the high performing middle manager' may become a reality, combining awareness of both personnel and process. O'Sullivan offers a developmental structure based upon the 'fit' of people, tasks, information processes and structure with the degree of 'congruence' between information, knowledge, power and rewards.

ACTION

List those factors which you consider affect your own approach to leadership at work. How far could Terrell *et al.*'s 'tools' provide effective support, and does O'Sullivan's emphasis on personnel and process account for the factors in your list?

Teachers as leaders and managers

Although, traditionally, the concept of leadership equates with senior management, the growth of managerialism post-1988, the requirements of managing curriculum change and the growing emphasis on the notion that 'all teachers are managers' (Buckley and Styan 1988) have all increased the emphasis on the importance of middle management. This view is seen overtly in the TTA's development agenda for national standards for subject leaders (TTA 1998b).

Leask and Terrell's (1997) examination of middle management leadership skills and qualities stresses the importance of both the visionary and the transformational roles in securing school improvement – even at middle management levels. The inception of a new National Curriculum for Initial Teacher Training (NCITT) has also echoed the need for newly qualified teachers to demonstrate increased self-management and leadership skills (DfEE 1998b; TTA 1998c), while the demand that all areas of the curriculum should be led by designated staff implies that even newly qualified teachers (NQTs) need to be ready to take on curriculum leadership responsibilities from their first day at work! In this scenario, leadership is no longer the prerogative of the headteacher or principal, with individual responsibility increasingly emphasized.

Murgatroyd and Reynolds (1984: 322) stress that leadership 'can occur at a variety of levels in response to a variety of situations and is not necessarily tied to possession of a formal organizational role.' Indeed, staff in smaller schools are overtly aware that this is a key part of their professional expectations. If we reflect further on Hersey and Blanchard's overview (see Tables 2.5 and 2.6 and Figure 2.2), we might see why Murgatroyd and Reynolds argue that leadership is the capacity to inspire followership, something which might reasonably be an ambition and assumed function of all teachers, in relation to their pupils and students. Murgatroyd and Reynolds's use of the term 'non-executive leadership' reflects the reality of staffroom situations as seen through:

- changing the beliefs and perceptions of colleagues;
- offering alternative ideas to refute long held beliefs;
- overcoming the fear of failure in others;
- reducing reliance on authority which is external to the group.

It also reflects the government's concern to see curriculum leadership (in terms of teaching and learning skills and competences at least) as a high level, high reward activity worth developing, e.g. through the advanced skills teacher (AST) concept (DfEE 1998c). An examination of the nature of leadership brings us to consider the nature of 'followership'. The following two chapters examine how leadership can be exercised in order to inspire and enthuse others towards ongoing objectives and organizational visions, a process important to both leaders and those they seek to motivate.

⬤ Suggestions for further reading

Fullan, M. (1992) *What's Worth Fighting for in Headship?* Buckingham: Open University Press.

Gronn, P. (1996) From transactions to transformations, *Educational Management and Administration*, 24(1).

Hall, V. (1996) *Dancing on the Ceiling: a Study of Women Managers in Education*. London: Paul Chapman Publishing.

Handy, C. (1993) *Understanding Organizations*. London: Penguin.

Leithwood, K., Jantzi, D. and Steinbach, R. (1998) *Changing Leadership for Changing Times*. Buckingham: Open University Press.

Ouston, J. (ed.) (1993) *Women in Education Management*. Harlow: Longman.

Sergiovanni, T. J. (1995) *The Principalship: a Reflective Practice Perspective*. London: Allyn & Bacon.

3 Managing ourselves and leading others

> It is only by individuals taking action to alter their own environments that there is
> any chance for deep change . . . Moral purpose needs an engine, and that engine
> is individual, skilled change agents pushing for changes around them, intersecting
> with other like-minded individuals and groups to form the critical mass necessary
> to bring about continuous improvements.
>
> (Fullan 1993: 40)

Focusing on individuals

In many respects, individuals are the key to effective management. It is largely through encouraging individual participation and developing the often very different personal talents and skills of members of a team, group or organization – whether involved in car production, selling advertising space or educating people – that organizations become more effective and successful. While we would challenge the assertion that educating people bears strong similarities with producing cars, e.g. in terms of philosophy, vocation and ethos, it is clear that motivation and commitment can be crucial in both activities, especially in relation to quality. However, achieving these is no simple task – as Ofsted and the TTA have discovered in trying to enhance school improvement and develop teacher commitment while simultaneously policing and inspecting education, and demanding greater accountability.

In a professional context where it is increasingly stressed that effective management is 'all about people' and that individuals are the key 'building blocks' in successful organizations, this chapter identifies and explores the skills and abilities which each of us is likely to need if we are to manage both ourselves and others when working in people-driven organizations. As a basic principle, we suggest that teams, groups and, ultimately, whole organizations need to value the individuals working within them if they are to be fully successful. In addition, individuals make more effective team members as they come to appreciate their own skills, talents and development needs – in other words, become better 'self-managers' (Pedler et al. 1986). We suggest that this can be achieved by:

1 Identifying and utilizing the key skills needed to manage others on a one-to-one basis.

2 Recognizing the importance of self-management and identifying particular skills which enable us to manage ourselves and deal with management pressures more effectively.

Clearly, some fundamental management development needs are implicit in both 1 and 2 above: for example, the need to understand how people are motivated; the need to see how every individual in an organization can help or hinder institutional success; and the need to develop communication and other interpersonal skills. Mescon *et al.* (1985) argue the need for parallel developments in these spheres – the ability to enhance organizational effectiveness alongside the ability to establish individual support and enhancement strategies. For Mescon *et al.*, organizations are the sum of the efforts and qualities of individuals and, consequently, individuals and organizations need to be fostered simultaneously. Brown and Taylor (1996) have also outlined how staff and organizational development-based strategies like 'Investors in People' can move individuals and their organizations forward simultaneously.

In Chapter 2 we considered the multiplicity of terms and perspectives used regarding leadership, management and administration. Glover *et al.*'s research (1998) suggests that many middle managers (often the key team leaders in educational organizations) tend to retreat from management into administrative 'paper-shuffling' tasks which make high demands on their time, thus creating greater potential for stress in themselves and others. We cannot fully lead or manage others effectively unless we are aware of the way in which we function both as individuals *and* as team members. This does not necessarily imply introspective self-examination, but emphasizes the need for awareness about our approach to work and how patterns can be adapted to meet new contexts. The way we work tends to revolve around several key elements implicated in interpersonal relationships, e.g.

- *Role*: how clear we are about our formal function within an organization.
- *Responsibilities*: how we turn the idea of 'role' into 'on the ground' practicalities.
- *Delegation*: how and to what extent autonomy and responsibility is moved 'down the line'.
- *Decision making*: how efficiently and effectively individuals participate in the process.
- *Managing time*: how we develop both short/immediate term coping strategies 'on-the-day' plus longer term strategies, regardless of our personal feelings.
- *Managing stress*: how we cope with the various work-related pressures – of context, relationships and processes.

REFLECTION

Try to identify how far you are clear about your own role in relation to the above issues.

Recent systems change has brought a new focus on individuals. While many educational organizations have traditionally utilized sequential planning and thinking about change (which often meant tinkering at the margins – in accountants' terms, the concept of 'historic' management), the post-1988 era reflects an impetus for far more fundamental and dramatic change, with a far greater focus on individual responsibility for success, albeit within an institutional context. In short, the pressures and responsibilities on individual staff have increased, with a concomitant emphasis on the importance of effective self-management, e.g. the processes of managing role, managing decision making, managing time and the consequent management of stress, as outlined above.

This means that understanding the extent of our own talents, skills and limitations is increasingly vital. The 'Peter Principle' (Peter 1972) argues that people move up organizational hierarchies to the level at which they become incompetent managers. Staffroom cynics would, no doubt, acknowledge that this happens only too readily in a more managerialist education service! If this kind of notion is to be countered, it is vital that the management processes mentioned so far are tempered by an understanding of how we, ourselves, and others think and use ideas. Creative thinking and flexiblity of approach can help us lead and manage people in changing contexts – promoting capability, personal responsibility, and empowerment rather than incompetence. The key to managing ourselves is thus twofold: first, recognizing the nature of the context within which we work; second, understanding appropriate ways to handle any given situation.

The art of delegation

The delegation of 'tasks' is not simply about 'hiving off work to someone else': some degree of thoughtful planning rather than ad hocery is essential in order to ensure that objectives are achieved without detriment to either individuals or the organization. In effect, our desire to delegate needs to be accompanied by a change in the trust–control balance in relation to those involved (Handy 1993). As Adair (1986) argues, a fundamental of good management practice is the ability to distinguish between *delegation* – a statement of the work to be undertaken and the standards by which it will be judged – and *abdication* – a 'shedding' of work and interest.

Hunningher (1992) notes that the main inhibiters to effective delegation identified by managers are:

- 'Nobody can do the job as well as the I can.'
- 'Delegating the work means it will be done badly and I'll get the blame.'
- 'Since I have little idea how the work can be done effectively, I had better do it myself.'
- 'I don't want the staff to think that somebody else is doing my job.'
- 'I can only be seen to be part of the team if I keep doing the job myself.'

Hersey and Blanchard's (1977) typology of effective leadership, considered in Chapter 2, may be significant here, in that it acknowledges the need for people to operate within a supportive and developmental context so that they become aware of the implications and practice of effective delegation:

in short, the importance of being concerned with both relationship (i.e. the focus on getting along with others) and task (i.e. getting the work done effectively). Teachers often experience a tension between what may be called their professional ethic on the one hand and their need to produce specified outcomes on the other, a difficulty which tends to be exacerbated by the fact that delegation can often occur for mundane and pragmatic reasons in a changing policy context.

As an exemplar, the following cameo examines delegation issues in one school following an Ofsted inspection when the head of science felt unable to cope because of what she saw as lack of support from departmental colleagues.

Cameo   Will it ever be manageable?

Jane Biggs was an effective head of biology who during the early 1980s took on more responsibility within the science department at Greenacres. However, in 1990, following the appointment of a new headteacher and a reorganization of curriculum areas, she agreed to become head of science. Her first two years were relatively successful as she built the four subject areas into a coherent whole, but following on from the introduction of the National Curriculum, local management of schools and strategic planning within the school, she felt that she was 'going under'.

The head suggested that the three subject leaders with whom she worked were not taking enough 'science' responsibility and suggested that Jane delegate some of the work. Her response was to ask the head of physics to maintain the stationery stock for the department, the head of chemistry to liaise with the local higher education institution (universities and colleges) (HEI) to arrange for the students on teaching practice, and the head of environmental studies to maintain the 'greenery' displays throughout the school.

The head, reviewing the situation, suggested that this was not the sort of delegation which would give her time for creative thinking and was not offering any development to the staff concerned. Jane's response was that the head obviously felt that she was incompetent, that she was being shown to be an ineffective woman manager and that he was giving her yet more to do because the delegated work had to be supervised.

In your view, what mistakes had the head made?

For Hunningher, effective delegation requires an initial careful selection of task and people followed by action. However, several questions need resolving first:

- the nature and type of challenge for the person taking on additional work;
- the skills and training required by that person;
- the need for clerical or peer support;

- the need for redefined job descriptions;
- agreement on a system for monitoring and evaluation.

All this is, however, premised on the capacity for and use of trust – another personal quality which individuals need to develop for effective management (Handy 1993). Trust is, nevertheless, double-edged: as Handy points out, it requires confidence that the individual is capable of undertaking the job effectively; it is effectively a leap in the dark, is a fragile commodity, and to be fully effective, must be reciprocal.

REFLECTION

Think of three situations in which you have been delegated work. How far were the precepts listed above followed – or was the delegation purely pragmatic?

While much of the discussion so far has been about 'managing the job', the ultimate aim of management development is to help people to undertake new challenges and roles where they can carry overall responsibility rather than merely complete ever more complex and detailed 'tasks' allocated by others.

Defining and managing roles

The progressive development of an increasingly mobile, well educated and affluent society has brought with it the potential for each of us to have opportunities and access to a wider range of more complex and potentially rewarding roles and responsibilities – whether through work, or within families or communities. Managing a diversity of roles does, nevertheless, bring significant pressures. Role performance is dependent on two sets of influences which, in many respects, interact with each other:

- an individual's personal 'forces' (i.e. personality, skills etc.);
- the situational 'forces' (i.e. the context).

Examining the concepts of role theory – the situational forces – can be helpful in our attempts to understand the 'why' and 'how' of individual performance and, in general, allows us to make reasonably accurate predictions and 'guesstimates' about how those whose work we manage are likely to react in any given circumstances. The cameo scenario above might have been very different if the head had recognized Jane's insecurity and bolstered her self-esteem before seeking a different form of delegation.

Organizations, as personified by their employees, are likely to have particular 'role expectations' of any new manager joining the workforce. Crucially, role expectations may or may not coincide and, furthermore, a particular manager's 'role set' (i.e. the group with which he or she works most closely) is likely to have particular expectations about his or her beliefs, attitudes and behaviours. Such differences in expectations may be regarded as minimal or overwhelming, and can affect those involved in various ways. For example, individuals may experience the following.

Role ambiguity

Individuals feel (rightly or wrongly) that insufficient information is available regarding their role: role definition is, consequently, unclear. These difficulties are often experienced by those undertaking 'liaison' and 'coordinating' roles in organizations.

Role conflict

An individual's job makes conflicting demands – commonly where that person is uncomfortable with particular role requirements. This can be seen where, for example, a head of department in a college of further education comes under pressure from senior managers to close a course, but is perceived by colleagues as the torchbearer for their future security.

Role overload

An individual manager is unable to meet the range of roles required, in both variety and quantity. This is another form of role conflict, often perceived as 'the last straw' and frequently experienced by middle managers who – 'caught in the middle' – often assume increased responsibilities during periods of staffing retrenchment.

French and Caplan (1970) distinguish between qualitative overload (i.e. work which is too difficult) and quantitative overload (i.e. too much work to do), while French *et al.* (1965) found earlier that qualitative overload was a particular source of stress for managers in higher education. Interviews, medical examinations and questionnaires completed by 122 university administrators and lecturers (divided into two groups) indicated that low self-esteem was related to work overload. Results were, however, different for the two groups. While qualitative overload was not significantly linked with low self-esteem among administrators, there was significant correlation for lecturers. In other words, the greater the 'quality' of work expected of lecturers, the lower their self-esteem because they felt unequal to the task. If this was true 30 years ago, it raises questions about current pressured circumstances, where we see a multifaceted need to lead and develop staff *and* manage resources against the background of increased demands for quality assurance and improved outcome indicators. We return to this theme when considering stress management.

REFLECTION

How far is this kind of overload reflected in your own sector of education? Does the emphasis on 'standards' and 'quality' in teaching in schools suggest that teachers are suffering from qualitative overload?

Role underload

This form of role conflict often occurs when organizational expectations fall short of a manager's own needs and role expectations: it is often a problem experienced at lower levels in hierarchical organizations when, for example, assistant year heads or assistant subject leaders feel that they are only being given routine administrative tasks.

Role clarity

This occurs when managers see their roles as straightforward, unambiguous and 'black and white'. The potential for inhibiting change and preventing role development arises, with notions of 'it isn't my role' coming to the fore.

Role incompatibility

This is a likely occurrence when the expectations of members of a role set are clearly identified but are, nevertheless, incompatible with each other – typified in primary schools where the role of curriculum coordinator sits uneasily with those of class teachers.

Role pressure and role strain

Handy (1993) distinguishes between 'role pressure' (i.e. beneficial stress) and 'role strain' (i.e. harmful stress), pointing out that some of the strategies for dealing with role strain are based on 'coping with' rather than 'solving' problems. For example, we may use

- repression (refusing to admit that a problem exists);
- withdrawal (opting out of the situation);
- rationalization (learning to live with the situation).

In order to meet these pressures, Handy and Aitken (1986) suggest that role switching can be a positive way of dealing with the difficulties.

Role switching

This is a strategy often used in both secondary and tertiary educational sectors, where senior and middle managers gain experience of a range of roles, e.g. pastoral, curriculum, financial and strategic in turn. Handy and Aitken suggest that if ambiguity is limited by careful definition and open agreement, if conflict can be reduced by reducing role overlap and if overload is minimized by agreed prioritization, then role issues need not interfere with an individual's well-being or organizational effectiveness.

ACTION

Consider an area of your work where tensions are created by role problems and assess how far the Handy and Aitken solutions provide a resolution. List any factors which are likely to encourage or inhibit success.

As individuals, our ability to understand, analyse and refine our own role may influence the ways we delegate so that others may enjoy the same degree of role clarity we would expect for ourselves. Recent research into subject leadership indicates that when decision-making processes are led by middle managers difficulties may arise, especially when delegated roles are mismanaged because of the tension between maintaining good relationships with the team and getting the task completed (Glover *et al.* 1998).

Making and taking decisions

The process of decision making seems to be problematic for many managers – particularly when they are new to the post. While this strategy of making decision taking a shared process may help to promote a stronger sense of 'ownership' and enhance the nature of organizational development, problems can also arise with collective rather than individual manager-led decision making. First, the process can take up much valuable time, and, second, issues which in some cases should be settled on a one-to-one basis become a collective responsibility – often to the detriment of more important activities. The nature of the decision to be taken is, therefore, important.

It is sometimes suggested that one strategy for resolving such difficulties might be to characterize various decision-types within a typology of decision making. The argument goes that specific procedures could then be applied to assist with the process. The minutes of staff meetings are typical of the messiness that can arise – leading to a misplaced 'hierarchy of decision making'. For example, there may well be massive concern over small changes to, say, lunch hour arrangements or arrangements for a social function, while highly significant curriculum delivery arrangements pass by either unchallenged or with minimum discussion. Vroom (1974) has stressed the variation in the types of decision made and the need for information systems to back up effective decision-making processes. Although his proposed system appears complex, it is based on assessing the nature or type of decision needed and an awareness of a set of 'rules'. Among the attributes which can be identified in any problem, Vroom includes:

- the importance of the quality of the decision for organizational development;
- the extent to which sufficient information is available;
- the extent to which the problem is structured;
- the extent to which acceptance by others (called 'subordinates' by Vroom) is critical for success;
- the extent to which others will follow a lead.

He also contends that the quality of the outcome will depend upon:

- the rationality of the decision;
- the acceptability of the decision to others ('subordinates');
- the time taken to reach the decision.

The rules for ensuring that quality decisions are made will include, according to Vroom, an assessment of:

- the context, implications and likely impact of the proposed change;
- the relationship between the decision and organizational goals;
- the way in which implementing a decision affects organizational structure.

Vroom argues that we need to note the difference between decision quality and decision acceptance, implicitly suggesting that we might profitably assess how often we fail to implement quality decisions because of the need to compromise or gain acceptance of the change.

ACTION

Think back to two or three recent decisions you've made in a work situation. How far does Vroom's analysis help you to evaluate decision quality against criteria of effectiveness and time used.

Obviously, it is unwise (or even impossible) to hold up the decision-making process while you have a philosophical debate about the most appropriate action to take! However, research into strategic planning processes shows that effective decision making can be facilitated by the availability of effective management information systems, an in-depth awareness of how others think and clarity of management structure – back to delegation and role. Much of this is impossible without effective time management which creates opportunities to utilize creative thinking for leadership rather than waste it on administration.

Managing time

Time is also a unique resource . . . one cannot rent, hire, buy or otherwise obtain more time. The supply of time is totally inelastic. No matter how high the demand, the supply will not go up . . . time is totally perishable and cannot be stored.

(Drucker 1967: 21)

The manager has four major resources – people, equipment, money and time – time is irreplaceable.

(Hunningher 1992: 186)

While a good deal of attention has been paid to 'time management' issues in business settings, it remained relatively ignored in education until business practices became more influential – partly because the use of teachers' time was ill-defined and partly because 'overtime' did not formally exist. Being a teacher simply 'took as long as it took'. School-based and site-based management, along with the identification of directed time, has focused attention increasingly on time usage, efficiency and the pressures arising from perceived bureaucratic overloads both within organizations and from national imperatives.

During the past decade or so, educationists have become increasingly concerned with specifying time spent, in relation to the length of the school day, e.g. directed time, and curriculum time for both students and staff pursuing 'self-supported' studies beyond 'standard' time allocations. Despite this, the value of effective time management in education remains unrecognized in certain respects. As Drucker has suggested, scarcity value is what makes time such an important resource and 'discretionary time is one of the scarcest and most precious of commodities' (Drucker 1967: 42).

Managing one's time effectively is a crucial aspect of both self-management and managing others. The rhetoric of effective self-management is often based on the value of being 'proactive' and a 'self-starter': clearly, such attributes are highly dependent on having a sense of time and how it can be most productively used. Lakein (1984) argues the need to be clear about our personal lifetime goals – thinking in both macro (life) and micro (day-to-day) time spans – if we are to use time effectively. Post-1988 legislative changes and ongoing funding limitations mean that educationists generally, and teachers in particular, need creative approaches to using both personal and professional time to pursue both organizational and individual agendas. The framework for initial teacher education (ITE) stresses this need for balance and the value of partnership, in-school mentoring and opportunities for reflection and mutual gain – even if it is difficult to achieve (Devlin 1995).

Clearly, our inability to manage our personal time effectively seriously diminishes our ability to manage time in others. One way of clarifying how far we are effective managers is to evaluate how our work time operates. Drucker (1967) considers that time management comprises a three-step process which is the 'foundation of executive effectiveness':

- recording time;
- managing time;
- consolidating time.

In common with other management writers, Adair (1983) suggests that a time log is an essential prerequisite to establishing effective time management skills. Recording and then analysing how present time is spent allows us better to plan and manage future time. Adair suggests:

- developing a personal sense of time based on 'where time goes';
- planning ahead to allow programmed deadlines;
- programming more demanding tasks for the time of day when you function best;
- use odd minutes to 'capitalize on marginal time';
- avoiding clutter;
- ensuring that you 'do it now'.

This may seem a counsel of perfection. Arguably, compared with those in business settings, teachers have too much 'directed' time and too little 'discretionary' time: they are 'tied' to particular classes or groups with only limited strategies available to 'block' time to maximize its value. While local management of schools (LMS) has provided some localized opportunities to adjust staffing ratios, facilitate 'time blocking' and provide more non-contact time in the secondary sector, the issue is far less flexible and often more complicated in primary schools, where there are fewer staff, multiple roles and curricular monitoring responsibilities.

> **ACTION**
>
> List some of the ways in which the use of time might be improved within your own department or school. Prioritize the items on your list and then consider what might stop such suggestions from being implemented.

Adair (1983: 68) suggests that people can be categorized as early-morning 'larks' (the more introverted) and the late 'night owls' (the extroverts). Such assertions remain open to debate, but the underlying principle that it is important that we recognize when we are most alert is valid – both in knowing our own strengths or preferences and when dealing with colleagues. It is not just time, but the attitudes stimulated by pressures which count.

The 'Pareto Principle' (named after the Italian economist Pareto) states that the significant items of a given group form a relatively small part of the total. This principle is also known as the '80:20 rule' or 'the vital few and trivial many', since, for example, it argues that 20 per cent of a given sales force brings in 80 per cent of the company's business. Managing time by applying the Pareto Principle implies that prioritizing a few essential elements is likely to result in greater overall achievements – even if managers, whether in industry or education, are constantly burdened with the 'trivial many'. If viewed from the 'time availability' angle, we might consider that 80 per cent of our creative work could be done in 20 per cent of our time – importantly, though, the 20 per cent which constitutes 'prime time'. While unhelpful if applied with rigidity, this perspective fits with Murgatroyd and Morgan's (1992) comment that 'working smarter, not harder' should be a key outcome of effective management.

> **REFLECTION**
>
> Consider how you already organize, even informally, your time according to the kinds of principles detailed above, e.g. Adair's recording, analysing and planning. Does the Pareto Principle offer any insight into your own work context?

A series of research investigations summarized by Turner (1996) points to 'time' as the most frequently identified inhibiting factor for those undertaking management responsibilities in education, with the second factor being stress – often a consequence of difficulties in reconciling role overload with time.

● Managing stress

> Of itself, stress is neither good nor bad . . . it depends on how it is experienced. Stress can be stimulating or energizing, in which case it is positive and beneficial, or it can be the cause of feelings of anxiety, distress or discomfort; here it is a negative and harmful condition.
>
> (Gray and Freeman 1987: 4)

As Gray and Freeman point out, stress is a biochemical response to a potentially threatening situation (stressor). It may be envisaged as a continuum, with successful stress management dependent on an individual's ability to identify and respond to the place where he or she is on this stress continuum. The level of stress experienced arises from both the environment and the circumstances within which we operate as individuals, as well as our own particular abilities to cope with it. The relationship between pressure and performance can be identified via the 'stress/performance curve': with experiences at either end being described as:

- *rustout* (where the individual receives too little stimulation/tension);
- *burnout* (where the individual receives too much stimulation/tension).

As Farber (1991: 35) has noted, in an extensive study of stress in American teachers, burnout can be especially destructive, with

- a sense of enthusiasm and dedication, giving way to
- a sense of frustration and anger in response to personal, work-related and societal stressors, which then engenders
- a sense of inconsequentiality, leading to
- a withdrawal of commitment, leading to
- a growing sense of personal vulnerability (with multiple physical, cognitive and emotional symptoms), which if not dealt with may escalate and lead to
- a sense of depletion and loss of caring.

Although it may seem helpful to try to determine how much stress people can withstand, this is highly dependent on individuals themselves, their personalities, the context within which they operate and how they perceive stressful situations. Friedman and Rosenman (1974) identified individual personality types, labelling them 'type A' (the coronary-prone personality) and 'type B' (the more relaxed personality), and argued that a clear link exists between coronary heart disease and personality type. Research has indicated that headteachers tend to score higher as 'type A' individuals (Kelly 1988).

It is generally conceded that this type A/type B categorization provides some insight into the identification of stress-prone personalities. There are, nevertheless, reservations about deriving general health–stress link explanations in this way, even though the concept of a 'feelgood' factor which is more than physical health may be associated with the alleviation of stress. One of the most significant of the emotional factors is that our work should maximize our feelings of well-being or self-esteem: the development-focused model of appraisal, for example, was intended to explore these feelings against the background of inhibiting factors which may be work-related.

One way of assessing the impact of various factors which induce stressful situations is via a 'stress audit', in which the context, structure, controls, demands and relationships in our work are assessed as potential causal factors. Results may be aggregated for a group or team, and then at a higher level for the organization, to identify those common factors which leaders can endeavour to improve. However, such audits indicate that individuals and groups require conducive physical and emotional environments within which to develop fully.

Brown (1993), in a succinct summary of stress management issues, argues that the right links need to be made in relation to stress management issues. For *individuals*, it is vital that a stress audit is linked to an overall appraisal review; for *organizations*, a continuing stress audit needs to be linked to group and institutional development; and for *LEAs*, a system is needed which both identifies and compensates for stress across the system. When completing an audit, individuals tend to *minimize* those situations where they feel valued: there is evidence that 'feeling valued' may be a compensating factor helping people to overcome other deficiencies and the particular demands of a work situation (Travers and Cooper 1995). There is also evidence that until individuals begin to recognize fully the levels of stress that they are experiencing, they will, albeit subconsciously, rationalize it and hide it from both themselves and others at work (Watts and Cooper 1992). In extensive research into secondary school management, Torrington and Weightman (1989) have identified 'valuing' as one of seven key issues 'central to effective management'. While 'valuing' does not eliminate stress, it can help stressed individuals to be more open about it. The other key management issues noted by Torrington and Weightman are:

- school culture and ethos;
- control and autonomy;
- coordination and cohesiveness;
- resources;
- participation;
- change.

This list indicates the kinds of components involved in setting the cultural tone, removing stress and enhancing teaching effectiveness. The importance of valuing individuals – and of being valued ourselves – is closely linked to the organizational culture created and the way that people work together, since 'when the culture works against you, it's nearly impossible to get anything done' (Deal and Kennedy 1983). Although a cultural network may incorporate many roles, those who effectively set the values framework are effectively what Schein (1985) has called the 'culture founders' – leaders charged with disseminating values while valuing others.

Elliot Kemp's (1983) model of the three key components of stress – the environment, the person and the person–environment interface – helps to illuminate Torrington and Weightman's 'valuing' findings. Fear, worry and loss of sleep are characteristic behaviours arising from person-related stress, while role issues are characteristic problems where the person–environment interface is concerned. Elliot Kemp classifies stress according to the balance between *perceived demands* on the one side, and *perceived personal resources* on the other, which the individual believes he or she possesses to meet such demands. These result in:

- *Distress* or limited challenge: where personal resources outstrip the demands of the role and responsibilities (e.g. the second in department unable to secure promotion);
- *Eustress* or comfort: where there is personal comfort that one has sufficient resources to meet the demands of the role (e.g. the course leader who thoroughly enjoys work);
- *'Challenge eustress'*: where demands, while being met, are extending the personal resources of the role holder (e.g. the primary school deputy head carrying considerable administrative burdens).
- *'Dysfunctional distress'*: where demands outstrip the personal resources to handle the situation (e.g. back to Jane in the cameo).

ACTION

Bearing in mind your current role and responsibilities, try to

- identify a list of factors which you feel contribute to the pressures you face in your role;
- compile a list of elements which you find help to reduce the pressures or 'stresses' of your role;
- assess your position on the Kemp continuum.

Kemp's comfort and challenge situations are related to medical research evidence which suggests that individuals need a certain level of stress to function effectively. In some circumstances, stimulation and pressure helps creativity and innovation enormously, making stress beneficial. A stress reaction can also have positive effects, triggering the extra energy required in particular circumstances – the 'adrenaline flow' idea – making stress what Selye (1956) has called 'the spice of life'. However, the relationship between pressure, stress and performance is a complex one, with negative or harmful stress resulting from either too little or too much stress. While it does not remedy the stress-causing situation, Cranwell-Ward (1987) has suggested ten personal coping strategies for dealing with the resulting imbalance when stress becomes too great a problem:

1 Review your relationship with your job regularly.
2 Develop your self-management skills.
3 Improve your emotional management.
4 Manage relationships more effectively.
5 Improve your problem-solving approach.
6 Develop your physical stamina.
7 Assess your outlook on life and develop a more positive stance.
8 Develop techniques for reducing the negative effects of stress.
9 Develop an effective approach to managing change.
10 Seek outside help if necessary.

According to Frogatt and Stamp (1991), we can all develop strategies for dealing with work-induced stress in more positive and productive ways: first, people should get to know their own *personal* limits and capabilities; second, they should consciously develop personal skills and resources to meet any demands they *choose* to take on, rather than have imposed on them; third, they should become *actively aware* of relevant life stages, life events and the non-work pressures facing them so that they do not overly stretch their mental and physical coping skills. Similarly, Toffler (1970) has argued that we need to develop our own particular 'stability zones' during periods of significant upheaval and stress. When confronted with instability and/or change in some part of our professional or personal lives, Toffler suggests that the people most successful at managing stress are those capable of maintaining stability in *other* parts of their lives. And, as Handy (1993) notes, 'a stability zone can be a place or time for rebuilding energy resources', since 'Decisions use energy. New situations imply new decision rules. If one is to manage stress it is important to conserve energy, to reserve energy for important problems and the strategic decisions' (Handy 1993: 377).

Managers may have a particularly difficult role in dealing with overly stressed staff, particularly where team-based support is limited or non-existent. Cook (1992) argues that, while dealing with such issues demands tact, a range of management strategies are available which can both help colleagues to deal with their stress and help the organization to resolve stress-inducing situations *more* rather than *less* productively. First, he argues, managers can help others to review those routines and practices which appear to trigger stress; second, they can help them set more realistic and achievable goals; third, they can help them recognize their limitations as well as skills, a strategy demanding considerable tact; fourth, they can help colleagues to find 'recharging' time and space; fifth, they can try to ensure that things stay in perspective. While such strategies may prove useful, depending on circumstance, it is important to recognize that high levels of stress may demand clinical as well as managerial support.

This leads us to consider once again the impact of the dynamics of the educational environment at the present time on stress levels in schools and colleges. Ouston *et al.* (1996) show how Ofsted inspections have engendered stress among school staff, illustrating how they 'feed off' each other's anxieties. Given the endemic nature of educational change, we might argue that determining individual 'stability zones' has become an essential prerequisite for survival – and an issue for managers to acknowledge as important. One way of managing personal stress is to identify sound personal strategies for attaining individual goals.

While management cannot be predictive, individual managers (as well as other staff) may be able to create their own 'comfort zone' by trying to establish relatively clear ideas about their own roles within the organizational structure and their own personal ambitions. While employment conditions, and to a lesser extent individual job descriptions, may help to define organizational roles, responsibilities and accountabilities, they are not usually much help in indicating the knowledge, skills, attitudes and values expected from a particular post-holder. Fulfilling these expectations in a creative, valued and valuing way is a function of the organizational culture in which we work. It is also a reflection of the extent to which we feel motivated – whether as individuals or as team members – as well as how we can also motivate others. We consider these issues in the following chapter.

Suggestions for further reading

Bell, J. and Harrison, B. T. (eds) (1995) *Vision and Values in Managing Education: Successful Leadership Principles and Practice*. London: David Fulton.

Day, C., Hall, C. and Whitaker, P. (1998) *Developing Leadership in Primary Schools*. London: Paul Chapman Publishing.

Handy, C. (1990) *Inside Organizations*. London: BBC.

Nelson-Jones, R. (1996) *Relating Skills*. London: Cassell.

Pedler, M., Burgoyne, J. and Boydell, T. (1986) *A Manager's Guide to Self Development*, 2nd edn. Maidenhead: McGraw-Hill.

Travers, C. and Cooper, C. (1995) *Teachers Under Pressure: Stress in the Teaching Profession*. London: Routledge.

4 Motivating and managing others

One vital component which is difficult to chart is morale and motivation . . . the morale and motivation of both teachers and pupils probably affects the change process more than any legislation or any report.

(Goddard and Leask 1992: 40)

Motivation and education

Unlike industry and business, education has traditionally paid very little attention to 'motivation' and job satisfaction. Although pupil motivation issues gain increasing attention, most studies of teacher motivation concentrate on 'new' teachers rather than what Huberman (1993) calls the 'evolution of motives' which comes later in teachers' careers. Nevertheless, in a context where the 'measurement' of institutional and individual performances is becoming a major focus, a key question for heads and other education managers is how they can help colleagues to give their best – how can they help to 'motivate' them?

In some ways, concepts of 'teacher professionalism' and 'teacher autonomy' have acted as a brake on management development in schools and colleges in the past, contributing to a lack of concern over motivation. Apparently, teachers didn't need motivating: like nuns they 'had a vocation' and, anyway, as highly committed professionals they 'could look after themselves'. During the past twenty years, however, increasing interest in human resource management (HRM) has made motivation increasingly important in the management of education. This changing focus is partly due to economic imperatives, the pace of change and altering organizational structures. We are now witnessing, whether in business or education:

- *increasingly devolved responsibilities* to smaller, self-managing, autonomous work groups, where each individual counts and is, ideally, highly valued;
- *a global focus on entrepreneurialism, competition and 'the market'*, bringing 'down-sized' organizations with 'leaner, flatter hierarchies', setting a premium on safe, long-term and permanent jobs as well as providing new challenges;
- *increasing emphasis on 'efficiency', 'economy' and 'value for money'*, stemming partly from increasingly sophisticated technological developments – bringing the threat of deskilling or redundancy for some and opportunities for others.

Given that education is predominantly a 'people business', motivating others – whether students or staff – is a key skill and major priority. Heads of primary schools – likened by some to the heads of small businesses – need to maximize both individual and organizational potential, a task which can be very difficult where the institutional ethos does not support, for example, incentive payments for additional curriculum responsibilities. Undoubtedly, though, as in industry, education managers are confronted with the need to 'get the best' from colleagues in a fast-moving world, with constrained resources and what seems like endemic, but often disjointed, innovation.

REFLECTION

Can you recall what your own motives were for taking your first job in education? What motivated you towards becoming an education manager? Where has reality fallen short and how is this related to aspects of motivation?

Motivation at work

Motivation of its members is one of the most critical tasks facing any organization . . . the concept of motivation is probably the most confused, confusing and poorly developed concept in organizational psychology.
(Smith *et al.* 1990: 29)

Like theories about management and leadership, motivation is a contested concept with no agreed, single definition: it is multifaceted and has been described as comprising 'all those inner-striving conditions described as wishes, desires, drives . . . . an inner state that activates or moves individuals' (Steiner 1965: 14). Despite difficulties over its precise nature, motivation is pivotal for managers because it concerns:

- *the goals* influencing our behaviour;
- *the thought processes* we use to identify our needs and drives towards particular decisions, goals and behaviours;
- *the social processes* which encourage a continuation of, or changes in, our behaviour patterns.

Mitchell (1982: 81) defines motivation as 'the degree to which an individual wants and chooses to engage in certain specified behaviours', and identifies four characteristics:

- It is an individual phenomenon: each of us is unique.
- It is normally within our own personal control: we choose how we behave.
- It is multifaceted: the two most important factors being 'arousal' (i.e. what gets people moving) and the choice or direction of our behaviour.
- It is concerned with the internal and external forces which influence our choice of action rather than with the behaviour itself.

In a review of teacher motivation, Whitaker (1993a: 122) asserts that it involves 'inspiring others; providing realistic challenges; helping others to set goals and targets; and helping others to value their own contributions and achievements'. This is implicit in the results of research undertaken by Harris *et al.* (1995), which stresses the importance of a strong vision for 'downward transmission of values' to the classroom level. Views about the role of motivation at work have often grown out of underlying assumptions about 'what makes people tick' and how they should be managed or led.

ACTION

Before reading on, make a note of what you consider motivates you personally in your present job or role. Then compare your own list of motivating factors with those which follow.

Handy (1993) has suggested that most managers utilize five motivational assumptions:

- *Rational-economic assumption.* Here, people tend to be viewed as essentially passive, readily manipulated and controlled largely through economic incentives like extra payments or fringe benefits. Education has traditionally offered limited scope to motivate in this way – with few opportunities to provide 'fringe benefits'. However, recent policy initiatives like 'advanced skills teachers' (AST) and 'beacon schools' – both of which attract additional funds – may be indicative of a fundamental policy change and, increasingly, schools and colleges are providing short-term incentive allowances for specific task-limited roles.
- *Social assumption.* Here, people are seen as social animals, gaining their basic identity and meaning through social rather than work relationships. Managing such people involves mobilizing social relationships, with leadership style and group behaviours very important. Working parties or task groups established in schools or colleges for specific tasks are indicative of this approach: groups then gain socially from the experience, continuing to operate by finding new tasks or a *raison d'être*. There is, for example, the PTA committee which meets in the pub as the 'Friends of the School' long after the last of their offspring have left school!
- *Self-actualizing assumption.* Here, people are seen as primarily self-motivating and self-controlling. They are 'mature' and able to integrate personal and organizational goals – though their motivation may be influenced by external pressures. Examples in education might include those teachers who always seem keen to undertake further training/development – almost regardless of topic – so as to 'be prepared' for that next promotion.
- *Complex assumption.* Here, people are viewed as highly variable, having numerous motives and responses to various managerial strategies. The degree of motivation often depends on personal assessments of how far situations satisfy particular needs at any given moment. Education managers might successfully persuade colleagues to take on apparently 'high status'

roles (involving no extra payment!), with the possible outcome that 'status' eventually becomes an insufficient inducement, and demands for money, time or special privileges may follow in order to maintain continuation or provide 'compensation'.

- *Psychological assumption*. Here, people are viewed as complex and mature, continually evolving and passing through various psychological and physiological stages of development – striving towards their 'ego ideal', which lies beyond basic hunger, sexuality and aggression drives. In education, managers utilizing this assumption recognize the complexities of motivation and that colleagues are at different motivational stages – with, perhaps, individual satisfaction deriving initially from money, then status and, later, influence/power, or even a combination of all three.

Arguably, each of these assumptions may significantly (albeit subconsciously) influence the leadership and management strategies we use. The danger is that we stick to one motivational 'style' or assumption rather than seeing ourselves as having a repertoire of 'approaches': a headteacher who tends to adopt 'rational-economic' assumptions might, for example, tend to see 'deals' and 'fringe benefits' as *the* way to motivate colleagues (even if education doesn't really facilitate such an approach and colleagues are not 'switched on' by them) – and then wonders why they don't produce results! Another leader, utilizing 'self-actualizing' or 'psychological' assumptions, may see professional development and improved work environments as the key. While such a strategy may be very successful for some staff, it is not the only solution: motivating others is not usually as simple or straightforward as this might imply.

For example, Leithwood's (1990) analysis of teachers' career cycles indicates how different motivational strategies may influence their drive for achievement at various career stages:

1 Career launch (motivated by newly qualified enthusiasm).
2 Stabilization (driven by maturing commitment; feeling at ease).
3 Diversification (encouraged by new challenges and concerns).
4 Professional plateau (reappraisal: cynicism? stagnation? less striving?).
5 Retirement preparation (serenity? disenchantment?).

Thus, knowing 'where people are at' is important: a deputy on a 'professional plateau' may find new challenges difficult to deal with and may be hard to motivate, whereas a highly motivated, newly qualified teacher may be overly willing to take on new responsibilities.

REFLECTION

How easy have you found it to identify what motivates you? What implications might this have for you when trying to motivate others, whether students or staff?

Motivation theories

Motivation theories were developed largely after the Second World War to meet the growing need for more effective industrial and commercial organization, and are usually divided between content and process theories. Content theorists try to explain what motivates us, whereas process theories examine the dynamics of motivation, focusing on the processes which influence how people decide on, develop and pursue particular behaviours. In effect, content theories concentrate on what motivates us, while process theories focus on how we are motivated.

Content theories

Maslow's hierarchy of needs

Of all the content theories, those based on 'need' have been particularly influential. Maslow (1943), considered something of a 'motivation guru' when his work on the 'hierarchy of needs' was published, identified five types of need. He argued that 'a satisfied need is no longer a motivator' and suggested that lower order needs must be satisfied before higher order ones can motivate behaviour. Maslow's five need levels are often shown as a pyramid in ascending order:

- *Self-actualization needs (the highest level)*, involve realizing one's full potential – what Maslow describes as 'becoming everything that one is capable of becoming'. Achievements take many forms and vary between individuals.
- *Self-esteem or ego needs*, i.e. the need for self-respect, confidence, personal reputation and esteeming others.
- *Social or love needs*, i.e. the need for affection, a sense of belonging, social activities, friendship and giving/receiving love.
- *Safety and security needs*, i.e. the need for security, freedom from pain, physical attack, predictability, orderliness.
- *Physiological needs (the lowest level)*, i.e. 'homeostasis' (the body's automatic efforts to function normally) and covers the basic need for food, water, sleep, sex.

Maslow's model assumes, first, that we are motivated by having unsatisfied needs; second, that once satisfied, a need no longer motivates; and, third, that higher order needs are less likely to be satisfied than lower order ones. Despite its popularity, Maslow's work has been criticized because his 'hierarchy' theory:

- has not been confirmed by research evidence;
- does not explain how some rewards or outcomes can satisfy more than one need, e.g. higher salaries can be paid at all levels;
- may be too culturally specific (i.e. middle class) rather than universally valid;
- does not recognize that people value the same need in different ways and takes no account of altruistic behaviour, i.e. satisfying others' needs;
- fails to account for non-work situations, i.e. needs can be satisfied socially and elsewhere;
- doesn't account for different value systems and gender issues;

- appears overly simplistic, e.g. it doesn't account for achievement, power and affiliation needs (McLelland 1961);
- offers a number of hierarchical levels which appear too restrictive to explain all needs;
- does not clearly define terms like 'self-actualization'.

Although these criticisms may appear theoretical, they do remind us that even seemingly seductive explanations like Maslow's model may not readily explain the complexities of motivation and the behaviour of our colleagues.

McGregor's Theory X and Theory Y

Maslow's ideas gained wider publicity through the popularity of McGregor (1960), who suggested that motivation is affected by two sets of contrasting assumptions about people and work: Theory X and Theory Y. According to McGregor, Theory X assumes that most people

- inherently dislike work and are lazy;
- are self-centred and lack ambition – indifferent to their organization's needs, they have to be coerced, directed, controlled or threatened in order to achieve at work;
- prefer to be directed, wish to avoid responsibility and, above all, want security.

By contrast, Theory Y assumes that most people

- are, by nature, physically and mentally energetic – work is as natural to them as rest and play, and laziness results from poor experiences at work;
- do not need to be externally controlled or directed – people can exercise internal self-control and self-direction when working towards objectives to which they are personally committed;
- will seek and accept responsibilities under the right conditions;
- have the capacity to exercise a high degree of creativity, imagination and ingenuity, and only become passive and resistant to the organization's needs because of the way they have been treated.

McGregor was convinced that Theory Y brought about more effective management (though he also felt that there were occasions when Theory X behaviour might be appropriate). While both Theory X and Theory Y are clearly over-simplifications of reality, McGregor argued that, in essence, a Theory Y approach could be successful and effective in motivating others.

Argyris (1964) has argued that too many organizations are stuck with Theory X thinking patterns, perpetuated through limited and routinized jobs and the rejection of new, more creative ideas, thus failing to encourage staff to develop mature patterns of work behaviour.

Herzberg's two factor theory

Unlike Maslow's or McGregor's theoretical approaches, Herzberg's (1966) work is based on actual research with groups of engineers and accountants. His

Table 4.1   'Hygienes' and 'Motivators'

'Hygienes' or 'job context' *factors arise from*	*'Motivators' or 'job content'* *factors arise from*
Supervision	The nature of the work
Interpersonal relations	Responsibility
Working conditions	Advancement

'motivation-hygiene' theory offers a more sophisticated analysis of the significance of higher and lower order needs, and had a major impact on the nature of job structuring in organizations from the 1960s onwards.

His study outlined a range of factors which produced 'job satisfaction' and 'job dissatisfaction' among workers. In short, he noted that while certain factors were associated with satisfaction (what Herzberg called 'motivators'), others were clearly linked with dissatisfaction (what he called 'hygienes'). They were not, however, simple 'mirror images' of each other: motivators were linked with the nature of the job (i.e. job content) and hygiene factors were linked with work environment (i.e. job context).

So, while 'poor company administration' was linked with dissatisfaction, 'good company administration' was rarely linked with satisfaction. While 'recognition' was frequently linked with satisfaction, a 'lack of recognition' was rarely associated with dissatisfaction. For Herzberg, job satisfaction and job dissatisfaction resulted from different causes (see Table 4.1). Herzberg pointed out that while hygiene improvements might prevent dissatisfaction, they would not increase work commitment and satisfaction. Consequently, even if pay and other hygiene factors are high, people may still not give their best efforts or feel motivated. In educational terms, this may help to explain why some staff seem to complain constantly about poorly furnished and overcrowded staff common rooms, but then take newly refurbished, spacious and comfortable provision for granted.

While they are superficially attractive, Herzberg's theories have also encountered several criticisms:

- Research evidence is not conclusive either way: is there a difference between an engineer and a teacher?
- Hygiene factors and motivators tend to depend on individual circumstances and preferences: think of the impact of smoking on organizational happiness.
- Herzberg's findings could be explained by human nature, e.g. we may blame 'the organization' when things go wrong (hygiene factors) but take personal credit for successes (motivators) – a frequent response in the appraisal of an underperforming colleague.
- In reality, the difference between 'job content' and 'job context' factors may be blurred, since one person's motivator could be another's hygiene factor.

Herzberg also suggested that the redesign of jobs to increase motivation and performance should concentrate on motivators. The 'job enrichment' movement grew largely out of his conclusions. He identified seven loading factors which would help to achieve job enrichment and which are often used in human resource management in education:

- *Remove controls*, e.g. allow department heads or curriculum leaders to plan without undue reporting back.
- *Increase accountability*, e.g. ensure that department heads or curriculum leaders present an annual report.
- *Create natural work units*, e.g. support heads of department and curriculum leaders in building teams of involved staff.
- *Provide direct feedback*, e.g. ensure that curriculum leaders are kept informed of 'client' comment.
- *Introduce new tasks*, e.g. offer key staff opportunities to integrate their work with others.
- *Allocate special assignments*, e.g. ask middle managers to undertake strategic reviews of areas of work.
- *Grant additional authority*, e.g. give specific external relations responsibilities to key middle managers.

In 'job enrichment', the job is first enlarged and then a range of traditional managerial functions are left to an individual's own judgement. Other strategies arising out of the movement included 'job rotation' (i.e. scheduling a person's time to include a variety of tasks) and 'job enlargement' (i.e. changing production processes and methods to ensure that people perform a complete range of tasks).

ACTION

Using Herzberg's theory, evaluate your present role and responsibilities, identifying any factors associated with satisfaction (motivators) and dissatisfaction (hygiene factors). On the basis of this experience, does Herzberg's theory seem valid for you? Do Maslow or McGregor offer complementary or alternative explanations of your attitude?

Process theories

In addition to content theories, several process theories have been developed – among them equity (or exchange) theory, expectancy theory and goal theory. Process theories focus on the complexity and dynamics of relationships and the processes of motivation.

Equity theory

Equity theory (or 'exchange theory', as it is also known) argues that people's motivation at work is affected by whether they feel fairly treated: most people balance what they put into work with what they get from it and then compare their rewards with those gained by others (Adams 1965). In effect, we each calculate the costs and benefits of working in a particular organization and check whether we are being treated equitably with others. The theory operates on the assumption that individuals are motivated to reduce inequity and unfairness by:

- changing their work conditions and/or the rewards they get;
- changing the level of effort they put in;
- changing (or appearing to change) what they do in order to alter the impression others have of them;
- comparing themselves with different individuals or groups in the organization, effectively reconstructing their view of equity and inequity;
- changing their job or their work situation within the organization, or, in the extreme, changing the organization they work in.

In education, as institutions face budgetary constraints limiting the room for financial reward, this theory may increasingly appeal to managers attempting to ensure rewards match efforts.

Expectancy theory

This is the most influential of the process theories and is based on the assumption that people are motivated by what they regard as the likely impact of their actions (Vroom 1964, 1974). Expectancy theorists argue: first, that individuals examine, in a rational way, the prospects for different rewards which might arise from adopting various courses of action; second, that individuals decide to act in a way which is (a) likely to be successful and (b) most likely to produce the highest reward for them personally. Not surprisingly, people appear to be most highly motivated when each of the following elements is present:

- they feel confident of achieving a high level of performance;
- the attraction of the reward is high;
- they think they will receive rewards if they perform well;
- they feel they will be fairly rewarded by comparison with others around them.

Despite the apparent complexity of the calculations involved, expectancy theorists accept that people don't necessarily consciously engage in the process of decision making outlined above: they accept that it is a subjective process.

Goal theories

These theories (see Locke and Latham 1990) argue that increased motivation and performance occurs where people agree specific and difficult goals and when feedback is given on their subsequent performance. They argue that both direct (e.g. time-limited) and indirect (e.g. verbal praise) incentives may increase motivation, especially when it is part of participative goal-setting backed by guidance. In goal theory, feedback is seen as crucial if motivation is to be maintained. Goal theory may, therefore, be regarded as potentially valuable in educational organizations if collegial and collaborative work climates exist and the focus is on participation rather than coercion.

REFLECTION

Do you think that working in a 'service' organization like education rather than a business organization *per se* makes a difference to the way you and your colleagues are motivated? How far do you consider the needs of individuals can be recognized and used as motivators in educational institutions?

 ## Developing motivational strategies

Various motivational strategies are utilized by managers – whether in educational or business organizations and whether consciously or not. Armstrong (1988) outlines three common approaches to motivation, but admits that while each has its merits, they are also 'essentially simplistic' solutions to what are fundamentally complex issues:

- *The 'carrot and stick' approach*: based on the idea that people work for rewards: the better you pay them the harder they are likely to work. If they do not work satisfactorily, then punish them.
- *Motivating through the work itself*: based on the idea that giving people fulfilling work will raise their level of job satisfaction, thus improving their performance levels.
- *The 'one-minute manager' system*: based on the idea that you should set goals for staff; give them positive feedback when they do things right; and negative, but considerate, feedback when they do something wrong.

Clearly, a complex range of motivational strategies is needed by managers – though it is also vital to acknowledge that individuals themselves will ultimately determine whether (and by how much) they actually wish to become motivated. The crucial element is finding an appropriate 'motivational mix' – one that is appropriate for the individual concerned, fits the nature of the work, is ethical and meshes in with the organizational culture. Finding this mix can be extremely difficult.

ACTION

The following is an extract from an Ofsted report on a failing secondary school (though it could easily reflect a college or other educational establishment). Assume that you are the recently appointed headteacher and are being asked by the governors to outline the ways in which you might motivate the school's demoralized staff. What would be the main points of your argument?

'Staff morale was very low about Christmas time but the present senior managers are respected and this is having an influence as staff believe that progress is being made and that there is hope for the future. Crisis management and day to day survival has been the theme for much of the year but now there is an active move in a number of areas or plans that will lead to development. Leadership from middle management is varied. A number of heads of department are comparatively new in post, others are, or have been ill, and the school has suffered from lack of clear direction.

It is important to remember that each motivational strategy has the potential to demotivate if used in inappropriate circumstances and motivational problems may arise when there is little or no fit between individuals' needs and work characteristics. Consequently, in attempting to devise motivational strategies, diagnoses of a person's basic growth and social needs are important: different needs may demand different strategies to satisfy them. As Hunt (1979) notes, individuals are also likely to have different 'motivation profiles' which are related to both their age and their professional stage of development. Scott (1997), in addition, points to the multiple criteria used by participants involved in the process of educational improvement: expectations determine action.

Torrington and Weightman (1989: 45) recognize these varying expectations and aspirations, and stress that motivation through 'valuing' is a 'complex social interaction requiring the others' views to be considered at all times. It is their needs as people, not just job holders, that have to be met, because the job is held by the complete person, not the part which comes to school.' They go on to suggest that the following elements are key strategies in managing motivation:

- being considerate and courteous to others;
- providing clear feedback, whether formal or informal;
- delegating in a 'real' sense, rather than simply giving out jobs/tasks;
- adopting genuinely participative approaches to decision making, where colleagues' views really count.

Lastly, a comprehensive range of potential motivation strategies which are built around individual growth needs have been suggested by Kakabadse et al. (1988) (see Table 4.2). While some of these approaches are encountered under other guises elsewhere in the book, Table 4.2 provides a relatively full picture.

ACTION

Try to compare your answers to the previous Action with the comprehensive list outlined in Table 4.2, assessing the practicability of Kakabadse et al.'s list as an answer for the governing body of the failing school.

Table 4.2 Possible motivation strategies

Results-focused appraisal	Where job effectiveness is evaluated by measuring actual accomplishments against previously determined goals; provides a framework for reward
Job enrichment or 'vertical job loading'	Where individuals have greater autonomy, responsibility and job control
Quality circles	Where participative problem solving and decision making is emphasized and teamwork is used to identify and solve specific quality-related problems
Management training	Where reappraisal of professional skills, attitudes and job behaviour is undertaken
Situational leadership	Where 'appropriacy' of leadership style to circumstance is evaluated
Autonomous workgroups	Where groups are given discrete tasks and significant autonomy to decide how to complete them – an essential ingredient in work design technology
Organic organizational design	Where challenging, but self-limiting, job experiences are set or project groups with specific and limited purposes are established
Job tenure	Where jobs are 'for life' (a double-edged sword in motivational terms) and either stimulate positive attitudes and performance because of job security, or the reverse
Staff benefits or rewards	Where rewards are not tied to specific jobs or individual performances, but are part of a general 'package'
Job design by accountabilities	Where jobs are identified according to each job holder's accountabilities

Source: based on Kakabadse *et al.* (1988).

The implications for education managers

Several writers on educational management consider the implications of motivational theories for managing schools and colleges. Dean (1995), for example, suggests that the following elements are positive motivators for teachers:

- students' development and learning;
- enthusiasm for their subject matter;
- recognition, interest, praise and encouragement;
- a chance to contribute and shine;
- the chance to take responsibility;
- challenges to their professional skill;
- the inspiration of others;
- career prospects.

Trethowan (1987) identifies several positive motivators which, when carefully chosen to suit individual needs, may be valuable in dealing with apparently apathetic behaviour. He also suggests that many of the following teacher-motivators are appropriate motivators with pupils and students:

- overt achievements;
- recognition by management;
- the job itself;
- delegated responsibility;
- advancement;
- personal growth;
- cash, particularly related to specific achievement.

By contrast, Day *et al.* (1990) outline below various ways in which teachers may become demotivated. While Day *et al.*'s focus is on professional development, the issues are fairly readily transferable to other motivational circumstances:

1 People are simply told that 'they must . . .'.
2 People are put into a threatened position.
3 Activities and responsibilities are not well planned.
4 It is felt that the plan is a 'gimmick' promoted by a senior member of staff to further his or her own ends.
5 People feel that the plan is mounted merely to satisfy higher authority.
6 A lot of hard work is involved without any apparent or obvious results.
7 Initial moves are badly organized, with consequent initial negative feedback.
8 People feel alienated from the school or from whoever is responsible for the plan.
9 The head/leader assumes the role of the 'expert', and there is a lack of opportunity for teachers to develop, or to exercise, responsibility;
10 There is group pressure from colleagues to 'opt out' (adapted from Day *et al.* 1990).

REFLECTION

To what extent is the *prevention of demotivation* more important than the *promotion of motivation* in the leadership of an organization known to you?

Since all of us have our own individually determined needs and drives, the task of managing to motivate others – whether pupils, students or staff – is not easy. Realistically we need to focus on 'the art of the possible' – getting to know what makes each person 'tick' individually – since despite the various models available, ready-made motivational formulae are non-existent. West-Burnham (1990) suggests six pointers, which, he argues, will help to motivate those working in education:

1 Make rewards valued and appropriate.
2 Ensure the link between effort, performance and outcome is seen in individual and subjective terms.
3 Negotiate outcomes; don't set them arbitrarily.
4 Managing motivation means understanding individuals and managing the variables.

5 Interpersonal skills are vital in identifying and understanding other people's perceptions.
6 Key practical activities associated with motivating colleagues are job design, appraisal, target setting, feedback and review.

For West-Burnham, appraisal and professional development are the key elements involved in motivation. He asserts, 'Managers cannot motivate: they have to operate procedures which allow them to identify, support and reinforce individual perception and this is best done through appraisal linked to professional and personal development' (1990: 85–6). Linked with this, Thompson (1991, 1992) has argued that we must begin by recognizing the complexities involved in motivation. In an examination of gender issues, she asserts:

> Comparative studies of men and women in 65 occupations found that most men work for money and career advancement. Men are always looking up the ladder to the main chance whereas women seek job satisfaction, a good working atmosphere and flexibility to fit family life into their careers . . . Research suggests that these attitudes are shared by teachers too. Women teachers value classroom teaching and put it as a priority . . . They are more hesitant about career moves unless they have assessed their readiness . . . In comparison, men teachers show little interest in this kind of self evaluation, do not mention their home situation and see their future in terms of promotion moves.
>
> (Thompson 1992: 260)

REFLECTION

How far are Thompson's comments borne out by your own experience?

As education has become more 'business-oriented', motivation has become an increasingly complex and central issue for those in leadership roles. While managers cannot directly motivate, they can establish a working climate where people feel motivated. Above all, what we can call manager-awareness of how to value others' contributions – whether pupils, students or staff – seems to be the key element in 'managing to motivate' – despite the complexities involved. Shearman (1995) suggests that much might be gained from re-examining, within the educational context, the role of motivation, while Peters and Waterman's (1982) well publicized 'attributes of excellent companies' *In Search of Excellence* was rapidly taken up in the early years of the post-1988 revolution – particularly because motivation plays such a pivotal role in their checklist:

- a bias for action;
- staying close to the customer;
- autonomy and entrepreneurship;
- productivity through people;
- a hands-on and value-driven approach;
- sticking to the knitting;

- simple form, lean staff;
- simultaneous loose–tight properties.

Viewed as an underlying philosophy, their 'hands-on, value-driven' dictum might be seen as crucial in school processes for achieving objectives: without motivated staff and students, goals would be unachievable. At the same time, though, personal satisfaction must be balanced against organizational needs – potentially a cause of tension where well developed appraisal systems identify personal targets, which are then inhibited by limited resources and the need to meet whole-school objectives. The emphasis on organizational excellence also raises questions about the place of the individual. Some education management writers are critical of Peters and Waterman's business 'excellence' strategies, suggesting that they are more akin to manipulation than motivation and recommending that educationists should not 'uncritically disseminate the standard management writing as "good practice" for schools' (Bottery 1994: 129). The following cameo illustrates the complex issues involved.

Cameo   **Motivating issues (part 1)**

The school management team were discussing a formal request from Bill W that he should be allowed to serve as a magistrate on the local bench – with absence from school on 18 half-days a year. Replacement costs would be paid.

'I don't see why he should,' responded John, the deputy head responsible for curriculum. 'He teaches two GCSE groups, remember, and we can't guarantee that we'll get supply staff – anyway he's too cynical for words . . . He's one of the union group who undermined the changes in tutorial arrangements last year remember! We've got too much on with the inspection – anyway, everyone will want to "get out and about" if we let him go.'

'I don't agree,' said Rosemary, the deputy responsible for personnel. 'Let's look at it this way . . . if he's cynical – and I don't think he is really, he's just inclined to question what we're doing – then we have to try to bring him round to our side. In his favour he's a good teacher – he's served the kids well for, what, about 12 years, he's supported the school – and we know that if there's a regular arrangement, then Jill B wouldn't mind doing the supply: she likes him and they work well together.'

'There's more to it than that though,' interposed Jenny, the senior teacher responsible for the sixth form. 'Bill's got no future beyond this school now. He's 53 and he won't move on now: but y'know he's got real gifts, he listens to the older kids – they respect his views. I think we should give him a chance to use his skills, and we could use him for the personal and social education (PSE) programme – that law and order module – he'd be good!'

What decision would you reach? Why?

> **Cameo   Motivating issues (part 2)**
>
> The headteacher recommended to the governors that Bill W should be allowed to work as a magistrate outside the school.
>
> Two years later, Bill was interviewed by a union researcher investigating career structures. Responding to the question 'Do you feel valued by the school?', he answered 'I do now. Thinking about it, I s'pose it's because I've been able to . . .'
>
> Does this response alter your original views?

The headteacher in the cameo reached the right decision, we hope, and Bill felt that while he had 'plateaued' at school, he still had benefited from personal development opportunities that also helped him professionally at work in terms of role and relationships. In Chapter 3 we outlined the mechanics of decision making, and stressed the importance of decision quality and reflected on our capacity to make 'right' decisions, in the 'right' way and for the 'right' reasons. Part of the problem is that different participants see problems very differently. Leadership is, in part, about building effective teams so that decisions, while perhaps not totally acceptable to all participants, are at least accepted and worked upon.

Suggestions for further reading

Everard, K. B. and Morris, G. (1996) *Effective School Management*, 3rd edn. London: Paul Chapman Publishing.

Guest, D. (1984) What's new in motivation, *Personnel Management*, May, 21–3.

Huberman, M. (with Grounauer, M. M.) (1993) *The Lives of Teachers*. London: Cassell.

Maslow, A. (1970) *Motivation and Personality*. New York: Harper and Row.

Nias, J. (1981) Teacher satisfaction and dissatisfaction: Herzberg's 'two-factor hypothesis revisited', *British Journal of Sociology of Education*, 2(3), 235–46.

Robertson, I., Smith, J. and Cooper, M. (1992) *Motivation: Strategies, Theory and Practice*. London: Institute of Personnel Management.

Vroom, V. and Jago, A. (1988) *The New Leadership: Managing Participation in Organizations*. Englewood Cliffs, NJ: Prentice Hall.

5 Leading effective teams

Team leadership is the only form of leadership acceptable in a society where
power is shared and so many people are near equals.

(Belbin 1993: 107)

Rhetoric or reality?

The concepts of 'teamwork' and 'flatter hierarchies' are often portrayed as
essential ingredients in the restructuring of education. While these features
have become acknowledged cornerstones in business practice, they are increasingly recommended as key levers for maximizing school improvement and
effectiveness. As yet, however, there is relatively little research evidence or
'homegrown' theory about the impact of teamwork in teaching – a profession which, despite the rhetoric, inevitably retains a heavy reliance on the
individual abilities of teachers in classrooms to generate organizational success.

Nevertheless, teams are in many respects essential building blocks in developing organizational efficiency at a macro level – whether in educational
institutions or businesses. Over the past few decades, teamwork has become
very much part of the rhetoric of education – even if cynics sometimes argue
that the rhetoric fails to match the reality. This view may stem partially from
the difficulties faced by educational institutions attempting to establish a
delicate balance between promoting holistic institutional development through
team-based efforts and maximizing individual potential – whether in pupils,
students, teachers, support staff or managers.

While asserting that if we are to understand groups and teams we need
first to understand individuals, Adair (1986) nevertheless acknowledges the
difficulties of being simultaneously both an individual and a group member.
Pointing to the 'psychological contract' between individuals and the group
they belong to, he notes: 'Achieving a balance between the interests and
self-expression of each individual on the one hand and of the group on the
other, is one of the most challenging tasks of leaders' (Adair 1986: 59). For
Handy and Aitken (1986), groups exist to achieve purposes, and they identify
five reasons why individuals participate in them:

- to share in a common activity;
- to promote a cause or idea;
- to gain status or power;
- to have friends and 'belong';
- because it is part of their job.

The Ofsted Framework (Ofsted 1995a) and early inspection reports articulate the centrality of clearly defined organizational aims, demonstrating how they should guide the practicalities of educational development planning. A strong emphasis is placed on leadership and the collective responsibility of all stakeholders in promoting organizational effectiveness. Responding to both the internal and external pressures affecting school development does, however, require an understanding of teamwork and team leadership roles in planning, implementing and evaluating. For example, Bennett's (1995) scrutiny of how so-called 'middle managers' exercise team membership and leadership shows that a clear understanding of role and function promotes successful schooling.

Defining differences

So far we have used the terms 'group' and 'team' interchangeably. Some refining of ideas is essential before we move on to consider team development issues. Schein (1969: 36) has argued that a 'psychological group' is 'any number of people who

- interact with one another,
- are psychologically aware of one another, and
- perceive themselves to be a group.'

Offering his own definition, Adair (1986) specifies six key factors which make up a group:

1 A definable membership.
2 Group consciousness.
3 A sense of shared purpose.
4 Interdependence.
5 Interaction.
6 Ability to act in a unitary manner.

This provides us with a useful starting place for examining the work of groups, since it embraces several cardinal elements in group management. Although numerous definitions of key group qualities are possible from a management perspective – whether in education or business – the concept of 'purpose' is fundamental and leads us to consider one particular kind of group in more detail: the team.

The terms 'group' and 'team' are often used interchangeably by management theorists to describe individuals cooperating to achieve a given task. However, while 'group' tends to be a generic term covering two or more people working together, 'team' is used predominantly when a group is deliberately constructed and there is a clear focus on its processes and level of performance. In addition, there is often a hidden presumption that 'teams' are limited in terms of size, whereas groups are not limited in terms of number of individuals. As Chaudhry-Lawton *et al*. (1992: 137) comment:

Experience suggests that teams of over ten and under three perform less well. In smaller teams it is more difficult to bring together the range of skills and approaches that lead to the significant enhancement of problem-solving, creativity and enthusiasm found in teams of five to seven people.

According to Woodcock (1979: 7), teams provide unique opportunities, since 'they can make things happen which would not happen if the team did not exist'. He likens the team to a family which:

- provides help and support;
- coordinates the activities of individuals;
- generates commitment;
- provides a 'place to be', so meeting a basic human need to belong;
- identifies training and development needs;
- provides learning opportunities;
- enhances communication;
- provides a satisfying, stimulating and enjoyable working environment.

ACTION

Based around Woodcock's team attributes, which key questions would you ask to ascertain how the 'team' with which you work see its 'team character'? What answers would you anticipate, and why?

In examining the differences between groups and teams, Babington Smith and Farrell (1979) define teams by reference to two essential elements: the common task and complementary contributions. They point to the dangers of assuming, first, that teamwork is always central to task achievement and, second, that all workgroups are teams. In addition, we would suggest that teams are frequently distinguishable from groups when three elements are present:

- they share a common purpose and agreed values which help to regulate behaviour;
- they have a sense of 'team-identification';
- they have interconnecting and interdependent functions.

REFLECTION

Using your own organization as a 'case study', what seem to be the key differences between groups and teams? How is a clear distinction drawn?

 ## Teams and team development

Although numerous management theorists have attempted to identify how groups and teams develop over time, it is difficult to track a group's movement from initial unclear and ambiguous relationships towards more stable, integrated relationships and structures where norms and behaviour appear to be understood by all team members. Consequently, issues of team building and team development have become important research drivers in business because of the potential impact that team cohesiveness has on task achievement.

ACTION

Can you identify the various team-building stages when you last joined a new work group or team? How comfortable was the process and when did you begin to feel you 'belonged'?

Despite differences of view over team dynamics, there appears to be general consensus that the route to team or group cohesion is likely to be both traumatic and problematic. Clearly, lack of smooth progression and control in team development reflects the intricacy of the issues involved. Nevertheless, problems may seem inevitable, since many writers accept that teams pursue fairly predictable 'development routes' and sequences. Schutz (1966), for example, argues that teams face three 'stages of concern' and indicates key questions which need resolution at each stage:

- *Inclusion*: how far do I feel that I am part of this group/team?
- *Control*: how far am I at ease with the degree of influence that I have in this group/team?
- *Affection*: how far am I comfortable with the level of intimacy there is in this group/team?

According to Schutz, groups constantly 'recycle', revisiting phases of development as they attempt to confront and resolve problems. Schein (1969), adopting a variation on this approach, suggests that in early group/team meetings, 'self-oriented' behaviour is demonstrated, whereby members focus on their own needs, identities and roles, and that this predominates over concerns for other group members or group functions as a whole. He also identifies four principal self-oriented concerns raised by members and characterized by a good deal of conflict and issue-switching:

- *Identity*: who am I and what will I be in this group?
- *Control/influence*: how far will I be able to control/influence others?
- *Needs/goals*: will the group's goals satisfy my needs?
- *Acceptance/intimacy*: how far will the group like and accept me?

If we move from 'group' to 'team' characteristics, Tuckman (1965) provides a generally much better known team development model, incorporating four phases:

- *Forming*: characterized by uncertainty and anxiety.
- *Storming*: characterized by conflict and internal dissent.
- *Norming*: characterized by the development of cohesion and satisfaction as 'group' members.
- *Performing*: characterized by a central focus on task completion, with interpersonal difficulties resolved.

In fact, Tuckman and Jensen (1977) later added a further stage to Tuckman's four-phase model:

- *Adjourning*: where the team is likely to disband because the task has been achieved or because team members leave. As break-up is anticipated, team members reflect on their time together, preparing themselves for change.

Arguably, teams in *educational* organizations tend to have a longer term focus, rather than being simple task or project groups – although the increasing pressures of external initiatives mean that more 'one-off' teams are established in education to match new requirements.

Tuckman's model is often claimed as valid because it appears to be verified by research and seems to explain several issues associated with problematic workgroups which fail to become teams. For example, groups may end up working only at 'half power' when they have failed to work through early developmental issues, while working parties may be relatively inefficient and show impaired performance because their leadership remains unresolved. Furthermore, teams often pull in different directions because their purpose or mission remains unclear and their objectives are confused. Alternatively, they may become vehicles for personal aims (with unstated or hidden agendas), which then hinder team cohesiveness and achievement.

A common thread in much of the writing on team management and development focuses on the early stages of group formation and the need for individuals to accommodate their existing beliefs, attitudes and values with those of their team members and what appear to be 'group norms'. Woodcock (1979: 7), for example, comments that during these early stages 'People conform to the established line . . . because they are too scared to suggest changes.' Later, however, 'greater openness is encouraged with conflict surfacing and common ground being sought' (p. 7). Kakabadse *et al.* (1988: 360) point out that during the 'storming' stage 'differences in beliefs and values may lead one group member to be antipathetic towards others'. These are, however, eased at the 'norming' stage, as 'individuals are likely to give each other feedback on what they see and assess. By doing tasks, norms of behaviour and professional practice begin to be established (p. 361).' Similar tensions in the initial stages of team development are identified by Francis and Young (1979), who note that people seek to find out about one another, wanting to uncover attitudes, values, style, and the other person's readiness to be contacted. This testing process continues until each person makes a decision concerning the character of his or her involvement. This 'testing out' process and the pressure to establish norms or require new members to conform to norms are important aspects of team formation or induction, and it is vital that the degree of psychological pressure and strain on individuals during this stage is not underestimated.

ACTION

By reflecting on the earlier action point when you joined a new work team/ group, try to assess how relevant Tuckman's sequences were. Did your group reach the 'performing' or 'mature' stage? How influential was (a) the nature of leadership, (b) participant commitment and (c) work context?

Team-building issues

Reviewing the process of team building in business organizations, Francis and Young (1979) assess the characteristics of effective teamwork and its impact on both the individuals and the team concerned. Taking a group dynamics approach, they consider the implications for individuals and team quality and identify five 'benefits of team building', which involve a capacity for:

- managing complexity;
- giving a rapid response;
- achieving high motivation;
- making high quality decisions;
- developing collective strength.

Adair's (1986) examination of the dynamics of group functions which make these benefits possible outlines three interlocking needs which have to be managed skilfully if progress is to be made:

- *Task*: the need to accomplish something;
- *Team*: the need to develop and maintain working relationships; and
- *Individual*: the personal needs of individuals which come with them when they enter groups.

He poses a number of questions for the leader in developing each aspect. For example: 'Is the task clear?', 'Does the team clearly understand and accept its objectives?', 'Have individual targets been agreed and quantified?' Adair's checklist (see Table 5.1) provides the kind of format potentially useful to leaders when trying to sustain effective teamwork.

Within a school setting, Johnston and Pickersgill's research (1992) shows that team building may be inhibited by headteachers who perceive themselves as responsible for both school successes and failures. For them, team building is a way of changing institutional cultures so that responsibilities become shared. They contend that planned personal and interpersonal development (for all staff) is crucial and that, to be effective, there is a need to:

1 Manage time appropriately to enable planned and sustained group activities (e.g. through a training day).
2 Work selectively and differentially to build relationships and support individuals within the team.

Table 5.1 Checklist for organizing effective team activity

Task issues	Team issues	Individual issues
Purpose	Objectives	Targets
Responsibilities	Standards expected	Induction
Objectives	Size of team	Responsibilities
Programme	Social cohesion of team	Authority
Working context	Team spirit	Training
Resources	Team discipline	Resources
Targets	Grievance procedures	Performance review
Training	Briefing	Grievance procedures
Progress	Support	Reward

Source: after Adair (1986).

3 Control 'interruptability', which may take the head or principal away from team activities.

4 Promote staff confidence and morale.

5 Develop feelings of security for all team members.

Although we return to the concept of culture later, it is important to note here that current initiatives for educational improvement and effectiveness lay strong emphasis on team development. For example, the management of Education Action Zones requires schools, LEAs and industry to work collaboratively to set educational objectives, resource allocation and targets. Such teams do, however, transcend school and college boundaries and may require the acceptance of new ways of working – where 'traditional' interests are challenged by the need to meet local and pragmatic targets within a national framework, e.g. in lowering truancy rates, existing group norms may have to be reviewed.

Conformity and group norms

Conformity to group standards is affected by a range of elements, like group size, unanimity of the majority and group structure, with conformity often increasing as group size grows. In addition, conformity is greater in decentralized than in centralized networks. Asch (1951), in a laboratory study of conformity (defined as the tendency of individuals to 'give in' to the group), examined the difficulties facing individuals who resist other people's opinions. Asch's experimental evidence shows how individuals may be influenced against their better judgement by group pressures and, arguably, indicates the potential for individual problems when a new member joins a team, as well as the importance of ensuring that appropriate norms are established by a group during the 'storming' and 'norming' stages of team development. A few years later, Deutsch and Gerrard (1955) suggested that two kinds of pressure tend to push people towards conformity:

- *Informational pressure*, which occurs because we are never totally sure our beliefs/attitudes are correct. Consequently, we use others' beliefs and attitudes to validate our own views and opinions.

- *Normative pressure*, which arises because we like to be liked/wanted by others. We are aware that we put our acceptance at risk by disagreeing over issues of importance.

Hollander (1964) has further argued that those who persistently contravene group norms respond in three basic ways. While two responses are effectively opposites on a conformity continuum of group norms – 'conformity' and 'anti-conformity' – the third reaction involves an assertion of 'independence':

- *Conformity*: 'Tell me what you want me to do and I'll do it.' Here, the group structures the conformist's behaviour.
- *Anti-conformity*: 'Tell me what you want me to do and I'll do the opposite.' Here, although the individual's response depends on the nature of group norms, he or she rejects them.

Cameo   Square pegs

Ferndale is a small rural primary school with four full-time teachers. The headteacher, Jane Harvey, decides to organize the four classes across consecutive age groups and to move from an organization based upon Key Stage 1 and Key Stage 2 to a team approach planning curriculum delivery across the four classes. For Jim Dale, who has been responsible for early years development and is paid an incentive allowance as head of early years, this appears to threaten his independence in planning and his relationships with the parents of younger children.

At the first meeting for the new team – replacing the usual weekly staff meeting – Jim states that he wishes to retain responsibility for all Key Stage 1 developments and that his 'bottom line is to remain in charge of all the work at that stage'. Jane was most anxious to support the views of the other two staff, who see the whole-school planning process as a way of meeting criticism over the lack of continuity which had been noted in the school's recent Ofsted inspection report. In the subsequent debate, Jim states that he is the victim of 'ganging up by the women' and Jane argues that 'we have to move forward to a system which is best not only for the children but also for our own professional development'. Anne Harris, her nominal deputy, feels that 'parents are still seeing us as an infants and junior school but really we're all one . . . and continuous'.

Eventually, Jim agrees to change 'for the sake of the school and to go along with the others', but adds that 'it's really only because I don't want to rock the boat. I think the time has come for me to move on and to look for another job – after all when I'm in my classroom, at least I'm my own boss!'

Conformity, anti-conformity or independence?

- *Independence*: 'Tell me what you want me to do and I'll think about whether I want to do it or not.' Here, individuals are aware of group norms but do not allow themselves to be pressurized to conform or rebel. They prefer to think through the options and take what they see as appropriate action.

Hollander explained that the tendency is for individuals persistently to adopt a particular type of response to group norms and that groups differ in their tolerance of 'deviance'. The implications of this are shown in the cameo opposite.

Teams, roles and performance

Much of the research into teams revolves around identifying factors capable of improving team performance – thus building on group dynamics in achieving tasks and implying the importance of conformity issues. Central to this focus is the study of the team roles adopted when teams work towards specific goals. Clemmer and McNeil (1989) urge that these goals can only be met if problem solving, effective meetings and team cohesion, persuasion and influencing are used by team leaders. This means that various individuals may have to undertake different tasks, with leaders acknowledging the particular contributory skills of each person. In an investigation of group development in the late 1940s, Benne and Sheats (1948) developed a classification of group roles and an associated framework for reviewing behaviour in group situations. Their research (which was firmly located within the group dynamics movement) focused on unstructured group situations and identified several team member roles (or 'functions', as Adair calls them). These are summarized in Table 5.2.

Table 5.2 'Roles' in team organization

Group task roles	Group building and maintenance roles	Individual roles
Initiator–contributor	Encourager	Aggressor
Information-seeker	Harmonizer	Blocker
Opinion seeker	Compromiser	Recognition-seeker
Information-giver	Gatekeeper–expediter	Self-confessor
Opinion giver	Standard setter	Playboy
Elaborator	Observer–commentator	Dominator
Coordinator	Follower	Help-seeker
Orienter		Special interest lobbyist
Evaluator–critic		
Energizer		
Procedural technician		
Recorder		

The use of the word 'role' may seem a little misleading here. If you think of your own work with a particular working party you may be aware of three features:

- *Expectations*: we act differently according to our expectations of a meeting (e.g. the compliant information-seeker at a pastoral meeting may become much more of an initiator at a finance group meeting).
- *Functions*: we use different combinations of the functions in each column according to the composition of the group (e.g. the encourager in a subject team meeting may become a follower in the curriculum management group where he or she is still developing alliances).
- *Complexities*: at any one time we are working towards a complex mixture of task, team building, team maintenance and individual objectives (e.g. think back to Jim Dale in the cameo).

Although Benne and Sheats's contribution is recognized (for example, in identifying role variety and in developing sensitivity training), they can be criticized for allowing their focus on 'task' and 'maintenance' functions to predominate, to the detriment of 'individual' contributions (Adair 1986). According to Adair, Benne and Sheats tend to assume too readily that individuals will subordinate themselves to the group or risk being perceived as nuisances. He argues that each individual's perspective and needs are vital components in developing group effectiveness: they stand alongside task and group maintenance needs. This is especially true in education, where team activities in teaching are often peripheral to 'core' classroom work and where established roles predominate in people's minds, e.g. the 'Head of PE' role has higher status than the 'meeting initiator' role. Their framework is helpful, however, in promoting thought about the ways we function within teams.

A better known and well used model is offered by Belbin (1981, 1993). While not arguing that people 'act' out particular functions, he suggests they have an inherent 'self-perception' which determines their intuitive way of acting in team situations. Much of Belbin's work builds on the idea of role and personality matching in team building – a potentially important frame of reference when considering team roles and when analysing deficiencies as part of the process of improving team performance. Belbin has specified nine 'team roles' (see Tables 5.3 and 5.4), each of which relates to the particular psychological and social attributes of individual team members.

Belbin's observations of team working indicated that teams comprising high-flying, high-achieving individuals were not necessarily the most successful, often because they failed to 'gel' and became internally competitive, particularly where there were several individuals who wish to, for example, 'shape' or 'coordinate' (Belbin 1993). The most successful teams were those with members who had a complementary range of skills and abilities, plus

Table 5.3 Potential team roles

'Action-oriented' roles	'People-oriented' roles	'Cerebral' roles
Shaper	Coordinator	Plant
Implementer	Teamworker	Monitor/evaluator
Completer/finisher	Resource investigator	Specialist

Source: after Belbin (1993).

Table 5.4 Useful people to have in teams

Type	Typical characteristics	Positive qualities	Allowable weaknesses
Implementer (previously 'Company Worker')	Translates ideas into practice; conservative and predictable; dutiful; 'gets on with the task'	Organizing ability; common sense; integrity; hard working; self-disciplined; loyal	Tends to lack flexibility; limited adaptability; unresponsive to new ideas
Coordinator (previously 'Chair')	Calm, confident and controlled; coordinates team resources; driven by objectives	Enthusiastic and welcoming; strong task focus; welcomes all contributions without prejudice	Ordinary; not particularly creative, inspirational or intellectual
Shaper	Highly strung; outgoing and inspirational; 'makes things happen'	Has drive and enthusiasm; ready to challenge current rhetoric, ineffectiveness, inertia and complacency	Tends to be impulsive, impatient, sensitive to criticism; can provoke, irritate others; likes to be 'in charge'
Innovator (previously 'Plant')	Individualistic synthesizer of new ideas; often serious minded	Imagination and intellectual ability; knowledge-focused; creative and unorthodox	Prefers ideas over people; 'head in the clouds'; tends to disregard practical issues
Resource investigator	Extrovert; identifies ideas and resources from outside team; questions and explores	Networking capacity; positive; curious and communicative; cheerful; good at sustaining team; responsive to challenges	Tends to lack self-discipline; impulsive; quickly loses interest
Monitor-evaluator	Critical thinker and analyst; tends to be sober, unemotional and prudent; constantly reviews team	Interprets complex data; judgement, hard-headed and objective; discretion	Tends to be overly critical and negative; can be intellectually competitive and cynical; lacks inspiration and ability to motivate others
Team-worker	Socially oriented; loyal to team; sensitive and perceptive of others' feelings and needs	A good listener; stable, extrovert and responsive to others; promotes team spirit and harmony	Indecisive at crucial moments; may not be sufficiently task focused
Completer-finisher	Driven to complete tasks on time and to high standards; painstaking, orderly and conscientious	Concern with detail; 'getting it right'; driven by targets and purposeful; able to 'follow-through'	Tends to worry over small issues; perfectionism; reluctant to 'let go'; compulsive; may lower others' morale
Specialist (new role added to original eight)	Has prior knowledge and specialist skills	Contributes specialist expertise as team input	Tends toward narrow and overly specific vision

Source: after Belbin (1981, 1993).

the flexibility to adapt roles and behaviour to changing circumstances. As Belbin (1993: 21) argues, 'The types of behaviour in which people engage are infinite. But the range of useful behaviours, which make an effective contribution to team performance, is finite.' He argues that team effectiveness can be improved because his research shows that:

1 A range of distinct 'team roles' can be identified.
2 Individual roles can be predicted through psychometric testing.
3 Leaders tend to prefer or adopt one or two particular team roles.
4 Combining team roles in particular ways tends to produce more effective teams.
5 Team roles are not necessarily linked or associated with individuals' functional roles (e.g. as accountants) in the organization.
6 Specific factors increase the likelihood of more effective teamwork and management, e.g. if individuals correctly recognize and/or predict their best role(s); if individuals become more self-aware about their potential contribution; and if individuals work to their team strengths rather than allow their weaknesses to interfere.

REFLECTION

Using Belbin's outline, try analysing how a work team you know well operates in terms of role. Is there a link between group dynamics and team effectiveness? If so, what are the key elements?

Belbin's (1981) early work on teams and 'team inventories' has been criticized as being both overly simplistic and biased, especially in terms of gender, leading to stereotyped approaches to team creation and recruitment, as well as driving a focus on specific 'types' of people in particular 'roles' to create 'dream teams'. The distortions of labelling people as 'completer-finishers' or 'plants' misses one of the fundamental aspects of team 'roles', since, to some degree, we are *all* potentially capable of undertaking the full panoply of roles – depending on context, task, training etc. As Belbin argues, however, some roles do appear more 'natural' to us as individuals because of personality and intellectual factors. Consequently, it is important not only that we consider how roles are performed within teams over time, but also that we accept the possibility of rebalancing our role contributions to compensate for perceived team deficiencies or limitations elsewhere.

Although Belbin's role categorization is by no means definitive, it has undoubtedly become an extremely widely used aid to team review and team building – especially in commerce and increasingly in education. However, as educationists we do need to sound a cautionary note: Belbin's work was based on research in a particular commercial and business sector and was undoubtedly gender-skewed, in that it used (almost exclusively) male managers at Henley Management College. It may not, therefore, have universal applicability to gender or, indeed, education. For example, when Bowring-Carr and West-Burnham (1994) examined the Belbin categorization in an educational context, they found that school management teams tended to score low on both monitor-evaluator and completer roles.

REFLECTION

Are there individuals within your team (or one you know well) who exhibit what Belbin calls 'allowable weaknesses' without seeming to contribute the 'positive qualities' – or vice versa? How are they handled?

Using the parallel imagery of sports teams in their review of what they describe as 'high performing teams', Margerison and McCann (1990: 10) have argued that:

> Successful managers will work through their team and their success will depend upon the team succeeding: a team is more than a number of brilliant individual advisers. It is a group of people who understand each other, who know individual strengths and weaknesses and who co-operate with one another.

The simplistic 'single goal' for the team and the industrial parallels they draw are not necessarily readily identifiable with the more complex aims and missions usually found in education – although their model does stress the importance of the idea that 'at the heart of every team is the linking function'. While Margerison and McCann refer to Belbin's work, they do not directly link their roles with his categorization, arguing that 'people do not take the position of the leader who has been appointed as the basis for obedience. They look for the performance as the basis for their support' (1990: 13).

Leadership, teams and effectiveness

Much recent work on team effectiveness has been focused on the ways leaders operate with their teams in ensuring secure development and progress. Within education, this emphasis reflects the often high value placed on situational and transformational leadership, although the Audit Commission (1991), Dimmock (1993) and Webb and Vulliamy (1996) all show that team involvement in educational institutions is necessarily limited by the fact that the leader takes (or ratifies) the final decision in the interests of the organization as a whole.

Moreover, educationists are heavily reliant on their own individual skills and knowledge, which in many circumstances may actively contradict or even undermine notions of teamwork. Identifying differences between large and small educational organizations, Dunning (1993) considers that most teaching heads in small schools (with perhaps three or four teachers) are trapped between, on the one hand, administrative demands and timescales and, on the other, the need to give teams time to develop. Consequently, headteachers tend to take on yet more tasks which, in reality, should be shared. MacGilchrist et al. (1995) show how this tendency can actively inhibit organizational well-being, e.g. where those in leadership positions produce development plans which have little or no sense of staff 'ownership'.

By contrast, Roberts and Ritchie (1990) show how secondary school structures might be developed to ensure that administrative loads are effectively shared, with developmental opportunities being fostered by senior managers. Howarth and Jelley's (1995) examination of middle managers' roles as team leaders in promoting quality subject teaching argues that this only becomes possible when administrative loads are managed in such a way as to enable teams to concentrate on *developmental* rather than *routine* issues.

It is possible to place team problems in four categories, i.e. those associated with goals, roles, processes, and relationships. In promoting team development, leaders thus need to analyse the 'driving' issue(s) and respond accordingly. This notion builds on Murgatroyd and Gray's (1984: 40) conception that 'leadership is essentially a description of a particular form of relationship between people sharing common aims which they seek to achieve by different objectives'. They identify four criteria related to the quality of relationships which they see as important in evaluating school leadership and, by implication, the work of teams:

- *Empathy*: the ability to see another problem as if it were one's own.
- *Warmth*: the ability to share problems.
- *Genuineness*: the ability to develop effective interpersonal relationships.
- *Concreteness*: the ability to recognize the reality of the problem or issue.

Taking it further, they argue that pupil achievement is a product of four separate factors, also connected with personal qualities:

- the quality of pupil–teacher relationships;
- the quality of peer relationships;
- the strength of positive self-concept;
- the strength of self-control.

Murgatroyd and Gray claim that both the criteria and factors are stimulated by classroom leadership and that classrooms largely act as 'mirrors of the organization of the school as a whole'. The extent to which team development, team cultures and social cohesion exist appears increasingly significant as a factor in school effectiveness. Indeed, the idea that classroom relationships and management approaches reflect school relationships and management approaches as a whole is a compelling one and one which is closely associated with the curriculum and the idea of 'mission' outlined by Stoll and Fink (1996).

The more effective teams within education carry with them the shared values of the organization, and 'ethos' – whether explicit or implicit – is a driving force for individuals, groups and the whole school or college. Communication between individuals, teams and the organizational environment does not, however, simply 'happen'. As Margerison and McCann (1990) indicate, it is the exploring, advising, organizing, controlling and linking aspects of team management which can make the difference. Without effective communication, team cohesion has little chance. We turn to this in the next chapter.

ACTION

Consider a recent (staff) meeting you attended in the light of our comments about leaders facilitating team development. In what ways do the minutes of the meeting, for example, reflect team organization and development? How could greater team effectiveness be promoted at such meetings?

If teamwork is to be beneficial for schools and colleges, it must provide clear benefits for all those involved: pupils and students as well as staff, groups as well as individuals. Although some argue that educational team-work has major benefits (see Bell 1992; Bell and Rhodes 1995, for example), many organizational and personal ambitions based around teamwork can remain unachieved because those involved fail to match their potential. Teams are dynamic and ever-changing, moving away from immature, weaker relationships (it is hoped) towards stronger, productive ones. There are, however, dangers that teamwork can become an end in itself – emphasizing the 'country club' culture where membership becomes more important than task (Blake and Mouton 1978). In addition, teams may fail to become fully integrated and may ultimately become dysfunctional – now a key issue under local financial management in some schools (Levačić 1993, 1995) – or they may become subject to micropolitical agendas (Hoyle 1986) or interdepartmental in-fighting and 'baronial' politicking (Ball 1987). Indeed, teams can fall victim to a number of major failings through, for example:

• an over-emphasis on tasks;
• too little emphasis on processes;
• too much time on discussion and debate;
• too little time for 'problem-solving' action which counts;
• too little emphasis or time spent on celebration, reinforcement and recognition of achievement;
• too much time 'responding' and focusing on reactive behaviour;
• too little emphasis on 'anticipatory' and proactive thinking;
• too little time developing their team skills and behaviour (based on West-Burnham 1992).

While some have argued that much organizational work (in education as well as business) is not dependent on teamwork, but is operational and demanding of individual rather than group skills (see, for example, Critchley and Casey 1986), the range and pace of organizational change is undoubtedly making team-based approaches an increasingly central component of organizational life which helps to 'oil the wheels' for institutional success.

● **Suggestions for further reading**

Adair, J. (1986) *Effective Team Building*. London: Pan.

Belbin, R. M. (1981) *Management Teams: Why They Succeed or Fail*. Oxford: Heinemann.

Belbin, R. M. (1993) *Team Roles at Work*. Oxford: Butterworth Heinemann.

Bell, L. (1992) *Managing Teams in Secondary Schools*. London: HMSO.

Bolam, R., McMahon, A., Pocklington, D. and Weindling, D. (1993) *Effective Management in Schools*. London: HMSO.

Crawford, M., Kydd, L. and Riches, C. (eds) (1997) *Leadership and Teams in Educational Management*. Buckingham: Open University Press.

Wallace, M. and Hall, V. (1994) *Inside the SMT: Teamwork in Secondary Schools Management*. London: Paul Chapman Publishing.

Part II
Changing and learning

6 Effective communication

The management of meaning and mastery of communication is inseparable from effective leadership.

(Bennis and Nanus 1985: 33)

Mechanisms and complexities

Effective communication is essential for effective management. As Bennis and Nanus's comment above indicates, communication has meaning beyond mere words and is a key attribute possessed by successful leaders. Too often, however, it is an area neglected in management development, even though the new managerialist emphasis on 'reputation management' and 'relationship marketing' has undoubtedly raised its profile (Greener 1990; Cram 1995). Yet in far too many schools and colleges communication skills are still perceived as weak: 'Communication is complex and in many schools is ineffective' (O'Sullivan *et al.* 1997).

Good communication in education is vital, not simply because it is a complex and multifaceted process, but because it occupies so central a role in both teaching and learning processes and in the task of leading the educational mission. As Sergiovanni (1987: 116) has argued, 'the *meaning* of leadership behaviour and events to teachers and others is more important than the behaviour and events themselves. Leadership reality for all groups is the reality they create for themselves, and thus leadership cannot exist separate from what people find significant and meaningful.' Because the nature of

Table 6.1 Factors affecting communication

Communication giver	Transfer	Communication receiver
Clarity of expression	Clarity of transfer	Receptiveness/commitment to receiving message
State of mind/mood at time of initiation	Immediacy of transfer	State of mind/mood at time of receipt
Language and emphasis	Language and emphasis	Interpretation of language
Contextual pressures	Contextual 'noise'	Contextual pressures
Perceived relationships	Interpretation *en route*	Perceived relationships
Non-verbal emphasis (body language)	Interpretation of image/stance	Individual responsiveness to non-verbal messages

communication has such an impact on relationships, task definition and focus, there is considerable potential for complexity and misunderstanding in everyday communication – as Table 6.1 tries to indicate.

We begin by examining the nature of communication and then examine its role in motivation and facilitating group relationships. Communication is about both *content* and *process*, about ideas and strategies, and about the way thoughts link with action (Bell and Maher 1986). If what we say as leaders or managers is to be effective, it needs to be consonant with our non-verbal communication and body language (Pease 1990); it needs to be consistent with earlier messages; and it needs to stand out from system 'noise' which acts as a barrier to effective interaction and communication. Consequently, awareness of inhibiting elements, in both ourselves and others, becomes crucial if problems are to be overcome. Major communication barriers include:

- hearing what we want to hear;
- ignoring conflicting information;
- being aware of our perceptions of the communicator;
- recognizing that words mean different things to different people;
- acknowledging that there is often little awareness and understanding about non-verbal communication (Armstrong 1994).

These difficulties can be minimized by following basic (and in truth often seemingly obvious) communication 'rules' – depending on the particular circumstances. However, while the rules may appear simple, their application can often become a highly complex matter. We are, for example, recommended to communicate

- in clear, unambiguous, short and simple ways;
- in a style which is acceptable and understandable;
- in ways which ensure that requests for action are easy to understand and execute;
- in ways which show concern for others;
- in consistent ways (Bell and Maher 1986).

Adair's (1983) examination of how group-based communications fails emphasizes that since communication clarity is central, it is helped by:

- having a clear understanding of what you want to say – the message objective;
- giving reasons which explain changes of practice or process;
- incrementalizing the explanation;
- relating aims to purposes and understanding the interaction.

When each of these elements is in place, quality communication is more likely, but is not guaranteed, since we still need to ensure that what we say is both heard and understood rather than just received.

ACTION

Consider three 'communications' – either verbal or written – you have received recently. How effective were they as communications, judging by Bell and Maher's and Adair's criteria above?

Lyons and Stenning (1986) have identified various activities which can help us determine our own communication capabilities. They focus on establishing clear communication and ensuring that purpose matches approach. For example, educational leaders at a range of levels need the capacity to communicate in various 'modes': giving basic information and instructions, explaining policy decisions, making requests and negotiating solutions, each of which demands an appropriate communication 'vehicle' – which may mean a chance encounter, a formal interview, a quick handwritten note or chairing a meeting.

Communication *appropriacy* is the key element here, since good communicators send messages in the most effective manner at the most appropriate time – while acknowledging that nothing is foolproof. We also need to remember that communication is about *how* we say something as much as *what* is said: we all transmit subliminal messages through, for example, our body language and nuanced language. Some writers have used the concept of 'a loop arrangement' between communicator and recipient to reinforce this point about appropriacy. For example, Laswell (1948) considers the 'five Ws' as crucial – *who* says *what*, to *whom*, in *which* way and with *what* effect – while Rasberry and Lemoine (1986) point to what they see as a four stage loop moving through:

1 Intended message.
2 Language encoding.
3 Transmission process.
4 Received (decoded) message.

This process can, however, sometimes overcomplicate matters and lead to changed meanings. Messages are undoubtedly influenced by the motives and socio-culture of both parties: while most of us still equate 'communication' with the written word, the spoken word has become increasingly central – particularly in organizations (especially educational ones) which are seen as 'people places'. The development of new communications and information technologies (C&IT) has created the potential to offer real communication immediacy in both spoken and written words: not only through e-mail and the Internet, but also in the way C&IT supports direct person-to-person communication through video conferencing, even if these developments simultaneously create new communications pitfalls.

Communication, information and technology

There is clear evidence that the Internet becomes a powerful conduit for learning only when individuals have their own identity . . . and a clear sense of communication with other learners.

(Heppell 1998: 40)

Recent dramatic developments in C&IT and management information systems (MIS) indicates their vast twofold potential for education: first, in reducing human involvement in the more laborious, complex and often time-consuming teaching, administrative and management tasks; second, in facilitating effective and speedy communication and learning at various levels, both across the organization (the intranet) and beyond the organization (the Internet). Despite its fundamental impact on global society, the presence of C&IT in general and the Internet in particular means, as Brighouse (1998, para. 60) has argued, that:

> We are only in the foothills of possibility. It must be the equivalent of the invention of the printing press as to the effect on the educational process. It does not mean the educational process is not the core and main activity. It just means that the possibilities in what we can do in unlocking people's talent are being yearly extended.

It is becoming clear that the growth of 'the information age' (part of what is often referred to as 'global megatrends': see, for example, Naisbett 1984; Beare and Slaughter 1993) has significant management implications. Jones and O'Sullivan (1997) point to several 'information megatrends' which, in educational settings, impact especially on those with middle management responsibilities:

- Globalized communications (e.g. Internet, e-mail, computer conferencing, digital communications).
- Exponential changes in capacity/cost ratios (i.e. things get cheaper, quicker).
- Symbolic knowledge is replaced.
- Established, organizational wisdom is challenged.
- Growing focus on quality, quantity and standards.
- Information-sharing and open access, to anything, anywhere, by anyone.
- Integrated media, e.g. computer-tele-video conferencing, interactive TV.
- Increases in 'information crime', e.g. hacking, viruses, plagiarism, 'chip piracy'.
- The growth of the 'information black market', for buying and selling knowledge and information.

These trends coincide with changing organizational pressures, where, for example, some schools and colleges are being downsized and delayered for budgetary reasons (Holbeche 1995), while others, which are deemed 'failing' (Ofsted 1997a), may become 're-engineered' by 'starting all over, starting from scratch' (Hammer and Champy 1993: 2). Such changes have major communication implications.

As the list above demonstrates, technology involves a delicate balance of both human and physical resources (Handy 1996). In facilitating the decentralization of administration down to the lowest possible unit (whether school, department or individual), more flexible approaches are being developed on an evolutionary basis, driven by need. However, new technologies are not unproblematic. For example, Riffel and Levin (1997) articulate how repeated problems over retraining and redeployment can result in problems for organizations because of C&IT's 'ripple effect', when what begins as individual interest metamorphoses into full-scale organizational approaches. Clearly, this has major implications for the ways in which internal communications work.

Riffel and Levin argue that new technology is only advantageous when, rather than simply becoming an adjunct to existing activities and improving specific tasks, it provides a clear organizational platform for improving teaching and learning communications. As part of this, an appreciation of the potential impact on support and ancillary staff is essential, as well as an understanding of its impact on teachers and other education professionals. This perspective is echoed by Heppell (1998), who argues that current definitions of learning, communication and C&IT are too narrow.

Because C&IT and MIS enable organizations to store and retrieve vast amounts of information in coherent formats, data processing and the tracking of trends and relationships become readily accessible. This is a key benefit in an age when target-setting, benchmarking and tracking are central. Moreover, the inception of a National Grid for Learning (NGfL) as an online learning resource facility for both staff and students supports this role (BECTA 1998; DfEE 1998d). For Buchanan and McCalman (1989) these are examples of the benefits of 'visibility theory'. In a review of new technology, they assert that information systems are valuable because they

- encourage *information sharing* among managers;
- increase *confidence and motivation*, facilitating access to better quality information;
- improve *management visibility* because information is more transparent;
- improve *communication responsiveness* and collaborative working by integrating knowledge availability, confidence and visibility, thus reducing the likelihood of micropolitical conflicts.

REFLECTION

In what ways are Buchanan and McCalman's assertions applicable to your own professional context?

The problems of managing information technology as a means of communication are as important in education as they are in the commercial world. Lancaster (1993), in a review of schools' early usage of C&IT, examines its impact in terms of management implications. He argues that C&IT will serve an institution well only if it effectively frees up staff time, saves money for use elsewhere and provides an improved information base for decision making and discussion.

REFLECTION

How far are Lancaster's recommendations about the benefits of C&IT apparent in your own workplace? What seems to be inhibiting such developments?

Despite C&IT's positive profile and potential, information 'gatekeeping' and communication 'blocking' too often remain a feature in many organizations. As the pace of C&IT developments quickens, key leadership tasks are, first, to identify organizational and communications blockages and, second, to initiate C&IT-related staff knowledge, training and development strategies. Despite this, the overwhelming pace of C&IT development itself will remain a communication block for most people in the foreseeable future: in a bureaucratic environment, for example, systems managers may be the only people able to benefit fully from C&IT's capabilities. It is essential that those leading organizational change recognize the need for a more expansive view of C&IT learning and capability.

Group-based communications

Effective leaders need to be effective communicators with both individuals and groups – especially in communicating their ideas and 'vision'. Deal and Kennedy's (1982) work on organizational culture accentuates the primacy of communication in transmitting values systems – in short, 'the way we do things here'. Other writers (e.g. Southworth 1994; Hayes 1996) contend that values-led communication in primary schools is crucial, since teacher-to-teacher talk, for example, provides a role model for pupils. Even so, 'cultural' transmission raises all the difficulties associated with group dynamics and the propensity for the development of sub-cultures where colleagues may not wish to articulate the 'dominant' culture.

In their evaluation of leadership dimensions, Beare *et al.* (1989) contend that leadership vision demands two kinds of communications skill. First, leaders must articulate the principles behind their ideas in order to gain support from their staff. Second, leaders need to transmit meaning: glib catch phrases are of limited value unless they are translated into the realities of the workplace. Both elements require high levels of interpersonal skills and communication, especially when planned changes are anticipated, as the cameo opposite indicates.

One issue arising out of the resolution of the cameo's central problem was a review of the school's communication channels. Leavitt's (1951) work on communication (see Mullins 1993) has pointed to the leader's strategic role in communication networks: the nature of the network effectively controls how communication works. As Figure 6.1 shows, centralized networks (e.g. 'chain' and 'star') often require group members to channel their communications through a central individual, while in decentralized ones (e.g. 'circle' and 'all channel' or 'fully connected' networks) information will probably flow more freely between network members.

Although there is little research clarity about the precise impact of different communication networks, it is generally accepted that, for simple tasks, wheel and 'all channel' networks perform well and 'circle' networks less well. 'All channel' networks again perform best in complex task situations. Chain networks may benefit the individuals at the head of the chain, but are generally of limited organizational value and are not good at gaining employee motivation. In essence, then, this appears to show that while centralized communication networks are generally effective at facilitating simple tasks, decentralized ones enable more complex tasks to be dealt with more successfully.

Cameo   Working together?

The headteacher of a large rural secondary school was concerned about the daily visit made to his room by the head of environmental studies. Although the head felt sure that conversations were intended as a casual chat and review of progress in an unusual teaching area, rumours reached him that other school staff saw the daily meetings as a blatant attempt to 'bend the boss's ear'. In an effort to break this practice, the head suggested a weekly meeting with colleagues in the science faculty, at which the head of environmental science would be present – but that to make time for this, the daily reporting had to stop!

For the first two weeks the new arrangement went well: all the group involved were kept up to date with developments in the environmental science area, and the seeds of greater curricular integration began to be sown. During the budget preparation round which followed, it was decided to alter the formula to the advantage of the science group. While this decision was, as it happened, totally unrelated to the head's meeting with science staff, other staff considered that the faculty had been using the meetings to their own advantage.

By the fourth week the head had been approached by other faculty heads – in maths and humanities – wishing to know why the scientists were being favoured: 'It's gone from one twisting your ear to eight of them having a go!' was the assertion. As a result, a pattern of meetings with all faculties was evolved so that the head could hear everyone's plans and problems. The revised scheme proceeded for half a term, but then the daily visits by the head of environmental science began again: 'Because I need to tell you about things that the others in the group don't understand and I don't like this delegation business.' Back to square one!

How would you have handled the situation?

Some of the specific costs and benefits regarding these approaches have been articulated in, for example, Lewis's (1975) and Baron and Greenberg's (1990) representations of the links between communication and organizational structures. Table 6.2 offers a 'shorthand' review of these links and their possible strengths and weaknesses, though it is essential to add a health warning. While it may provide a useful overview, if taken literally so simplified a diagrammatic representation can encourage an overly rigid approach to organizational and communication analysis and, importantly, ignores a range of other more subtle – but nevertheless crucial – influences.

While, in general terms, hierarchical and collegial structures may impact differentially on organizational communication, there is likely to be higher staff commitment if the overall structure (whatever its shape) encourages

A 'star' (centralized)		Enables communication from the periphery to a central figure and vice versa; efficient pattern for providing quick answers to simple problems; person at centre may find role fulfilling, while those at periphery do not; with complex tasks, central person can become saturated
A 'chain' (centralized)		Creates clear communication links or stages; can inhibit fast communication because a chain is only as good as its individual links
A 'circle' (decentralized)		Facilitates sequential information flow from person to person, group to group; tends to be used where more autocratic leadership persists; while communication links are clear, delays in communicating ideas and information quickly can occur
'All channel'/a star within a 'circle' (decentralized)		Facilitates a 'completely connected' network; considered inherently more democratic than other networks; enables communications to flow freely across/around the network, with everyone talking to everyone else and high levels of personal satisfaction; structure can, however, create overly complex communication processes, causing difficulties over achieving simple objectives and solving simple problems

Figure 6.1   Communications networks

Table 6.2   Organizational and communication links

Characteristic	Star	Chain	Circle	All-channel
Speed	Fast, but only for simple tasks	Fast for simple tasks	Often slow	Flexible
Accuracy	Good for simple tasks	Often good	Often poor	From poor to excellent
Morale	Can become very low	Low at end of chain	Can be high	Often very high
Leadership stability	Very pronounced	Marked	None; can be team focused	Variable
Organization	Often stable	Emerging stability	Can be unstable	From flexible to unstable
Flexibility	Low	Low	High	High
Performance	Good for simple tasks; poor for complex ones	Good for simple tasks	Good for simple tasks and some complex ones	Very good for complex tasks

feedback and continuity of communication (see Table 6.3 as an illustration of this point). Inevitably, this influences the timing, nature and value of face-to-face communication, as well as its 'controllability' – a key issue for managers and leaders at all levels.

Table 6.3 Approaches to feedback in various organizational settings

Formal	Collegial	Political
Hierarchical communication	Matrix or round-table communication	Pockets of communication
Line relationships	Cross-table relationships	'In' people relationships
Sifted downward transfer	Open 'team' transfer	Closed transfer
Sifted upward response	Open 'team' response	Closed response

ACTION

Gauging how poor communication inhibits organizational effectiveness is helpful in identifying effective communication. Over several days, try to record any situations where insufficient or poor quality information has created problems for you. When have problems arisen? Is there a pattern? How might difficulties be overcome?

According to Adair (1983), capable managers try to *prioritize* their communications across their organization. He suggests that they should do so according to 'three concentric circles of priority' regarding information-giving:

● The *'must knows'*: 'the vital points necessary to achieve the common aim'.
● The *'should knows'*: 'the desirable but not essential'.
● The *'could knows'*: 'the relatively unimportant'.

While Adair acknowledges that those working in industrial organizations may feel comfortable with these priority categories, he accepts that in strongly people-driven organizations like education a more open communications structure is generally assumed as the 'norm'. Comments like 'senior staff only tell us what doesn't matter' or 'we never find out till after the decision's made' reflect the sense of negativity sometimes felt by teachers and principals when they perceive that policy makers neglect or ignore their views.

Handy (1993) also stresses the centrality of communication effectiveness, noting that our interactions are largely determined (at least initially) by how we *perceive* others, i.e. by the things they do and say. Non-verbal cues are especially helpful in determining others' intentions and expectations: Handy asserts that, in many cases, non-verbal communication gives us vital information. He lists several typical failures, arguing that 'it is perhaps worth admiring the fact that any sensible communication takes place at all' in organizations (1993: 86–7). As well as removing communication blockages, he adds that managers need to take *positive* steps to overcome possible failure, by, for example:

- using more than one communication net or group;
- encouraging two-way rather than one-way communications;
- keeping as few links in the communication chain as possible.

REFLECTION

How realistic are Handy's 'positive steps' in your organization, especially when 'keeping people informed' often means proliferating paper?

Beyond mere words: transactional analysis

A key communication skill – especially in face-to-face situations – is the ability to 'read' or detect how our behaviour impacts on others, which, in turn, helps us derive a clearer understanding of our own 'people skills'. The use of non-verbal communication and body language is recognized as increasingly powerful, particularly in 'people-centred' organizations and especially in one-off meetings like interviews (Pease 1990). Moreover, the one-to-one communication 'transactions' emphasized in transactional analysis (TA), which are traditionally a key focus in management development programmes for businesses, are now becoming increasingly important in education management development (see Steward and Joines 1997, for example).

Originating with Berne's (1964) *Games People Play*, TA's core concept is its description of the three 'states of mind' which influence our behaviour with others. Berne's three behaviour categories – or 'ego states' as they have become known – are labelled as parent, adult and child. Importantly, these concepts are not necessarily congruent with specific functions normally associated with real parents, adults and children, but are behaviours only generally associated with these roles. Each ego state indicates the different roles (Barker 1980):

- *Parent*: sets limits, gives advice and guidance, makes the rules.
- *Adult*: gathers data, sorts and plans decisions accordingly.
- *Child*: centre of our feelings, source of creativity, conditions authority relationships.

While TA's impact and value remains contested (and is more complex than can be indicated here), reflection on our own perceptions and feelings in various professional situations could help us to determine TA's applicability to a range of interpersonal situations like mentoring, induction, appraisal and professional development. The 'strokes' concept (developed out of Spitz's 1945 work) is an important aspect of TA and argues that our need for (positive) 'strokes' conveys our basic (childhood) needs for physical contact and comfort, something which Berne argued is felt by everyone, whether child or adult. As adults, we learn to adopt less tactile forms of recognition for acknowledging and valuing others than we use as children, e.g. a smile, frown, compliment. Sometimes, however, ignoring or insulting people means only negative strokes are given.

Berne's strokes classification indicates that the kind of 'stroke balance' people get when young influences us later in life. He suggests that because, periodically, we need to replenish our 'stroke reservoir' or 'credit bank', we will all actively take steps to do so. Barker argues that by developing our own 'positive strokes matrix', using a classification of 'given', 'asked for' and 'refused', we can identify how frequently we receive positive and negative strokes. This can also help us understand their impact on our own and others' people management skills. For example, teachers who constantly seek recognition ('ask for' positive strokes) but almost never get them (are 'refused' positive strokes) often feel both insecure and under-appreciated. However, our tendency to overuse compliments (positive strokes) can also create problems, especially in public situations, and might appear insincere. Moreover, 'group strokes' can be interpreted as a cover for allocating additional workloads, being seen by more cynical colleagues as a sop when other rewards like time or salary enhancement are unavailable.

ACTION

Do TA approaches appear to have any applicability to the attitudes to work of your colleagues in different workgroups? What influence does the relevant group leader seem to have in TA terms?

Resistance, conflict and communication

Whether it involves individuals or groups, the breakdown of communication and the resulting atmosphere of conflict is both an important and a difficult area, and strategies which re-establish effective communications have a major role to play in its management. Handy (1993) uses the basic concept of 'difference' in identifying the nature of conflict and, using a pluralist perspective, he distinguishes between three kinds of difference:

- that arising from 'argument';
- that arising from 'competition' between participants;
- that which reflects genuine 'conflict'.

Handy recommends four strategies for working through differences productively within groups at the 'argument' level of conflict:

- shared leadership – offering open discussion;
- confidence and trust in others – letting them express their views;
- challenging tasks – involving interpersonal activity;
- the full use of group member resources.

These strategies can often be seen working across education – e.g. in planning for subject progression in primary and secondary schools or in curriculum meetings planning new subject combinations in further and higher education – although where people seek to enhance self- or peer-esteem or wish to gain senior management support, competition may become apparent. Handy notes that at the productive or 'fruitful' level, some degree of competition may be helpful: first, in setting standards; second, in stimulating and channelling energies; third, in 'sorting things out', distinguishing better from worse.

Much depends, however, on how 'closed' or 'open' the competition becomes – and how far needs are fully appreciated at an interpersonal level. This point is particularly pertinent *vis-à-vis* competition over power and influence, where a win–lose scenario (or 'zero-sum game') is likely to arise because the competition is often perceived as 'closed' – even though in reality, it may be open. Ideas have to be presented and understood in ways which do not involve loss of face and so that both parties gain from resolving difficulties. Handy sees conflict as 'harmful difference', which is characterized by:

- poor communication, laterally and vertically;
- intergroup hostility and jealousy;
- interpersonal friction;
- escalation to arbitration;
- proliferation of rules, regulations, norms and myths;
- low morale over apparent inefficiency.

He argues that two basic management strategies are available to deal with conflict: the 'control by ecology' strategy (often seen as fruitful competition), which harnesses the cultural forces within an organization; and the 'regulations' strategy, which uses formalized control through mechanistic approaches and is much more of a feature of the past two decades. The latter features in at least two types of meeting in education: the working party (marked by informality and common purpose) and the staff meeting (marked by formality and limited participation). Armstrong (1994) advises that those who wish to resolve conflict need to:

- listen actively;
- observe as well as listen;
- help people to understand and define the problem;
- allow feelings to be expressed;
- encourage alternative solutions;
- get people to develop their own implementation plans.

ACTION

Using Handy's framework, analyse a recent 'conflict' situation in your institution, identifying how far the 'ecology' or 'regulations' approach is being used and with what success. Could a change of leadership tactics be valuable?

Schacter (1951) has indicated that where a member of a close-knit team disagrees significantly or displays apparently 'deviant' behaviours – whether in team meetings or elsewhere – communication with the individual is, at least initially, likely to increase dramatically in order to 'problem solve' and

'bring the person round'. Where the 'deviant' behaviour persists, communication efforts are likely to peak, the group 'cuts its losses' and communications rapidly decline, with individuals sometimes being told openly of their
'rejection'.

Its importance in organizational health terms means that communication
quality has preoccupied much 'business'-related research – especially where
group members are at odds with colleagues. Leavitt and Pugh's (1964) research,
for example, has shown how the quality of communication can deteriorate:
while, initially, logical arguments are used to 'retrieve' a 'deviant', failure can
lead to progressive threats and have even been followed by physical violence
as efforts are made to 'bring people round'.

REFLECTION

What strategies prove successful in your institution (or one you know well)
for bringing 'deviant' colleagues into line?

Recognizing the existence of power groups and developing management
strategies to meet objections in conflict situations are important in themselves (Ball 1987), but managing the 'micropolitics' in an organization may
help even more in pre-empting conflict. Micropolitical groupings often
develop (or regroup) when policy matters are being discussed and when
participants have a greater or lesser degree of vested interest in the outcomes
(Hoyle 1986).

Clearly, communication is fundamental to the operation of this process –
both in developing power group affiliations and in facilitating transactions
within the organization. Hoyle submits that 'we all know it goes on', but
that we frequently avoid acknowledging the importance of micropolitics,
because it is not viewed as a wholly rational process and because people
feel 'unprofessional' if they get involved. Ball's (1987) analysis of the ways
micropolitics works in schools argued that the politics of leadership stems
from different approaches to participation – adversarial, authoritarian, managerial and interpersonal – while Hoyle (1986) defines micropolitics as 'the
strategies by which individuals and groups in organizational contexts seek to
use their resources of authority and influence to further their interests'. He
suggests that micropolitics is distinguished from management by various
strategies used to further personal professional interests, e.g.:

- dividing and ruling;
- co-opting and displacing;
- controlling information;
- controlling meetings.

These arise because the leader's formal, legitimate decision-making role may
be challenged by alternative kinds of democratic and professional forms of
decision making – often considered appropriate in educational circles but
much less likely in business. The management of communications as a means
to policy-making ends within education provides plentiful examples of both

the exercise of power and the impetus to try to 'mould' people, practice and philosophy. Relationships and ways of working within various sections of an organization may differ significantly, producing in-house climates of either cooperation or conflict, plus associated winners and losers.

In an examination of managerial power, Kanter (1979) has underlined the importance of using it 'correctly' to achieve effective organizational perform-ance and organizational change. Distinguishing between productive (i.e. 'cor-rect') and oppressive (i.e. 'incorrect') uses of power, she examines the particular concerns of women managers: to achieve success in many micropolitical environments, women need to be very careful over *how* they communicate as well as *what* they say. She also considers that meetings are crucial forums for both men and women managers, since it is here that the 'power games' get played out.

Negotiation and conflict resolution

Negotiation skills have become increasingly important in the context of a more marketized education service. In many schools and colleges, however, their value frequently remains underplayed and undervalued. Lowe and Pollard's (1989) examination of the value of combining effective negotiation and listening skills suggests that 'frame of mind' is as important as what is said. Successful negotiations place issues and principles rather than personal animosities and pressures at the centre of discussion so that the 'push–pull' approach is avoided and win–win becomes possible (Fisher and Ury 1981; Kennedy 1989). Organizational conflict is often generated by:

- poor communications;
- interpersonal rivalry;
- intergroup rivalries;
- increasing reliance on arbitration;
- a proliferation of rules;
- low morale (Handy 1993).

When conflict arises initially over tensions about objectives or territory, immediate outcomes may be 'fruitful competition' (persuasive argument and discussion) or 'conflict' (which needs controlling). Fruitful competition ('control by ecology') generally arises when:

- common goals exist (clear and shared organizational/group purposes);
- there is openness about how to progress towards clear goals;
- failure is not punished but is seen as productive learning.

Conflict, however, is often controlled by regulatory strategies:

- *Arbitration*: particularly helpful for highly specific issues.
- *Rules and procedures*: although part of 'bargaining', can constrain and inhibit permanent solutions.
- *Coordinating devices*: 'boxing the problem' by marginalizing people into 'new' roles.

- *Confrontation*: being 'upfront' and challenging.
- *Separation*: providing a 'cooling off period'.
- *Neglect*: ignoring issues which seem trivial or unresolvable, but can stifle productive work (Handy 1993: 311–12).

ACTION

Consider recent tension(s) generated either between individuals or within a group you know. Were they resolved through 'fruitful competition' or 'control'?

Everard and Morris (1996) consider how far conflict is avoidable. They suggest that if it moves from being individually focused to group based, attitudes can harden and 'win–lose' situations prevail. Creating 'win–win' solutions can be difficult, however, because personal attitudes are often the hardest management 'nuts' to crack. In addition, options for resolution may be constrained by the professional context, organizational ethos and, ultimately, even the framework of individual and employment rights, since resort to the last can sometimes inhibit 'common sense' solutions. Armstrong (1994) highlights four negotiation stages:

- *Preparation*: setting objectives, obtaining information and determining strategy.
- *Opening*: revealing your bargaining position.
- *Bargaining*: spotting weaknesses in the other person's case and convincing them of the need to 'move'.
- *Closing*: recognizing the impossibility of further compromise.

Although Armstrong's approach is more formal than Lowe and Pollard's, it is becoming an increasingly important feature as education managers begin to take on more formal personnel management responsibilities. Mulholland (1991) offers a similar framework, but one built on achieving goals rather than resolving win–win, win–lose, lose–lose types of conflict. This process begins by assuming that agreement will be reached, and Mulholland suggests that both parties should compare and contrast their options, judge and evaluate the ideas, clarify and test the views expressed, and then establish and reiterate goals as the criteria for successful closure.

The ability to negotiate and settle issues reveals much about how communication skills are used, the communications environment and process, and how far progress is achieved without either party losing face. Such skills are fundamental in developing good relationships at both individual and team levels.

Meetings and interviews

Meetings can be an extremely effective communication vehicle and a vital component in productive decision making. They are also an area where detailed guidance and practical strategies may prove instructive (see Everard and Morris 1996) and where meeting patterns and activities may reflect overarching managerial and organizational approaches as well as the quality of team development. Effective meeting skills help to preserve the clarity of organizational purposes, enabling managers to 'hover' or 'helicopter' metaphorically above meetings, identifying the processes at work and ensuring interactions remain productive. Both individual and team roles emphasize the way meetings, whether formal or informal, are integral elements in team processes and how, if handled appropriately, they can be major team-building vehicles.

ACTION

Try 'helicoptering' over a meeting you are attending and record how ideas are successfully or unsuccessfully transmitted. Is success related to people's understanding of communication processes? How far are 'micropolitics' evident?

Armstrong (1994) argues that effective communications and meetings management skills can be integrated through:

- taking everyone's views into account;
- ensuring ideas are clearly articulated;
- ensuring information is exchanged;
- ensuring that aims and objectives are coordinated;
- encouraging synergy (collective creativity is greater than individual contributions).

In this set of ideals, communication does not simply 'happen', but requires some degree of individual 'management': the chair's role is crucial in this. Understanding the meeting's *purpose* is vital so that the overarching agenda is clear to participants. Everard and Morris (1996) suggest that we should 'classify' meetings along the following lines in order to determine appropriate communication strategies:

- decision taking regarding policy and practice (e.g. departmental meeting to plan exam strategy);
- collecting views, information and proposals (e.g. a working party focused on improving external relations);
- giving information and briefings (e.g. a pastoral staff 'two-minute' update at staff meetings);
- generating ideas (e.g. a cross-institutional brainstorming session led by senior manager on improving boys' attitudes).

Bell and Maher (1986) outline a similar set of purposes, but add a 'persuasion/influence' category – potentially significant in education, where 'professional' relationships are emphasized above authoritarian approaches.

ACTION

Try to classify various meetings you have attended recently. What predominates? What is most productive?

Both sets of authors identify a similar range of factors that enhance meeting effectiveness and offer pragmatic and practical advice (which parallels much group and team theory). While these factors (e.g. context and environment, layout and seating, the need for agenda clarity, firm but open and democratic chairing, the need to utilize participants' known skills) all relate to motivational and team development theories, the essential element is that agreement is reached over *how* the organization or section or meeting should move forward.

Hayes's (1996) study of collaborative decision making, in which heavy reliance is placed on securing agreement, identifies three strategies for achieving outcomes and maximizing potential for agreement:

* leader uses a 'pre-decision' which is not open to negotiation, but allows others to comment (disagreement is effectively pre-empted);
* leader offers several options and participants select one (thus enhancing opportunities for agreement);
* leader lets all speak, encouraging collegiality and participation (which means leader must then accept the outcome).

This identifies a clear link between Hayes's suggested strategies and the Tannenbaum–Schmidt (1973) decision-making continuum discussed in Chapter 2. While many issues may readily be resolved in meetings or in one-to-one sessions, the potential for misunderstanding or even misrepresentation always exists. In some instances, written records of agreements (e.g. minutes, *aides-mémoire*) can be appropriate strategies for limiting misconceptions – even though these can readily be 'massaged' to control information flows and decision making.

It is often in interview or 'semi-formal interview' situations (which increasingly occur in educational organizations) that 'environmental conditions', non-verbal communication and body language become extremely important indicators of organizational ambience and the degree to which productive communication exists. The way in which interviews are conducted, from initial welcome through formal 'interview' to post-interview treatment, can provide (potential) employees, visitors or students with remarkably clear insights into an organization's tenor, ethos and culture.

Seemingly superficial aspects, like how room layout can be used (whether consciously or not) to facilitate or inhibit effective and efficient communication, give actual or potential employees clear, if often subliminal, messages (Collinson *et al.* 1990). Who sits where, who dominates and the implications this has for others (e.g. notions of panel 'democracy', encouraging candidates to relax, give their best) give out messages which help participants to determine their strategies for action and communication – whether in interviews, meetings or one-to-one situations. Savage (1987) suggests that the most important barriers to interpersonal communication, often seen most overtly in interview situations, arise from:

- language (mis)interpretation;
- attitudinal problems stemming from different value systems;
- different perceptions of the issue/problem;
- an undue emphasis on status (the power problem);
- selective perceptions (bias for or against);
- the presence of environmental and internal 'noise';
- the selective retention or rejection of material;
- the withholding of information (knowledge is power);
- the tendency to pre-judge before interviews are completed (or have even begun);
- poor listening and questioning skills.

Learning to listen

It is in the area of listening skills that managers frequently find themselves especially criticized. Listening is a fundamental aspect of effective communication (Riches 1994, 1997a; Armstrong 1994), yet it still remains relatively neglected in much of the education management literature, though less so in commerce. Rogers and Roethlisberger (1952) have argued that ineffective listening is the greatest barrier to productive communication: because of time pressures and a preoccupation with other issues, managers are often tempted to adopt selective or 'on–off' listening and what might be called 'false' listening (where, technically, the words are heard but the mind is not attentive), leading to complaints that 'he [or she] never has time to listen' and 'just isn't interested'.

Consequently, a first requirement for effective listening is to acknowledge the barriers. Armstrong (1994) argues that communication difficulties often emanate from poor listening skills – especially in one-to-one situations. He suggests that several principles are fundamental for developing good receptive skills:

- concentrate on the speaker, noting both verbal and non-verbal communication;
- be responsive, show you are listening;
- ask questions for elucidation;
- allow people to comment without interruption;
- evaluate as the conversation proceeds;
- try to minimize interruptions.

ACTION

Analyse whether message clarity, transmission and reception was successful in an interview or formal meeting situation you have been involved in recently. What does the analysis say about people's communication skills?

Hargie *et al.*'s (1994) examination of the ways in which education managers utilize interpersonal communications found that managers often overrated their own ability to communicate effectively and indicated that this tendency is displayed more frequently by men than women. In 'people-oriented' organizations like schools or colleges, consequently, difficulties most frequently occur over listening to and motivating staff and dealing with conflict. These can affect the ways in which higher social values are maintained, as exemplified in difficulties with 'opinionated' parents, awkward staff, overly dominant individuals or those simply opposed to change. Hargie *et al.* note that leaders frequently say they feel relatively insecure about their listening skills and ability to empathize, handle aggression and make decisions, often anticipating particular difficulties with individuals or sections of the organization which other colleagues considered had 'special' access or privileged channels of communication.

Although we may endeavour to simplify the communication 'loop' in day-to-day work, it is important that the need for reflective communication and appropriate skills training and development is not ignored. Because human relationships are intricate and complex, some people feel there is little time to reflect, 'manage' or plan our responses and approaches, and rely instead on 'gut reactions'. Although learning from experience is very important (if often unconscious), the need for reflective communication is also central. As Duignan (1989) stresses, valuable learning can stem from failure if handled appropriately: the responses we store in our subconscious help us develop appropriate strategies for use in similar, future situations. We now move on to consider organizational relationships as a whole and the peculiar nature of organizations.

Suggestions for further reading

Adair, J. (1988b) *The Effective Communicator*. London: The Industrial Society.
Brighouse, T. (1991) *What Makes a Good School?* Stafford: Network Educational Press.
Raspberry, R. W. and Lemoine, L. F. (1986) *Effective Managerial Communication*. Boston: Kent Publishing.
Riches, C. (1997) Communication in educational management. In M. Crawford *et al.* (eds) (1997) *Leadership and Teams in Educational Management*. Buckingham: Open University Press.
Wheatley, M. J. (1992) *Leadership and the New Science*. San Francisco: Bennett-Koehler.
Whitaker, P. (1993b) *Practical Communication in Schools*. Harlow: Longman.

7 # Organizational cultures

Because culture is created by its participants, it inevitably changes as participants change, although it can also be a stabilising force, particularly for longer-standing members. It presents, therefore, the paradox of both being static and dynamic.

(Stoll and Fink 1996: 83)

● People and structures

While, in superficial and physical terms, many schools and colleges might appear to have changed little over the past half century, recent policy initiatives have undoubtedly generated significant organizational changes. The post-1960s move to comprehensivization encouraged the creation of larger, more hierarchically structured institutions, whereas the post-1980s push towards 'self-management', marketization and 'privatization' has brought about a restructuring of education focused on 'leaner, flatter hierarchies' (Mullins 1993), 'delayering' (Holbeche 1995) and 'team-based working' (Belbin 1996).

Although recent education management policy developments have often generated an increased understanding of the linkages between organizational structure, role and salary, they have also increased anxieties about the impact of organizational structure on employees (e.g. work overload, performance-related pay, appraisal and gender/equality issues). Leavitt (1978) provides a relatively straightforward representation of organizations as complex systems (see Figure 7.1), which consists of four elements, each interacting with the others and with the external environment:

- *Technology and control*: techniques for controlling and processing information, e.g. accounting.
- *Structure*: patterns of organizational authority, responsibility and communication.
- *People*: attitudes and interpersonal relations.
- *Tasks*: problem-solving and improving organizational performance.

More simply perhaps, Child (1984) identifies two elements fundamental to organizational structure:

- *The basic structure*, which signals the behaviour expected of the members of the organization, i.e. how an organization's work gets divided up, assigned

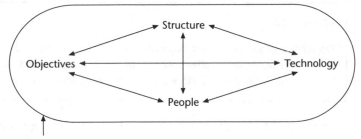

Figure 7.1 Leavitt's diamond.

and coordinated (e.g. as seen in the recent development of the role of curriculum leaders in the primary sector);
- *The operating mechanisms*, which indicate to individuals what is expected of them and also seeks to motivate them, i.e. by specifying the kind of behaviour expected in greater detail; motivating individuals and attempting to ensure they strive towards organizational goals (e.g. achieving this through development planning, schemes of work and annual reviews).

Organizational structure is often represented formally, e.g. through an organization chart which, theoretically, distinguishes between a 'tall' hierarchy (more bureaucratic, with more organizational levels) and a 'flat' hierarchy (more democratic, with fewer organizational levels), and indicates the span of control (i.e. the number of people reporting to a manager and who is responsible for their work). The concepts of span of control and hierarchy are closely related: flat hierarchies generally have broader spans of control, while taller hierarchies have narrower ones. In other words, the broader the span of control, the fewer the hierarchical levels. Both elements are often exemplified in staff perceptions about their 'place' in the organization. Current management 'fashion' often praises the concept of the 'horizontal organization' where:

- work gets organized around processes rather than functions;
- key performance objectives are identified;
- hierarchies are flattened by minimizing things which do not 'add value';
- teams rather than individuals are the organizational building blocks (Handy 1993: 117).

In such structures, Handy (1993: 117–18) notes:

it is the job of the centre to set standards but not necessarily to specify how they should be delivered. The unit is then judged, after the event, by its performance against those objective standards. Some call this 'process re-engineering', but that is only to give a modern name to an ancient principle.

REFLECTION

Do recent changes in your organization's structure reflect a particular focus on leadership or team effectiveness, or do imperatives act as 'drivers' (e.g. finance, national policy)? How are relationships affected?

At this point, we need to explore the range of working relationships within organizations. The way concepts like authority, responsibility and accountability are interpreted will influence our understanding of organizational life. Terms are often used interchangeably and it can be helpful to explore their key elements. Huczynski and Buchanan (1991) offer the following definitions:

- *Authority*: a form of power where the actions of others are ordered through commands, which are effective because those being 'commanded' accept this arrangement as legitimate.
- *Responsibility*: an obligation placed on a person occupying a specific position.
- *Accountability*: when followers perform given tasks because they are members of an organization. Accountability requires that each person reports on how he or she has discharged the responsibilities given.

In the exercising of these functions, three 'people relationships' are identifiable:

- *Line relationships*: between leader/manager and follower (e.g. head and deputy head).
- *Staff relationships*: between postholder and support services (e.g. teacher and special needs coordinator).
- *Functional relationships*: between members of the team in fulfilling a task (e.g. the assessment working group).

In the context of educational relationships, the greater the tendency for leaders to exert authority, the greater the likelihood that all working relationships will be hierarchical, and the greater the likelihood that bureaucratic approaches will be stressed. Where leaders work alongside their team(s), using implicit authority, there is a greater likelihood of 'team-based accountability' and a stronger likelihood of supportive functional relationships – often seen in newly structured education-based teams. These include:

- *Matrix structures*: where specialists with different functions/from different disciplines (e.g. production, marketing, research; or, in educational terms, information technology, literacy, assessment) come together in an inter-disciplinary team headed by a project leader (perhaps on a short-term, task-focused basis).
- *Collateral structures*: where staff work in a loose, organic structure designed to coexist alongside the bureaucracy on a permanent basis. This is sometimes a feature in further education, where course development task teams work within managerial accreditation systems.
- *Network structures*: where a small central core of staff direct and subcontract out to others major organizational functions like advertising or distribution. This is sometimes seen in education where, for example, secondary schools 'import' part-timers for specific roles.

Table 7.1 Organizational culture

Theory A (American)	Theory J (Japanese)
Short-term employment	Lifetime employment
Specialized career paths – narrowly defined roles	Non-specialized career paths – developing transferable skills
Individual decision making	Consensual decision making
Focus on individual responsibility	Emphasis on collective decision making
Frequent formal appraisal	Implicit, informal appraisal
Rapid promotion (often stemming from high turnover)	Collective responsibility
Segmented concern for people	Comprehensive concern for people

Source: after Ouchi (1981).

- *Entrepreneurial structures*: where groups of staff effectively operate as small-scale businesses within a 'parent' organization. In education this operates through self-funded units – often in further and higher education.

In his review of organizational structure (see Table 7.1), Ouchi (1981) contrasts major American companies (Theory A) with major Japanese companies (Theory J). Although essentially focused on business organizations, Ouchi's comments provide insights for those currently managing in more market-driven education settings because they illustrate how the concept of 'organizational culture' is expressed by its impact on employees.

Such distinctions should not be applied rigidly, especially in education: many organizations incorporate elements of both approaches. Indeed, Bolman and Deal (1984) refer to the 'conceptual pluralism' existing in organizations where differing approaches and philosophies effectively work alongside each other.

We have so far used the words 'organization' and 'culture' relatively loosely. While we often assume we know what 'organization' means, we are often unsure of its precise definition – if there is one! Huczynski and Buchanan (1991: 368) define organizations as 'goal-oriented systems seeking effectiveness and efficiency', and note that our organizational position (put crudely, whether we are managers or managed) influences perceptions of organizational structure.

Working in education gives people access to very particular forms of organization and allows us, over time, to occupy very different roles – thus facilitating very different perspectives on 'the organization' and its purposes. We can even be members of different 'organizations' within a single institution, while simultaneously being members of various other 'external' organizations – both 'social' and 'work-oriented'. The most effective organizations may integrate successfully both social and work elements (Japanese companies have a reputation for this). Adair (1986) argues that the ingredients familiar in effective groups are also applicable to the wider organization:

- a sense of membership;
- group consciousness;
- shared purpose;

- interdependence;
- interaction;
- unitary action.

Clearly, however, organizations are more than the sum of individual groups and, overall, organizations may not place the same emphasis on human values that Adair identifies in individual groups. Organizational structure and culture have, nevertheless, a major influence on effective leadership and development.

Commercial organizations often express their central *raison d'être* in terms of their profit-making capacity – with individuals and organizational groups being important insofar as they achieve those ends. However, a growing number of companies acknowledge the value of pursuing social purposes as a subset of their economic drive, e.g. The Body Shop refuses to test its products on animals, while The Cooperative Bank has an overtly ethical investment policy, although cynics might comment that a social conscience could even be profitable.

The nature of post-1979 Thatcherite reform has meant that, at one extreme, educational organizations are now often characterized as little different from commercial organizations – seen as functioning in a market as part of 'public entrepreneurship' (Osborne and Gaebler 1992) and 'New Public Management' (Dunleavy and Hood 1994). An alternative view argues that public sector organizations are not (and should not be) profit-centred and market-driven, but are in reality more people-centred than the commercial sector – and, importantly, that this makes a significant difference to the way they are and should be managed. However, it is not that simple: educational organizations may demonstrate, in different measure, features of both categorizations. They are confronted with all the dilemmas and difficulties of both the 'market' and the 'service' ethos – an issue considered by Hall (1996) in her exploration of the pressures facing women headteachers working in the new 'education market' and Grace (1995) in his examination of school leadership.

However, being people centred does not mean that service organizations can avoid being clear about their purposes – their goals, targets, aims and objectives. As Everard and Morris (1996: 137) point out, 'a sense of purpose is like gravity – a continuous force that moves the organization is a particular direction'. This 'continuous force' of purpose may also be seen as a foundation for the development of organizational culture or ethos – already summarized as 'the way we do things here' (Deal and Kennedy 1982), but in many respects, an almost indefinable 'something' which people can feel rather than define.

For Schein (1985: 6), the essence of culture is 'the deeper level of *basic assumptions* and *beliefs* that are shared by members of an organization, that operate unconsciously, and that define in a basic "taken-for-granted" fashion an organization's view of itself and its environment.' By contrast, Greenfield (1973) argues that organizations have no character of their own because of the 'subjectivity' of groups and the fact that, ultimately, groups are only gatherings of individuals. If this is so, organizational ethos or culture can only exist by common consent and any emphasis on organizational values will reflect conglomerate power relationships or underlying agreements between individuals rather than any 'collective will' overall.

> REFLECTION
>
> How far can your own institution be said to have a 'common culture', or can different ones be detected? If so, what characterizes them and which factors influence cultural change where you work?

Organizational models

The systems approach

The systems approach offers a model of organizational purposes and processes which provides a framework for analysing the ways in which individuals, organizational structures and culture(s) operate. Organizational systems can be seen as either 'open', where organizations interact with their environments, or 'closed', where they do not. While educational organizations are generally perceived as 'open' systems, those labelled 'closed' are seen as trying to limit community and stakeholder influence.

During the 1960s and early 1970s, for example, 'unresponsive' and 'un-manageable' schools were labelled as 'closed' – a technical impossibility. However, in the post-ERA (Education Reform Act 1988) context, schools and colleges are regarded as interacting with, for example, in reputation and marketing terms, their local communities and stakeholders. As a linear model, the systems approach is considered logical, rational and amenable to a measurement-led 'hard data' or quantitative focus. Although variations in input and organizational processes affect outputs, the model encourages input costs to be matched against outputs, thus encouraging a focus on concepts like efficiency, cost-effectiveness and value for money. Viewed 'mechanistically' (see Table 7.2), the systems debate focuses on: (a) the capabilities/abilities of pupils/students as 'inputs'; (b) the work of the institution as 'process'; and (c) the achievements of individuals (however these may be measured/assessed), as 'outputs'.

The systems model is reflected in the structuralist approach in FitzGibbon's (1996a) work, which sets out a framework with inbuilt motivators for improvement and which underpins much current work on target setting pupils' potential for achievement. It has, however, been criticized precisely because of its linearity and focus on measuring inputs, processes and outputs and possible inflexibility. There has been growing acknowledgement that the

Table 7.2   The systems model

Inputs	Educational processes	Outputs
Personal knowledge, values, goals, money	Influence of structures, people, technology, tasks	Personal, social and market changes; skills, knowledge, values; creativity; communication, social responsibility etc.

model has failed to enhance understanding of organizations sufficiently, because it assumes a tidiness in organizational relations, goals and structures which does not necessarily exist. The application of scientific or systems management concepts (Fayol 1916) to education has made some educational institutions into very large organizations. The organizational complexity seen in some large comprehensives, and in tertiary and higher education, is not readily appreciated, but does testify to complicated efforts to reconcile course provision, wide-ranging needs and the drive to expand student numbers within the demands for an educational economy focused on cost-effectiveness and efficiency.

ACTION

List those features in your own institution which might be linked with a 'scientific' approach, rating them for their contribution to (a) organizational development and (b) interpersonal relationships.

The pace of environmental change in organizations has brought the possible benefits of bureaucratic, hierarchical and seemingly rigid organizational structures into question. Bennis (1969) colourfully describes bureaucracy as 'a lifeless crutch that is no longer useful', while Argyris (1957) considers that just as individual personalities mature, so bureaucracies also become less suitable working environments over time. Argyris argues that managerial practices in formal organizations can even inhibit maturation processes, creating 'a lack of congruence'. He challenges managers to provide a working environment which allows its workforce to mature as individuals – thus moving away from bureaucratic organizational structures.

The cultural approach

The bureaucratic approach of classical management theorists contrasts with more humanistic and open approaches based around 'subjective' perspectives on organizations. In this perspective, people become central, with organizational culture and nature depending on individual attitudes and perceptions. The management challenge stems, first, from the need to create situations where individual ideals, aspirations and practices can be harnessed for organizational benefit, and, second, from the need for organizational leaders to formulate and transmit their 'vision' of the organization's mission, its aims and the ways its people might contribute to corporate life.

At this point, we need to reiterate that our emphasis is shifting from systems to people, an idea Handy (1993) takes up in using the concept of 'culture', which combines both mechanistic and humanistic approaches. Building on the work of motivational theorists like Maslow and McGregor, this concept emphasizes what in management-speak is called 'human resource management' (HRM), where the combined strengths of individuals are enhanced (e.g. through training and development) and 'empowered' to achieve agreed organizational goals.

As we have seen, there are differences of view about how far organizational culture exists and what it comprises (see, for example, Greenfield 1973; Deal and Kennedy 1982; Schein 1985). Although it is difficult to define, Stoll and Fink (1996: 82) suggest that culture 'describes how things are and acts as a screen or lens through which the world is viewed'. Because every school is a complex and unique organization with its own peculiar culture, this means that each cultural picture will be very different. This perspective implies less overall control and much flatter management structures, with fewer layers of management and control than the systems model – reflecting what are seen as the more subjective elements in Ofsted inspections.

Hannagan (1995) suggests that systems develop according to the management of the following elements (see Table 7.3).

Table 7.3 Elements of systems management

Element	Explanation
Sub-systems	The smaller working units (e.g. the science department)
Synergy	The interrelationships between units (e.g. cross-curricular initiatives)
Open and closed systems	The extent to which schools interact with their environment (e.g. links with local industry, community organizations etc.)
Boundaries	The ways in which schools define their limits (e.g. in dealing with out of school problems)
Information and resource flows	The channels/connections within the system (e.g. for encouraging bids for additional funding)
Feedback	The monitoring processes which enable goals to be maintained/achieved (e.g. through individual appraisal and departmental/curriculum reviews)

Source: after Hannagan (1995).

ACTION

Consider how curriculum change is managed in your own organization according to Hannagan's management elements: how far does it suggest you work in a scientific or a human organization?

In effect, both scientific and human approaches can be found in most organizations, reflected through organizational structure (i.e. roles and responsibilities) as well as organizational culture (i.e. the level of interaction and collaboration).

Culture: exploring the concept

In an exploration of the concepts surrounding school culture, Prosser (1991) identifies five kinds of culture:

1 The wider culture of national norms.
2 The culture appropriate to different types of institution.
3 The genetic culture (likened to human individuality) which identifies one institution from another.
4 The culture as tone or 'feel' – exemplified in displays, litter etc.
5 The culture or ethos as seen by outsiders: a sum of all aspects and 'what people say about the place'.

Handy's (1993) model of organizational cultures directs us towards understanding the personal relationships between leaders and led, whereas Bush's (1995) typology goes beyond the leader-led pattern and endeavours to summarize the totality of organizational culture. Distinguishing between the two is not easy, however, although such a conceptualization offers a useful 'shorthand' for understanding cultures. Before we consider these in detail we need to establish some criteria which will help us determine the applicability of the Bush model.

ACTION

Ask several of your colleagues how they perceive their working culture: is it mechanistic or people centred? How do they identify the elements and how far do they indicate that the organization's culture is 'mechanistic' or 'people-centred'? Do their responses indicate that a common perception about culture exists?

Bush (1995) suggests that the best way to ascertain an organization's *nature* is to ask five questions:

1 Who sets the goals?
2 How are the decisions made?
3 What is the stated, and real, organizational structure?
4 How are links to the environment managed?
5 What are the 'messages' about management style?

The concept of 'organizational culture' is especially important in educational institutions because of their 'people-centredness' and high dependence on the nature and effectiveness of interpersonal relationships. Handy (1993: 181) asserts that 'earlier management theory, in its search for universal formulae or cure-all remedies, did a great disservice in seeking to disseminate a common organizational culture', and identifies four cultures – initially based on business organizations – showing differing responses to the people and environments involved. However, as Handy and Aitken (1986) argue, they are equally applicable to education (see Figure 7.2).

It is important to note that organizations – especially larger ones – will embrace a mix of cultures even if one predominates, and the 'cultural mix' at any given time may be influenced by factors like institutional size, workflow, environment and history. Although Handy and Aitken (1986) note that

Structural image	Characteristics
Web	*Club culture* Sometimes described as a 'power culture'; is indicative of centralized control and power, often via a single leader supported by a powerful 'inner group'. The kind of culture found traditionally in 'family firms'; generally has a limited bureaucracy, focusing instead on trust and choosing 'the right people'. Is capable of being a fleet-footed organization, but can suffer if grows too large with too many 'links' in the web.
Temple	*Role culture* Reliant on a formal demarcation of roles/responsibilities: seen as a typical 'bureaucracy' with narrow band of senior managers. Focus is on procedures, performance and role-bound behaviour (job descriptions), as traditionally exemplified by large public sector organizations. Seen as strong in stable environment, offering security and predictability to workforce, but problematic in times of change.
Net	*Task culture* Often a matrix organization and focused on teamwork and 'problem-solving'. Project-focused groups form and reform, using participants coming from a range of organizational levels and status, depending on the specific task. Some links in the 'net' stronger than others; influence *vis-à-vis* task is often based on expertise rather than status. Kind of culture which is good where flexibility, speed of response and sensitivity to environment is required, but control of staff and direction can be difficult.
Cluster	*Person culture* Least common as an organizational culture, even though many staff may be personally attracted to elements of it. Culture where individualism is prevalent with few effective 'controls', thus 'making the organization the resource for the individual's talents', i.e. organization seen as serving personal needs. Few organizations could operate where this kind of culture was strong, although individuals (especially those with particular skills/expertise) may have a person culture mindset – and are not usually easy to manage.

Figure 7.2 Organizational cultures (after Handy 1993).

teachers see themselves as 'task culture afficionados', educational cultures vary, with primary schools being predominantly 'almost pure task cultures' and secondary schools (especially larger ones) showing 'a predominance of the role culture'.

As part of the increased interest in 'corporate culture' over recent years, management theorists have focused on the 'uniqueness' of organizations: what makes one institution highly successful and another less so? Greater recognition is now given to the apparently less tangible, but crucial, organizational realities, like 'values', 'philosophy' and 'ideology'. Although these aspects are less apparent in Handy's work, they are increasingly emphasized.

Nowadays it is generally acknowledged that organizational culture comprises both the tangible and the intangible. Moreover, the organization's values system, which is focused on 'where it wants to be' (i.e. its 'vision'), is seen as an important, if elusive, element. Bush's (1995) typology, which utilizes both organizational and philosophical elements and draws on a range of management theorists, is set out below in brief:

- *Formal models*: marked by a focus on 'structures' and 'systems' and with elements of former scientific management philosophies. The fundamental emphasis is on compliance to rationality – the idea that if aims and objectives are clearly defined then all processes must be geared to their achievement (Packwood 1989).
- *Collegial models*: based on varying degrees of consensus, but with the aim of developing shared, team approaches offering equality of input and shared involvement. A model with strong dependence on relationships but requiring considerable time in order to ensure that all issues are agreed (Nias *et al.* 1989).
- *Political models*: reflect the 'micropolitical' power which may underpin relationships in schools and colleges. It relies upon power struggles and the use of influence to ensure personal or group objectives which may be at variance with the organization's overall objectives (Hoyle 1986; Ball 1987).
- *Subjective models*: stress the importance of each 'subjective' individual within the organization. There is little cohesion and attaining organizational goals may be inhibited by a complex of individual agendum (Hodgkinson 1993).
- *Ambiguity models*: characterized by a lack of goal clarity; an incomplete understanding by participants of the way in which the institution works; inconsistent organizational activity; and a fragmentation of activity. The fact that action B follows action A cannot be seen as an intended consequence but as 'just happening', since 'an organization is a collection of choices looking for problems, issues and feelings looking for decisions in which they might be aired, solutions looking for issues to which they might be the answer and decision-makers looking for work' – exemplifying 'loose coupling' (Weick 1989; Orton and Weick 1990) and 'garbage can' approaches (Cohen and March 1989).

Table 7.4 summarizes the essential features of the Bush typology and answers the fundamental questions we noted earlier.

Bush stresses the importance of 'conceptual pluralism' (Bolman and Deal 1984): the existence of a variety of alternative approaches within the same organization or in the interpretation of the organization by the individuals concerned. Clearly, conceptual pluralism may make it difficult to classify group and organizational cultures tidily. For example, while a team leader may believe that he or she is 'consultative' in approach, team members may feel that the leadership is largely autocratic and that they are only consulted over 'details' rather than 'issues'.

This prompts us to consider the differences between the reality and rhetoric of organizations, a problem which may lead to organizational dysfunction because misperceived and/or misunderstood views of philosophies and practices are acted upon. Furthermore, various aspects of different cultures may

Table 7.4 An analysis of organizational culture

Type	Goal-setting	Decision-making	Structure	Relationship to environment	Cultural form
Formal	Imposed	Authoritarian	Hierarchical	From senior members	Boss–worker
Collegial	From within	Consensual	Round table	From group	Team
Political	Power complex	Strongest influence	Interest groups	From most powerful	Conflicting groups
Subjective	Personal	Personal	Individualistic	Random	Law to him or herself
Ambiguity	Interaction of complex influences	Loose coupling of events	Variable and randomized	Random	Incoherent

Source: based on the typology of Bush (1995).

coexist at any given time within different parts of the organization – adding to the complexity.

> **ACTION**
>
> How far can issues/problems facing your own area of work/institution be explained by: (a) conceptual pluralism; (b) a reality and rhetoric mismatch; and (c) its 'formal' organization or role culture structure?

So far we have considered culture as a positive attribute: by implication, anything capable of inhibiting the culture may be seen as inhibiting the organization. 'Every staff room has one cynic' and we can all recall colleagues who use their 'negative power' 'to stop things happening, to delay them, distort or disrupt them' (Handy 1993: 131), and act as thorns in the flesh of policy developers and implementers. Ganderton (1991) suggests, however, that 'subversive' roles may be important in promoting reasoned action, opening up discussion and neutralizing structural power, while Ranson (1994) notes that such people are often energetic, imaginative and creative and only become destructive when their activities undermine core organizational values.

Vision, mission and culture

Hargreaves and Hopkins (1991) lay particular stress on shared values in educational institutions and, in doing so, emphasize a theme found in much contemporary writing on managing change. For example, a key feature in Peters and Waterman's (1982) assessment of 'excellent' companies is the shared values system – or, in their terms, 'hands-on, value-driven' management. For them, 'clarifying the value system and breathing life into it are the greatest contributions a leader can make' to a community of like-minded people driven by common goals (p. 22).

Both Peters and Waterman developed their ideas on leadership and culture within a rapidly changing environment. For example, Peters (1987) argues that 'managing chaos' means leaders must 'learn to love change', communicate a vision of the future and be 'flexible of mind', always ready to challenge conventional wisdom. Waterman (1987) also suggests that because the future is less predictable than the past, the old axioms 'universally accepted as true' no longer apply. He argues that vision and shared values – kept deliberately simple – are vital because even well defined strategies may be undermined by events, may need to respond to changing priorities or may come to nothing.

While 'vision' does not always have a good press, many management writers see the concept as a fundamental leadership quality and prerequisite for effective change management – regardless of context. Although the concept may be extremely slippery to pin down, successful organizations do need to articulate, communicate and display a picture of 'what they might become' to both their staff and the wider community.

Educational research which has explored these issues in England was largely initiated by Rutter and his research team working in the Inner London Education Authority during the late 1970s. They found that when a sense of shared purpose and organizational loyalty existed, organizational effectiveness was increased (Rutter *et al.* 1979). Subsequent work on what has become known as 'educational effectiveness' argues for the validity of this assertion – exemplified in the stress on a vision for the school or college as outlined by Mortimore *et al.* (1988) in a similar study of primary schools, and by MacGilchrist *et al.* (1997), who note the importance of shared understandings in developing the 'intelligent school'.

Deal's (1985) commentary on the reinvigoration of inner-city American schools highlights the sense of purpose shown in the schools where he worked alongside teachers in building up organizational self-esteem. The ability to appreciate the problems being faced, alongside a willingness to celebrate successes – however modest – was fundamental to institutional progress. Stoll and Myers (1997) also show how the link between vision and changing cultures is essential for improving so-called 'failing schools'. Using assemblies to demonstrate 'sharing', graduation ceremonies as positive 'statements' and community relationships as 'opportunities': all were seen as fundamental contributions to developing institutional self-belief. Following on from Fullan and Hargreaves (1991), Brighouse (1991) argues that we need to interpret 'vision' as 'atmosphere' and 'shared values' when focusing on school life. He goes on to articulate the leadership qualities required across various organizational levels if 'vision' is to be communicated successfully:

- keep it simple;
- avoid transferring the blame to actions beyond your control;
- concentrate on issues which reinforce the professional culture;
- practise being brave;
- empower others;
- build corporate visions;
- decide what not to do;
- find some allies.

REFLECTION

Is there any evidence within your school or college that vision has been a driving force in development. If not how has this been inhibited?

This leads us to consider the issue of changing institutional cultures, where the aim is to establish a regenerated vision and build on education's organizational framework (Handy and Aitken 1986), as well as to consider Bush's (1995) more holistic approach to what might be called 'moving cultures'.

'Moving cultures'

Cultures are dynamic, not static. The concept of 'moving cultures' builds on an analysis of what currently exists, a vision of what might be achieved and the associated strategies which might help to 'move the culture' and achieve organizational change.

Day *et al.* (1998: 57) assert that 'It is clear that the preferred management culture for effective schooling – paradoxically given more emphasis by the introduction of a National Curriculum – is *interdependence* rather than dependence or independence' (authors' italics). This focus finds an echo in Rosenholtz's (1989) research into 'learning enriched' and 'learning impoverished' schools, which she characterizes as 'moving' or 'stuck' – a reflection of their culture (see Table 7.5).

Taking up Rosenholtz's categorization, Hopkins *et al.* (1994) identify five 'expressions' of school culture by using two dimensions: improvement–decline (dynamism of improvement) and effectiveness–ineffectiveness (outcomes). Taking into account both the Rosenholtz and Hopkins typologies, we suggest (see Table 7.6 and Figure 7.3) a cultural model for educational

Table 7.5 Moving and stuck educational institutions

'Moving' institutions	*'Stuck' institutions*
Learning 'enriched'	Learning 'impoverished'
Collaborative goals and shared approaches	No clear goals or shared values
Acceptance of uncertainty: acceptance of risk taking and creativity	Emphasis on maximizing certainty: teacher emphasis on school = routine
Interactivity: positive teacher attitudes	Isolation: teachers rarely talk to each other
Leaders as facilitators: supporting teachers and removing organizational barriers	Leaders as gatekeepers, with focus on detachment and self-reliance
Leaders: foster collaboration as opposed to competition	Leaders: avoid risk taking and 'play safe'
Holistic focus: looking out and beyond as well as within	Insular focus: inward-looking, often with accompanying sense of powerlessness

Source: after Rosenholtz (1989).

Table 7.6   Improvement and effectiveness: identifying educational cultures

'Type'	Dimensions	Characteristics
Motivating	Effective *and* improving	Collaborative and actively responsive to change; capable of rapid development when and where necessary
Cruising	Currently effective – but not necessarily improving	Complacent and cosy: living off its 'good reputation'
Drifting or wandering or fading or strolling	Moving towards or midway on both dimensions: importantly, depending on the organization's existing direction and trend, there is a danger it will become directionless	May have ill-defined aims and targets for development: average but . . .
Struggling	Ineffective, but endeavouring to improve	Recognizes and accepts that change is needed, but has limited strategies, structures and 'know-how' in place
Declining	Ineffective and 'drowning'	Apathetic and losing heart: 'cannot change' (i.e. may not accept or recognize what needs to be done); may be moving fast, but in the wrong direction

institutions which reflects the shifting sands of educational development, improvement and decline.

Hargreaves (1995) has also offered two complex dimensions in his analysis, with the first dimension being based around the way that staff and pupils are welded into a corporate organization through control or encouragement as a social entity. The second dimension is based on aims related to people or

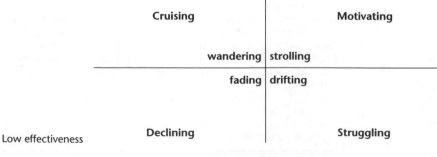

Figure 7.3   The dynamics of educational cultures.

High

(relaxed, caring)	(pressured, controlled)
Welfarist	**Hothouse**

Social
cohesion

Anomic	**Traditional**
(insecure, alienated, at risk)	(custodial, formal)

Low   High

Social control

Figure 7.4 'Types' of school culture (after Hargreaves 1995).

task. Taking these into account, a school may be seen as tending towards the instrumental (marked by social control and attention to task) or the expressive (marked by social cohesion and attention to people). The organization may then be classified as one of four 'types':

- *Traditional*: low social cohesion, high social control (custodial, formal).
- *Welfarist*: high social cohesion, low social control (relaxed, caring, cosy).
- *Hothouse*: high social control, high social cohesion (pressured, controlled).
- *Anomic*: low social control, low social cohesion (insecure, alienated, at risk).

When these four characteristics are transposed into diagrammatic form, the likely differences along the control–cohesion continuum are more readily identified (see Figure 7.4). Once again, however, it is essential that such ideal typologies are not overly rigidly interpreted. Reality is not that predictable.

The cameos on page 124 are extracts taken from the general statements at the start of relatively recent Ofsted reports – one primary and one secondary school. They reflect the concepts of moving cultures and pose questions about vision, direction and the achievement of change. As you read through the cameos, consider how the evidence fits with the culture patterns we have considered earlier and attempt to identify what changes are necessary.

The concept of organizational 'vision' is frequently referred to as the institutional 'mission statement': this, however, equates to more than organizational aims and has rather more to do with the organization's *raison d'être*, the culture by which it works and the criteria by which it is judged. If it is a genuinely collaboratively driven statement of focus, the mission statement can be a valuable organizational tool, in that it provides an overview framework for future organizational planning and a check for reviewing where it is going or has been. However, mission statements in education are often decried and referred to as mere 'politically convenient rhetoric', thus ensuring any potential value they may have becomes neutralized. Despite this, Stott and Walker (1992) assert the value of linking a clear vision of 'what we're about' with organizational planning processes. Moreover, the most successful mission statements are those expressed in simple, unambiguous terms and identifying key priorities which are capable of regular review by all staff according to their areas of responsibility.

Cameo **Moving cultures: the secondary school**

Context

The newly appointed headteacher inspires confidence and there are clear indications of first class leadership. Her clear sighted vision informs discussion and planning papers. The process of planning for development has begun well and the three clear priorities formulated by the teaching staff – achievement, learning, environment – inform the thinking and actions of the team. A manageable rolling programme of improvement has begun; there is a determination to find solutions and to target funds in a difficult and worsening financial situation.

Strategic and development planning

However, the planning process has yet to address a range of serious deficiencies in curriculum, staffing, resources and response to pupils with special educational needs (SEN). The development plan currently lacks clear specific targets with precise deadlines and monitoring arrangements. The neglect of appraisal has undermined staff accountability. There are no precise targets for middle managers (Ofsted Report).

Cameo **Moving cultures: the primary school**

Context

Leadership and management of the school is rooted strongly in good relationships and mutual trust. The headteacher has created a united team of teaching and non-teaching staff, all of whom have the best interest of the pupils at heart and give generously of their time to the school. Informal understandings are strong.

Strategic and development planning

The school's aims are brief and do not provide a clear educational direction. The development plan gives no details of the use of resources, training requirements or financial implications, nor is it checked systematically for its impact on standards of attainment. The school has few subject policies and schemes of work to support teaching and learning. The school should: develop further the planning role of the governing body; establish a clear direction for the school; ensure the governors' involvement in the formulation of a strategic development plan (SDP) which identifies priorities; set up mechanisms and procedures to monitor and evaluate the delivery of the curriculum (Ofsted Report).

Consultation and collaboration

For an agreed vision and shared vision to have any value or meaning, it is essential that the organizational atmosphere is conducive to participation and consultation. The primary sector has, we might argue, much to offer in this respect because of its tradition of collegial and task-oriented cultures. The compartmentalization of secondary and tertiary education, by contrast, encourages 'balkanization' or at best, only a 'contrived collegiality' (D. Hargreaves 1994). The notion of 'conceptual pluralism' (Bolman and Deal 1984) may be applicable here since one person's collegiality may be seen as another's 'micropolitical perspective' (Glatter 1982).

An example of this can be seen in the more 'traditional' ways of managing meetings. For example, is a head of department necessarily the best person to chair proceedings? If not, how can the most effective distribution of roles in meetings be renegotiated, especially for specific types of agenda? One method has been to use a non-threatening, self-perception inventory approach which seeks to identify the characteristics of an individual matched to the task needs. Once people realize that they are suited to one or more types of organizational role – and are appreciated for their contribution – mutual respect may grow because they are not attempting to fulfil roles for which they are clearly unsuited. This, however, is an 'easier said than done' situation: it is the more holistic culture created through strong day-to-day relationships – with open debate and involvement, appreciation of individual viewpoints and a recognition of counter argument – which really underpins consultation.

> **ACTION**
>
> Consider the strengths and weaknesses of your own immediate working group, and in relation to your organization as an entity, in developing a consultative approach.

In undertaking the above activity, you may have concluded that collegial forms of consultation are inhibited by

- the lack of time;
- the incompatibility of individuals;
- decision making without reference to the opinion offered;
- the opinion lacking clarity and relevance.

The most frequent cry is that *'they' consult but don't implement* – in other words, consultation is merely a sham. Despite this, there are several practical strategies or devices which may help to support more open management and more effective consultation. These include greater use of matrix approaches for specific tasks or projects, whereby relatively short-lived but highly focused teams are established to address specific issues. Handy's (1993) examples of basic managerial structures are indicative of relationships from the 'grass-roots' to the executive.

A task-focused matrix enables individual status to become subsumed because the team is 'commissioned' for its skills and the task to be pursued. At its simplest, a matrix may occur where a cross-section of departmental staff are given a specific task in formulating an assessment policy; at its most complex it may involve all staff as equal members of several teams undertaking interlinked areas of work, e.g. the personnel, assessment and servicing committees of a division of the LEA service. It is an attempt to harness the skills of the members of groups without 'status inhibition'. If utilized as a permanent organizational structure, however, a matrix can create splintered forms of operation, leading to cliques and somewhat rigid team behaviour.

The evolution of the working party was partly a response to task-centred production teams in engineering practice. In some establishments, a staff forum provides an opportunity for colleagues to air their views in a situation which, at least overtly, is not status-ridden. A recent development has been the attempt to integrate the organization's overall mission, together with the process of consultation in an annual review of institutional development at sub-department, department and whole institutional level.

The importance of working relationships is summarized by David Hargreaves (1994) who, using Toffler's (1990: 386) concept of 'a moving mosaic' – comprising 'many shifting see-through panels, one behind the other, overlapping, interconnected, the colors and shapes continually blending, contrasting, changing' – to describe newer types of organizational structure, articulates five models of joint activity:

- *Individualism*: marked by a concern for role and classroom boundaries.
- *Collaboration*: marked by voluntary association, e.g. to produce materials.
- *Contrived collegiality*: marked by formal systems imposed by administrators.
- *Balkanization*: marked by the insulation of one working group from another.
- *The 'moving mosaic'*: marked by flexible groupings of teachers working together through a variety of collaborative styles.

Moving cultures and 'moving mosaics' do, however, hinge on the ways in which organizations plan for and cope with change. Change is endemic in the life of schools and colleges, which have to respond to new initiatives and environmental pressures and influences. While leaders may have a 'vision' for the school or college's future, there is also an imperative to manage change so that the 'vision' is readily achievable *and* achieved. The consultation process is not sufficient in itself: it is essential that it is backed by collaborative action. This may be seen in terms of the ways in which personal and organizational change is led, managed and facilitated.

Suggestions for further reading

Anthony, P. (1994) *Managing Culture*. Buckingham: Open University Press.
Harris, A., Bennett, N. and Preedy, M. (eds) (1997) *Organizational Effectiveness and Improvement in Education*. Buckingham: Open University Press.
Middlewood, D. and Lumby, J. (eds) (1998) *Strategic Management in Schools and Colleges*. London: Paul Chapman Publishing.
Mintzberg, H. (1994) *The Rise and Fall of Strategic Planning*. London: Prentice Hall.
Pheysey, D. (1993) *Organizational Cultures*. London: Routledge.
Stacey, R. (1993) *Strategic Management and Organisational Dynamics*. London: Pitman.

8 Managing change and creating opportunities

Change is too important to leave to the experts.

(Fullan 1993: 39)

Change flourishes in a 'sandwich'. When there is consensus above, and pressure below, things happen.

(Pascale 1990: 126)

The changing context

Educational management is inextricably linked with change: indeed, we might say that effective management equates with productive change. In a context increasingly driven by political concerns to meet the needs of a 'Learning Society' and 'Learning Age' and to deal with global economic challenges (Dearing 1997; DfEE 1998f), change management skills are crucial. Problems often arise, however, when change is resisted because it seems revolutionary and threatening rather than evolutionary and 'natural'. Educational change is often made more difficult because, as Kogan (1978: 47) has argued, 'The school system . . . is exceedingly strong in its ability to generate and sustain its own policies. The continuities are far stronger than the changes.' Consequently, leading organizational innovation is a complex enterprise and managing planned change (rather than dealing with imposed crises or coping with contingencies) becomes a challenge to both leaders and followers.

> **ACTION**
>
> After identifying a change which has affected your work, list the internal and external factors which have influenced its progress, assessing how (and why) it was change you wanted or resisted.

In essence, there is little difference between 'managing' and 'managing change' (Bush 1995). Indeed, as Hoyle (1986) notes, if management is about 'moving' institutions rather than helping them 'tick over', then a 'theory of management' equates with a 'theory of innovation'. Harvey-Jones (1988: 96) reinforces this view, arguing that *speed* (i.e. movement) rather than *direction* is an essential management prerequisite: adaptability is essential for successful change, even if 'adaptation . . . ultimately can only be made on an individual and personal level'.

Consequently, 'the great leader who can suddenly engender in people a vision and lead them to an entirely new world' is, for Harvey-Jones, simply management 'mythology', whereas 'openness' achieved through 'creating the grain' (via climate, readiness and need) rather than working against it is the management ideal (p. 96). While acknowledging that change may engender fear, Harvey-Jones recognizes that 'in the process of change, it is equally important to be clear about those things that one wishes to hold on to, as well as those which one wishes to see changing' (p. 96). So what do we mean by 'change'? And how does 'change' differ from 'innovation'? Some of our difficulties in determining precise meanings are demonstrated by the fact that definitions are value-laden and need to be contextualized.

REFLECTION

How far does the concept of 'bringing about change' differ from allied ideas of bringing about *innovation* and *development,* or from contemporary notions of *improving* or *becoming effective?*

Hoyle (1972) considers that 'change' is a generic term covering a broad range of concepts (e.g. innovation, development, renewal), which incorporates a sense of unintended or accidental movement, whereas the term 'innovation' indicates intentional and deliberate processes. In general, however, such distinctions are rarely so finely drawn by those writing about change and its management.

The rhetoric and public imagery of 'change' is that of 'benefit for all': a longstanding assumption that change is 'good in itself' and equates with progress – otherwise why would people engage with it? However, the reality may be very different. Change can frustrate, confuse and destroy as well as challenge, stimulate and enhance (Fullan and Hargreaves 1991; Fullan 1993). It is often forgotten that it can also require significant levels of *long-term* commitment if it is to be successful (Van Velzen *et al.* 1985; Hargreaves and Hopkins 1991). Furthermore, the idea that change is essentially a rational, technocratic activity which can be mandated is clearly thought through and leads to measurable outcomes is one that has been increasingly challenged and found to be misleading. As Pascale (1990: 20) has argued, 'not surprisingly, ideas acquired with ease are discarded with ease', a view reinforced by Fullan (1993: 22), who notes that 'Mandates are not sufficient and the more you try to specify them the more narrow the goals and means become.'

In considering the purpose of educational change and who benefits, Fullan (1991) asks what school reform is for. He addresses the question in two ways by asking 'What are schools for?' and 'What is reform for?' Clearly, if educational institutions only have very limited influence over pupils then managing educational change is highly problematic. If what educational organizations do is seriously constrained or undermined by societal pressures, then there is little scope for initiating real change. However, the growing body of 'school effectiveness' research appears to indicate that 'schools *do* make a difference' (Brookover *et al.* 1979; Reynolds and Cuttance 1992; Teddlie and Stringfield 1993). Fullan argues that to understand educational change we need to develop an overview of the sources and purposes of change – along with a clear picture of *who* actually benefits. In particular, he asserts that we need to learn two lessons:

1 That educational innovations should not be taken for granted: they are not ends in themselves.
2 That educational change has often been of 'first order' rather than 'second order' change, i.e. has focused on improving what already exists rather than altering the fundamentals.

REFLECTION

How far does your organization's management structure inhibit or encourage 'second order' change as opposed to the 'fix it'/'first order' kind?

Models of change

Bennis's (1969) well-known typology of change, extended by Chin and Benne (1974) identifies three change strategies linked to organizational culture:

- *Empirical–rational (bureaucratic model)*. Assumes that people are responsive to rational explanations and demonstrations; typically this strategy involves using education, training and publications to disseminate knowledge/research findings, e.g. curriculum development 'agencies' which share good practice across the system.
- *Normative–re-educative (collegial model)*. Assumes that effective innovation needs changes in attitudes, relationships, values and skills. Typically, this strategy involves using consultants/change agents. Although this strategy was used in introducing appraisal, its success was limited by failure to ensure staff 'owned' it. 'Quick fix' consultants also fail to support the re-educative process.
- *Power–coercive (political model)*. This strategy relies on access to political, legal, administrative and economic resources and has featured in many changes driven by legislation and directive, e.g. the 1988 Education Reform Act regarding the National Curriculum; teachers' pay and conditions regarding directed time.

Theoretically, those leading change simply match their managerial strategy with an appropriate change perspective. Unsurprisingly, however, change is more complex than that. For example, as Hopkins *et al.* (1994) stress, strategy means more than a plan to be operationalized: it must be overtly acceptable to become real. They argue that change involves three key elements:

- technology – the way change is achieved;
- politics – the recognition that change involves a combination of power and influence;
- culture – the social norms which condition the likely acceptance of change.

REFLECTION

What links can you identify between your institution's organizational culture and the way change gets managed?

Ferguson (1982) suggests that we change in four basic ways:

- *Change by exception*: where our belief system remains secure but allows for 'the exception which proves the rule'.
- *Incremental change*: where change is so gradual that we are unaware it is occurring.
- *Pendulum change*: where, periodically, one approach is abandoned in favour of another.
- *Paradigm change*: where insights and new information facilitate new forms of understanding or an integration with earlier understandings to create new perspectives and interpretations.

REFLECTION

What route to change most often arises in your own organization or area of work?

At this point, we need to ask whether Bennis and others' models are applicable across a range of social and political contexts. Astuto and Clark (1980: 61) argue that during periods of turbulence we need 'an agenda *to* change rather than an agenda *for* change', while Heller (1994) asserts that, in future, the key management concern will be enhancing collaboration and cooperation – both within and beyond organizations. For Schrage (1990: 40) collaboration is central because it is 'the process of *shared creation*'. However, even this may not be enough. Stability and collaboration are diminished when 'client responsiveness' drives development, and this, in turn, may strengthen the case for normative–re-educative approaches to enhance flexibility.

While periods of stability may generate more formal and rational models, periods of uncertainty often engender more ambiguous organizational cultures, resulting in limited information flows, confused complexity and sometimes limited certainty. At one extreme, Cohen and March (1989) see such organizations as subscribing to a 'garbage can' organizational model and exhibiting problematic goals, unclear technology and fluid participation. A prerequisite for meeting demands for a millennial 'third wave' of rapid change may be more flexible and adaptive organizations (Toffler 1981), and in such a context 'collegial' management models are considered more conducive to change, while 'bureaucratic' ones emphasize stability and continuity – leading to stagnation?

While the flatter, broader management structures which support collegial management appear fundamental for longer-term responsiveness and strategic management (Grundy 1993), we argue that organizational structures need to be designed to promote both stability *and* growth. In other words, schools and college organizational structures need to be flexible enough to adapt to a changing world, yet secure enough to accommodate changes without being destabilized by them (Mintzberg, 1994). Some three decades ago, Toffler (1970) acknowledged this dilemma, arguing that the 'disorienting nature of change' meant 'adhocracies' were essential to deal with a rate of change moving out of control.

Although Bennis's (1969) typology offers one rationale for change, other writers have also examined the processes involved. Kurt Lewin's action-research, which emphasizes the 'unfreezing–moving–freezing' of group standards (Lewin 1947), has also provided a metaphor for the change process. Highlighting the change agent's role and group participation in effecting strategic change, Lewin saw positive relationships between the acceptance of innovation decisions and the degree of group member participation in decision making. He argued that both notions – the change-agent and the adopters' role in decision making – encourage more dynamic conceptions of change. His model is problematic, however, because the 're-freezing' concept implies that organizations could readily assume that change could be revolutionary, sporadic and then 'completed'. This does not accord with experience.

Schön (1971) identifies three change development approaches:

- *The centre–periphery model.* Where change ideas are generated centrally by task teams and then disseminated 'out' to the system/organization as recommended good practice. A model often used when standardized curriculum packages are needed or in curriculum reorganization situations.
- *The proliferation of centres model.* Where ideas/strategies are generated rapidly in various locations across the system/organization in response to particular challenges or needs. This approach has characterized professional development strategies used to introduce teachers to new ways of delivering a given curriculum initiative.
- *The learning systems network model.* Where ideas are continuously modified and information is 'networked' rapidly across the system/organization. This model is apparent in the work of innovative subject departments and in 'action-research' staff development, where in-class experimentation in curriculum delivery is then shared among the whole staff.

Havelock's (1971) ideas that change comes about in three ways are closely linked to Schön's, although his models focus more strongly on the research origins which support change:

- *The research, development and diffusion model (RD&D).* This model offers 'a process whereby ideas and tentative models of innovations are evaluated and systematically reshaped and packaged in a form that ensures benefit to users and which eases diffusion and adoption' (Havelock 1971). Imitating medical and agricultural change models, it stresses the central importance of technology. 'Change' was identified with 'unproblematical progress'; seen as a 'good thing' and developed by 'experts' at the centre. Essentially, it offered an apparently 'user-proof' package: the introduction of Key Stage assessment tests exemplifies RD&D, with government 'contracting out' the task of implementing good practice to research centres/agencies.

- *The social interaction model*. This model enables research and development to be undertaken in a working unit and is dependent on the collective will for change. It relates well, for example, to the traditional rhetoric of primary school organizational patterns where planning for curriculum delivery is undertaken by a whole school team. Havelock's idea was extended into Schön's 'proliferation of centres' model, where good practice in one group is emulated by others.

- *The problem-solving model*. This is the most individualistic of Havelock's schema, based around problem-solving situations which occur in daily life and using individuals as the initiators of change. Although consultants provide support, individuals retain control of the change process. This model is familiar to all those who ask themselves whether they might teach more effectively by altering approaches or using different materials.

It is possible, of course, for organizations and groups to develop a hybrid version of all these approaches – often without recognizing that this is happening.

ACTION

Try to analyse several areas, sectors or departments in an organization you know well using the models outlined above. You may find it useful to develop a grid of characteristics: what does the analysis tell you?

The 'realities' of change

In order to consider how far change rhetoric and intention matches change realities and outcomes, it is important to ask what that 'reality' is. While teachers often complain about the pace of change and its impact on class-room life, it is important to see its operation at both individual and institutional levels. Fullan (1991) approaches this issue by distinguishing between 'the daily subjective reality of teachers' (individual perceptions about change) and the 'objective realities' (measurable outcomes for the organization). Rejecting both passive and isolated professionalism, he argues for 'interactive professionalism', where teachers as 'continuous learners' would find that 'help would be the natural order of things' (Fullan 1991: 142).

Best *et al.* (1989) also consider 'subjective meanings' in their review of secondary school pastoral issues. They argue that because each teacher has a unique perspective on his or her role and institution, this creates multiple realities which are identifiable across all institutions: 'there are, if you like, as many "realities" as there are teachers, and it is arguable that any kind of categorisation of perspectives does violence to the subtlety and uniqueness of each teacher's understanding of his world' (Best *et al.* 1989: 108). While this adds weight to Greenfield's (1973) assertion that individual subjectivity is greater than any organizational imperative for change, we need to remember that external influences regarding National Curriculum delivery and national schemes of assessment have increased the pressures for 'objective' outcomes, increasing the drive towards greater commonality of practice in schools and colleges.

REFLECTION

What evidence do you have for the existence of subjective and objective realities in your organization?

Greenfield rejects what he considers to be a simplistic notion of the concrete realities of organizations, because 'the drive to see the organization as a single kind of entity with a life of its own . . . blinds us to its complexity' (1973: 555). He argues that 'the more closely we look at organizations, the more likely we are to find expressions of diverse human meanings' (p. 572). The subjective perceptions of those involved, each of whom may invest each event with their own (different) meanings, are what are important. Clearly, this is potentially a highly complex model of change – not a single process but as many processes and perceptions as there are staff. For change to succeed, Greenfield argues that two clear, but often neglected, tasks are needed:

- 'mapping' people's versions of reality;
- discovering the stresses/disjunctions which threaten people's definitions of reality.

These tasks then imply a third:

- developing people's commitment to new goals and ways of achieving them.

We can argue that such tasks are vital regardless of organizational culture. However, views change over time; some individuals become convinced or cynical; emergent patterns of success or failure arise from change (or lack of it); and the necessary dynamics of leadership have to be adapted to meet these issues. Such concerns are implicit in Fullan's (1991) stages for introducing change.

Initiating, implementing and institutionalizing change

Initiating change

People initiate change for numerous reasons: personal status; bureaucratic self-interest; concerns to meet perceived but currently unmet needs; concern to comply with external pressures and so on. While acknowledging that 'countless variables' or combinations of factors are involved, Fullan (1991) identifies eight factors associated with successful change adoption (see below with our examples):

1 Existing quality innovations (e.g. the growth of ICT).
2 Access to innovations (e.g. commercial pressures to give education access to the Internet).
3 Advocacy from central administration (e.g. government emphasis on the primary literacy hour).
4 Teacher advocacy (e.g. in adopting modular examinations).
5 External change agents (e.g. in the curriculum work of the Health Education Council).
6 Community pressures or apathy (e.g. in developing anti-bullying strategies).
7 Funding for new policies (e.g. in 'pump-priming' Education Action Zones initiatives).
8 Problem-solving and bureaucratic orientation (e.g. in coping with increased student numbers).

Fullan emphasizes planned or 'action-oriented' change when there is evidence of 'relevance, readiness and resources'. He notes that much research around initiation decisions is timebound – often having taken place 'when failure and confusion were widespread' – but accepts that, more recently, improvements have occurred in linking change initiation strategies with identified needs.

REFLECTION

How far are Fullan's eight factors implicated in recent change initiatives in your institution? Can you see any pattern in the variables and can you find factors which Fullan does not note?

A key problem for those engaged in cultural and organizational change is that initiation is the easy part: too often the expected post-initiation 'implementation-dip', where morale and 'stickability' are threatened, acts as an inhibitor – particularly when externally driven and newer change imperatives draw the attention of those involved in change away from partially completed change attempts, thus threatening the prospects of 'completion'. However, as Fullan (1991: 49) has noted, 'change is a process not an event', making the notion of completion irrelevant.

Implementation issues

Implementation, an especially complex and intricate process, involves many more people than those involved in the planning stage. Fullan identifies various 'interactive factors' affecting implementation and divides them into three sections: the characteristics of change; the local characteristics; and external factors. He acknowledges, however, that 'individual roles and lists of factors, while helpful to a point, seem no longer adequate' to explain the intricacies of implementation. Fullan identifies six implementation 'themes':

1 *Vision-building*: designed to permeate the organizational value system; a concept also utilized by Leask and Terrell (1997), who see it as stemming from personal pedagogic beliefs.
2 *Evolutionary planning*: designed to blend top-down and bottom-up approaches; a concept also outlined by Murgatroyd and Morgan (1992) and seen in the introduction of quality management systems in schools.
3 *Monitoring/problem-coping*: designed to chart and maintain progress; a concept built upon by Louis and Miles (1992) and seen as an 'open' approach to problems.
4 *Restructuring*: designed to meet widespread development needs; a concept which Huddleston and Unwin (1997) take up in their continuum of didactic-to-experiential teaching strategies in FE and HE.
5 *Staff development/resource assistance*: shown in a variety of curriculum initiatives and the introduction of performance indicators for primary schools (Strand 1997).
6 *Initiative-taking and empowerment*: offering flexibility as change is adapted to meet individual circumstances.

In assessing implementational issues, Smyth and van der Vegt (1993) identify four, often conflicting, pressures which impact differently on change situations:

- pressures for increased centralization and steering implementation activities;
- pressures from implementers for greater local autonomy;
- pressures from inside an organization to respond as a unified entity;
- pressures from internal interest groups who have identified both the incentives and disincentives of the proposed changes.

We might consider that, in certain respects, Fullan offers us a somewhat simplistic approach to implementing change. Local financial management (LFM) is an example of first-order change which has not been entirely successful in securing improved educational outcomes, because of staff pressures emphasizing stability, parental pressures about school 'choice' and wider community pressures about unfulfilled expectations regarding school improvement.

Considering long-term continuation issues, Fullan (1991: 88) argues that 'the longer the external resource support, the less likely the effort will be continued after external funds terminate', a concern reminiscent of Ouston *et al.*'s (1992) comment on 'honeypot' management, where schools gain change-focused funding for limited periods. Aside from 'bidding fatigue' experienced by some schools, it was clear that schools were anxious about how the funding would be found once pump-primed resourcing finished. More recently, Johnson (1998) shows that once schools supported by a special budgetary initiative had utilized their funding allocation, they had no intention of continuing the work.

ACTION

Are Fullan's comments about 'continuation' pertinent to your own experience? How has external funding for change been dealt with in your organization?

In practical terms, Miles (1986) argues that effective implementation requires:

- clearly defined change management responsibilities;
- the empowerment of individuals and the school as a whole, without top-down pressures;
- both pressure *and* support;
- adequate and sustained professional development support;
- rewards (more than just praise) for teachers early in the change process.

Institutionalization issues

Many factors are implicated in successful or failed change. These include whether participants have the vision, commitment and persuasiveness necessary to move from implementation to what Miles (1986) calls 'the institutionalization of change'. Because vision needs to be tempered by knowledge of the context, an especially strong commitment to change can sometimes inhibit the process, alienating others. Fullan (1991: 62) warns that where innovators cannot negotiate a way through, they may become 'as authoritarian as the staunchest defenders of the status quo'. Examining the issue of rational decision making, he acknowledges that 'the social world can be altered by seemingly logical argument' (p. 46), but recognizes that some problems are unresolvable. We cannot analyse every problem and posit all the alternative solutions because, *de facto*, 'implementation planning is itself a process of innovation' (p. 98). During institutionalization, success depends upon harnessing these aspects, alongside:

- embedding change in a school's organization and structures;
- eliminating practices which compete with or contradict the change;
- developing strong links with other change efforts;
- spreading good practice and assisting those in need through local facilitators (Miles 1986).

Loucke-Horsley and Hergert (1985) also produce practitioner focused guidelines regarding change implementation and institutionalization, many of which are implicit in Fullan and Hargreaves's (1991) list produced for the Ontario Teachers Federation:

- Taking action is preferable to planning: protracted needs analysis is worse than none at all.
- Heads are not the key to school improvement: other people are also important.
- Creating ownership at the beginning is unrealistic: like trust, it builds up over time and through completing tasks which show that improvement is possible.

- Helping and supporting teachers after planning and initial in-service work is more crucial to success than all the pre-implementation training.
- Coercion isn't always bad: 'a firm push' plus lots of help can launch a project well.
- 'Imported' new programmes/practices offer viable, cost-effective alternatives to major in-house development efforts (Loucke-Horsley and Hergert 1985).

REFLECTION

How far do these factors adequately explain successful and unsuccessful changes within your own institution? Are any explanatory factors missing?

Change and leadership

Education leaders take ultimate responsibility for managing change and are accountable for its institutional impact. Weindling and Earley's (1986) leadership research, which considered 'how heads manage change', found similar findings to those identified in Hersey and Blanchard's (1977) model. For example, organizational changes made soon after a new leader's arrival were 'frequently concerned with communication and consultation'; several new heads also 'deliberately chose to make early changes', which they considered were cosmetic and in non-controversial areas but recognized that 'It was important to be seen by the staff as someone who gets things done, as it shows you mean business' (1986: 333).

Fullan (1992) notes the emphasis often placed on both the 'leader as initiator' and 'maintenance of stability' roles: teaching staff often have expectations about their leader's ability to establish a delicate balance between both organizational continuity and organizational change. However, they also experience major pressures because 'in the field of educational change, everyone feels misunderstood . . . the role of principal has, in fact, become dramatically more complex, overloaded, and unclear over the past decade' (p. 1). The role is full of inherent dilemmas because much of the leader's time is spent 'on administrative housekeeping matters and maintaining order' (Fullan 1991: 146–7) and, even though this protects the organization from unrealistic or ill-conceived change projects, it can also 'effectively screen out much needed changes'.

ACTION

How far is there a 'preoccupation with organizational stability' in your institution or area of work? What effect does this have on the potential for curriculum change and/or organizational routines?

After analysing various leadership studies, Beare *et al.* (1989) offered what they call 'emerging generalizations' about leadership, which they suggest can help those striving for excellence (and, by implication, successful change management):

1 Emphasis should be given to 'transforming' rather than 'transactional' leadership.
2 Outstanding leaders have an organisational vision.
3 Vision must be communicated in ways which secure commitment among organisational members (i.e. they draw others in by 'magnetic commitment' rather than coercion).
4 Communicating vision demands communication of meaning (whether through symbols, words, actions or rewards).
5 Issues of value ('what ought to be') are central to leadership.
6 The leader has an important role in developing an organisation's culture.
7 Studies of outstanding schools provide strong support for school-based management and collaborative decision making within a framework of state and local policies.
8 There are many kinds of leadership forces (technical, human, educational, symbolic and cultural) and these should be widely dispersed throughout the institution.
9 Attention should be given to 'institutionalising vision' if leadership of the transforming kind is to be successful (i.e. the principal should work with others to 'implant the vision' in the structures and processes of the school).
10 Both 'masculine' and 'feminine' qualities are important in leadership, regardless of the leader's gender.

(Beare *et al.* 1989: 108)

REFLECTION

Are Beare *et al.*'s 'emerging generalizations' in tune with leadership approaches to change experienced in your area/institution?

Choices for change

We consider the range of management models (e.g. bureaucratic, collegial, political, subjective and ambiguity) elsewhere and link them to the opportunities and implicit choices for change they suggest. However, in an examination of 'choice' in relation to educational leadership, North (1988) questions how far leaders are free to make 'rational choices'. In other words, how far do organizational structures and cultures constrain their efforts to make decisions about change? North considers that the rhetoric of choice does not *de facto* match the reality. While legislation like the 1988 Education Reform Act often lays particular emphasis on 'rationally planned choices', North notes that, in practice, the individual leader's

perceived ability to make a choice between a range of theoretically possible courses of action is so constrained by the school culture available
that it may be realistic to deny that seemingly-available choices are, in
practice, available. It is not just a question of most problems having
fixed and moving elements, but of far more restricted options than
implied by rational processes of deliberative action.

(North 1988: 164)

After quoting the 'private views' of heads, North recommends that institutional leaders reject 'the strategy of bringing about organizational change
based upon a rigid, predetermined blueprint in favour of working to a rough
outline map flexible enough to allow substantial adaptations to be made in
the light of experience' (1988: 170).

ACTION

Is there evidence in your work situation that change is developed by using
'rational choice' opportunities, or does it happen via a flexible 'rough outline
map'? What implications does this have for your own approach to work?

Cohen and March (1989) examine the concept of what they call 'choice
opportunities'. Adopting a 'garbage can' version of the ambiguity management model, they emphasize that the complexities and uncertainties of life
in educational institutions create what are effectively 'organized anarchies'.
For them, educational organizations are characterized by problematic goals,
unclear technology and fluid participation in their decision making, all of
which is overlaid by rapidly changing demands. The key to understanding
such organizations is to view 'choice opportunities' as 'garbage cans'. Cohen
and March's 'garbage can' theory is especially useful in organizations plagued
by: goal ambiguity and conflict; poorly understood problems which 'wander
in and out of the system'; a variable environment; and decision makers faced
with multiple tasks and ideas. Consider the principal's choice opportunities
for change in the following cameo.

Cameo Challenging change

Amy Scott is principal of a college of further education in a small market
town. The college has 290 full-time students studying a range of General
Certificate of Education (GCE) Advanced and General National Vocational
Qualification (GNVQ) courses and is in competition with two comprehensive
schools in the town and surrounding area, both of which have sixth
forms offering a similar range of courses. There is some overlapping
timetabling of minority subjects, but the college is conscious it is losing
its 'market share'. In addition to this, a range of issues confront the
principal, e.g. severe budgetary restraints for the coming year, increasing

staff turnover in the 'wrong' areas and the need to revise curricula and
undertake staff development in some areas to address criticisms in recent
Further Education Funding Council (FEFC) quality audits.

In relation to the 'market share' issues, the principal asks Tom
Broadwood, her vice principal, to undertake a survey of both existing
and potential students to ascertain the strengths and weaknesses of the
college's 'offer'. This indicated some concerns over the lack of pastoral
care in the college, particularly for students who have difficulty with the
more academic demands of certain courses. After talking to her senior
management team, Amy proposes that all full-time staff should have
a time allocation for specific tutorial support work, but this is being
opposed by three groups:

1 The vice principal and the head of engineering, both of whom have
   been in post for over twenty years, argue that students should be seen
   as mature individuals, who don't need the kind of 'nannying' offered
   by schools.
2 The staff representatives feel that the tutorial demand will 'steal'
   time from that allocated to normal teaching work – to the detriment
   of results by which the college is judged.
3 The science, engineering and IT technicians feel that the use of
   laboratory bases for tutorial activities will hinder their maintenance work

During a period of negotiation, Amy secures the support of the college
governors and the local employment office manager, who has been
coping with the college's high rate of student drop-out. The head of
engineering signifies his intention to take early retirement if a suitable
financial package can be arranged, and the academic board points out
that without more attention to learning and social skills students will be
unable to complete their courses satisfactorily. The staff representatives
on the college management committee agree to renegotiate the
conditions of service to include a greater element of self-supported
study, which will release some teaching hours.

Amy realizes that the complex pressures may be shifting in her favour.
While her preference is to utilize more collegial and transformational
management approaches, she feels the time may have come, for the
good of the college, for her to be more dogmatic and assertive.

The transactional element has already become clear, but is the solution
likely to be of the garbage can variety?

The 'garbage can' concept offers a highly pragmatic approach to change.
The 'loose-coupling' metaphor (Weick 1989) is yet another way of conceptual-
izing organizational ambiguity. Loose-coupling, defined by Weick, happens
where 'events are responsive but . . . each event also preserves its own identity

and some evidence of its physical or logical separateness . . . their attachment may be circumscribed, infrequent, weak in its mutual effects, unimportant and/or slow to respond' (p. 120). He argues that loose-coupling is highly applicable to educational organizations which should be committed to experimentation and innovation and where 'retrospective sense making' is seen as the key to success.

REFLECTION

How inevitable is it that educational organizations are 'loosely-coupled' given the tradition of teacher autonomy that exists? Are the 'loose-coupling' and 'garbage can' concepts complementary or competing metaphors?

Given that leadership at various levels can significantly influence the scope for change, and the realities of complex change processes are not entirely clear, we are likely to find a variety of approaches in most change situations. Davies and Morgan (1989) recognize this and endeavour to integrate several theoretical strands. They suggest that organizational change often becomes driven by bureaucracy once earlier changes are institutionalized. Debate around the unresolved issues may then be pursued through collegially focused discussions, influenced by participants' political alignments. Resolution can occur, at least partially, through the dynamics of the moving organization, leaving more formal systems to develop again.

Change and corporate culture

Culture . . . is the assumptions which lie behind the values and which determine the behaviour patterns and the visible artefacts such as architecture, office layout, dress codes and so on.

(Schein 1983: 14)

Because corporate culture is based on taken-for-granted assumptions and beliefs about 'the way things are done around here', it is, in many respects, an elusive concept to pin down. Traditional ways, old habits and corporate cultures established over many years are difficult to change, and attempting to do so quickly may prove extremely disorienting and painful for those involved. Although they were writing for a business audience, Deal and Kennedy's (1982) comments on organizational culture may resonate with education, especially in the current 'new managerialst' context, where there is a political emphasis on closing/restructuring failing schools. They argue that large-scale corporate change is justifiable in five specific contexts:

1 When organizations have strong values which do not fit the changing environment.
2 When the organization's sector of the economy is very competitive and moves with lightning speed.

3 When the organization is mediocre or worse.
4 When the organization is about to join the ranks of the very largest companies.
5 When the organization is small but growing rapidly.

Importantly, they caution that changing cultures costs a lot – in terms of time, effort (i.e. people) and money. Given the rapidity of change and emphasis in education, it is likely that a number of 'corporate' cultures have found themselves 'out of step', e.g. 'have strong values which do not fit the changing environment'; appear 'mediocre or worse'; or are 'small but growing rapidly'.

REFLECTION

With Deal and Kennedy's comments in mind, do you consider educational organizations experience more difficulties in undertaking large-scale corporate change than businesses? If so, why?

Goldsmith and Clutterbuck's (1984) study of British companies argues that they can change their corporate cultures very quickly because employees' attitudes are constantly evolving. They see the key to success as the capacity of senior managers to build *and* communicate a unified image of the company's mission. In successful companies people are actively *shown* (by example) rather than *told* (by dictat) what the organizational goals are. Goldsmith and Clutterbuck (1984: 17) argue that leaders should positively exemplify appropriate behaviours and attitudes, since 'one of the strengths of many company leaders . . . has been their ability to adapt their behaviour to stimulate cultural change'.

Rossman *et al.* (1988) identify three cultural change processes based on a continuum from 'evolutionary' through 'additive' to 'transformational' change:

• *Evolutionary change*: which is implicit, unconscious and unplanned, with norms, values and beliefs fading and appearing over time.
• *Additive change*: which may or may not be explicit and conscious, since norms, beliefs and values are suddenly modified when new initiatives are introduced.
• *Transformational change*: which gives deliberate attention to changing norms, values and beliefs.

In terms of planned effectiveness and improvement efforts, cultural change is likely to be of the second or third kind, although, in many cases, rapid internally driven change can appear unrealistic and unviable if a culture of cooperation is to be maintained. A more common question for both education and industry may be: 'how do we innovate and change things when the prevailing climate is bureaucratic and traditionally oriented?' In answer, Handy (1993) reminds us that institutional cultures are generally subject to 'incremental change' rather than revolution, with some organizational cultures (usually the task-oriented sections of organizations) leading the way.

Kanter (1983) notes that even though many organizational cutlures are predominantly bureaucratic (what she terms 'maintenance' focused), there is potential to establish 'parallel' (task-oriented) cultures 'to energize the grass roots'. She also argues that these concepts (which reflect well-known conceptions of 'organic' and 'mechanistic' organizational structures, can operate simultaneously as 'equally formal structures' able to carry out 'specialized functions' within the 'integrated culture' of the organization (Kanter 1979).

This chapter has examined many key elements involved in the successful leadership of change, at individual, unit and whole-organizational level. While systems and sub-systems may operate in different cultural circumstances, with multiple and sometimes competing realities, there is much agreement that leaders need to exemplify the best aspects of change: demonstrating and articulating the benefits, enabling shared approaches to develop and tensions to be addressed. It is in such a context that much recent work on school improvement and effectiveness has developed.

Suggestions for further reading

Barth, R. (1990) *Improving Schools from Within*. San Francisco: Jossey Bass.

Beare, H., Caldwell, B. and Milliken, R. (1989) *Creating an Excellent School*. London: Routledge.

Fullan, M. (1993) *Change Forces: Probing the Depths of Educational Reform*. London: Falmer Press.

Fullan, M. (1999) *Change Forces: the Sequel*. London: Falmer Press.

Leithwood, K. A. (1992) *Teacher Development and Educational Change*. Lewes: Falmer Press.

Stacey, R. (1992) *Managing the Unknowable*. San Francisco: Jossey Bass.

Stoll, L. and Fink, D. (1996) *Changing Our Schools*. Buckingham: Open University Press.

9 Educational improvement, inspection and effectiveness

It is clear that the preferred management culture for effective schooling –
paradoxically given more emphasis by the introduction of the National Curriculum
– is *interdependence* rather than dependence or independence.

(Day *et al.* 1998: 57, authors' italics)

Pressure and support

The 1988 Education Act endeavoured to pressurize and simultaneously to
motivate schools towards more formal approaches to school improvement,
framed by a policy emphasis on rapid rather than evolutionary change within
a climate of greater school-based accountability. This emphasis was con-
solidated by the 1992 Education Act, which effectively 'disestablished' HMI's
classic role of 'collecting, synthesising and disseminating good practice and
providing data to inform policy making at national level' (West-Burnham
1994: 161), in favour of a rigorous national inspection framework overseen
by the Office for Standards in Education (Ofsted), whose mission was articulated as 'improvement through inspection'.

Tasked with assessing current educational practice through individualized
institutional inspections, Ofsted was to determine how every maintained
school 'lived' its philosophy, plans and organizational structure through producing improved school performance and pupil achievement. The new system,
so different from the old under which teachers might never meet an inspector
in an entire career, emphasized accountability through:

- a four-year inspection cycle for all schools;
- publishing standardized inspection procedures and explicit criteria (via the
  Handbook);
- inspecting all aspects of a school;
- training impartial inspectors;
- governor and pupil involvement in inspections;
- standardizing reports to governors and staff, with summaries for parents/
  community;
- specific time-limited Action Plans as responses to report findings (West-
  Burnham 1994: 163).

At Ofsted's inception, many were cynical about a system seemingly so focused on failure: Day *et al.*'s (1998: 215) comment reflects a frequently held view that 'any system of inspection which seems to attach more import-ance to failure than to success is unlikely to succeed in improving the quality of learning in schools'. Moreover, although the new inspection system implied that school improvement was a new concern, a thriving 'Effective Schools Movement' (ESM) had existed for some time, involving researchers, LEAs and individual self-evaluating schools (Reynolds 1992). While all were largely convinced that more overt and specific improvement strategies added value, the commitment to school effectiveness and improvement was sometimes driven by desires to face-down increasingly vocal criticisms over declining standards, 'progressive education' and comprehensivization which had 'placed schools in the dock' (Gray and Wilcox 1995).

Post-1979, successive Conservative governments saw the twin goads of pupil-led funding and external inspection as a stimulus to initiate rapid change – a view largely retained with the change to a New Labour govern-ment in 1997. However, echoing Fullan (1991), New Labour has emphasized that education will be subject to policy 'pressure' (the need to perform) *and* policy 'support' (opportunities for advice and additional funding), with LEAs resurrected as enablers and monitors of school improvement, though now also inspected by Ofsted.

REFLECTION

What, from your perspective, are the advantages and disadvantages of a national and institutional level system which links funding to overt improvement?

Inherent tensions are now becoming clear between central government's advocacy of higher standards for *all* pupils and the criticism that this dictum fails to acknowledge that schools vary in terms of intake, socio-economic context, resourcing and levels of local expectation. Despite tendencies to describe 'school effectiveness' in global terms, we need to distinguish between three allied concepts:

- *School effect*: the overall impact of schooling on achievement, usually on a large scale.
- *School effectiveness*: the impact of the various factors present in a given educational context, usually in a school or group of schools or colleges.
- *School improvement*: the strategies through which research findings are used to initiate change, again often in a school or group of schools.

Brighouse (1986) argues that two sets of 'pressure' face schools endeavouring to be effective: one internal (students, staff and organizational culture), the other external (the school in the wider local/national community). Both kinds of pressure influence perceived aims, processes and leadership.

External pressures stress the need:

- for resources (there are never enough);
- to improve, especially when national targets are at variance with local needs;
- to undertake increased administration in order to support identified targets;
- to conform to LEA plans (which bring together school–LEA improvement strategies);
- to meet local community expectations to maintain recruitment;
- to bid for additional financial support (locally or nationally) to support innovation.

Internal pressures stress the need:

- to motivate staff confronted by external pressures;
- to maintain the impetus for educational improvement and professional development;
- to retain students, despite problems;
- to plan, allocate and evaluate resources effectively to support improvement;
- for a curriculum which stimulates all students.

School effectiveness issues

Reid *et al.* (1987: 22) have argued that 'while all reviews assume that effective schools can be differentiated from ineffective ones there is no consensus yet on just what constitutes an effective school.' There are signs, however, of growing consensus regarding appropriate methodologies for investigating and assessing school effectiveness (McPherson 1992; Sammons *et al.* 1995). Despite the tendency to conflate various terms associated with the effective schools movement, Mortimore (1991: 9) suggests that an effective school is 'one in which pupils progress further than might be expected from consideration of its intake', while Sammons *et al.* (1995: 3) suggest it is one which 'adds extra value to its students' outcomes in comparison with other schools serving similar intakes'. For Hargreaves and Hopkins (1991), 'effectiveness' research findings comprise three perspectives:

- the *organization*, which may be external, e.g. the LEA, and internal, i.e. the school;
- the *process* by which the educational aims are achieved;
- the *outcomes* by which achievement might be measured.

REFLECTION

What does your own experience suggest are the significant factors in establishing the level of 'effectiveness' in your own institution? How do you encourage a positive learning environment?

It is important to acknowledge the timescale required in terms of the impact of added value on organizations: for example, Goldstein and Thomas's

(1995) assessment of a school's performance improvements in terms of added value points to the need for at least three years worth of data before informed judgements can be made. Recent years have seen numerous attempts to identify criteria for judging schools as either 'good' or 'bad', or a mixture of both. During the late 1980s we saw outbreaks of 'list-mania' regarding the ingredients of school effectiveness or successful schools. In an effort to cut through much of this, Scheerens (1992: 7–9) poses six questions designed to frame our evaluation of the various effectiveness studies:

1 From whose perspective is 'effectiveness' being judged?
2 Which area of activity within an organization determines effectiveness?
3 At which level of the organization is effectiveness to be judged?
4 Within what time span is effectiveness to be judged?
5 What data are to be used for assessment?
6 What standards or measures are to be used for effectiveness judgement?

Some of the more worthy attempts at identifying the key characteristics of 'effective schools' have included Rutter *et al.*'s (1979) now famous *Fifteen Thousand Hours* study, where pupil experiences in a group of inner-city secondary schools were assessed. For Rutter *et al.*, school effectiveness comprised:

1 A good school ethos.
2 Good classroom management.
3 High teacher expectation.
4 Teachers as positive role models.
5 Positive feedback and treatment of pupils.
6 Good working conditions for teachers and pupils.
7 Pupils given responsibility.
8 Shared staff–pupil activities.

Lightfoot (1983) characterizes 'goodness' in American high schools as:

1 Consciousness of imperfections.
2 Development of a visible and explicit ideology that involves staff and pupils.
3 Headteacher's role as voice of the school, providing vision.
4 Senior management holding teachers and their work in high regard.
5 An easy rapport between teachers and pupils.
6 Visible concern for the weakest members of the institution.
7 Opportunities fostered for pupils to form a 'vital' relationship with at least one adult.

Following on from Rutter *et al.*, Mortimore *et al.*'s (1988) examination of inner-city primary schools identified the important effectiveness elements as:

1 Purposeful leadership by the head.
2 Involvement of the deputy head.
3 Involvement of teachers.
4 Consistency among teachers.

5 Structured sessions.
6 Intellectually challenging tasks.
7 Work-centred environment.
8 Limited focus in sessions.
9 Maximum communication between teachers and pupils.
10 Parental involvement.
11 Record keeping.
12 Positive climate.

Focusing on 'successful schools' rather than effective ones, Brighouse and Tomlinson's (1991) contribution to the debate identifies the following key elements:

1 Leadership with curriculum as the main aim.
2 Emphasis on the quality of teaching and learning.
3 Clear goals and high expectations for both staff and students.
4 A supportive school climate.
5 Monitoring and evaluation as part of the culture.
6 Staff development and in-service support.
7 Parental involvement and support.
8 Community involvement and support.

ACTION

What aspects appear to be common to the above or, alternatively, only seem to stand out in one investigation? Do Scheeren's questions help to account for the differences?

Commissioned by Ofsted to review current knowledge on school effectiveness, Sammons *et al.* (1995) suggest that a common thread exists which combines leadership, high expectations and a supportive culture (summarized in Table 9.1). While not claiming exhaustiveness, their overview of effectiveness factors nevertheless consolidates the range of research evidence previously available.

Clearly, however, recognizing the characteristics of effective schools does not mean that they can be readily 'grafted on to' schools. The assumption that to know the faults is to achieve success is clearly wishful thinking. For example, Goldstein and Myers (1997) indicate the tensions which arise when research apparently offers an 'off-the-shelf' model for change, especially when it is then hijacked by government and when a belief in school effectiveness strategies conveys a message that 'failure' is the institution's fault alone.

Both Rosenholtz (1989) and Barth (1990) offer alternative views of what constitutes school effectiveness. Both criticize 'list logic', which, according to Barth, is simply 'a list sweepstake to see whose is the best list'. Both stress the uniqueness of socio-economic context and organizational school culture. Barth's model of effectiveness sees schools not as places 'for important people who do not need to learn and unimportant people who do', but as places where students discover – and adults rediscover – the joys, difficulties and

Table 9.1 Eleven factors for effective schools

1 Professional leadership	Firm and purposeful
	A participative approach
	The leading professional
2 Shared vision and goals	Unity of purpose
	Consistency of practice
	Collegiality and collaboration
3 A learning environment	An orderly atmosphere
	An attractive working environment
4 Concentration on teaching and learning	Maximization of learning time
	Academic emphasis
	Focus on achievement
5 Purposeful teaching	Efficient organization
	Clarity of purpose
	Structured lessons
	Adaptive purpose
6 High expectations	High expectations all round
	Communicating expectations
	Providing intellectual challenge
7 Positive reinforcement	Clear and fair discipline
	Feedback
8 Monitoring progress	Monitoring pupil performance
	Evaluating school performance
9 Pupil rights and responsibilities	Raising pupil self-esteem
	Positions of responsibility
	Control of work
10 Home–school partnership	Parental involvement in their children's learning
11 A learning organization	School-based staff development

Source: Sammons *et al.* (1995: 3).

satisfactions of learning. His is a model of school effectiveness dependent on the creation of 'a community of learners' or, in Rozenholtz's terms, the building of 'learning-enriched' as opposed to 'learning-impoverished' environments.

ACTION

Consider a curriculum change which you have been involved with and assess the strengths and weaknesses of change context: do these compare more with the list logic or the cultural model?

Reflecting on the ways that change is facilitated or impaired, added to our awareness of organizational micropolitics and power structures, highlights what, for us, are three necessary but not sufficient fundamentals for an 'improvement culture':

• developing shared values as a prerequisite for change;
• understanding change management processes;

- creating a review and evaluation system integrated into ongoing planning processes.

Rightly, however, Sammons *et al.* (1995) express caution in relation to interpreting findings and generalizing from effectiveness research – especially regarding the 'key determinants' of success and particularly when studies are often small scale. They point to:

> The dangers of interpreting correlations as evidence of causal mechanisms ... reciprocal relationships may well be important, as may intermediate causal relationships. Thus, high expectations may enhance student achievement, which in turn promotes high expectations for succeeding age groups. Improved achievement may benefit behavioural outcomes which in turn fosters later achievement. Conversely, lower expectations may become self-fulfilling, poor attendance and poor behaviour may lead to later academic under-achievement which exacerbates behavioural and attendance problems and so on.
>
> (Sammons *et al.* 1995: 1)

Despite assertions that there is only a limited relationship between resourcing and student achievement (Hanushek 1988, 1989), the evidence suggests that an essential baseline level of resourcing is crucial in improving schools (Sammons *et al.* 1995). As Gray (1990: 213) advises, 'adequate levels of resourcing ... seem to be a necessary but not a sufficient condition for a school to be effective ... in twenty years of reading research on the characteristics of effective schools I have only once come across a record of an "excellent" school where the physical environment left something to be desired.'

School improvement

Although Fidler (1997) tells us that 'what counts as school improvement is a highly contested issue', Stoll and Fink (1996: 42) identify it as 'a systematic and sustained effort aimed at change in learning conditions in one or more schools, with the ultimate aim of accomplishing educational goals more effectively.' However, we are warned by Scheerens (1992) that many of the factors identified in school improvement research are probably so context-bound that they are not readily transferable. He cites as evidence:

- the possibility of training leaders;
- the value of assessment procedures in securing progress;
- the modification of the school climate as changes develop;
- the possibility that the organizational structure itself may promote or inhibit improvement.

Scheerens is also especially sceptical about the impact of three politically motivated 'tinkering' devices:

- education as a market commodity;
- judgement simply on specified outputs;
- the publication of results to enhance the marketability of schools and colleges.

He questions the 'self-renewing' capacities of schools, suggesting that school development planning rather than enhancing school improvement via its culture may lead to mechanistic approaches to improvement.

REFLECTION

Review an 'improvement initiative' in your institution and assess how far 'school effectiveness' findings have been influential and how far improvements have been facilitated through effective change management strategies.

We suggest that a fundamental and recurrent requirement for improvement appears to be an acceptance of a set of shared values which all stakeholders hold about the school and its aims and objectives. Achieving and inculcating a set of values may, in turn, depend on the nature of leadership, the culture of relationships and the communication of a vision which is understood by both students and staff. Improvements which lead to enhanced outcomes demand not only strategic and tactical planning, but also development planning, and are seen by Hargreaves and Hopkins (1991) as ultimately *empowering* schools. In addition, school improvement needs effective change management strategies, a process which, in practical terms, comprises three stages: first, establishing targets; second, rational planning to achieve objectives; third, monitoring and evaluation.

Establishing targets

The establishment of clear aims against which plans can be developed is often seen as an essential precurser to school improvement, and these aims, depending on which are identified, then need to be translated into specific objectives. These are, in turn, explicitly defined, prioritized and then implemented on the basis of 'rational planning' approaches. As part of this, there is a strong expectation that schools engage in long-term planning, with strategic thinking placed in a specific time frame – with each year's budget set in the context of longer-term organizational development.

In many respects, this model can be seen as an educational equivalent of formal 'business-based' strategic planning processes. The approach has, however, been subject to criticism in the corporate sector as inapplicable to organizational environments characterized by uncertainty and ambiguity – a key concern for educationists too. Mintzberg (1994), among others, sees fluid and informal 'emergent' strategic management processes as a more practicable and effective alternative to rational planning strategies which lay down precise future targets and routes. The importance of constant feedback has also been stressed by Hargreaves (1995), who argues that we need constantly to recast plans as circumstances change.

Table 9.2   Rational planning process

Audit	Establishing the present situation
Planning	Considering alternative tactics and strategies to meet aims
Linking	Matching component plans to the development plan
Prioritizing	Establishing which plans are logistically and financially possible
Implementing	Putting the selected plans into operation
Evaluating	Measuring progress towards aims as a result of implemented plans
Repeating	Continuing the process so that development becomes a continuous activity

Rational planning to achieve targets

Rational planning processes are essentially sequential: objectives are agreed and information is obtained on the available alternative methods through which objectives might be attained. The selection of the most appropriate course of action, e.g. whether resources should be used for improving information technology (IT) or for building repairs, is dependent on knowing the costs of taking action balanced against the benefits which might accrue. Ends are thus clearly linked to means. Systems to ensure that decision making is based on perceived organizational priorities then stem from this rationality. Consequently, rational planning, although variously presented, tends to follow common themes and a cyclical process (see Table 9.2).

The School Development Plans Project (Hargreaves *et al.* 1989), which established ground rules for the involvement of all aspects of school management in an openly discussed and developed system, stressed the importance of identifying criteria for success as a planning feature. Hargreaves and Hopkins's (1994) work exemplifies this strategy in detail, and considers how school development plans require action planning to be concerned with the detailed implementation of key elements in the plan as well as the costs involved at classroom levels. Schools need to plan their developments at whole-school and departmental or sub-unit levels across time, since a single budget cycle is too constraining for fully achieving such aims.

Monitoring and evaluation

During the target implementation period (e.g. a school year), institutions are, ideally, also concerned with evaluating completed plans for the previous year and with utilizing that evidence to inform strategic review and planning for the following year. The distinction between monitoring – i.e. checking the progress of plans as actioned – and evaluation – assessing the impact of those plans – is an important one. Monitoring is often a management function, while evaluation requires the broader vision of leadership. There is evidence that many schools have only an imperfect understanding of monitoring and evaluation processes (Glover and Law 1996; Ofsted 1998a). Ofsted and the DfEE have highlighted the importance of review through:

• *Target-setting*: based on school and LEA generated data (DfEE 1996, 1997b).

- *Evaluation*: based on enhancing the skills of policy makers in schools as they compare their strengths and weaknesses with achievements in other schools in similar circumstances (Ofsted 1998a).

The requirements of Educational Development Planning (DfEE 1998a) bring both techniques together under the guidance of LEAs: schools need to establish the targets by which their role in progressing towards overall objectives is judged, with almost all objectives being rooted in the improvement of classroom-based teaching and learning. Much of the recent analysis by those adopting more mathematical views of improvement measurement (e.g. Gray and Wilcox 1995; Goldstein and Thomas 1995; Cheng and Cheung 1997) points to the difference between individual departments and pupils – itself often a key element in the Ofsted inspection process.

Improvement through inspection?

The school effectiveness movement has had a major impact on the evolution of a national system of assessment, measurement and reflection, even though its value remains highly contentious. Some have argued that the rhetoric of inclusivity implicit in school improvement and effectiveness work is not being matched by the actuality of practice (Elliott 1996; Slee *et al.* 1998) and that the very narrowness of its focus means that we should 'recognise the inevitability of the failure of the school effectiveness research and school improvement movement, even in its own terms of reference' (Slee and Weiner 1998: 7). There is also criticism that 'the fundamental weakness of the Effective Schools Movement (ESM) analysis is that it ignores the "context" in which educational events happen' (Rea and Weiner 1998: 30).

Using a series of intensive interlinked investigations in each school (Ofsted 1995a), Ofsted endeavours to pursue its strategy of 'Improvement through Inspection' – a conception of Ofsted's role not always readily shared by the recipients of its scrutiny. Statistical profiles and documents on each school enable inspection teams to develop initial organizational profiles related to resources and context as a framework for their later judgements. While the effectiveness of a school's resource management is underpinned by evaluations of its administrative efficiency and planning, Ofsted argues that it limits this rather mechanistic focus by inspecting pupil behaviour and personal development as part of a range of reviews, e.g. subject, organization, teaching and learning quality, assessment, recording and reporting, special needs, management and administration, guidance and welfare, as well as school–parent, agency and community links.

Ofsted has argued that its mission actually *complements* the drive towards school effectiveness and improvement. However, even if the Agency is seen by some as central and supportive for this task, it is heavily criticized by others for establishing an inspection process which can undermine schools' fragile achievements (TES 1999). Since its earliest days, Ofsted has been accused of utilizing inspection findings too simplistically as potential 'cure-alls' for ailing schools – providing even successful schools with 'summaries which . . . adopt a sales-pitch discourse by offering self-study DIY packages of information and value-added strategies' (Rea and Weiner 1998: 26).

Despite this negative picture, there is evidence that senior managers can find the process developmental (though this is less the case for teachers) and that schools are becoming increasingly adept at managing Ofsted inspection processes to maximize their own aims, e.g. by utilizing them as a check on their own self-review (Ouston *et al.* 1996; Fidler 1997). However, while post-1992 school inspection processes build on concepts of organizational culture, teaching and learning, organizational environment and relationships with stakeholders, it is clear that the current inspection process still strongly emphasizes the need for and value of rational planning as a feature of effectiveness – an issue which raises questions among many school leaders and teachers 'at the chalkface' about Ofsted's understanding of the nature of their task.

REFLECTION

What do you see as the major difficulties in using such a framework approach for a national system?

Initial reviews of Ofsted's impact (Gray and Wilcox 1995; Ouston *et al.* 1996) raise three main concerns:

- that a consistent approach is needed between schools, yet this can only be met by the use of descriptors which might form the basis for mechanistic assertions;
- that criteria for judgements are based upon knowledge of best practice, yet for a variety of reasons these may not be attainable within all schools;
- that Ofsted's structure provides for the use of suggestions which could help to improve practice, yet these suggestions are not always offered to schools.

Consequently, while the inspection framework itself (Ofsted 1995a) offers guidance to schools on improvement strategies, the inspectorate's role is not 'advisory', e.g. through providing working plans as supports for improvement. Although one of Ofsted's reporting aims is to help schools move towards improvement through a rational system, evidence from early inspection reports indicates that inspection tends to inhibit or constrain schools from adopting their own philosophy and cycle of auditing, planning, prioritizing, implementing, monitoring and evaluating. Many teachers and heads remain sceptical about the link between rational planning and school effectiveness. There is, however, evidence in early Ofsted reports analysed by multiple regression techniques that:

- strong links exist between schools which pursue rational planning procedures and high scoring attributes for school quality overall and the quality of teaching and learning;
- schools which have developed rational planning within departments, as well as at whole-school levels, are also more likely to be successful;

- pupil background (as reflected in the percentage of pupils with free meals in a school) is an apparent factor affecting the quality of learning, but the impact on the quality of teaching is much less – in short, schools do make a difference (Levačić and Glover 1995).

The following cameo illustrates these issues/dilemmas:

Cameo   All dressed up . . . ?

Staff at Merelands High were worried about their approaching Ofsted inspection two terms hence. One group of staff, led by a longstanding deputy (employed at the school since the 1970s, when it was a secondary modern), suggested that the school should be seen 'as it is, warts and all', with little attempt to 'dress up for the inspection'. This, they argued, would highlight how the years of underfunding had impacted on the shabby buildings, a poor library and the generally disaffected intake from a deprived environment.

The newly appointed head considered this a negative view, seeing Ofsted as an opportunity for managing successful change. She knew there would be criticism of those elements already identified by 'the group', but was also conscious that other staff felt disenchanted by the cynics' views. This, she felt, could be used as a catalyst for successful change.

'Working only from the positive' and asking those who wanted to plan for the inspection to join her on a working party, she aimed to identify school features which were more successful than others, and which could contribute to a 'vision for the future' – based on the idea that if all the strengths and weaknesses of the school were listed, with associated proposals for growth and development identified, then various working groups could demonstrate more positive attitudes and plan within the limits of what could be controlled by the school.

In the event, the process gained momentum when the deputy head, finally fearful of public criticism in the coming inspection, both requested and got early retirement. Reports of the main working party and, six weeks later, those from working groups formed the basis of a staff conference and a revised budget developed with the help of an LEA advisor/critical friend.

Priorities were established: 'those that cost nothing but our effort' set alongside those which would bring great benefit for limited expenditure were actioned as soon as staff gave their views, while those which would pull on resources were assessed in the light of the budget. The improvement process was by no means complete when Ofsted arrived, but attitudes were changing and expectations rising, with the prospects for increased intakes.

The key question the head asked herself was, would this have happened without Ofsted?

If we reflect on former HMCI Sheila Browne's comments on Her Majesty's Inspectorate's (HMI) role some two decades ago, they demonstrate that, despite Ofsted's rigour, the potential problematics of inspection are little changed:

> However frequent their visits, HMI have always had to remember that their selective observation can never match the collective knowledge of the head and teachers; it is they, after all, who day by day with their pupils are and make a school or college . . . A full inspection report is never the last word.
>
> (Browne 1979: 37)

Although Ofsted considers that leadership and management in most primary and secondary schools is good, there is concern that in secondary schools 'the weakest aspect of leadership and management is the monitoring and evaluation by schools of their own performance. This is improving, but could be further improved in two out of three schools' (Ofsted 1998c). This view echoes Chief Inspector Chris Woodhead's annual report (Ofsted 1997a), which, in somewhat negative language, argued that some heads 'fail' because they:

- are rarely seen in classrooms;
- fail to monitor teaching enough to know staff strengths and weaknesses;
- fail to bring about improvements in teaching;
- are unable to delegate and spend too much time on routine paperwork;
- fail to assess whether the school is getting good value for money;
- create a lack of a sense of purpose through weak leadership;
- fail to give clear objectives and targets, causing staff to waste time;
- add to discipline problems by not establishing clear rules for pupils and by failing to support staff when they try to discipline children.

ACTION

What are the key strategies you think would alleviate or overcome the problems Ofsted identified above? Are any issues reminiscent of those in your own organization and how are they being tackled?

While issues for improvement may be clear to 'insiders' who understand the institution's 'culture' or 'ethos', they are bound to be less clear to 'cultural outsiders' like Ofsted inspectors. Although a school's stated aims may be shown to 'fit' with the Inspectorate's criteria for effectiveness and improvement, staff may in reality fail to utilize them sufficiently well as a basis for professional interaction. For example, although one school's Ofsted documentation was rated as superb, its Ofsted inspection report noted that 'it needed to live by what it said – and it needed to know that it had said it.'

While the actual experience (rather than anticipation – some might say dread) of inspection may make it a more positive experience for schools, it can be of *long-term* value only if a report's main findings and key issues provide a valuable basis for future action, rather than 'hoops to be jumped through'. However, while 'at risk' or 'failing' schools are held to action plans, 'successful schools' may in future not be subject to external scrutiny but held to ongoing institutional development plans. Ultimately, improvement is about maintaining momentum. As Stoll and Fink (1996: 166) comment:

> A cruel irony is that there is very little evidence that external assessments actually improve the quality of education. In fact, there is substantially more evidence of their negative effects on teaching (Haladyna et al. 1991; Smith 1991) and many examples of teaching to the test, where test content drives what is taught. None the less, governments have spent millions on such strategies while cutting proven approaches like staff development.

● Performance indicators: measures and markers

> One of the limitations of school effectiveness research is that it is comparatively easy to track progress and assess value-added by using statistical data such as base-line scores and examination results. Assessments about the effectiveness of a school, therefore, have often been based around narrow sets of quantitative measures.
>
> (MacGilchrist et al. 1997: 3)

It is sometimes said that 'we need to measure what we value rather than value what can easily be measured'. It remains the case, however, that while policy makers have often found quantitative measures seductive because hard data can be manipulated and communicated in 'headline grabbing' ways, qualitative measures may be less readily malleable (Finch 1986). Nevertheless, Mortimore et al.'s (1988) study of junior school effectiveness was an early exemplar of efforts to *combine* a range of measures – by testing reading, writing, speaking and maths skills, as well as reviewing attendance, self-image, behaviour and attitudes to different school activities. Since 'measuring change is a challenge' (Stoll and Fink 1996: 172), no matter which approach is used, Gray (1990) has argued for a limited, but balanced, combination of methodologies, highlights academic progress, pupil satisfaction and pupil–teacher relationships as key effectiveness indicators and emphasizes that we should not rely on too narrow a definition of achievement.

A former Secretary of State for Education is said to have favoured three organizational indicators for successful schools: litter, graffiti in the toilet areas and the angle at which most students hold their heads. Such judgements may appear overly simplistic: Wilson and Corcoran's (1988) study of 571 American high schools (incorporating both objective and subjective performance indicators) acknowledges the inherent complexity created by performance measures, accepts that generalizability is inhibited by each school's uniqueness and recommends that indicators should, if possible, be simple, measurable and representative. Gray (1990: 217) offers us eight general principles for constructing performance indicators in educational setting, and suggests that performance indicators should:

1 Be about schools' performance.
2 Be central to the processes of teaching and learning.
3 Cover significant parts of schools' activities (but not all).
4 Reflect competing educational priorities.
5 Be capable of being assessed.
6 Allow meaningful comparisons: over time and between schools.
7 Allow schools to be seen to have changed their levels of performance by dint of their own efforts.
8 Be few in number.

These criteria may be met by basic data like examination achievements and students' course completion rates, although more consistent reporting policies also facilitate the development of other indicators, e.g. truancy rates and exclusions. The key criticism of such data is that false impressions about achievement get created: only with a fuller knowledge of the impact of institutional policies and practices on each cohort can we make clear judgements. Gray sees our obsession with detailed indicators as obscuring the real purposes and achievements of education, which is about developing individuals within different teaching and learning contexts. In reality, performance indicators may simply measure symptoms rather than deeper causes: ideally, perhaps, improvement strategies should be aimed at the latter.

Gray concludes that indicators need to relate to context: for both individuals and organizations. He suggests that 'too many questions drive out good answers' and proposes three indicators which have the potential to focus on quality, performance and the need for comparative data. For Gray (1990), a good school has a high proportion of pupils who:

1 Make above average levels of academic progress.
2 Are satisfied with the education they are receiving.
3 Have established a good relationship with one or more of their teachers (a key process indicator).

Gray's indicators, though simple, enable senior managers to bridge the divide between objective and subjective data via investigations and data collection which have the potential to show how links are made between systems (e.g. management information), relationships and quality assurance procedures. Arguably, it is only by *merging* or *integrating* both methodologies and both perspectives, on effectiveness and improvement – 'particularly through the study of those historically ineffective schools which turn the corner and start to improve' – that real progress will be made in this complex area (Gray *et al.* 1996: 8).

Towards school self-evaluation

An improving school is a self-evaluating school.

(Stoll and Fink 1996: 171)

While we have paid a lot of attention to the operation of externally driven inspection systems (Ouston *et al.* 1996), many schools find internally organized monitoring and evaluation processes increasingly valuable. Reid *et al.* (1987) have shown, for example, how self-review and evaluation is encouraged by teacher research processes – a feature emphasized more recently in the TTA's 'teacher-as-researcher' initiative (TTA 1996a).

Evaluations based on 'bottom-up' staff perceptions of institutional organization and achievement often avoid the negativities characteristic of imposed evaluations – particularly if the process is facilitated by school based review support materials like GRIDS (1988), a system of school-based review or school self-evaluation which, through its use of practical handbooks, supports in-house development. Participants identify organizational strengths and weaknesses, target improvement areas and focus on quality, thus developing both systems and people in order to maximize organizational potential (for a further exploration of the quality-related areas, see Oakland 1989; Murgatroyd and Morgan 1992; West-Burnham 1992). We revisit the concept of quality assurance elsewhere.

Stoll and Fink (1996: 169) see school self-evaluation as central because 'real improvement comes from within and is not externally imposed or mandated', but accept that it is no universal panacea, since weak rational planning processes may make improvement strategies ineffectual: 'An inherent danger . . . is that a school might not always identify its weaknesses. Insiders may be too close to problems to diagnose them adequately or may have limited expectations about what is possible with particular pupils.' Both Willms (1992) and FitzGibbon (1996a) explore the diversity of ways in which objective data can be generated. When the frequency with which features occur is related to particular intake situations, teachers are able to chart progress – in reading improvement, for example. However, more sophisticated analysis derives from grouping sets of frequencies related to, for example, student satisfaction or parental perception. We need to be cautious, however, in equating one set of data with another: there may be no causal links and analytical techniques are being developed to ensure that where links seem apparent they are statistically significant rather than just serendipity.

The post-Ofsted era has seen increasing sophistication in the collection and deployment of 'objective' (i.e. quantitative) data as performance indicators, particularly via commercially developed surveys (e.g. on pupil satisfaction, commitment and loyalty) with feedback to schools to inform development cycles, with more in-house surveys, with more 'teacher-researcher' led classroom research (TTA 1996a) and with improved databases tracking pupil progress and linked to LEA and other networks.

In addition, the growing emphasis on subjective (i.e. qualitative) approaches is helping schools to improve their grasp, by using cultural or 'ethos indicators' to assess how institutions support effectiveness (McBeath et al. 1992). There are, however, costs and benefits in both subjective and objective approaches: a key issue for practitioners and researchers is finding an appropriate methodological balance which can offer individual as well as groups of schools meaningful success indicators.

Teacher-led research is particularly important in terms of its potential impact: its importance lies in its accessibility and potential for value-addedness at classroom levels, enabling teachers to 'feed' their own pedagogy. For example, Wikeley (1998) stresses that the importance of 'ownership' lies in improving subject departments and notes that 'reported' research is of limited value in convincing staff that personal change is needed: personal professional learning is the key to greater effectiveness.

ACTION

Devise an evaluation programme for a newly introduced learning process within a subject area in your institution, e.g. increased use of supported self-study. How would you ensure that your results are valid, generalizable and credible?

Suggestions for further reading

Beare, H., Caldwell, B. and Milliken, R. (1989) *Creating an Excellent School*. London: Routledge.

Earley, P. (ed.) (1998) *School Improvement after Inspection? School and LEA Responses*. London: Paul Chapman Publishing.

Fullan, M. G. and Hargreaves, A. (1992) *What's Worth Fighting for in Your School?* Buckingham: Open University Press.

Gray, J., Reynolds, D., FitzGibbon, C. and Jesson, D. (1996) *Merging Traditions: the Future of Research on School Effectiveness and School Improvement*. London: Cassell.

Ruddock, J., Chaplain, R. and Wallace, G. (1995) *School Improvement: What Can Pupils Tell Us?* London: David Fulton.

Sammons, P., Hillman, J. and Mortimore, P. (1995) *Key Characteristics of Effective Schools: a Review of School Effectiveness Research*. London: Institute of Education.

Slee, R. and Weiner, G., with Tomlinson, S. (eds) (1997) *Effectiveness for Whom? Challenges to the School Effectiveness and School Improvement Movements*. London: Falmer Press.

10 Leading and managing in learning organizations

People with a high level of personal mastery live in a continual learning mode. They never 'arrive'. People with a high level of personal mastery are acutely aware of their ignorance, their incompetence, their growth areas. And they are deeply self-confident. Paradoxical? Only for those who do not see that 'the journey is the reward.

(Senge 1992: 340)

The learning context

In the context of continuous social, economic and cultural change, framed by a concern with flexible organizational structures and responsive learning strategies, the central task of educational leadership is fostering, and then sustaining, effective learning in both students and staff. As Garrett (1987) points out, if an organization is to survive and develop, the rate of learning inside it must be equal to, or greater than, the rate of change in the external environment. This has major implications: if institutions are incapable of 'learning' and changing, they will not thrive. Hopson and Hough (1985: 7) argue that because 'We live in a transient society where the only constant phenomenon is change', it is clear that 'the only security is the knowledge that tomorrow is going to be very different from today'.

We begin by examining the nature of the learning context within which educational leaders at all levels need to operate and the concept of the 'learning organization'. The post-1988 educational management climate requires that schools and managers respond to the implications of wider and rapid economic change, which is progressively repositioning it away from a corporate 'dependency' culture, towards a market-led 'enterprise culture' (Shipman 1990). Indeed, current technological imperatives indicate that change is 'probably accelerating, not slowing down', and reflects the kinds of challenge already confronting business organizations, e.g.

- the need to 'thrive on chaos' and 'learn to love change' in uncertain times (Peters 1987);
- the need for organizations to become 'learning companies' (Pedlar *et al.* 1996), 'learning institutions' (Handy 1989) and 'learning organizations' (Swieringa and Wierdsma 1992) in 'the Learning Age' (DfEE 1998e);

- the need to understand that personal learning is complex and that 'life-long learning' needs to become a reality (Argyris 1991; Senge 1992).

 ## Towards organizational learning

Despite the plurality of definition and the sense of bafflement felt over the notion that organizations are capable of 'learning', the concept of 'organizational learning' is relatively longstanding within business (e.g. Argyris and Schön 1981; Revans 1982; Honey 1991; Swieringa and Wierdsma 1992; Pedler *et al.* 1996). Although taken up a little more recently in education (e.g. Southworth 1994; Boud 1995; Clark 1996), interest in the concept has been stimulated by, for example: the demanding pace of change; emphases on competence, professionalism and the role of professional development; policy maker perceptions about education's failure to maximize student potential; and policy drives to pursue higher standards and 'educational improvement'. There is also a growing consciousness that because education is expensive in resource terms (Reimer 1971), it could become subject to 'cultural lag' if it fails to maintain pace with the information explosion and technological revolution (Garrett 1987; Lofthouse 1994a) with face-to-face approaches being overtaken by more cost-effective, Internet-based provision.

Two decades ago, Carl Rogers (1980) outlined the perceptions which seemed to frame 'traditional' conceptions of teaching and learning. He characterized what, nowadays, we might call a 'teaching organization' rather than a 'learning organization':

1 Teachers possess the knowledge; pupils are the recipients.
2 Teaching imparts knowledge to pupils; tests and examinations measure how much they have received.
3 Teachers possess power; pupils obey.
4 Classrooms operate through teachers' authority.
5 Pupils cannot be trusted; they do not work satisfactorily unless teachers control and check them.
6 Pupils are best controlled when in a state of fear.
7 Democracy is explained but not practised in classrooms; pupils do not formulate personal goals but have them determined for them.
8 The intellect rather than the whole person is central; emotional development is not necessarily part of learning (adapted from Rogers 1980).

In *Teaching as a Subversive Activity*, Postman and Weingartner (1971: 17) argue that institutions should 'enable the young to receive an education in learning how to learn', since 'what students mostly do in class is guess what the teacher wants them to say', ensuring that their learning is framed by the 'hidden' curriculum of schooling. Postman and Weingartner argue that, instead, they need to question taken-for-granted assumptions: 'This is why we ask that the schools should be "subversive", that they serve as a kind of "anti-bureaucracy bureaucracy", providing the young with a "What is it good for?" perspective on their own society' (Postman and Weingartner 1971).

Some two decades later, in *The Age of Unreason*, Handy (1989) asserted that 'Education needs to be re-invented' through an injection of 'upside-down thinking':

> Our schools first need to be re-designed . . . But education will not finish with school, nor should it be confined to those who shine academically at 18. Learning, too, as we have seen, happens all through life unless we block it. Organizations therefore need, consciously, to become learning organizations, places where change is an opportunity, where people grow while they work.
>
> (Handy 1989: 168)

Identifying several distinct 'sorts of intelligence or talent' in people, Handy suggests that the term 'the learning organization' means two things:

- an organization which encourages learning in its people;
- an organization which itself 'learns'.

He outlines the precepts of 'a theory of active learning', where learning is 'the theory at the heart of changing', distinguishable from 'more trivial definitions'. Echoing Postman and Weingartner's focus, Handy regards 'active learning' as:

- not just knowing the answers;
- not the same as study;
- not measured by examinations;
- not automatic;
- not only for intellectuals;
- not finding out what other people already know (Handy 1989: 50).

Much of this echoes Ferguson's (1982) futures prescription, which argued that 'the old paradigm of education' should be replaced by 'transpersonal education' and a 'new paradigm of learning' stressing 'the nature of learning rather than methods of instruction. Learning, after all, is not schools, teachers, literacy, maths, marks, achievement . . . Learning is kindled in the mind of the individual. Anything else is mere schooling' (Ferguson 1982: 316). Just as society changes, so learners also need to change: Ferguson's 'new learning' paradigm emphasizes learner autonomy and 'lifelong learning' (see Table 10.1).

REFLECTION

Consider, at this point, how far your own organization or area of work focuses on maintaining the 'Old Paradigm' – or is moving towards the 'New Paradigm'.

 ## Creative thinking

> The capacity to be creative is intensely human. It is essential for survival. It is, therefore, all the more surprising that creativity is generally neglected in mainstream education.
>
> (Fryer 1996: 1)

Table 10.1 Paradigm shift

Old (education) paradigm	New (learning) paradigm
Content emphasized – acquiring the 'right' information and giving 'right answers' once and for all	Learning emphasized – focusing on 'learning how to learn', asking questions etc.
Learning is a product, a destination	Learning is a process, a journey
Hierarchical: rewards conformity, discourages dissent	Egalitarian: dissent permitted; sees students and teachers as autonomous partners
Relatively rigid structure; prescribed curriculum	More flexible structure; mixed teaching and learning experiences
Compartmentalized; age segregation; focus on 'appropriate' ages	Flexible; integrated age groupings; age no block to progress/access
Guessing and divergent thinking discouraged as insufficiently rational	Guessing and divergent thinking encouraged as supporting creativity
External world emphasized: inner experiences seen as inappropriate	Inner experience valued: focus on whole learning context
Left brain emphasis: analytical, rational and linear thinking;	Whole-brain focus: holistic, non-linear, intuitive right brain thinking encouraged
Labelling (remedial, gifted, minimally brain dysfunctional etc.) becomes self-fulfilling	Labelling has only minor prescriptive role; less emphasis on permanent and fixed evaluation
Concern with norms	Concern with individual potential and overcoming limitations
Abstract 'book knowledge' emphasized	Abstract knowledge complemented by experience and experiment
Technology's dominance threatens dehumanization	Appropriate technology supports teacher–learner relationships
Teacher imparts knowledge and instructions	Teacher learns too – from pupils
'Efficient environment' and institutional convenience emphasized	'Learning environment' and contexts conducive to learning emphasized
Bureaucratically determined and tangential community input	Community links and inputs encouraged
Education as social necessity: inculcates basic skills/training	Education as lifelong process: moves beyond schooling
Performance seen as a priority	Self-image as a generator of performance is a priority

Source: adapted from Ferguson (1982).

While many educationists may not agree with Fryer's comment, it remains the case that 'creative thinking' has, until relatively recently, been seen as an implicit and unspoken rather than an overt and declared aspect of education. Indeed, it appears that a substantial minority of children (30 per cent) find that schooling produces boredom rather than stimulates creativity, with some 70 per cent of British high school children 'counting the minutes' until their lessons end (Barber 1994).

Armstrong (1994) has defined creative thinking – an overt 'skill' expected of many leaders – as 'imaginative thinking which generates new ideas' and new ways of looking at things. Consider, for example, de Bono's (1967) 'lateral' thought processes, so named because they make sideways links rather than relying on consequential and logical 'vertical thinking'. In education, creative thinking might be exemplified by the way one headteacher in a deprived inner-city primary school decides to use resources to retain a teach-

Table 10.2   Hemispheres of the brain

Brain's left hemisphere emphasizes	Brain's right hemisphere emphasizes
Language	Rhythm
Logic	Music
Number	Images
Sequence	Day-dreaming
Linearity	Colour
Analysis	Connections

Source: after Whitaker (1995).

ing assistant and a teacher in each classroom rather than to establish smaller classes with one teacher in each.

Conventional approaches to education have paid only limited attention to the way the brain works – a situation which, fortunately, is changing, even if only slowly. While the complexity of brain processes and its influence on creativity and learning processes is increasingly recognized (e.g. Cropley 1992; Fryer 1996), the acceptance that our brains have two hemispheres which operate with different purposes may have major implications for the way we both learn and think of ourselves (see Table 10.2).

Even though there is little clarity about how our brains work and how creativity is generated, as Abbott (1994: 73) points out, the process is highly dynamic: 'The brain learns when it is trying to make sense; when it is building on what it already knows, when it recognises the significance of what it is doing; when it is working in complex, multiple perspectives.' Whitaker (1995) notes that while traditional teaching methods place a particular emphasis on left brain functions, e.g. memorizing facts, determining single 'correct' answers and logical sequences, developing right brain functions and approaches (e.g. using imagery, imagination, rhythm) can add a further dimension to learning performance (Buzan 1982). For Armstrong, the main barriers to creative thinking are:

- allowing the mind to become conditioned into following a dominant – and often totally logical – pattern;
- restricting free thinking – 'thinking the impossible' – by rigidly drawn boundaries;
- failing to examine the basic assumptions which may hamper new ideas;
- reducing ideas to 'either/or' when elements of both might be used;
- using logical structures which might be constricting;
- tending to value conformity rather than imaginative thinking;
- fearing that suggestions might lead to being 'put down' by others.

Lateral thinking has become an increasingly acceptable strategy for assessing organizational development: brainstorming, for example, is now commonly used in seeking possible solutions to problems, although the main inhibiting factor is that, as individuals, we are not always very creative about personal ways of thinking and working. As Armstrong notes, it is easy to find ten ways of saying 'no' to anything new, though in doing so we deny ourselves opportunities for creativity as a result. It is important, though, to try to link creativity with clarity: creative thinking is most successful and effective where ideas are clearly communicated. The implications of creativity make it important that ambiguity is avoided so that our willingness to challenge current ideas and our readiness to offer solutions is based on evidence and argument.

Leadership, teaching and learning

Effective teachers are those that provide pupils with maximum opportunities to learn.

(Silcock 1993: 13)

While they acknowledge that there are difficulties in pinning down the concept, Aspinwall and Pedlar (1997) argue that those charged with leading 'learning schools' need to be committed to developing the following four key principles:

- lifelong learning for all;
- collaborative learning, where difference and conflict are used creatively and positively;
- developing a holistic understanding of the school;
- strong external and community relationships.

Each of these requires that teaching and learning processes are well led and managed, although this is not necessarily an easy process:

The problem with talking about 'learning organizations' is that 'learning' has lost its central meaning in contemporary usage. Most people's eyes glaze over if you talk to them about 'learning organizations'. Little wonder – for, in everyday use, learning has come to be synonymous with 'taking in information' . . . yet, taking in information is only distantly related to real learning.

(Senge 1992: 13)

If a teacher's role is help others to develop their learning capacities, it follows that management activities, organizational structures, systems and processes need to intersect to maximize teaching and learning opportunities. Buckley and Styan (1988: 1) contend that this needs to be facilitated through management training for all those involved in facilitating the learning process: 'Learning, if it is to be effective, needs to be managed. Thus all teachers are managers.' This theme was taken up in the School Management Task Force (SMTF) report (DES 1990) and, more recently, has been part of the TTA's development of national standards for headship, subject leadership and teacher training/induction (TTA 1998a, b, c).

'Leading' and 'managing' learning is not, however, that simple. Teachers may be adept at creating and 'managing' learning opportunities, but they cannot directly 'lead' or 'manage' others' learning:

The manifest purpose of the teacher's role performance is to produce learning in students, but this cannot happen directly. The best the teacher can do is to induce students to engage in activities deemed instrumental in the covert psychological processes he hopes to affect . . . opportunities for slippage are enormous.

(Perrott 1982: 17)

ACTION

Before reading on, record how much time you spend during an average or typical day in 'managing the learning' of others. What tends to inhibit the process?

Education organizations are different from commercial organizations because 'teachers perform multiple roles . . . an important factor in distinguishing schools from other organizations' (Buckley and Styan 1988: 7). Echoing this, Shipman (1990) reminds us that educational leadership and management 'cannot be confined to the classroom and staffroom' and calls for a 'synoptic view of management', where:

- promoting learning is the focus of management;
- management training improves teaching quality and raise levels of attainment;
- school management has an evidence base from studies of school excellence which can support improvement;
- managing teaching and learning through the curriculum involves paying attention to breadth, balance, continuity and progression.

According to dictionary definitions, 'learning' is both knowledge gained by study, instruction or scholarship and the act of gaining knowledge. For Bass and Vaughan (1966: 8), it is a 'relatively permanent change in behaviour that occurs as a result of practice or experience', while managing learning and teaching involves helping others to enhance their knowledge, skills, abilities and understanding of the world around them. Consequently, rapid technological and social change means that *how* people learn becomes as important as *what* they learn: indeed, knowing *where* and *how* to find answers is becoming as important as knowing *what* the answers are, if only because the nature of 'truth' and what counts as knowledge changes as the pace of technology quickens.

This focus on 'transferability' has to accommodate relatively recent political demands for more quantifiable knowledge and skills: for example, the National Curriculum and National Vocational Qualifications. Meeting such demands requires a range of effective management strategies – in classrooms and organizationally – since 'teaching and learning are not readily managed . . . the teacher can teach, but some children won't learn' (Shipman 1990: 4). If Shipman is correct, identifying effective learning and teaching strategies to maximize individual and organizational potential becomes crucial and teachers need to understand the implications of their own teaching and learning strategies, their own preferred 'teaching styles' as well as others' preferred 'learning styles'.

Although they accept that 'learning how to learn' is a vital future skill, Nisbet and Shucksmith (1986: 8) argue that the current context for learning means that, as learners, we all also need to possess 'a seventh sense... metacognition [reflection], the awareness of one's mental processes, the capacity to reflect on how one learns, how to strengthen memory, how to tackle problems systematically – reflection, awareness, understanding, and perhaps, ultimately, control.'

● A focus on teaching

To teach is to learn twice over.

(Joseph Joubert, *Pensées* 1842: 22)

As this quotation indicates, it can often seem that our need to teach something ensures that we at least learn, even if our pupils or students don't. Differences between teaching and learning strategies and individual teaching and learning styles are often characterized as a polarization of 'traditional' versus 'experiential' approaches. While the rhetoric in education is frequently that a *range* of strategies is utilized to match different learning needs (groupwork, teacher talk/lecturing, discussion, practical activities etc.), the prevailing orthodoxy within classrooms remains largely focused on transmissive and teacher-centred approaches. As Hargreaves (1982: 195–200), in his review of comprehensive education, noted, 'traditional' approaches imply that:

> The teacher's authority ultimately rests in the authority of his subject. For such a teacher his subject expertise is absolutely central to his identity. He thinks of himself, not as a teacher, but as a mathematics teacher, or a history teacher and so on ... One of the most striking characteristics of teachers is their addiction to didactic talk. Teachers are qualified in their subjects; they know; and they are not satisfied until they have told their pupils what they know.

REFLECTION

How far are didactic or transmissive approaches pre-eminent in your own area of work, and what prevents greater use of experiential methods?

Transmissive approaches tend to dominate because

- they fit the existing organizational frameworks, replicating tutors' own learning experiences;
- teachers and lecturers are visibly accountable for what they (try to) teach learners;

- they present few organizational or teaching problems, objectives are readily designated, teaching programmes designed and students examined because 'known knowledge' is transmitted (Bennett 1976);
- they are 'tidy' by comparison with more 'messy' experiential approaches and are more efficient in terms of tutor time, allowing learners to cover the same material at the same time and same pace;
- they create a power-status relationship between tutors (in control) and students (as passive recipients);
- they maintain the emphasis on a long, formalized 'knowledge apprenticeships', reinforcing conceptions of education as a form of social control (Habermas 1972);
- they emphasize tutors' personal authority and professional status (Bernstein 1977);
- they are predictable, enabling objectives setting and assessment to be more efficiently organized.

In organizational terms, transmissive methods are defended because they offer managers:

- the potential for (management) control;
- a means of accountability;
- economy of teacher time;
- opportunities to check progress (e.g. through a syllabus checklist);
- opportunities for traditional timetable/rooming arrangements;
- ease of tracking, since checking knowledge transfer and retention in groups of students is quicker and much tidier than checking individual student learning.

Experiential learning

'Experiential learning' implies a seamless, unending process which goes on both within and outside formal education structures, yet the ubiquitous nature of learning by 'experiencing' or 'doing' belies its complexity and the fact that, despite considerable professional interest, it is not fully understood. Indeed, Lofthouse (1994a: 124) has argued that the growth of bureaucratic demands placed on schools has actively encouraged them to regress towards more traditional teaching and learning practices: a focus reinforced over the past decade with the growth of an accountability, 'back to basics' and 'standards' agenda which is pushing for a closer scrutiny of the cost and value of different learning and teaching strategies. Based on West-Burnham's (1992) identification of the polarities between transmissive and experiential approaches, it is possible to describe various combinations of teacher-student relationships (see Figure 10.1).

Experiential learning tends to be used as an umbrella term for a range of related approaches to learning: 'active learning', 'learning-by-doing', 'action-learning', 'humanistic learning', 'holistic learning' and so on. The focus on individual learners rather than on the learning material itself emphasizes the holistic nature of learning, and while different learning cycles are identified in various perspectives, each emphasizes the central notion that experience

Teacher				
Masters	Providers	←→ Teachers as ←→	Expert coaches	Facilitators
Do *to*	Do *for*	←→ Action ←→	Do *with*	Enables
Servants	Recipients	←→ Students as ←→	Participants	Active learners
Student				

Figure 10.1 Relative teacher and student roles (after West-Burnham 1992).

is the key to learning and personal control. Conventional approaches usually require students to 'know their place'; experiential modes undoubtedly diminish tutor centrality, facilitating greater learner 'empowerment' and personal control. Even so, its ubiquitous nature belies its underlying complexity: despite considerable academic research and practical inquiry, it is an area of learning that remains little understood (Markee 1997).

However, as with any other learning approach, if experiential learning is to be effective, it needs to be well organized and purposeful, with a basic objective of helping learners to construct their own learning agenda and 'learning cycle'. While levels of tutor control and direction vary depending on the specific situation, in line with transmissive approaches, tutors need to offer supportive learning structures, reflected in a more coherent understanding of learning styles and processes.

Learning styles

According to Gregorc (1982), our learning styles are determined largely through how we *perceive* and *order* information – ranging from the concrete (rooted in the physical senses, emphasizing the observable) to the abstract (rooted in emotion and intuition, emphasizing feelings and ideas), although most people prefer one particular mode. Furthermore, our ability to order information is both sequential (i.e. storing information in a linear, logical, step-by-step way) and random (i.e. storing it in a non-linear, holistic and kaleidoscopic way), though again most people have a preference. Gregorc argues that while individuals may use all four learning approaches to some degree, we generally utilize one or two (see Table 10.3).

Like Gregorc, Honey and Mumford (1988) emphasize that learning is as much about developing personal competence as about accumulating knowledge. Building on Kolb *et al.*'s (1971) work, they identify four ways of learning (i.e. by feeling, watching, thinking or doing), noting that we tend to prefer one or two, thus creating a unique, personalized approach to learning (see Table 10.4).

The growing emphasis on preferred learning styles in much management literature has not overtly infiltrated educational practice. Even with increased stress on measuring ability and tracking achievement, educationists often remain sceptical about individual learning styles, although we know that a poor match between teaching strategy and learning style(s) can inhibit student achievement, can provoke misinterpretation about potential and can

Table 10.3 Individual learning approaches

Concrete sequential	Likes organizing facts and direct experience; accuracy; task-oriented work and orderly, quiet, working environments
Abstract sequential	Matches concepts against experience; logical, analytical and evaluative thinker; articulate communicator; often dislikes speedy decision making and group work
Abstract random	Intuitive problem solver, comfortable with emotions and imagination; needs rapport to be effective learner; less comfortable with highly structured tasks
Concrete random	Experiential, intuitive problem solver; impulsiveness; independent, divergent and original thinker; inhibited in traditional settings (smallest group)

Source: after Gregorc (1982).

encourage behaviour 'problems'. Nevertheless, while we might pinpoint many of the key ingredients which support or frustrate effective learning, the process itself still remains messy, unpredictable and hard to pin down, even by researchers. Postman and Weingartner (1971) suggested that 'good learners':

- enjoy problem-solving;
- know what is relevant for their survival;
- rely on their own judgements;
- are not afraid to be wrong and are able to change their minds when necessary;
- think first, rather than appear to be fast answerers;
- are flexible and adaptable to situations and challenges;
- have a high degree of respect for facts;
- are skilled in inquiry;
- do not need to have absolute and final solutions to every problem;
- do not get depressed by the prospect of saying 'I don't know'.

Understanding a learner's capabilities and the drawbacks associated with the experiential methodology are essential if this approach is to be successful

Table 10.4 Ways of learning

'Reflector'	Reflects on concrete experience; prefers to see range of options/opportunities and draw conclusions; dislikes pressure for 'the solution'
'Theorist'	Logical learner who reflects on data and information; tends to dislike unstructured situations; likes to develop ideas through discussion; enjoys planning and detailed evaluation/reflection
'Pragmatist'	Likes to get results; good independent thinker and worker; enjoys solving problems in personal way; tries out possibilities, enjoying practical, purposeful approach to, for example, training and development
'Activist'	Enjoys experimentation and exploration of new ideas; interactive and responds to challenges, taking risks if necessary; enjoys active learning, e.g. role play and competitive teamwork

Source: after Honey and Mumford (1988).

(Dennison and Kirk 1990). Conventional teaching and learning methodologies are increasingly attacked as incompatible with concepts like the 'learning organization' and the 'learning age': criticized for their rigidity and for encouraging 'a pedagogy which tries to answer questions not yet asked by potential learners' (Dennison and Kirk 1990: 17). Yet, while effective experiential learning and 'learning on-the-job' are seen as a better match for post-millennial demands, these approaches are also criticized for lacking clear objectives and coherent structures. A common complaint when experiential learning strategies fail learners is that there was 'too much activity and not enough learning'. It is important, therefore, for those managing learning and teaching to recognize the potential value (and setbacks) of both approaches. Whatever the method being used, we still need to clarify our curriculum focus, specify learning outcomes, establish coherent structures and develop a review process: in short, we need a rational but flexible framework for learning.

The learning process

Learning should not only take us somewhere, it should allow us to go further more easily.

(Bruner 1960: 17)

The concept of the 'learning cycle' is a useful shorthand to describe learning processes (see, for example, Kolb 1984; Handy 1989), especially since reflective and experiential learning lays stress on new learning approaches. Kolb *et al.*'s (1971) four-stage experiential learning cycle describes a series of discrete mental processes and argues that we make sense of concrete experiences by reflecting on them, developing our ideas and then acting on the basis of our new learning. This is a particularly important aspect of professional development learning. Kolb *et al.*'s approach, built on by others, can help to identify problems or issues, assemble possible strategies, then choose and evaluate what seems to be the best approach (see Figure 10.2).

In applying an experiential learning cycle to a classroom scenario, Whitaker (1995) has argued that we should try to distinguish between 'incidental' and 'deliberate' learning, while Brookfield (1987) asserts that the Kolb process requires further refinement so that we adopt a more 'critical' approach, involving:

- identifying and challenging assumptions;
- identifying and assessing context;
- imagining and developing alternatives that might explain or expand thinking;
- developing a 'reflective scepticism' in considering alternatives.

REFLECTION

Do Kolb's learning cycle (and Brookfield's and Whitaker's amendments) reflect your approaches to learning and development? How has your learning developed, e.g. when developing curriculum areas or teaching?

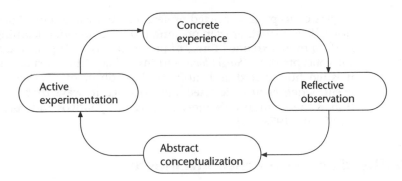

Figure 10.2 Experiential learning cycle.

Focusing on the notion of critique, Friere (1972) has suggested that three key elements are central to the learning process (see Table 10.5). These elements are an encouragement to identify our own learning issues and questions rather than be 'spoon fed' with ready-made answers. Too often, however, learners get trapped by what Friere (1972: 26) calls 'the banking concept of education', where 'students . . . accept their ignorance as justifying the teachers' existence' – thus taking us back to more transmissive and didactic forms of teaching and learning. In addition, it is important that learners become more aware of how and why learning differs. This may mean distinguishing between *'shallow'* or *'surface'* learning (i.e. the kind of learning which involves *remembering facts* without understanding why) and *'deep'* learning (i.e. the kind of learning which involves *understanding meanings*) (Entwistle and Entwistle 1991).

Linked to this, Argyris and Schön (1981) have distinguished two levels of learning complexity as part of their exploration of the learning process: *single loop learning* (where simple changes are made when an activity does not work well) and *double loop learning* (where we actively question the underlying assumptions informing an activity). Too often, patterns of teacher development reflect 'single-loop' learning approaches, where individualized teacher theories get developed and tested in isolation from colleagues, reflecting

Table 10.5 Three key elements in the learning process

Praxis	A continuous process of experience and reflection, incorporating critical thinking; by discovering how and why certain activities fail or succeed, we are able to improve our future actions
Problematization	The ability to focus on the frustrating and difficult aspects of learning which need to be changed; if we ignore this aspect, cognitive dissonance or learned helplessness results
Conscientization	The process whereby learners become more aware of the social, political and cultural context for learning, developing their capacity for understanding, thus learning to influence their futures

Source: after Friere (1972).

Hoyle's concept of 'restricted professionality', which closes down on professional dialogue rather than opening it up. Double loop learning, by contrast, leads to more extended forms of professionalism. Argyris and Schön explain the concepts thus: '*Single loop* learning is like a thermostat that learns when it is too hot or cold and turns the heat on or off ... *Double loop* learning occurs when error is detected and corrected in ways that involve modification of an organization's underlying norms, politicos and objectives' (Argyris and Schön 1978: 34).

● Multiple and corporate intelligence

> When applying the notion of multiple intelligence to an organization as opposed to an individual, successful organizations are those that understand the *interdependent* nature of the different intelligences and strive to develop and use their 'corporate intelligence'.
>
> (MacGilchrist *et al.* 1997: 25, authors' italics)

The notion of 'interdependence' is increasingly important in the literature on effective and successful organizations. McMaster (1995), for example, arguing for the importance of the concept of 'corporate intelligence', suggests it is indicative of an essential interdependence and intersection of key elements to create a whole organization. For him, corporate intelligence means that 'more information, more richness of interpretation, more creativity in processing information, and more generative ability can be integrated beyond what any single individual can do' (1995: 3). This moves us towards the notion of synergy (where the sum becomes greater than the constituent parts) and away from more individualized and mechanistic perspectives on the nature of learning and intelligence. It challenges the Newtonian world picture, in which the learning process is seen as essentially rational and dependent on a disaggregation and fragmentation of each element for analysis (Senge 1992; Wheatley 1992). However, as Bohm (1980: 1) noted two decades ago:

> fragmentation is now very widespread, not only through society, but in each individual; and this is leading to a kind of general confusion of the mind ... The notion that all these fragments are separately existent is evidently an illusion, and this illusion cannot do other than lead to endless conflict and confusion.

Although 'intelligence' is not an easy term to define – neither easily observed nor readily measured – the concepts of intelligence and of intellectual development have been strong threads running through educational provision, with success usually determined by demonstrable intellectual excellence via examinations, used as performance indicators and gateways to future opportunities in both education or the workplace. Goleman (1996) warns, however, that while the 'academically' intelligent may become highly successful, they may not necessarily have appropriate levels of emotional intelligence and maturity: this may, he argues inhibit their development and effectiveness. Other writers, like Gardner (1993), stress the importance of being emotionally literate and of accepting that learning occurs in a variety of ways and not simply through our intellect (the mind). He argues that intelligence is about more than cognition and intellect. He considers that everyone has the capacity for seven kinds of intelligence (Gardner 1983):

- linguistic (words);
- logistical mathematical (numbers and reasoning);
- spatial (pictures and images);
- musical (tone, rhythm and timbre);
- bodily-kinaesthetic (the whole body and the hands);
- interpersonal (social understanding);
- intrapersonal (self-knowledge).

Traditional academic skills, according to Gardner, are no longer sufficient . . . assuming they ever were. In addition to intellectual intelligence, students (and, at least as importantly, their teachers) need a range of practical, coping skills, e.g. for problem solving. Handy (1997) also acknowledges that intelligence takes a variety of forms and proffers his own 'provisional' list of eleven intelligences:

1 Factual intelligence (the 'know it all' facility possessed by, for example, 'Mastermind' quiz addicts).
2 Analytic intelligence (the ability to reason and conceptualize).
3 Numerate intelligence (the ability to be at ease with numbers of all sorts).
4 Linguistic intelligence (a facility with language and languages).
5 Spatial intelligence (an ability to see patterns in things).
6 Athletic intelligence (physical skills, exemplified by athletes).
7 Intuitive intelligence (an aptitude for sensing and seeing what is not immediately obvious).
8 Emotional intelligence (self-awareness and self-control, persistence, zeal and self-motivation).
9 Practical intelligence (an ability to recognize what needs doing and what can be achieved).
10 Interpersonal intelligence (an ability to get things done with and through others).
11 Musical intelligence (an easily recognized ability, whether in opera singers, pianists or pop groups).

Asserting that we each possess our own individualized range of intelligences, Handy accepts that they may not necessarily correlate or complement each other. For example, those traditionally deemed 'intelligent' may demonstrate factual, analytic and numerate intelligences, all features which, he notes, can 'get you through most examinations and entitle you to be called clever'. Beyond these, however, lies a wider range and combination of intelligences which, conventionally, have received only limited attention. Only now, framed by social and political imperatives to develop 'learning skills' for an 'information age', are they becoming valued.

We need to consider what the recognition and acceptance of 'multiple intelligence' means for those managing education and what the practical implications are for schools and colleges. Before doing so, however, we need to acknowledge that many schools already demonstrate longstanding (albeit

REFLECTION

How have you conventionally conceived your own 'intelligence(s)'? How and why might you have constructed such a view of your intelligence 'strengths' and 'weaknesses'?

implicit) commitments to nurturing 'multiple intelligence', i.e. to valuing more than a cluster of academic intelligences. This remains, however, often less explicit and overt than it now needs to be. For MacGilchrist *et al.* (1997: 104), multiple intelligence is essentially the:

range of collective capacities schools have that enable them to achieve their goals successfully. It involves the use of wisdom, insight, intuition and experience as well as knowledge, skills and understanding. These intelligences provide something analogous to the fuel, water, and oil in a car. They all have discrete functions but, for their success, need to work together.

Identifying 'nine intelligences' to be found in 'successful schools' (see Table 10.6), they suggest that such institutions are 'intelligent schools'. While accepting that their list is not and cannot be finite, they argue that effective organizations use these nine intelligences to address simultaneously 'the core business of learning, teaching, effectiveness and improvement'.

ACTION

Try to identify practical examples which show how far your own institution actively engages with and nurtures the above corporate intelligences. Where are the gaps and why might they exist in your organization?

Cynically, we might argue that effective educational organizations have always engendered the development of 'multiple intelligences' and have been empathetic in addressing the differing needs, abilities and intelligences of those studying and working within them. For some, the 'new language' of intelligence might merely be seen as repackaging performance, effectively masking earlier good educational practice. Others might argue that, even if this were the case, such an approach 'raises the stakes', disseminating good practice and opening up professional debate about educational values and purposes, e.g. about the nature of intelligence. Rather than supporting more technicist approaches, it might, in turn, actually counterbalance the drive towards measuring and quantifying performance (e.g. via league tables) which currently frames educational development. 'Intelligent schools have the capacity to "read their overall context" in a way that they are neither overwhelmed by it nor distanced from it but are in a healthy relationship with it and know they need to respond to both its positive and negative aspects' (MacGilchrist *et al.* 1997: 105).

Table 10.6   The corporate intelligence of the intelligent school

1 Contextual intelligence	Understands the relationship between the school and the wider community
	Able to read internal and external context
	Flexible and adaptable
	Knows 'no quick fixes'
2 Strategic intelligence	Uses contextual intelligence to establish clear goals
	Establishes shared aims and purposes
	Puts vision into practice through planned improvements
3 Academic intelligence	Emphasizes achievement and scholarship
	Values pupils' engagement in and contribution to learning
	Encourages the 'can do' factor
4 Reflective intelligence	Monitors and evaluates the work of the school
	Uses data to judge effectiveness and plan improvement
	Uses data to reflect, in particular, on pupils' progress and achievement
5 Pedagogical intelligence	Emphasizes learning about pupils' learning
	Ensures learning and teaching are regularly examined and developed
	Challenges orthodoxies
6 Collegial intelligence	Views the staff as learners
	Improves practice in the classroom through teachers working together
7 Emotional intelligence	Values expression of feelings
	Understands others and how to work cooperatively
	Individuals understand themselves
	Encourages motivation and persistence, and understands failure
8 Spiritual intelligence	Has compassion
	Values the development and contribution of all members of the school and its community
	Creates space to reflect on ultimate issues
9 Ethical intelligence	Has clear values and beliefs
	Has a sense of moral purpose and principle
	Is committed to access and entitlement for all
	Has high but not complacent self-esteem

Source: Reprinted by permission of Paul Chapman Publishing from MacGilchrist *et al.* (1997) *The Intelligent School.*

Managing curriculum issues

While it may have 'philosophic fascination', curriculum is complex and difficult to define.

(Lofthouse 1994b: 143)

Richmond (1971: 87) reflects these difficulties in arguing that: 'Curriculum is a slippery word. Broadly defined, it means nothing less than the educative process as a whole. Narrowly defined, as it usually is, the term is regarded

ACTION

Reflecting on your own experience, try to create your own working definition of 'curriculum'.

as being more or less synonymous with the syllabus, a scheme of work or simply subjects.' Multiple realities and perceptions create major difficulties for those charged with managing and prioritizing curriculum choices and developments. While effective curriculum planning and organization is best supported by agreed terminology, planning and monitoring (Caldwell and Spinks 1992; Hilditch 1993), this requires discussion about fundamental values, what constitutes 'useful' and appropriate education, whether curriculum has a moral dimension and so on – no easy process. The situation becomes even more complex because we need to translate principles into practice and understand what influences curriculum planning, e.g. availability of teaching expertise, administrative support, physical resources, accommodation, internal organizational 'status' of subjects and departments.

While some curriculum influences, like financial resources or timetabled hours, are relatively easily measured, 'organizational status' or 'tutor expertise' is less readily quantified. Curriculum management and development is consequently more piecemeal and incremental and less rational and coherent a process than is generally supposed. This inevitably impacts significantly on our ability to 'manage' teaching and learning effectively, whether as classteacher or headteacher. Even more importantly, personal values and ideological judgements may strongly influence both the curriculum itself and teaching and learning processes.

Davis (1976) identified three perspectives (see Table 10.7) which demonstrate how educational thought influences curriculum management and organization: each perspective reflects different assumptions and value positions.

REFLECTION

Are any (or all) of Davis's perspectives pertinent to your own area/department or across your organization? Where or what are the exceptions and why might this be?

 ## Curriculum policy decision making

Curriculum decisions are based, whether explicitly or not, on underlying assumptions and values. The complexities of decision making and the curriculum's central place in education mean that managers retain multiple perspectives or 'frames' when gathering data, judging ideas and deciding what to do next (Bolman and Deal 1984). Stakeholder involvement (e.g. government, parents, interest groups, industry) adds to the complexity of curriculum deci-

Table 10.7 Curriculum perspectives

	Classical perspective	*Romantic perspective*	*Modern perspective*
Approach	Class teaching	Individualized learning	Flexible grouping
	Teacher-dominated	Child-centred	Inquiry-centred
Philosophy	Autocratic	*Laissez-faire*	Participative
	Certainty	Confusion	Probability
Ideology	Conservative	Abdication	Liberal
	Disciplined	Freedom	Responsibility
Focus	Subjects	Methods	Processes
	Skills	Discovery	Creativity
Relationships	Competitive	Cooperative	Growth
	Other-directed	Inner-directed	Self-fulfilling
	Doing things to	Doing things for	Doing things with

Source: adapted from Davis (1976).

sion making challenging managers; particularly extensive information and knowledge about ideological preoccupations is needed (Duignan and Macpherson 1992). Even though historically the curriculum has been relatively free from centralized control, policy initiatives over the past two decades have, first, exacerbated centralization–autonomy tensions, leaving schools and colleges 'hovering' in the middle, and, second, increased the pace of curriculum change, despite the presence of the National Curriculum (Finegold *et al.* 1993).

Echoing Callaghan's famous 1976 Ruskin Speech, the *Better Schools* (DES 1985) White Paper had emphasized centralist tendencies in terms of: curriculum objectives and content; examinations and recording assessment; management and professional effectiveness of the teaching force; and school governance and parental/community involvement. These tendencies were echoed in initiatives like TVEI (Technical and Vocational Education Initiative), GCSE (General Certificate of Secondary Education) and ROA (Records of Achievement), with the policy drive re-emphasised in 1988 through the introduction of a National Curriculum, national testing at 7, 11, 14 and 16 and the Secretary of State's accumulation of numerous new powers (Leonard 1988). However, despite centralization, considerable levels of decentralization still remained 'in the system', through:

- high levels of teacher and institutional autonomy over pedagogic matters;
- flexibility over specific aspects of curriculum content;
- diffused decision making through the use of governors at all levels of the education system;
- delegated decision making regarding financial resources.

Institutional diversity, classroom autonomy, teacher interpretation of central directives, loose connections between the reality and the rhetoric of policy interpretation and the 'loose coupling' between intent and actual action: all are able to inhibit central control (Weick 1989). There was, nevertheless, an implicit concern that the centralizing and centrally driven initiatives like the 'literacy hour' could endanger the educational mission if it removed scope for professional decision making (Barber 1997).

While policy rhetoric (whether in education or business) may claim to be 'rational' and 'systematic', the reality is often that events on the ground may be driven by the 'disjointedness' of change which is 'beyond certainty' (Handy 1996). This can be seen in the variety of teaching–learning practices, lack of consensus and fudged policy agreements at institutional level and the often limited feedback associated with monitoring developments. Recent initiatives like the primary 'literacy hour' and target-setting within educational development plans may, however, be indicative of a more rampant centralization.

REFLECTION

What evidence is there in your own area of work of simultaneous 'centralization' and 'decentralization' within education? What kinds of management difficulties do these implied tensions seem to create?

These tensions are exemplified by Ferris *et al.*'s (1993) research, which argues that primary school curriculum reform was undertaken far too quickly on too broad a front, bringing 'change without consolidation' – similar to what Fullan (1991) calls 'innovation without change'. Designing and planning a curriculum which meets legal requirements and acknowledges institutional constraints, yet provides more than a minimalist learning experience, is a key management challenge. An essential prerequisite for effective teaching and learning is, consequently, a well planned and managed 'entitlement' curriculum, with publicly agreed characteristics and rooted in equity and access to the curriculum, regardless of race, gender, religion, social background and physical (dis)ability.

In practice, however, an 'entitlement' curriculum is an ideal which few educational institutions are able to 'manage': meeting deceptively easy 'entitlement' aims is more difficult than it might appear. Limitations in practice arise partly from limited resources, but more fundamentally perhaps because institutions are unable (and sometimes unwilling) to shake off traditional curriculum assumptions.

ACTION

Can you identify the major attitudinal, organizational and practical barriers to curriculum entitlement regarding 'equality of access to the curriculum' within your own organization?

Curriculum planning and development

Lawton (1983, 1990) has outlined five levels of curriculum decision making – national, regional, institutional, departmental and individual – and suggests that decisions at each level 'knock on' to other levels. For example, even if curriculum control is top-down, curriculum innovation in institutions may still develop 'bottom-up' and, even if it is slower, curriculum development may also permeate outwards (regionally). Similarly, decision making across curriculum areas is interrelated: for example, introducing Records of Achievement impacts on both aims/content and pedagogy.

ACTION

Analyse an area of your own work where decisions about one aspect of the curriculum have impacted significantly on other areas (and potentially even levels).

Whatever the tensions between centralizing and decentralizing forces, the curriculum still has to be 'managed' in ways that help educational effectiveness. We now consider two approaches to curriculum planning: those related to achieving aims (incorporating rational, behavioural and cultural models) and those related to the learning process. We begin with models related to achieving aims.

Rational model

Tyler (1949) attempted to bring order to what seemed a haphazard approach to curriculum development. His model was essentially linear in approach – moving through four stages of specifying objects, planning content, outlining methods/learning experiences and, finally, measuring and evaluating success. Wheeler (1967) argued that a cyclical model linking evaluation with objectives formulation on a continuous basis was more appropriate to capture the dynamics of school life, while Kelly (1989) considered it far 'too simple a model'. Indeed, Kelly went even further, suggesting:

> we must . . . acknowledge the interrelationship of all four elements, since the practical experience of most teachers suggests that every one of these four elements is constantly being modified by every other and that the business of curriculum planning must be seen as one of constant interaction between the elements.
>
> (Kelly 1989: 16)

Bartlett's (1991) research into the management of major curriculum change in Australia found that linear models predominated where bureaucratic approaches to policy development were adopted, which often meant that bureaucratic institutional responses resulted.

Behavioural model

Bloom (1956) concentrated on behavioural objectives, where learner behaviour is described in measurable terms. The rationality here is based upon achieving the necessary learning skills. Bloom's *taxonomy of educational objectives* details 'hierarchies' of behavioural objectives, suggesting that the curriculum can be defined in terms of pre-specified and measurable changes in learner/student/pupil behaviour. His taxonomy has been criticized for presenting a very narrow view of the teaching and learning process, and while it might be an appropriate model for 'training' in specific skills, e.g. word processing or basic arithmetic, it is not broad enough to encompass the full range of 'education' – like English literature, history or philosophy.

REFLECTION

What are the advantages and disadvantages of an approach which sets out to 'programme' learning in this way? Are we returning to this model?

Objections to the behavioural objectives model usually include the following concerns:

- it takes a narrow and mechanistic view of human nature;
- it fails to allow for individual interests, ambitions and autonomy;
- it regards education as instrumental with extrinsic objectives, rather than appreciating the need for intrinsic rewards;
- in common with other rational models, it doesn't take account of the various value systems within which people operate (Kelly 1989).

Cultural model

The idea of a curriculum based around a common culture has also been advanced (e.g. Broudy *et al.* 1964), with the aim of immersing learners in a 'culture of learning'. Though regarded as American in origin, this view has a long history within England – from Matthew Arnold in the nineteenth century and Raymond Williams in the 1950s and 1960s (with his view of a 'common curriculum' for a democratic society) to Lawton's more recent 'cultural analysis' model.

Skillbeck (1989) maintains that curriculum planning models must be culturally contextualized – through 'situational analysis' – and argues that once educational institutions are reconciled with their social context they can plan (and by implication manage) their curricula accordingly. His suggested sequence of planning stages is:

1 Situational analysis, based on both external influences (e.g. community/parent expectations, subject matter taught, teacher-support systems, resource flows) and internal influences (e.g. pupils, teachers, material resources and perceived issues/problems) on the institution.
2 Goal formulation, for the institution within its community.
3 Programme building.
4 Interpretation and implementation, according to the needs of the students.
5 Monitoring, feedback, assessment and reconstruction.

In effect, Skillbeck's model can be seen as another variety of the 'rational' model, because it focuses on rational analysis and informed choice in deciding and achieving objectives, although it recognizes the importance of flexibility – allowing for continuous feedback within changing situations. Rosenholtz's (1989: 104) comment emphasizes the importance of context: 'It is far easier to learn to teach, and to learn to teach better, in some schools than in others'. Senge (1992: 209) notes how shared conceptions within that context become vital: 'You cannot have a learning organization without shared vision. With a pull towards some goal which people truly want to achieve, the forces in support of the status quo can be overwhelming. Vision establishes the overarching goal.' It is clear that both Rosenholtz's and Senge's comments indicate how teaching and learning processes need to take account of the environment within which they take place. We now turn to models related to the process of learning which attempt to recognize the value of context.

Process models of learning

The emphasis on taking greater note of situational factors and the need to accommodate a variety of learning outcomes has brought increased interest in process models of curriculum development which stress *procedures* and *interactions*: means rather than ends; broad principles rather than 'products' and 'behavioural outcomes'.

While it considers 'learning outcomes' and 'objectives', the process model focuses on intelligent development rather than quantifiable knowledge – thus linking with participative teaching and learning methodologies. Process approaches effectively become guidelines which may prove appropriate for specific contexts and learning needs: in essence, they are concerned with the 'how' rather than the 'what' of people's learning. According to Preedy (1989), process models assert the importance of:

- institutionally-based curriculum planning;
- the teacher/lecturer's role and professional judgement in interpreting the curriculum;
- the need to focus on the whole curriculum rather than simply a fragmented, subject-based approach;
- curriculum negotiation which tries to accommodate different perspectives, e.g. between teaching colleagues, between teacher and student and between students.

This view places students as active partners in the learning process and therefore aligns with more collegial and democratic approaches to curriculum management.

ACTION

Assess the curriculum plan available for your own area of work against the models above and consider how far 'curriculum pragmatism' is being used in their development.

● **Reviewing progress**

Both the 1981 and 1988 Education Acts required education managers to *monitor* (i.e. collect information), *evaluate* (i.e. make judgements about how worthwhile or effective an activity is against values and principles) and *review* (i.e. take decisions about changes in the light of evaluation).

Despite this formality, it is clear that monitoring, evaluation and review processes are still not fully integrated with practical, day-to-day management and implementation: too often they become a 'bolt-on/drop-off' aspect of management. Monitoring is fundamental to effective curriculum management and the provision of learning opportunities. A curriculum audit provides education managers with an effective method of monitoring provision in preparation for action planning and, like the Ofsted framework for inspection, needs to include policies, provision, access, teaching and learning styles, staffing, grouping and so on.

REFLECTION

How is the process of institutional review used to achieve and maintain coherence in your organization?

Following a curriculum audit, the development of a curriculum action plan establishes key curriculum development targets, normally within an overall institutional plan. Curriculum-focused plans:

- establish states and levels of curriculum participation and responsibility;
- identify and assess resource needs;
- outline priorities and timescales for development, implementation and review;
- suggest approaches and methods of monitoring and evaluation;
- assess training needs;
- incorporate curriculum management and development into whole institution/organization development plans.

Ideally, the plan helps to 'complete the cycle' – echoing elements in the audit checklist, with auditing and planning processes mutually supportive and consistent. A development plan is likely to comprise:

- curriculum change priorities;
- long-, medium- and short-term targets;
- the means of achieving the targets;
- mechanisms for monitoring and evaluation.

It is important to remember that, although central, the curriculum audit and action plan is only part of an institutional development plan. While curriculum provision and resource allocation requires annual audits, other aspects of institutional life also affect learning opportunities; these need to be part of a rolling organizational programme of specific audits conducted over successive years. West's (1990) summary of audit practices across schools within one LEA indicates that effective monitoring was achieved through:

- classroom visits by a designated member of staff;
- mutual observation;
- observation of work in action;
- follow-up discussions;
- 'mark-ins' to ensure consistency;
- interviews to ascertain pupil perceptions;
- systematic sampling.

Five years on, these elements form part of Ofsted's inspection processes.

ACTION

Are audits undertaken and utilized in your institution? How might they be established or improved, and what targets would be appropriate?

Evaluating teaching and learning

Evaluation is a complex process, concerned with the values, judgements, fundamental ideological concepts and political concerns framing the curriculum and structures for teaching and learning. Different management models provide alternative frameworks for the concept of curriculum evaluation (Preedy 1989): where rational models are assumed, evaluation is likely to rely on positivistic, quasi-scientific, quantitative methods, e.g. those stressing the accumulation of 'hard' (rather than 'soft') data and 'objective' evidence. Where there is a political focus on 'power relationships' in management, evaluation may be viewed as an issue of 'who is in control', with debates over the nature of 'evidence'. Collegial, democratic or subjective management models tend towards more reflective, qualitative and impressionistic evaluation, where the interaction between curriculum, learner, teacher and context is stressed.

Concern about evaluation processes raises questions about its overall control and whether it is or should adopt a 'grassroots' or 'top-down' focus. Ultimately, however, it becomes a question of who controls the evaluation process. Adelman (1984) considers it so complex and multifaceted a process that it needs to incorporate several interrelated decisions over:

- *Goals*. What is evaluation for? What purpose?
- *Focus*. What aspects of courses, teaching, learning, administration are to be evaluated?
- *Methods*. How is information to be collected? On what basis are future decisions to be made?
- *Criteria*. Where do criteria arise from? What are they?

- *Organization*. Who does the evaluation? What resources are available? How is evaluation to be organized?
- *Dissemination*. How open/confidential will findings be? Who will see findings?

The answers to these questions determine where curriculum control lies. Consequently, the approach adopted indicates not only the degree of control but also the underlying management perspective on the value of evaluation. Despite the emphasis on learning processes, self-evaluation and profiling, the underlying focus in 'output' models of evaluation has remained and, recently, has been strengthened by National Curriculum assessment procedures and examination league tables, and bolstered by the emphasis on parental and political concern, and the competition between education institutions faced with potentially declining rolls.

Increased external demands on educational institutions generally, and schools in particular – from DfEE, Ofsted, TTA and LEAs for example – has also encouraged a climate where producing measurable 'objective' data is the norm, emphasized through the language of 'cost-effectiveness' and 'efficiency'. Alongside the demand for quantitative evaluation rests an increased interest in *process* evaluation – particularly with school-based development – because such approaches endeavour to incorporate staff perspectives and support a growing concern to involve everyone.

Suggestions for further reading

Huddleston, P. and Unwin, L. (1997) *Teaching and Learning in Further Education: Diversity and Change*. London: Routledge.

Markee, N. (1997) *Managing Curricular Innovation*. Cambridge: Cambridge University Press.

Nixon, J., Martin, J., McKeown, P. and Ranson, S. (1996) *Encouraging Learning: towards a Theory of the Learning School*. Buckingham: Open University Press.

Pedler, M., Burgoyne, J. and Boydell, T. (1996) *The Learning Company: a Strategy for Sustainable Development*, 2nd edn. Maidenhead: McGraw-Hill.

Senge, P. M. (1992) *The Fifth Discipline: the Art and Practice of the Learning Organization*. London: Century Business.

Swieringa, J. and Wierdsma, A. (1992) *Becoming a Learning Organization: Beyond the Learning Curve*. Cambridge: Addison-Wesley.

Part III
Tasks and responsibilities

⑪ Managing staff and promoting quality

No organization can rely on genius: the supply is always scarce and unreliable.

(Drucker 1988b: 17)

The institutional context

The nature and funding of educational organizations means that staff are *the* key institutional investment. Moreover, the growing complexity of educational institutions means that even relatively small primary schools may incorporate multilayered, interconnected roles and responsibilities, exemplified by a variety of working cultures and practices. All this means that effective staff planning and development are essential prerequisites for achieving and maximizing organizational goals. This chapter examines specific aspects of 'people management' (or, in 'management-speak', human resource management) and its influence on achieving organizational aims.

Despite the growth of site-based management, some disquiet remains about HRM in education and its links with the personnel practices, costs and ethos commonly associated with commercial organizations, e.g. performance-related pay, performance reviews and head-hunting focused on the organizational good (Seifert 1996a). For example, Bottery (1992) has asserted that the language of 'human resources' should be replaced with a focus on 'resourceful humans'. While some argue that recruitment and selection processes driven by business values are unethical in educational settings, the development of site-based management and educational funding changes has pushed recruitment practices towards maintaining staffing levels at the lowest costs, stressing 'value for money' concerns. Others argue, however, that while newly qualified staff may be inexperienced, they are cheaper and are often seen as having more energy, commitment and up-to-date knowledge than their more experienced (and expensive) colleagues, a point also made by HMI (DfE 1992).

While the staff planning, recruitment and development strategies of many commercial organizations are seen as expediting both short- and long-term aims successfully, market practices in education are also prompting increased interest in HRM, personnel investments and succession planning to facilitate the new 'targets-focused' emphasis articulated through, for example, the school improvement agenda. The fact that 30 per cent of 219 subject leaders in secondary schools surveyed by Glover *et al.* (1998) had gained promotion internally shows that such strategies can combine cost-effective organizational development with individual professional development. Drucker's (1989a, 1990b) comparison of commercial and service organizations details 'common explanations' often used for educational organizations which 'do not perform': for example, 'their managers aren't businesslike', 'people are not as good as they should be' and 'results are intangible and incapable of definition or measurement'. Drucker argues that such excuses are 'invalid and pure alibi', since 'service institutions are paid for promises rather than for performance'.

REFLECTION

Do Drucker's views about the service sector seem accurate to you? Is education now a 'service industry'?

The nature of educational work does, however, mean it is particularly subject to wide-ranging constraints (structured by legal, financial and technical obligations), demands and choices. As Hall (1997) notes, education managers must not only work within legal employment frameworks (e.g. the Employment Acts, Sex Discrimination Acts 1975 and 1986, Employment Protection Act 1978, Health and Safety at Work Act 1974), but also within those relating specifically to education (e.g. Teachers' Pay and Conditions Act 1987, Education Acts 1988, 1992 and 1997, School Teachers' Pay and Conditions Act 1991, not to mention the ever-growing mass of circulars). In addition, they must deal with both explicit and implicit demands arising from, for example, recruitment and selection, induction, appraisal, CPD, staff deployment and grievance and disputes procedures. Beyond this they need to try to realize their management philosophies in terms of active choices about management specifics – perhaps the most difficult element of all – highlighting the difficulty of maintaining a 'professional' focus in the light of an 'executive' workload (Hughes 1988). Taken at their two extremes, we might picture the starker choices as being between 'systems-led' and 'human relations-led' approaches (see Table 11.1).

Table 11.1 Contrasting approaches to people management

	'Systems'-led	'Human relations'-led
Organization	Systems-led and market-driven	People-led and values-driven
In-service development	Training for key staff	Training and development for all staff
Appraisal	'Control' focus: performance review	'Development' focus: professional development
Staff	'Human resources': a means to an end	'Resourceful humans': ends in themselves
Recruitment and selection	To 'fit' the organization	To 'develop' the organization
Organizational focus	Strategically driven with unproblematic goals	Emphasis on excellence with diverse goals
Ethos	Compliance and control focused	Consensus, commitment and collegiality
Driving force	Value-for-money and cost-effectiveness focused	Quality-achievement and effective learning focused

Recruitment and selection

> Good practice, then, is to ensure that the school's equal opportunities policy is
> alive and well and in the selection interview.
>
> (Riches and Morgan 1989: 41)

Changes in the organizational environment of education means that recruitment and selection processes nowadays need to be managed more effectively
(Middlewood 1997a). Changes have occurred in terms of recruitment and
selection over the past decade, largely because of:

- greater institutional autonomy and changes in the organizational
  environment;
- increased local financial control and accountability in a context where
  staffing is the overwhelming cost;
- a growing performance-linked emphasis in organizational management,
  with performance indicators (in terms of institutional, student and staff
  outputs), annual performance reviews/appraisals and performance-related
  pay (PRP).

Although much research into recruitment and selection in education has
been generic in focus (Middlewood 1997a), the future focus on tighter procedures is likely to provoke a much closer research scrutiny, especially regarding the link between selection procedures, training processes (e.g. as the
TTA's programme moves towards possible mandatory status with the NPQH)
and measurable performance outcomes. However, the existence and reinforcement of shared values and an inclusive organizational ethos or mission
which involves reference groups can also help to maximize staff potential,
an important concern for both new and existing employees alike.

However, as McDougle (1982: 4) argues, the effective induction or orientation of new staff can promote both organizational *and* personal well-being:
'a feeling of self-worth, a sense of pride and confidence in both self and the
organization, and a desire to succeed'. The process of recruiting and selecting
new personnel can be a vital contribution and investment in developing
an effective organizational culture and productive workplace. Peters (1987)
recommends, for example, that the new 'chaotic' working environment
demands that managers pay particular attention to recruitment, training and
team building by: involving everyone in everything; spending time on recruitment, training and retraining; and using self-managing teams. In addition,
Drucker (1989b) argues that individuals and organizations succeed best by
instilling a 'habit for achievement' and 'spirit of performance' in relation to
staff appointments.

A tension undoubtedly exists (both in education and industry), however,
between traditional, reactive perspectives where staff are recruited to 'fit'
existing plans (e.g. where recruitment is linked to an audit of forecast needs
for specific skills, numbers and expertise) and a more proactive perspective
where the (existing and potential) skills of current staff are recognized
and developed, thus avoiding 'reactive' and potentially unstable recruitment
strategies.

Hargreaves and Hopkins (1991) argue for the importance of establishing institution-wide educational development strategies, where staff training is facilitated on the basis of an agreed but flexible programme. Scheerens (1992) similarly stresses that policies should focus on staff cohesion and morale, with strengths directed at effective organizational development, while Chadwick (1988) summarizes an approach which identifies needs and uses recruitment policies to ensure effective 'fit' between organization and individual. For Mayo (1991), the recognition of a changing context is essential: a baseline audit of existing staff to identify current strengths, weaknesses and needs is vital. In our experience, too few educational institutions look closely enough at the analysis stage (Glover and Law 1996), perhaps because too many teachers retain taken-for-granted assumptions that skills and competencies are shared potentially by everyone. Increasingly, however, it is acknowledged that this may not necessarily be the case.

ACTION

How are staffing needs identified in your workplace? What might an audit of existing skills and competences show about your area of work?

Whether viewed from Hargreaves's or Chadwick's perspectives, the process of both analysis and audit requires a clear understanding of everyone's potential contribution. In recent years, the focus on HRM techniques in education has emphasized the importance of balancing:

- skills and competences (e.g. budgetary control);
- knowledge (e.g. teaching linguistics, employment law);
- attitudes (e.g. willingness to work collegially).

It remains difficult, however, to educate, train and develop these elements in isolation – clearly, many are developed 'on-the-job'. While employment conditions, and to a lesser extent individual job descriptions, are helpful in defining roles, responsibilities and accountabilities, they are often of only limited help in indicating the knowledge, skills, attitudes and values expected of individuals, although some may be met through the person specification.

Job descriptions and person specifications can represent valuable starting points for both interview panels and individual interviewees, e.g. as initial structures for personal professional profiles (Everard and Morris 1996). As Day *et al.* (1998: 171) comment, 'Prospective candidates are entitled to the clearest, most professional statement about what the school requires. The job description and person specification should supply this.' The danger is, however, that they are interpreted too rigidly. Morgan (1997) suggests that analysing the knowledge, skills and attitudes required for specific tasks provides a set of criteria helpful in selection processes, with job-simulation exercises (like assessing competence through in-tray exercises, role play, written responses and observed discussion) able to demonstrate how individuals match job criteria. Even if two- or three-day interviews feel like overkill they are potentially more equitable: selection panels can establish a more rounded picture of candidates 'off guard' and candidates can elucidate organizational 'rules', cultures and mores over a longer period.

REFLECTION

How does your organization operate selection interviews? How does it ensure the best person gets appointed?

Recruiting staff is, however, far from a foolproof process. In research exploring the haphazard nature of recruitment and selection processes, Morgan *et al.* (1983) analysed criteria used by interview panels: panel members frequently valued and stressed indeterminate 'personality' and 'experience' characteristics over evidence of identified skills for effective job performance. He cites classic 'old stager' governors who argue for decisions based on 'hunches' and complain about longwinded selection procedures, and notes the tendency among some governors to see scientific or rational approaches as no more effective than explorations of 'personal chemistry'.

While not referring to the quality of appointments, Morgan *et al.* suggest that scientific approaches, like competence analyses at assessment centres, can offer advantages. Although this is a view emphasized in the TTA's development of its national training portfolio (for further discussion of competence issues, see Chapter 12), it has also been criticized by the House of Commons' Education and Employment Select Committee scrutiny of the role of the headteacher (House of Commons 1998).

Draper and McMichael (1998) extend the scientific approach in analysing survey responses from 87 deputy headteachers who identified factors deterring them from seeking promotion. Although gender-related issues, stress and home commitments influenced decisions taken by female deputy heads, potential applicants generally pointed to deterrent factors like fear of dealing with others and reduced quality of life. Motivational factors included feeling ready to move on, capacity to do the work and meet new challenges. If selection is for the organization as well as for the post, then the impact of contextual and personal factors also needs full exploration at interview. Where organizations recognize and work to minimize negative factors, succession planning becomes both possible and advantageous because it:

● minimizes the time and money spent on combating unnecessary turnover;
● maintains morale by giving internal opportunities;
● fosters continuity in development and relationships;
● encourages new appointments at a junior level which mean they 'inherit the culture';
● recognizes that shared values are more readily maintained through stability.

Many might consider this approach inappropriate in dynamic educational environments, partly because it ignores the needs of those who are repeatedly overlooked. Where effective appraisal and professional development strategies exist this is less true, since advantages often outweigh disadvantages.

● Redundancy, redeployment and retirement

The rise of an accountability-focused quasi-market in education (Le Grand and Bartlett 1993) and the accentuation on parents as 'active choosers' of educational provision (Echols *et al.* 1990) have made the effective management of staff *performance* even more central to organizational success. As this changed professional landscape encourages closer scrutiny of teacher performance (e.g. via inspection and peer observation), examples of good and less good classroom practice become more overt.

Fullan and Hargeaves (1992: 18) note, for example, the 'problem of untapped competence and neglected incompetence', where the 'unseen pool of existing expertise is one of the great untapped reservoirs of talent – it can fuel our improvement efforts, and it is right under our noses.' They warn, however, that 'if you open up classrooms and find excellence, you also risk exposing bad practice and incompetence . . . Those teachers who are ineffective have either become so through years of unproductive and alienating experiences, or were ill-suited for teaching from the beginning.' They argue that, ideally, 'interactive professionalism' helps to expose problems 'more naturally and gracefully' than more punitive approaches.

The emphasis on teacher competence is, however, increasingly apparent with the inception of the DfEE's 'Advanced Skills Teachers' initiative (rewarding good practice with both praise and remuneration) and the labelling of 'failing teachers' (stigmatizing poor practice). Her Majesty's Chief Inspector (HMCI) Woodhead's annual report (Ofsted 1995c), which argued that 'the performance of a small minority of teachers is consistently weak', led to an immediate exposé of the '15,000 failing teachers' working in schools (some 4 per cent of teachers) and the development of specific teacher gradings rating teaching quality outcomes within Ofsted inspections. This compares with Bridges's (1992: 4) research, which found that although 'incompetence is a concept without precise technical meaning', some 5 per cent of teachers in American elementary and secondary schools are deemed as 'failing'. Such a context makes dealing with underperformance and poor performance a crucial but extremely difficult management responsibility (Foreman 1997).

The need for clear structures and formal procedures for dealing with poor performance and incompetence, whether in industry or education, has grown during the twentieth century and have become particularly important as attempts to end discriminatory practices have been pursued. While Norris (1993) argues that more closely structured processes (whether in recruitment, selection or staff development) may increase both the validity and reliability of staffing selections, the employment climate in education, with its growing emphasis on performance review, performance-related pay and performance indicators, also highlights the potential for a more litigious context. When faced with underperformance or performance discrepancy, Mager and Pipe (1989) suggest that managers first need to ask several key questions (with follow-up evidence gathering). They argue that these questions might comprise:

- What is the nature of the discrepancy? (e.g. evidence of underperformance; poor workload/skills match)
- Is the discrepancy important? (e.g. how far is it damaging the organization; are there time, money, relationship consequences?)

- Is it a skills deficiency issue? (e.g. what are the training needs; costs; availability; underperformer's attitude to training?)
- Is it an attitude problem? (e.g. are there workplace, peer, environmental pressures; a need for non-monetary rewards, status, title etc.; are there job design/conditions of work issues?)

In the post-1988 environment, governing bodies gained much wider responsibilities for both employment and staff performance, but they are also required to adhere to more clearly structured procedures (Hume 1990; Foreman 1997). For example, the dismissal of staff is now an overt aspect of governing body and school management responsibility under the 1988 Education Reform Act: 'The regulation of conduct and discipline in relation to the staff . . . and any procedures for affording to members of the staff opportunities for seeking redress of any grievances relating to their employment, shall be under the control of the governing body' (Schedule 3, para. 6.1).

Staff may leave institutions for a variety of personal and professional reasons, e.g. desire for change, promotion, retirement, personally acknowledged incompetence, overwhelming demands, end of contract, ill health, redundancy. Departure provides an opportunity for review, not simply of curriculum structures and staffing, but also of organizational culture and reflection on the way an institution is perceived by its 'insiders': an 'exit interview' or debriefing session with leavers (whether staff or students) offers a different perspective on the way the organization works. Promotion, (early) retirement and redeployment can all be perceived as difficult transitions by the individuals involved as they make major life adjustments: Mahoney (1991) suggests that even apparently liberating opportunities can represent a major loss of identity. Clearly, each specific situation needs sensitive handling.

It is, however, the question of dismissal on the grounds of redundancy, incompetence or misconduct which both provokes great personal distress and, in the context of devolved governance, creates potentially significant management complexities, especially for those running grant-maintained schools (GMS). While maintained schools may have LEA guidance and policy support for dealing with such matters, this does not obviate the need for governing bodies and education managers to ensure that their own policies, processes and documentation demonstrate good practice. Everard and Morris (1996) point out, employers need to show that an employee has been dismissed for one of the following reasons *and* that they have acted reasonably in all circumstances, following agreed practices and procedures (e.g. ACAS code of practice):

- incapability or lack of qualifications;
- misconduct;
- redundancy;
- continuing to work contravenes a statute (e.g. loss of licence in a job where driving is essential);
- another substantial reason.

Though they are focused on commercial practice, Armstrong's (1993) suggestions for alleviating the difficulties inherent in redundancy processes in humane ways may have increasing currency in education:

- plan ahead to avoid redundancy;
- use other methods to reduce staff numbers/hours of work to avoid or minimize redundancy effects;
- call for voluntary redundancy (not always easy in smaller educational organizations);
- develop and apply an appropriate and legally responsible redundancy plan and policy;
- provide help with finding new opportunities (e.g. the notion of *outplacement*; while common in business and sometimes used by LEAs which, pre-1988, acted as brokers, this is now a difficult option for individual schools or colleges).

The following cameo provides an opportunity to consider how far these suggestions might have made a difference.

Cameo   **Facing dilemmas**

Few 'human relations' or personnel issues are ever simple. One decision may have implications for other parts of the organization, as problems at Evenlode GM School, a seven-form entry comprehensive with a total roll of 920 pupils, including 105 in the sixth form, indicate. After a period when numbers grew, the catchment area had begun to decline and by 1995 the sixth form college in a neighbouring town was becoming more attractive than 'staying at school'. As a result the school was facing a shortfall of £140,000 in 1996. While every effort had been made to pare the budget, the inescapable fact was that four staff had to be shed from the full-time total of 46.

Only a limited redundancy policy was in existence and only one existing member of staff – a mathematician who was very much needed to maintain the curriculum – sought early retirement. The senior management team and the governors then attempted to develop and amend policy as they went along. Whichever criteria were proposed, different but inherent problems arose: 'last in, first out' would be detrimental to science; while curriculum needs indicated overstaffing in the technology area, the possible solution was problematic because two of the three deputies taught in the area, while the highest paid mainscale staff were recognized as highly effective sixth form teachers.

During these uncertainties, 15 high-achieving potential sixth formers moved to the college and problems worsened. In the event, five female members of staff went on to 0.8 timetables, the deputy heads moved from technology to become 'timetable fillers' and the sixth form subject offer was reduced so that the mathematician could be released. What price strategic management?

What could have been done to prevent or better manage this situation?

Your response may highlight the problems arising from both controllable and uncontrollable factors. Strategic plans have to be an organizational driving force and, whatever the implications for individuals, the organization's needs invariably come first: in a brave world, the governors might have questioned their decision in maintaining a sixth form if they were losing so many to the college. The important issue is that human relations approaches emphasize the importance of staff development to enable people to adapt to changing circumstances and, ultimately, to promote a high-quality educational experience for all students. Fundamental to this perspective is appraisal.

● Appraisal

It is generally accepted, whether in education or in commercial organizations, that performance feedback is fundamental for future personal and organizational development (Fidler 1992; Handy 1993). In many cases, the introduction of appraisal to education has brought greater openness and discussion and an improved professional development focus, facilitating mutual support as a foundation for effective personnel management. While the School Teacher Regulations (1991) located the aims for appraisal's introduction firmly around benefits to individuals (e.g. career and professional development, personal achievement and guidance, counselling and training), institutional benefits were summarized in the single aim: 'to improve the management of schools'. This apparently simple difference in emphasis masked, however, underlying tensions between the managerialist and developmental strands of appraisal: as Hall (1997: 152) notes, 'the potential of appraisal systems in education for identifying development needs is muddied by their accountability purposes of performance, potential and reward review.'

In his review of advantages accruing from mutually beneficial appraisal-driven discussion and planned professional development, Fidler (1989) notes teachers' concerns about threats to professionalism, unclear targets, uncertain rewards, evaluation difficulties and lack of time: all issues that can potentially be countered if organizations value developmental aspects of schemes and handle staff sensitively. This remains difficult to achieve, however, without effective long-term *management* support for staff in setting and achieving specific targets (Thompson 1991; Wragg 1996). A sense of 'ownership' by staff is also especially important for success (Smith 1995). While reflecting senior management perspectives, an Ofsted commissioned review of appraisal across seven LEAs and eighteen schools has noted the value attached to appraisal because it had improved:

- overall management and communication skills;
- professional dialogue;
- appraisers' management skills;
- the identification of staff potential;
- needs identification in relation to CPD;
- the targeting of CPD resources (Barber *et al*. 1995).

In assessing appraisal's impact on school policy development, Timperley and Robinson (1997) found that both appraisers and appraisees were keen to improve their interpersonal skills and mutual understanding of the way context, constraints and conflict management influenced appraisal: more evidence of the centrality of good communication in effective management practice. Hutchinson's (1995) review of the impact of appraisal in higher education also has messages for schools and colleges in its articulation of the possible tensions between appraisees' staff development expectations and the managerialist focus on target-setting of appraisers – a tension borne of confused purposes. Nevertheless, collaborative working in support of mutual understanding has been established, albeit patchily across many schools through extended observation, assessed team working and sustained mentoring – although the process of development has become fractured in many schools with the decline in national funding support and the failure of appraisal to become fully integrated with management processses (Thompson 1998).

The rationale for appraisal in education has been that 'cold' performance indicators cannot reveal the nuances of individual work performance, though recent government policy announcements indicate a revised view of the links between appraisal, performance and pay (DfEE 1998c). Despite these uncertainties, professional evaluation can be a valuable learning opportunity for staff if it is based on:

- a thorough preparation;
- observed teaching;
- a calm atmosphere;
- targets related to professional development;
- an understanding of inhibiting factors within the workplace (Poster and Poster 1997).

While national guidelines under the Teachers' Pay and Conditions of Service arrangements recognized these factors, they have contrasted with industrial models because they were not salary-linked. While Handy's (1993) review of an industrial model of appraisal relates techniques to the twin aims of career planning and compensation systems, educational appraisal has focused generally on enhancing professional development opportunities. However, recent national policy pronouncements appear indicative of an ideological shift *vis-à-vis* performance-related pay (DfEE 1998c). Despite its legal status in management, recent Ofsted reports also note the declining use of appraisal in schools and colleges (Ofsted, 1998c), partly as a response to 'overload' concerns (especially heavy during inspection periods) but, more importantly, reflecting teachers' disillusionment with target-setting, which then remains unsupported because of insufficient financial resources.

REFLECTION

What differences do you identify between the aims and practices of 'industrial' and 'professional' appraisal? In your experience, how effective is appraisal in achieving organizational aims?

Unless there is clarity of job or role definition, some elements within appraisal may be interpreted in ways which inhibit discussion and prevent mutual understanding. Although 'vague' job descriptions can provide flexible role frameworks, they may be open to wide interpretation. More detailed and specific formats are especially valuable where watertight role interpretations are needed. Early guidelines regarding teacher appraisal emphasized the need for:

- time to undertake appraisal;
- appraiser and appraisee training;
- adequate and agreed preparation;
- observation within a normal working environment;
- adequate and formative discussion;
- general and specific target setting;
- agreed statements of professional needs (DES 1989).

The fact that these guidelines were developed without emphasizing a uniform appraisal system appears to indicate a government deference to the concept of teacher 'professionalism', which acknowledged teachers' 'commitment, conscientiousness, efficiency, reliability, expertise and so forth' (Hoyle 1989: 62). For example, some schemes allow staff to be appraised by colleagues or line managers of their choice rather than the line manager accountable for the appraisee's work, with mutuality, formative discussion and professional needs emphasized as underlining appraisal purposes. While it has been seen as a force for genuine performance improvement, time and effort costs also need to be recognized.

The tenor of current debates over appraisal's value and future is clear from a recent DfEE discussion paper (DfEE 1998f) arising out the Ofsted/TTA appraisal review (TTA/Ofsted 1996). With a strong emphasis on target-led and performance-linked approaches, it recommends that appraisal:

- should be well integrated into the school's improvement agenda;
- should be complementary to other systems of monitoring and review;
- should take place in a clear and coherent cycle;
- should be supported by clear agreement about what quality looks like;
- should set targets which are prioritized and strategic, measureable, achievable, realistic, time-related (SMART);
- should develop links with pupil performance targets;
- must lead to high-quality staff training and development;
- must contribute to higher standards, not more bureaucratic burden;
- should enable LEAs to consider appraisal's place in their strategies for securing school improvement (DfEE 1998f: 1).

Fullan and Hargreaves (1991) argue that any scheme should be judged against three criteria:

- *Effectiveness*: does it achieve its aims?
- *Efficiency*: is it at minimum cost with maximum benefit to individuals and organization?
- *Economy*: will total benefits outweigh total costs?

They argue that if the answers to the three questions are not all positive, then appraisal's role in organizational improvement is limited.

> **ACTION**
>
> Try to summarize both the personal and the organizational advantages which arise from appraising a colleague who is prepared to reflect on the experience with you.

Williams and Mullen (1990) found that teachers wanted reassurance over several issues:

- the rationale for appraisal;
- the background knowledge of teacher appraisal;
- the practice of teacher appraisal;
- the introduction and development of teacher appraisal.

These concerns hinge on respect, confidentiality and competence: all are central to an effective CPD agenda. Although schools' appraisal schemes were initially introduced with LEA support in order to meet such concerns, it is clear that several fundamental tensions remain between, for example:

- identifying personal targets and the funding/development implications this provokes;
- confidential discussions and the subsequent transmission of targets to senior staff;
- perceived individual CPD needs and the prioritization of whole-school related objectives by middle and senior managers;
- the local demands for development-led appraisal and national demands for accountability-led appraisal.

In order to maximize individual, departmental and whole-school opportunities, increased awareness of value for money issues is fundamental. There is a need for the purchasing rationale and outcomes achieved to be reconciled – often simply by asking how far the activity met its aims.

Mentoring

The growth of initial teacher training (ITT) partnerships in recent years, alongside the resurgence of induction and peer support strategies, has stimulated the growth of mentoring – especially where positive opportunities are provided for review and reflection, enabling both mentee and mentor to feel valued (e.g. Wilkin and Sankey 1994; Cooper and McIntyre 1996; McIntyre and Hagger 1996).

> REFLECTION
>
> Construct a list of the personal pitfalls and benefits of being a mentor.

While mentoring responsibilities may fall to 'critical friends' in non-threatening and supportive situations, mentoring relationships are more precarious when competence is being judged in teacher training situations: mentees who see mentors as exercising long-term power may be tempted to become compliant rather than explore alternative perceptions.

Dart and Drake (1994) summarize the classic mentor's dilemma when they comment: 'The concept of the mentor includes both supportive and assessment roles.' However, others note difficulties stemming from handling criticism and maintaining mentoring relationships which are neither overly ambitious in terms of mentee expectations nor overly protective and undemanding (Glover and Mardle 1995). However, mentors also identified personal benefits, because they were required to make more explicit the usually implicit features of teaching (Hamlyn Report 1994: 24).

The quality of the mentor–mentee relationship is fundamental: only limited success is possible without a supportive framework. Leithwood (1992b) suggests a pedagogic framework where mentees move from acquiring survival skills towards achieving instructional expertise and then to participating in a broad array of decision making, while Heron (1986) identifies prescriptive, informative, cathartic, confronting and catalytic modes as a supportive framework. Glichman (1991), however, suggests three behaviours:

- *Directive*: mentor controls.
- *Collaborative*: mentor and novice develop strategies.
- *Non-directive*: novice 'knows best' in a given situation.

Devlin's (1995) research with long-serving mentors also identifies several key characteristics:

- 'a suitable, adaptable, sympathetic, understanding personality';
- 'an interest in their own evolution';
- 'good interpersonal skills';
- 'philosophical grasp of mentoring';
- 'experience of teaching'.

Some schools have recognized that mentoring responsibilities enhance careers, enabling staff to demonstrate both pedagogic and administrative skills, an emphasis taken up in terms of both status and salary through New Labour's introduction of the 'advanced skills teacher' (AST) (echoed in the TTA's concept of the 'expert teacher'), which enables those chosen to gain temporary promotion and higher salaries while remaining in the classroom.

● Quality assurance

> Quality cannot be imposed from outside – from outside the institution, outside
> the team, outside the individual. You cannot inspect in quality.
>
> (Bowring-Carr and West-Burnham 1994: 75)

To be fully effective, educational organizations nowadays need to demonstrate that they deliver 'quality' and 'high standards' (DfEE 1997a), particularly
in a quasi-competitive educational environment which demands collective
'responsiveness' and professional commitment to local learning communities. As Darling-Hammond (1989: 152) points out, 'It is the degree to which
teachers assume collective responsibility for instructional *quality* that determines professionalism.' For Tofte (1995: 470), quality in education is defined
by its ability to:

- provide teaching and challenging educational situations which are fit for
  students' needs, interests and expectations;
- work for continuous improvement in all processes to make students satisfied;
- work to maintain and/or add value to life.

Commercial organizations traditionally differentiate themselves through their
ability to deliver at a consistently higher quality than their competitors, with
both word of mouth recommendations and previous performance contributing
to expectations. Kotler and Armstrong (1991) identify several 'common virtues'
in relation to service quality which may also resonate with educationists:

- senior management commitment to quality;
- high service standards throughout the organization;
- careful monitoring of both in-house and competitors' service performance;
- commitment to satisfying both employees and customers.

ACTION

List the ways in which your school or college has formal, and informal,
policies which meet these objectives. Would external evaluation generate
any change?

In general, three major approaches to quality validation are utilized within
a British educational context, with each involving a review of existing practice
and the articulation of policies and procedures as a framework for organizational practice. At a basic level, this involves a commitment to meeting
simple targets, e.g. 'replying to every letter we receive within 48 hours'. More
comprehensively, there is a commitment to more extensive target-setting as
a form of organizational motivation. Although each approach stresses different elements, three main quality assurance approaches are used in schools
and colleges: total quality management, kitemarking (e.g. ISO 9000 series)
and Investors in People.

Table 11.2 The generic strategy model

Nature of access	Strategy	Curriculum offer	Comment
Open to anyone	Broad, open	Broad, non-specialist	Seek standards across the board
Selective, e.g. by gender/denomination	Basic, niche	Broad, but with particular ethos	Seeks standards on broad basis plus particular ethos
Open to anyone	Enhanced, open	Emphasis on specialism, e.g. agriculture	Develops standards in specialisms to add value to basics
Selective in some form	Enhanced, niche	Emphasis on specialisms	Develops quality in specialism

Source: after Murgatroyd and Morgan (1992).

Total quality management (TQM)

Building upon American and Japanese practices, and adapted to the British context by Oakland (1989), TQM integrates principles applicable to many organizations. Among the 'quality gurus' contributing to TQM's development are:

- Juran (1980), who believed that although companies might understand how to measure the quality of their products, they were unable to achieve quality because of a lack of understanding of the human situations. His solutions were based on targets, training and leadership.
- Deming (1982), who stressed that quality measurement was a necessary baseline for future improvement, and argued that this should be sustained by random checks used as the basis for a whole-organization commitment to improvement. Deming's principles focus on corporate openness and team development to secure improvement.
- Crosby (1986), who defined quality as 'conformance to requirements' (Crosby 1979: 15) and outlined the concept of 'zero defects', suggesting that the four 'quality absolutes' are definition, systems, standards and measurement, thus emphasizing a more mechanistic approach.

Murgatroyd and Morgan (1992), who have applied these principles in educational contexts with considerable success, begin with a 'generic strategy model' which recognizes that schools and colleges are affected by access policies as well as the curriculum services they provide. This then results in four situations (see Table 11.2).

Ideally, quality processes should flow out of each organizational strategic plan, incorporating concerns with culture, commitment and communications. The TQM approach is based around team development and achieving broader vision by all participants, but backed by sound measurement. While it does not directly provide accreditation and has a stronger HRM focus than its industrial counterpart, it has an underlying philosophy capable of being accredited through other approaches. TQM literature and training focuses on various principles:

- continuous improvement;
- leadership;

- teamwork;
- driving out fear;
- measuring variation as a key to achievement;
- breaking down barriers;
- constancy of purpose;
- a driving vision.

West-Burnham (1992), who has further developed TQM as a framework for quality improvement, stresses its link with moral, environmental, survival and accountability imperatives for developing organizational cultures. TQM emphasizes the development and maintenance of effective systems, while stressing that whole-organization commitment to improvement on a continuous basis must be accompanied by development opportunities. For example, 'systems' are stressed only insofar as they achieve 'right first time', and 'methods' insofar as they ensure 'prevention not detection'. It is only by being clear about strategy and valuing effective feedback systems that quality can come fully into play: Murgatroyd and Morgan (1992: 23) note that 'quality is a function of strategy . . . until you have defined the strategy your school is pursuing, quality is secondary.'

Kitemarking (e.g. BS 5750/ISO 9200)

This approach provides a 'kitemark of quality' based on an assessment of how organizational systems are developed to support consistency and quality in 'product delivery'. The thinking process behind accreditation is that staff should:

- explain what they are doing;
- say why they are doing it;
- do what they say they are doing;
- change those features which are not working properly, recording what has been done.

Assessment is undertaken by qualified independent registrars or counsellors and is based upon:

- a defined organizational structure (e.g. identified line management responsibilities);
- internal quality audits (e.g. mapping of strengths, weaknesses and development areas);
- management review (e.g. reviewing outcomes and key management issues);
- formal training (e.g. updating for all staff).

Critics of this kind of systems-based approach argue that it lacks flexibility and becomes too rigid in 'people product' situations.

Investors in People (IIP)

Although it is a more recent development, this approach is based on the application of TQM principles, focused on staff development philosophies. Providing organizational accreditation and supported and assessed by external mentors and assessors, it is systems-based insofar as appropriate staff development structures are required. However, it places greater emphasis on developing and achieving self-set targets within the framework of organizational improvement. This leads to a training and development focus for people management and a concentration on improvement through collaborative action. Brown and Taylor (1996) argue that this has a positive impact on school improvement where it underpins the organizational culture: it cannot be successful if bolted on.

REFLECTION

If your organization already has a quality assurance framework in operation, assess its success. If not, consider why no quality framework exists and what might be the most appropriate strategy given your organizational culture.

Some educationists remain sceptical about the potential for systems to ensure quality and there is some recognition that several key factors may be implicated in failure, e.g.

- lack of leadership commitment;
- incoherence in implementation planning;
- lack of clear data on which to build;
- lack of appropriate skills to sustain development (Murgatroyd and Morgan 1992).

In a review of the impact of quality management on organizational culture, Hall (1997) notes that TQM and IIP are predicated on the belief that the culture of educational institutions and the behaviour of individuals within them can be changed, and acknowledges that 'They claim to gain employee commitment through involvement and empowerment, but is this just rhetoric to obscure control? . . . the question remains whether they succeed in changing culture only at the level of visible behaviour while values and assumptions remain intact' (Hall 1997: 155).

Even when quality systems have been established, changes in personnel or failure to review and refocus commitment frequently enough may result in poor continuity and 'slippage'. The wider adaptation of people-focused approaches indicates, however, that effective quality assurance approaches are capable of motivating staff, especially when corporate activity produces tangible successes. For example, the DfEE's guidance on target-setting (DfEE 1997b) reflects the extent to which TQM techniques are becoming embedded, by arguing that 'successful schools set targets which are SMART':

- Smart (focused on the clear goal of learner achievement).
- Measurable (focused on learning progress and achievement).
- Achievable (i.e. within the institution's (time and money) resources).
- Realistic (i.e. for learners and in terms of the institution's overall aims).
- Time-related (i.e. in a realistic time-span and with a specifc end point/ date).

Problems arise, however, when staff feel insufficiently motivated to act: an issue which returns us to the need for appropriate leadership within a supportive and developmental culture that values staff contributions. The next chapter explores this aspect more fully.

Suggestions for further reading

Audit Commission (1989) *Assessing Quality in Education*. London: Audit Commission.

Bush, T. and Middlewood, D. (eds) (1997) *Managing People in Education*. London: Paul Chapman Publishing.

Preedy, M., Glatter, R. and Levačić, R. (eds) (1997) *Educational Management: Strategy, Quality and Resources*. Buckingham: Open University Press.

Rosenholtz, S. (1989) *Teachers' Workplace: the Social Organization of Schools*. New York: Longman.

Seifert, R. (1996b) *Industrial Relations in Education*. London: Pitman.

Sisson, K. (ed.) (1994) *Personnel Management: a Comprehensive Guide to Theory and Practice in Britain*. Oxford: Blackwell.

12 Managing resources and finance

Change, by definition, cannot be managed through a status quo level of
resources. It makes new demands, creates unsolved problems, and is resource-
hungry . . . above a certain floor, the level of resources is less important than *how*
resources are acquired and *where* they are applied.

(Louis and Miles 1992: 230–1)

The context for resource management

Resource and financial management are means to an end. Each aspect of provision in effective educational organizations, whether core staffing, equipment,
materials or specialist expertise, is deployed in order to facilitate learning
and educational achievement. As Irvine (1975) has noted, a budget system
should be an enabling mechanism rather than just a mechanical or technical
exercise: it should help managers to plan, coordinate, control and then evaluate their organizational actions more effectively.

Research into the impact of local financial management (LFM) suggests
that because senior staff are increasingly concerned with whole-school and
'corporatist' concerns, they have become increasingly separated from their
staff, who tend to take a more 'individualist' stance, focused on classroom
concerns (Bowe *et al*. 1992; Simkins 1994). Levačić (1995: 189) points out,
however, that staff often expect their senior colleagues to be 'corporate' on
their behalf:

> Financial management . . . is largely regarded by classroom teachers as
> one where they have limited interest and expertise. In their view, it is
> the principal's proper function to resource the learning core of the school
> and protect it from undue disturbance . . . Most principals concur with
> this and do not seek teacher involvement in budgeting except in resourc-
> ing the curriculum and in keeping them informed about the general
> financial situation of the school.

Although it is now more overt, schools have always provided a forum for a
'dialogue of accountability' (Thomas and Martin 1996): even though LFM
formally emphasizes key accountabilities and concerns, the tensions between
professionalism and managerialism, individualism and corporatism are not
entirely new, as Hughes (1972) has indicated. What have changed, however,
are the complexities which arise out of the overt linkage of financial investments

in education with learning outcomes, an issue which makes educational philosophy even more crucial.

At a time when education funding has diminished in real terms and some desirable (or even essential) goals cannot be pursued, financial decisions are being made by those 'closer to the clients' (Peters and Waterman 1982). The post-1988 and subsequent financial settlements effectively depowered LEAs as 'command and control' bureaucracies, emphasizing 'management by contract' over 'management by control' (Harland *et al.* 1993). This made schools self-managing educational institutions responsible for planning, commissioning and evaluating their own income and expenditure, supported by LEAs as 'enabling' authorities (Audit Commission 1989b). Some argue, however, that those at the 'chalkface' nowadays have much financial responsibility but little power. Compared with commercial organizations, education managers appear to 'have limited power to influence the total quantum of financial resources available to them', and face 'a much wider range of regulations, advice and incentives designed to constrain schools in the choices they actually make' (Simkins 1997: 163–4).

Although it is only one aspect of the 1988 Education Reform Act, LFM became a fundamental catalyst for the 'new education management'. Over the past decade, delegated responsibilities and devolved budgets have had a major impact on the *perceptions* of many 'at the sharp end' of education (Thomas and Martin 1996), thus facilitating change on the basis of innovative and locally based financial thinking (Levačić 1993, 1995; Simkins 1994). Consecutive Conservative governments argued that if schools and colleges became 'self-managing' (Caldwell and Spinks 1988, 1992), able to pursue open recruitment policies, then an 'education market' would operate, with stakeholder and 'client power' determining the fate of schools. This assumption has not, however, been entirely borne out by research: Halpin *et al.* (1997) indicate that devolved funding may actually encourage schools to adopt conservative strategies both developmentally and financially, and, in the case of former GM schools, actively 'opt into the past'. Knight (1993: 136) also argues that 'although financial delegation appears to give schools greater freedom for major innovation, there is little evidence yet that it is occurring'. Within this context, this chapter examines the impact of LFM and reflects on its influence in terms of educational philosophy and strategic management.

Education managers have utilized their resource and financial management responsibilities in a variety of ways (Simkins 1994), with many schools: taking on 'peripheral' (part-time, temporary) staff rather than 'core' (full-time permanent) staff in order to overcome fluctuating need and to support pressurized areas; identifying cost-saving strategies for recurrent expenditures like energy, site and grounds maintenance; and employing more administrative staff (e.g. bursars, receptionists) to release teaching staff (Mortimore *et al.* 1994). Even though these developments are often driven by cost-effectiveness and value-for-money concerns, this aspect of headteachers' and governors' financial management is seen as weak (Thomas and Martin 1996), with almost two-thirds of primary schools and half of secondary schools being criticized in the Chief Inspector's Annual Report (Ofsted 1995c: 24).

While financial stringencies may be alleviated by enhanced education spending into the new millennium, the New Labour government's emphasis on a 'bidding culture' which links funds to government-specified objectives and targets has, according to Dean and Rafferty (1998), created a 'lottery' where 'The winners are the councils which have learnt how to bid successfully. The losers are the children whose authorities don't know how to play the game.' This is a picture also evident in school-led bidding. This raises questions over how far such approaches deliver genuine outcomes or are simply 'bolted on' for a limited period. Within schools, 'bidding' may be a particular concern in secondary schools, where heads of department are expected to be more accountable for resources through their departmental development plans (Levačić 1995). In addition, Bradley's (1996) assessment of intended and unintended consequences in FE funding allocation systems found that policies based on targets, completion rates/results, course costs and core funding frequently focused on maximizing 'earning potential' rather than equity and course development concerns.

ACTION

How far does your organization's development plan: (a) set out its priorities clearly for all staff; (b) accurately cost priorities; (c) indicate who makes these decisions and with what criteria; and (d) indicate how (or if) consultation takes place over both priorities and decisions?

Prioritization and decision-making processes are often indicative of an organization's prevailing management culture and the constraints it faces. In the immediate post-LFM environment, educational organizations faced stark realities associated with prioritization in a resource-starved climate. Although the ERA framework required LEAs to devolve aggregate running costs (e.g. 90 per cent or more) to schools and colleges, with at least 75 per cent of funds related to age-weighted pupil numbers, a decade after its introduction some LEAs have still to comply fully (Dean 1998).

Whatever the allocation method, the dramatic reality facing most schools is that between 78 and 85 per cent of their budget covers staffing. Once on-going building and maintenance costs are included, funding to support the educational process *per se* (books, equipment and development activities) amounts to a tiny proportion of total funds: as little as £80,000 in a £1.8 million budget for a school of, say, 950 pupils. While these concerns may have changed resource management processes, we need to note that even before 1988, both curriculum and staff deployment decision making was located within the schools themselves (Simkins 1997). Moreover, nowadays, even with substantial devolution, these two areas remain the key influential elements in day-to-day resource management and are central pivots around which the impact of change and the quality of educational outcomes are evaluated (Knight 1989, 1993).

Financial decision making

Although decision-making processes vary from the highly formalized and autocratic to the more loosely defined and collegial, their essential purpose is to achieve clearly specified goals. Levačić (1995) has outlined a three-stage rational planning approach focused on meeting organizational aims in cost-effective ways:

- agree and articulate aims and priorities focused on organizational goals;
- collect and analyse data to inform choices which are based on monitoring and evaluating prior experience;
- select the best set of actions to achieve specified aims and objectives.

This contrasts with the political approach (Simkins 1989), where decisions stem from micropolitical tensions arising between power groups (Hoyle 1986; Ball 1987). As Wright (1980: 17) notes, resource allocation is about more than logic. Often, 'a department's share of scarce resources depends on the skill of its advocates in the use of essentially political tactics such as knowing how much to bid for, how far to pad estimates, how far to over/underspend, how to "read" the political climate, how to generate and utilise public support.' When political power is a significant force in resource allocation, decisions are usually based on existing power group relationships or minimal acceptable adjustments to previous budget in order to avoid confrontation. Political tensions often mean that funds may be allocated through weighted formulae based on relative micropolitical power rather than need. The infants department in a large primary school, for example, may be allocated a specific funding level because 'Miss X is a law unto herself: we need to keep her sweet', rather than because of relative pupil need.

REFLECTION

How far do resource allocation patterns within your organization, or one you know well, seem to be based on rational or on political approaches? How is the organizational culture affected?

Ofsted has defined an 'efficient school' as one which provides 'excellent value for money' because it 'makes good use of all its available resources to achieve the best possible education outcomes for all its pupils' (Ofsted 1995a: 121), a point echoed in recent writing on school development planning, school improvement and resource management (Thomas and Martin 1996). The cameo opposite, which details extracts from two school inspection reports, articulates Ofsted's concern with rational planning as a basis for quality practices.

As Simkins (1994, 1995) has noted, Ofsted's overarching focus is often 'disaggregated' in schools by their concern with some of the more specific aspects of resource allocation, the first four of which have been stressed by the Audit Commission (1985):

- *Economy*: obtaining a given standard of 'goods' at the lowest cost.
- *Effectiveness*: matching outcomes/results against the objectives/resources used.

Cameo   **Rational responses?**

School A

'To date, links between curriculum planning and financial planning have not always been precise or explicit. This is the consequence partly of the difficulty of financial prediction, and partly of a wish not to constrain the development of educational vision by subjecting it too early to financial considerations. However, separation of the two elements can lead to losses of efficiency, whether this is embarking on developments which cannot be sustained in the long run, or moving ahead with new developments at the cost of existing provision. In addition, time can be wasted on the development of plans which ultimately have to be postponed or abandoned because the resources are not available.'

School B

'The school development plan is very comprehensive and gives a very detailed picture of the school's priorities for development. Financial planning is becoming closely linked to the school's aims and priorities, with funding appropriately targeted. Governors are closely involved with the strategic management of resources and there are detailed policies for charging and pay. The school recognizes the importance of value for money and carefully assesses the benefits of expenditure on staffing, premises and learning resources.'

- *Efficiency*: securing outcomes at the minimum cost.
- *Equity*: ensuring a fair distribution of resources to support the learning process.

ACTION

How far are these four concepts used in financial decision making in your own institution? How are specific policies (e.g. special needs) affected and how far is funding use monitored?

Resource allocation: issues and judgements

Everard and Morris (1996), who distinguish between *resource-driven* and *needs-driven* approaches to resource management, suggest that we should plan with existing resources in mind and consider demands for greater funding effectiveness. This perspective echoes comments made by a 1970s grammar school headteacher whose school had recently been 'comprehensivized': 'It isn't easy to use seven classicists. What we want is one classicist, three scientists and three technologists!'

During the early 1990s and framed by New Right concerns that education was 'overadministered', successive Conservative governments endeavoured to modify LMS and LFM arrangements to reduce LEAs' central service budgets (advisory and inspection services, psychological services, special needs support and the cost of administration), so as to allocate funding directly to schools or colleges. While the Conservatives saw financially based pressures as an effective means of controlling LEAs, New Labour's rhetoric has been to combine both 'pressure and support' (Fullan 1991; DfEE 1997a), whereby LEAs have limited financial control but are used to facilitate and monitor allocated funds as a means of improving standards.

This remaking of education as 'new public management' (Dunleavy and Hood 1994), with its focus on 'stakeholder' and 'client' demand within a 'market place', brings several issues to the surface:

- If income is linked to student numbers, how do schools/colleges provide for special needs students who require a much higher staff : student ratio?
- How will 'minority' subjects be treated if institutions fail to recruit sufficient student numbers?
- Where does the issue of 'equity' fit in self-governing schools/colleges – *across* education generally and *within* institutions? For example, how do the needs of a primary pupil from a deprived inner-city area match with those of a primary pupil from the leafy suburbs?
- How are assumptions that 'educational need' is more expensive for 13–14-year-olds reconciled with needs for 7–8-year-olds, and so on?

REFLECTION

How far and in what ways are the advantages and disadvantages of LFM apparent within your own organization?

Focusing on equity issues, Simkins (1995) suggests schools need to consider:

- the relationship between resource deployment and pupil outcomes;
- the need for a 'foundation' entitlement for all pupils;
- the need for criteria for differential resourcing above the foundation level;
- the concept of minimum attainment linked to entitlement;
- the balance between efficiency and equity.

The key issue here may be how criteria against which expenditure plans are then judged are determined, an issue which the National Curriculum appeared to clarify, since schools would need to deliver a basic programme – or so it seemed. Primary schools, for example, in 'delivering', say, science attainment targets, in choosing between topic-based methods, subject teaching or a combination of both, needed strategically to assess the balance between teaching resources, staff skills, teamwork and the teaching environment.

While acknowledging that no single system is perfect, Levačić (1995) has outlined four funding allocation approaches, the last of which can undermine all the others (see Table 12.1).

Table 12.1 Strategies for resource allocation

Bidding allocation	Distributed according to competitive bids or an annual plan as part of a prioritized school development plan
Formula allocation	Distributed according to pupil numbers, staff and lessons taught, although rarely linked to subject development needs
Historic allocation	Distributed according to previous spending, even if this ignores current needs
Political allocation	Distributed according to personal and political bias: those with influence gain most, especially where finance is centralized. This approach may undermine all others

Source: after Levačić (1995).

Knight (1993) has also identified four allocation strategies (see Table 12.2), although these more specifically focused on issues surrounding departmental resource allocation. However, as Simkins (1997) notes, Knight's perspective tends to ignore a number of underlying questions about the nature and quality of available information available, the nature of the criteria used in decision making, the openness of the allocations process and where the responsibility for decision making ultimately rests.

Table 12.2 Strategies for resource allocation

Incrementalism	Based on historical allocation and the global sum available
Benevolent despotism	Based on senior management judgement of need and demand
Open market	Based on bids from potential recipients
Formula-driven	Based on a (often weighted) quantified measure of need, e.g. pupil numbers

Source: after Knight (1993).

REFLECTION

Which of these approaches (or a combination of them) appears to offer the best strategy for your area/organization – and why?

 Costs, benefits and value for money

If financial decision making is to be fully effective in measuring outcomes, the value of expenditure needs to be explicit and evaluated rather than simply implicit. Cost–benefit analyses, originating within business and social economics contexts, offer ways of assessing the impact of expenditure by ensuring that all elements of a proposed investment are costed, e.g. direct (teaching) and indirect (administration) staffing costs, rooms, materials, training. Although direct benefits are set against projected costs, it is also important to consider the indirect benefits of proposals (e.g. increased staff expertise, increased publicity, additional employer support). Where benefits equal or outweigh costs, decision making becomes easy; but even when immediate costs outweigh benefits, a project could still be seen as a 'pump-priming' investment for longer-term developments.

ACTION

Try a cost–benefit analysis for your own team, area of work or institution by quantifying the costs/debits of employing additional personnel for your team or organization and then listing the benefits/credits. What practical difficulties does this create?

At one level, cost–benefit decisions might appear to be dependent on individual perceptions. There is, however, a growing demand for good quality management information systems (MIS) to support decision-making processes: management information is a prerequisite for effectiveness and can counter personal prejudice. Establishing an appropriate system is crucial: MIS purchased by many LEAs at the inception of LFM neither matched school needs nor took account of organizational procedures, leaving 'no-win' situations for both LEAs and schools. Wild *et al.* (1992) found that only 20 per cent of IT applications supporting LMS brought the gains envisaged: more recent work indicates, however, that success rates are improving.

While financial decision-making processes may vary, priority ranking and alternative costings of proposals are also crucial, since each decision has opportunity costs, and allocating resources in one way 'costs' the alternative opportunity not taken up. Linking a cost–benefit analysis with the opportunity cost concept can facilitate comparative costings, e.g. between plans A and B. Ultimately, however, it is not simply a matter of determining value in a cost–benefit equation, since a variety of less readily quantified person-related factors are also implicated in decisions. In all of this, however, the process of evaluation remains fundamental.

Schools have not traditionally analysed how they have 'delivered the service' of education in terms of unit costs, such as 'passes per teacher hour', or value-added to pupils' achievements as a result of a year in primary education. However, growing government emphasis on quantifiable educational outcomes linked to financial inputs means that financially focused planning procedures are becoming increasingly used to forecast and measure costs against (likely) performance. D. Hargreaves (1994: 19), for example, has called for a national funding formula for schools to 'replace the present highly diverse and inequitable patterns of per capita spending according to local whim', and thus to enable better comparative data to be generated.

Jones (1986) has assessed 'value for money' in relation to the costs and benefits of course provision targeted at higher pass rates. While many consider such approaches are anathema in education, the development of Standard Assessment Tasks (SATs) has created at flawed benchmarking database which facilitates the evaluation of the more quantifiable aspects of teachers' work, even in primary schools, as well as the development of 'progress indicators' in school league table publications (DfEE 1997a). Such procedures will remain problematic and potentially discredited until they can overcome accusations that they present crude and contradictory statistics, resulting in distorted pictures which are baffling for both parents and teachers alike.

Applying value-for-money approaches requires a broader consideration of cost–benefit and opportunity cost issues, because both financial and educational factors are quantified. For example, analysing teaching group size indicates several value for money questions:

- the link between optimum group size and high(est) examination results/ outcomes;
- the link between additional spend and improved results;
- the link between 'peripheral' costs (e.g. additional accommodation, equipment and support staff) and outcomes;
- the links between the students' ability profile, the constraints influencing course delivery and the targeted pass rates;
- what counts as a fair or reasonable expectation.

Such issues are now examined as part of a growing statistical evaluation of educational expenditure, with attempts to use 'objective' criteria to assess how effective and efficient expenditure affects outcomes. Such information is basic to rational budgetary planning.

REFLECTION

How does your department, section or organization monitor its courses and/ or subjects? How are 'subjective' criteria for measuring performance assessed and are financial implications considered?

The budgetary process

As Handy (1993) has asserted, budgets are not simply financial statements: they facilitate the development and control of the budgetary process and are essential elements in organizational productivity and change. In this context, Handy emphasizes the value of participative budgeting and management, where decisions are 'owned' by participants, morale is maintained and organizational effectiveness is retained. While this implies that decision making is open, this situation remains an exception in many schools (Glover et al. 1996). Indeed, our earlier cost–benefit discussion suggests that no straightforward approach to the budgetary process exists. Questions that need to be considered include:

- Should the *average* or *actual* costs of additional staff be considered in assessing teaching arrangements?
- How are the *indirect* costs of the establishment to be absorbed? What is the value of a cost per pupil per hour?

- How are the *outcomes* estimated? Is the successful completion of, for example, an Outward Bound type course ever measurable?

If we accept it as a 'given' that collaborative planning is advantageous in institutional development, it is important that the issue is considered as part of an evolving system capable of being understood by all. Participative budgeting is complex, nevertheless, because we need simultaneously to *evaluate* the previous budget while we *implement* the current one and *plan* the next: the ongoing continuity of finance committee work in many institutions reflects this complexity. Further complications arise because some objectives are not readily quantifiable. For example, how can we develop performance indicators that enable us to 'measure' adequately young people's increased awareness of society's needs?

The budgetary cycle

To enable education-focused organizations to function efficiently, budget planning needs to operate according to a formal timetable. The days have effectively gone when finance was seen as a 'back of an envelope' issue in schools and an LEA prerogative: the formalization of responsibility at institutional level derives largely from the fact that, overall, the financing of education is now closely scrutinized and controlled by central government and its agencies. Accountability for the use of public funds now stems from the point of delivery and, in addition:

- the amount of money involved is now much greater than previously;
- the necessity for consultation is often more frequently recognized;
- the systems and mechanisms for the release and control of money are increasingly sophisticated.

Arnold and Hope (1983) have developed these ideas in their 'stepped' process, which indicates opportunities for collective management in identifying goals, choosing the basis of decision making, ranking alternatives and monitoring progress. They also identify the need for full information as a prerequisite for decision making, but suggest, nevertheless, that budgets are more than statements of intent. Initial school experience of budgeting, as reported by Levačić (1995), suggests that the management of decision making is now more regulated than previously. Table 12.3 indicates the complexity and continuity of the budgetary process.

ACTION

Using the four budgetary stages of goals, decisions, implementation and evaluation, try to construct a budget calendar for your institution. What is the link between the annual calendar of institutional meetings and the need for resource and budget decisions?

Table 12.3 The budgetary cycle in operation

Goals	Decisions	Implementation	Evaluation
Set in the year before the budget	Made before the budget is finalized	Notification and authorization of budget allocations	Undertaken in the year after the budget
Whole-school or whole-college, often with departmental interpretation required	Rational or political; cost–benefit calculation; allocation processes	Employing/ordering; receiving and checking; entering to stock; monitoring use	Budgetary control; assessment of use; assessment of effect; future strategies
Strategic framework	Interpretation of need related to framework	Use according to objectives of framework	Outcomes related to existing framework

 Budget functions

Handy (1993) stresses that a budget needs to fulfil several functions:

- planning;
- providing operational data;
- controlling;
- acting as a stimulant for change.

If the budget is viewed as a resource management tool, then its role is clearly wider than providing a simple income/expenditure statement: it is also concerned with allocations according to custom or priorities. Broadly, four basic budgeting approaches are delineated here:

- historic budgeting;
- zero-based budgeting;
- programme-planning budgeting;
- limited plan budgeting.

These approaches are not the same as the allocation strategies detailed earlier in this chapter: their concern is with charting the intended use of funds once allocated to a cost centre.

Historic budgeting

Under historic budgeting, each 'cost centre' or budget holder receives a share of funds according to *previous* expenditure. While allocations may be 'tinkered with', they remain substantially the same year-on-year, with the budget being related neither to *actual* expenditure needs nor to possible changes in organizational priority. System modifications can overcome some criticisms of this approach: for example, a central pool could retain about 20 per cent of the total funding, which is then open to needs-led bidding. For example, if English is subject-weighted at 1.5 within a given school (on the basis that it is a two-subject GCSE examination), and it is allocated 20 per cent of available teaching periods, it has an inflated budget share. We must remember, however, that when weighting increases for some subjects, available resources reduce elsewhere. Consequently, 'baronial' politics can become perpetuated within this organizational power structure and, however refined the formula, it cannot fully recognize institution-wide (i.e. 'whole-school') planning policies. As Wildavsky (1994: 508–9) has argued, historic budgeting 'has the defects of its virtues . . . comparing this year with last year may not mean much if the past was a mistake and the future is likely to be a bigger one . . . There is an incremental road to disaster as well as faster roads to perdition; simplicity may become simple mindedness.'

Zero-based budgeting

As one response to the difficulties inherent in historic budgeting, zero-based budgeting ensures that cost centres are required to calculate their financial needs afresh each year, knowing what their commitments will be. Arguably, 'the past, as reflected in the budgetary base . . . is explicitly rejected. There is no yesterday. Nothing is taken for granted, everything at every period is subjected to searching scrutiny' (Wildavsky 1994: 509). Meeting demands according to need should, then, become possible.

However, there may be problems with this approach: people may overestimate to ensure sufficient funds are allocated to a given area, while continuous negotiations can also develop, reflecting organizational power-group relationships. Hartley (1979), whose attempts to introduce the system into American schools used known-in-advance criteria for strategic planning and budgeting, argues that we should consider not only the budget's financial imperatives, but also its justification regarding both curriculum and environmental need.

REFLECTION

What difficulties do you anticipate in operating zero-based budgeting?

Programme planning budgeting

To overcome the 'manipulation' problems that can occur with other methods, Caldwell and Spinks (1988) attempted to establish a totally objective method of school-based financial planning. Costing the component elements of an institution's curricular offer can be a precursor to informed decision making about organizational priorities. They argue that if each element in the programme is costed and subject to collaborative prioritization, then institutional cooperation is enhanced and power politics shift towards greater collegiality, so that whole-institutional planning becomes a reality.

Limited plan budgeting

This approach attempts to combine the best features of several schemes. Although 'limited planning' ensures that a specific, basic curriculum is offered annually, decisions about crucial budget *changes* are also considered. Formula allocations are used for, say, 60 per cent of an organization's financial commitments, while plans are also proposed and funded for specific changes, e.g. to introduce a new PSE programme for year 10. Each programme-plan costing takes account of staff time, teaching materials/equipment, accommodation costs and an element for central services, with costs then set against resulting savings. As one development area is established, another is curtailed. While calculations may become complex and sometimes problematic, institutions usually cost-limit their plans *vis-à-vis* additional staffing, staff training and additional resources: that is, they concern themselves with marginal change.

ACTION

What arguments would you use in asserting the value of limited plan budgeting for your own organization or area of work? What would be the biggest difficulty in persuading others?

Entrepreneurial schools and colleges

If taken to their logical conclusion, LFM and LMS gives schools and colleges almost complete control over resource deployment. However, budgets have two sides – *income* and *expenditure* – and while the current educational and economic climate means institutions cannot readily reduce expenditure, there is increasing government emphasis on financial entrepreneurialism and 'income' generation.

Maintained schools are increasingly encouraged to supplement devolved budgets through sponsorship, fund-raising and even selling or hiring out skills, services and equipment, with nursery provision and after-school care developments being good examples of full-cost provision in disused classrooms, particularly where it ensures continuity of parental commitment. Moreover, colleges and universities increasingly provide consultancies and staff training for local companies, develop education–industry links and seek sponsorships, supporting the post-1988 focus on meeting wider local needs and improving community links (in addition to generating income).

ACTION

How far is your organization 'entrepreneurial'? What, if anything, does it do to generate income and how far are these activities (a) educationally focused, (b) income-focused? Is it easy to distinguish between them?

Whatever the degree of entrepreneurialism, the inescapable fact is, that, under current arrangements, educational institutions depend on student or pupil recruitment and need, therefore, to be fully aware of local community needs. Aldrich and Mindlin (1978) see two types of dependency relationship in this, which often work in tandem:

- *Resource dependency*: when the institution is reliant on its community for resources.
- *Information dependency*: when the knowledge the community has about the institution determines recruitment levels and the support available.

Issues of dependency and external relations will remain intricately interlinked issues while institutional funding is linked to student admission numbers. However, as Simkins (1997: 164) notes, 'it is just because it is so difficult to make a link between particular decisions about resource use and the learning outcomes which are achieved . . . that we need to think clearly about the principles and assumptions upon which such decisions are made.'

Financial monitoring and evaluation

A key problem in developing school-based autonomy is that staff may not understand the relevance of budgetary control and evaluation. Once the allocation has been made, they rapidly lose interest in the subsequent tracking of expenditure. Although an audit function means that each expenditure item must be legal, documented and quality assured, audit is generally less well understood in 'value-for-money' terms. Similarly, many staff often feel that the budget is only of value for the current year.

Concepts of 'overspend' and 'underspend' are also worthy of analysis here, as is budget *correction* as a way of ascertaining the skills base for resource management to achieve organizational objectives. Experience in 'opted out' schools suggests that budgets have become extremely significant for both teachers and managers in former GM schools, since they know now that neither central funding nor local (LEA) support is available to 'bail out' profligate schools (Bush *et al*. 1993). This is an issue recognized in both Ofsted's and the National Audit Office's reporting systems, where schools and colleges are encouraged to:

- develop clear financial procedures which ensure that, once money is allocated, it is spent according to intention;
- develop consistent audit control which will help to eliminate fraud and misuse of funds;
- develop an awareness of procedures for ensuring value for money purchasing;
- develop a system which ensures that the long-term effects of expenditure are monitored and evaluated.

In addition, central government emphasis on benchmarking (DfEE 1995a) has attracted a good deal of attention: after recording expenditure across various areas, benchmarking can be used as a way of measuring individual school performances against those with similar profiles. In theory, schools and colleges are able to assess their standing in relation to similar sized and situated organizations, although this raises various 'why?', 'what?' and 'to what effect?' questions. For example, one headteacher has used 'benchmarking data to review spending in different staffing areas and found that there was some duplication of management tasks. A revised management structure released funds for other priorities' (DfEE 1995a: 5). However, the methodology used in benchmarking may be subject to similar criticisms to those regarding Ofsted inspection and league table methodologies, where the plea is that 'judgements must be credible and fair' (FitzGibbon 1996b). Clearly, however, the need to ensure that resources are maximized for educational effectiveness is especially important within classroom settings, with a need for clear criteria in relation to successful resource utilization.

REFLECTION

If financial monitoring is undertaken in your area/department, how far is it a response to published procedures and/or driven by a 'local' concern to ensure value for money?

The longer-term impact of resource allocation is assessed via evaluation, with outcomes judged on the basis of quality output and resource utilization patterns, e.g. annual assessments of GCSE results against additional staffing expenditure or IT costs. Generally, however, evaluation is nowadays officially seen as comprising more than this and is concerned with using resources strategically as well as operationally to support school aims and objectives. This leads us to consider the *relationships* between stakeholders in education – those in schools, colleges and their communities – an issue we consider in the next chapter.

Suggestions for further reading

Caldwell, B. and Spinks, J. (1988) *Beyond the Self-managing School*. Lewes: Falmer.

Knight, B. (1993) *Financial Management for Schools*. Oxford: Heinemann.

Levačić, R. (ed.) (1993) *Financial Management in Education*. Buckingham: Open University Press.

Levačić, R. (1995) *Local Management of Schools: Analysis and Practice*. Buckingham: Open University Press.

Preedy, M., Glatter, R. and Levačić, R. (eds) (1997) *Educational Management: Strategy, Quality and Resources*. Buckingham: Open University Press.

13 Managing stakeholder relationships and partnerships

Successful public sector agencies need to adopt the same characteristics as successful private sector concerns. They need to be responsive to their customers and constantly in search of efficiency gains and quality improvements.

(Davies 1992: 9)

 ## The new governance

The past fifty years has seen a growing focus on external accountability in education. In particular, the educational restructuring of recent decades has been premised largely on New Right concerns to introduce an education market, reduce 'producer capture' (Baker 1993: 63) and move away from what were seen as 'permissive' and liberal philosophies which led to steadily declining standards. The Conservative government's remedy for the apparent educational malaise was to move 'back to basics' (Major 1994), which involved a stronger accountability emphasis, a return to traditional approaches to teaching and assessment (e.g. as polarized in the 'real books' versus 'reading schemes' debate) and a closer focus on meeting national economic needs (Edwards 1995).

Ranson (1991, 1994) has summarized the shift in responsibility towards the 'point of delivery', increased parent and governor power, and changes in institutional status as grant-maintained schools became 'properly independent of their maintaining LEA'. In trying to balance voter, local taxpayer and central government pressures as well as match government-prescribed performance criteria, LEAs have been pressed to metamorphose into enabling and facilitating agencies (Audit Commission 1989a). Governing bodies rather than LEAs are now, at least in theory, key educational power sources at a local level – accountable for management, curriculum, staffing, resource allocation and admissions policies.

The twin pulls involved in maintaining enrolment numbers and meeting 'market' demands in the 'new education management' (Grace 1995) mean that, in order to retain their particular market 'niches', schools and colleges have increasingly needed to focus on external relationships, as well as on both formal and informal aspects of marketing within their wider communities, in order to attract potential 'clients' and 'customers' alongside their other stakeholders.

Table 13.1   Educational environments

Environment	Characteristics	Example
'Placid randomized'	Little change or slow change; unrelated to other organizations; unpredictable	Rural comprehensive school with geographically limited catchment area
'Placid clustered'	Stable; with limited change, but affected by what happens to other organizations	Four schools within an area offering twelve forms of entry but with only the equivalent of ten forms in the age cohort
'Disturbed reactive'	Change dictated by what competing organizations do in response to wider change	Colleges of further education within a close urban area facing higher unemployment
'Turbulent reactive'	Constant readjustment to external changes, with inherent instability and possible closure	A 'failing school' within an urban area where there is surplus capacity and where restructuring is inevitable

Source: after Emery and Trist (1965).

It may be helpful, at this point, to clarify several key concepts. Stakeholders, as defined by Hannah and Freeman (1984), comprise any group who affect or are affected by an organization: in education, stakeholding begins with students and incorporates staff, parents, potential parents, employers and the wider community, covering all those who 'have a vested interest in education, its processes, and its outcomes' (Murgatroyd and Morgan 1992: 5). By external relations we mean those ways in which a school or college's ethos is represented to its local community, as well as its community focus in terms of accountability, responsiveness and responsibility (Scott 1989). The environment is that set of local and national circumstances which condition the resource base, expectations and responsiveness.

Research in this area has generally grown out of Emery and Trist's (1965) work, which argues, first, that organizations function within four types of environment (see Table 13.1) and, second, that 'uncertainty' (i.e. of role or funding) and 'clustering' (i.e. the influence of other local organizations) are major environmental influences on them. Our concern here is with the way in which external relations policies acknowledge the wider environment and are responsive to stakeholders.

REFLECTION

What kind of environmental 'picture' does your own organization – or one known well to you – display? What evidence is there that its philosophy and practice are affected by environmental pressures?

 Autonomy and accountability

[The] top-down approach is comforting to policy makers because it preserves the illusion of control and the pretence of accountability.

(Darling-Hammond 1995: 597–605)

According to Handy (1994), the range, pace and complexity of social change means that 'paradox has almost become the cliche of our times'. This perspective is echoed in Hargreaves's (1997) assertion that education is currently confronted by five paradoxes:

1 That parents now often give up responsibility for the very things they want schools to stress.
2 That there is both more centralization and more decentralization.
3 That greater globalism creates more tribalism.
4 That increased diversity and integration is accompanied by a greater emphasis on common standards and specialization.
5 That a stronger orientation towards the future is creating a greater nostalgia for the past.

This kind of complexity is summed up in Pascale's (1990: 110) comment that 'Paradoxes serve us by setting up polar opposites and affirming both sides. Two factors, mutual exclusivity and simultaneity, are essential for a genuine paradox.' Such paradoxes are reflective of the autonomy–accountability tensions currently framing educational development: while teachers have traditionally considered themselves autonomous professionals, the post-1988 reform agenda is a direct challenge to this status through strengthened accountability demands. The battleground between autonomy and accountability is characterized by the increased utilization of the language of educational control – seen in concepts like self-managing schools, site-based management, local financial management, parental choice, decentralization and restructuring.

Accountability is a complex concept which, clearly, takes a variety of forms (Kogan, 1986), with recent policy debates challenging *professional* models of accountability, while emphasizing *managerialist* models (Ranson 1994: 12). Ranson links this trend to three overlapping periods of development: first, the age of Professionalism (1945–75); second, the period of Corporatism (1970–81); third, as part of a more 'market'-driven era, the period of Consumerism (1979 to the present). We might argue, however, that so neat a periodization too readily masks the fact that the concerns and philosophies typical of each period are not simply 'sloughed off' as time passes, but remain influential to varying degrees within current educational debates and structures. Following on from Winstanley *et al.* (1995), Simkins (1997) has examined the differences between what he describes as 'hard' accountability (i.e. managerialist) models and 'soft' accountability (i.e. professional) models. He articulates the changing autonomy–accountability balance by using the concepts of 'criteria power' and 'operational power' (see Table 13.2).

The paradox of simultaneous decentralization and centralization of power indicates that nowadays 'school autonomy is exercised within a much firmer framework of central control' (Simkins 1997: 22) and, in addition, shows how formal patterns of power have changed at school level, with teacher power diminishing while headteachers, parents and governors are now, at least theoretically, both more powerful and more accountable. The realities of practice 'on the ground' may, however, create a different impression. While this depiction of accountabilities offers us a sense of the balance in environmental, community and stakeholder roles, they remain difficult to evaluate objectively since, as Glatter (1989) has argued, it is 'essentially artificial and pragmatic'

Table 13.2 The changing autonomy–accountability balance

Stakeholders	Criteria power	Operational power
Central government	Big increase in power	Determines framework and delegates
Local government (LEAs)	Loss of power to central government	Big loss of power to schools/ headteachers
Teachers/professional associations	Loss of power to central government	Loss of power to schools, heads, governing bodies
Headteachers	Has influence rather than power	Increased power: devolved from LEAs
Parents	Has influence rather than power	Increased power: active parental choice
Pupils	Effectively powerless	Effectively powerless

Source: based on Simkins (1997).

to assume that organizations can be distinguished sharply from their environmental context.

Governing body roles and responsibilities

As very much a centrepiece of the 'Thatcherite' legislative revolution in education, governing bodies have, at least theoretically, become key drivers of English educational development. Consequently, the changing governance of schools and colleges is bound to be a major issue for those leading and managing education. For example, during the five years following the 1986 Education Act (which considerably extended governing body power and accountability, particularly in relation to staffing and finance), over 75,000 parent governorships were filled.

While accountability to the local community rests with governors, post-1988 research indicates that headteacher–governor relationships can become increasingly problematic in relation to differential interpretations of philosophy and practice (Deem 1993). This is an issue highlighted by the shifting power relationship between stakeholders: the new balance between the 'local triumvirate' of schools, LEAs and governing bodies means, for example, that headteachers are often less able to dominate school governance in ways which many did before the reforms (Deem 1990).

Research also indicates that parents are often bewildered by 'the sometimes heavily politicised conflicts in which governing bodies become embroiled' (Bridges 1994: 15). Some parent governors, for example, are highly critical of what one New Right commentator has provocatively described as the 'articulate, adroit and literate "political" people' sometimes found on governing bodies (Seldon 1990). Despite this cynicism, the governor role remains crucial for both the rhetoric and reality of 'parental choice', even if a number of governors do consider themselves 'marginalised by manipulative heads, outranked by LEA nominated veterans, mystified by educational jargon and intimidated by paperwork' (Golby 1993: 52). Within the wider community, longstanding scepticism among parents about both the work and nature of school governance has been a difficult issue to address (Bridges 1987). It is, nevertheless, a crucial issue which requires sensitive handling on the part of senior staff. In the light of such concerns, Everard and Morris (1996) suggest that headteachers need to:

1 Raise governors' awareness of organizational processes.
2 Try to utilize user-friendly language with educational lay-people.
3 Remember that governors are a valuable resource when managing change.

Despite this advice, differences in perception are frequently evident between staff or parent perceptions of governors' roles and governors' own perceptions of their role, an issue highlighted in the following cameo involving a grant-maintained school.

Cameo Governing perceptions

'The Governing Body is the policy-making body for the school. The head is the chief executive working within this framework, and the sub-committees are responsible for discussions and investigation of those matters which are to be referred on to the Governors' (Chair of governors: grant-maintained school, explaining how he envisaged the relationship between schools and their governing bodies: Leverhulme Trust Investigation Evidence, 1992).

'Where the Head and Advisory Committee agree then the decision should be reported to the Governors without lengthy further discussion. Where there is disagreement, existing policy continues, unless the Head feels that she wishes to bring the matter to full Governors for discussion. Our role at Governor's meeting level is not to be concerned with detail, only with policy' (Minutes of governors' meeting).

The cameo indicates the need for clearly defined responsibility boundaries regarding a governing body's role, with an important distinction being drawn between *governance* (i.e. policy-making) and *management* (i.e. policy implementation). Echoing Hargreaves's 'paradoxes', Pascal's (1987) scrutiny of governing body 'democratization' in primary schools identifies four tensions:

1 Between governor *elitism* as a power base, and the *pluralism* of all stakeholders in a community.
2 Between *centralization* (i.e. with power centred on governors) and *devolution* (with day-to-day power delegated to senior staff).
3 Between *professionals* (paid experts) and the *laity* (lay volunteers) in controlling knowledge.
4 Between governors as school *supporters* and governors as a group to whom the school is *accountable*.

REFLECTION

How far are the above tensions evident in your own institution or sector?

While such tensions can be resolved to mutual benefit, individual or group agendas are also likely to surface when, for example, LEA governors have a strong political agenda or are replaced by other pressure groups. Reminiscent of research into group dynamics and team-building, Wirt's (1981) assessment of relationships between political bodies and their paid executives has identified five 'relationship' stages, which may throw light on governing body–school management relationships:

- *Quiescence*: professionals dominate, while laity supports.
- *Issues*: laity begins to question professionals.
- *Turbulence*: conflict between laity and professionals over control issues.
- *Resolution*: professional–laity conflict is investigated.
- *Closure*: professional roles are redefined.

Some school and college principals experience significant interventions in school management as their governing body reaches the third ('turbulence') stage, while others report that stage one ('quiescence') is allowed to predominate. Over time, 'case law' is likely to determine more clearly the legal role and power boundaries. It may be that targeted training may alleviate at least some governing body tensions, although many are effectively inbuilt and inherent within local educational policy-making and management structures. For example, governing bodies often remain reluctant to spend limited funds on their own training, even when it is earmarked for this purpose (Barber *et al.* 1995). In addition, active governor participation in development planning can help to diminish division and increase understanding (Cuckle *et al.* 1998).

Sallis (1989) considers that active governing body input is essential for healthy educational management and development, since it represents an external 'client' perspective and, reciprocally, acts as an institutional voice in the wider community. She stresses the value of both experiential learning and governor training in facilitating improved understanding of governor responsibilities, even though voluntary roles and limited time makes it potentially problematic. As Crawford *et al.* (1998) indicate, issues of time, obligation and workload could seriously inhibit future governor recruitment, especially in socially deprived areas, even if complex policy decision making can be facilitated through governor sub-committees with coopted school staff 'experts'. While individual governing bodies determine their own work patterns, some commonality of approach is apparent, with, for example, staffing, premises and curriculum sub-committees commonplace.

ACTION

How are members of your organization's governing body directly involved with the daily running of your institution? Are governors updated regularly on curriculum issues and what potential is there for improved governor involvement or understanding?

The institutional leader–governor relationship is complex and sometimes very difficult. Although not commonplace, Deem (1993) found that some governing bodies interpreted their roles as 'boards of directors', with head-teachers being chief executives responsible for setting and achieving financial and performance targets. In taking their 'external' stance, many governors are fearful of being 'manipulated', 'done to' or 'done for', and expect to have a clear and often decisive voice in governance: an issue which can lead to excessive demands being placed on headteachers (Riley *et al.* 1995). Though not necessarily borne out in reality, the division of responsibilities between headteacher roles (internal management, leadership and school organiza-tion) and governor roles (governance and accountability for, finance and organizational leadership, for example) does assume a high degree of consen-sus and collaboration between both parties (Ribbins 1989). But, as Riley and Rowles (1997: 89) have cautioned, 'As things currently stand, contradictions are built into the role of head and governor, particularly in relation to school management and quality.' If a relatively diverse governing body is to com-prehend educational life effectively it may be important to ensure that a basic platform of governor competence and development is in place. Turner *et al.* (1991) offer the following principles for effective governor training:

• governor involvement in devising their training programme;
• group-based training to enhance social values;
• issue-based training to focus on school or college life 'realities'.

As Riley and Rowles (1997: 82–3) argue, while 'The role of school governors will continue to evolve . . . There is undoubtedly a need for some reassess-ment, and possibly some redefinition, of the expectation of governors.' Despite their loss of power, the re-emergence of LEA 'policing' powers, when set against the emphasis on governor responsibilities for target-setting and benchmarking, suggests that governing body autonomy may, in future, become more con-strained and its accountabilities more closely determined.

Changing LEA roles

In summing up the dramatic post-1988 realignment of LEA-school relation-ships as 'the Kremlin is subjected to glasnost', Mann (1989) was explicitly acknowledging the shift in LEA responsibilities over recent years (see Table 13.3). In order to fill the gap left by LEAs, senior institutional managers have had to develop more specialist accountancy, personnel, project management and negotiation skills, as well as determine provider specifications for a range of goods and services. In addition, the creation of grant-maintained schools and City Technical Colleges (CTC) has influenced the policies, man-agement profiles, institutional marketing, recruitment and school–school relationships of all LEAs, and has had a considerable impact on the survival abilities of some LEAs particularly hard hit by 'opting out'. While growing governor power and increased central government control have thus squeezed LEA 'operational' and 'criteria' power (Simkins 1997), recent government commitments to school improvement and target-setting have also brought the potential for their phoenix-like resurgence.

LEAs are now, in theory at least, well placed to provide schools with com-parative information to inform school improvement strategies (Fidler and

Table 13.3 Changes in LEA responsibilities

From generic to specific support	Schools often now work directly with specific LEA personnel – finance, buildings – rather than through a single officer
From advisory to inspection roles	Moving to 'provider–purchaser' relationships between schools, LEAs and other agencies
From 'controlling' to 'enabling' roles	LEAs 'service' rather than control governing bodies and, despite joint responsibility for curriculum, admissions and appeals matters, are no longer *the* key decision makers.

Morris 1996) and have a key mediating role in target setting (DfEE 1997b) – even if school leaders now frequently see themselves 'in the driving seat' of the relationship. Moreover, although LEAs may be newly revived, the government's 'fair funding initiative' (DfEE 1998g) means that in future 'the local education authority monopoly will have to compete, for the first time, on a true market basis to survive' (Cooper 1998: 4). At present, however, many LEAs are still engaged in a struggle to reconcile issues emanating from the post-1988 restructuring of their roles:

- providing whole-LEA provision when some schools have 'opted out' for grant-maintained status;
- offering 'choice', while avoiding the creation of 'ghetto' or 'sink' schools;
- providing adequate post-compulsory education for minority groups which could actually be uneconomic and thus 'inefficient';
- maintaining community education philosophies on a declining resource base and when courses need to cover economic costs;
- delegating maximum levels of funding to schools, while maintaining a feasible 'service';
- maintaining 'flexibility' in the face of reduced options for flexibility as schools and colleges move towards centralized funding regimes;
- coping with less institutional dependency and smaller LEA advisory services as new inspection procedures developed.

Undoubtedly, the 'fair funding' regime will impact on many of these core functions. It may further the establishment of 'semi-privatized' LEAs, whereby they develop limited companies with private sector involvement, characterized by *out-sourcing* (i.e. privatizing specialist services and purely administrative tasks like payroll) and/or *in-sourcing* (i.e. collaborative partnerships with neighbours where external managers 'helicopter in' to help to reinvigorate services). This seems to bear out Mann's (1989) original view that LEAs would metamorphose into competitive service providers with very limited statutory power, a situation already apparent as many LEAs have been forced to marketize their relationships with schools (Law 1997b). Maden (1990) had argued that LEA–school partnerships were central if local government was to maintain its statutory 'service' responsibilities. She called for institutional planning processes to be linked into LEA monitoring services and collective agreements over common quality policies, so that LEA coordinating roles remained feasible, purposeful and beneficial. In the early post-ERA period, the Audit Commission (1989a) had seen LEAs as 'enablers':

- as *leaders*, offering a vision of what the education service might achieve;
- as *partners*, supporting schools and colleges develop new working relationships;
- as *planners*, for the efficient and effective use of resources;
- as *information-providers* in an education market;
- as *regulators*, inspecting and monitoring progress in schools and colleges;
- as *bankers*, administering funds to enable schools to deliver services.

Reflecting on LEA roles in past decade in *Whose School Is It Anyway?*, Riley (1998) notes that LEAs have adopted a spectrum of approaches:

- *Interventionist LEA*: doing the legal minimum in delegating responsibilities and resources to governors.
- *Interactive LEA*: actively maintaining a dialogue focused on supporting schools.
- *Responsive LEA*: only providing support services when requested by schools.
- *Non-interventionist LEA*: exercising minimalist functions regarding planning, special needs provision, inspection and advice.

Despite the implications of the 'fair funding' policy, post-1997 New Labour government initiatives seem to indicate a reinvigoration of LEA activity from progressive marginalization towards more interactive, tripartite relationships between schools, local and central government (DfEE 1998a, c). LEA involvement is particularly emphasized in terms of the right of access to schools, the control of premises, school target-setting, the provision of advisory services, the exchange of information, consultation and exclusion and discipline. In this changed LEA–governing body relationship it is stressed that:

> Governing bodies are responsible for the conduct of their school. That includes, in particular, ensuring that the school has in place an effective process for reviewing performance, identifying priorities, taking action, and monitoring progress, with a view to raising standards. The relationship between LEA and governing body should support this role. Where schools are successful, the governing body should have space to conduct their business as they see fit. But where there is evidence that the governing body is operating in a way which risks damaging the performance of the school, the LEA should draw its concerns to the governors' attention, and use its powers as necessary to ensure that the problem is addressed.
>
> (DfEE 1998a: para. 66)

Parents and markets: partners or consumers?

[One] of the essentials for educational advance is a closer partnership between the two parties (parents and teachers) to every child's education.

(DES 1967: 9)

The legal framework of parental choice in education has evolved over many decades. Although, for example, the 1944 Education Act spoke the rhetoric of parental concern regarding school choice and allowed for appeals to the

Secretary of State, the development of planned provision made it both a rarity and virtually ineffective at local levels.

Johnson's (1991) research indicates that parents often seek an education for their children which closely relates to their own previously – a particular concern of middle-class, grammar or independent school parents during the early 1970s, reacting against 'progressive ideas', 'comprehensivization' and 'child-centred' teaching. By the late 1970s, appeals had increased dramatically, with both Labour and Conservative parties acknowledging the growth of 'parent power', whether in defending or attacking the education service (Hargreaves 1997).

The 1980 Education Act acknowledged parental concerns by requiring that admission arrangements should by publicized; schools should admit pupils to the level of their physical capacity; and the local right of appeal should be maintained, even though local government (LEA) planning was to be maintained. These developments brought pressures for greater freedom even though the concept of 'choice' was more constrained than protagonists wished.

REFLECTION

How far do you consider parental choice is compatible with maximizing resource usage in an area?

Increasing 'parental choice' was an overt ambition of the 1988 Education Reform Act, with 'opting out' portrayed as a gateway to financial autonomy, independence and the potential of 'privatized' schooling via direct government funding (Walford 1990). Although the nature of grant-maintained (GM) status is set to change under the 'fair funding' review (DfEE 1998g) and research indicates that GM status has increased day-to-day responsibilities borne by governors and senior managers (Bush et al. 1993), in reality relatively few differences exist between GM and LEA schools where enhanced LMS autonomy exists (Halpin et al. 1991). While maintained schools may have less access to 'lump sum' funding, the 'missing' feature for GM schools is that LEAs are no longer automatic cushions in terms of personnel, premises and legal matters, an element compensated for by the fact that GM schools have become increasingly 'market-wise'.

While some schools now sample parental opinion via parental satisfaction surveys, relatively few schools consult students in any systematic fashion (Rudduck et al. 1995). However, there has been considerable research into the complex issues surrounding the ways in which education 'consumers' judge schools and colleges. Adler et al. (1989), working in Scotland, found that while parental judgements about secondary provision were largely 'happiness-based', there was also concern about school disciplinary structures. Carroll and Walford (1997) point out that the 'happiness' factor is related to peer group pressure: even when pupils have realistic choices, they often opt for the nearest comprehensive school to be with peers. Similarly, in an examination of parental appeals following the 1980 Education Act, Stillman and Maychell (1986) found that they displayed a threefold division of concerns:

- *Process*: will the school experience promote happiness?
- *Outcomes*: what about examination results, discipline, truancy?
- *Geography*: what about access and safety issues?

There is evidence that, over time, these factors change in importance: Glover (1992) found parental attitudes changed between the time pupils entered and left a large comprehensive, with parental judgements progressively coming into play throughout school life. Public relations policies may founder, however, if schools direct their efforts *only* at meeting external perceptions, even if these and their community links are important for schools.

Some writers (e.g. Hammond and Dennison 1995) suggest that, although educational marketing is increasingly complex, parents and students have a fairly restricted set of choice alternatives (whether through geography, costs etc.). This enables institutions to evolve specific 'niche' strategies to meet needs in particular sections of their 'market'. The costs of meeting the needs of potential clients involve matching the 'product' and 'packaging' with the available *funds* and the likely *costs* – effectively a cost–benefit analysis. The degree to which schools and colleges are justified in using often limited resources to widen 'market share' does, however, pose ethical questions about managing public services. Insidious advertising (like that developed by the school which caused uproar when it offered double-glazing incentives to its parents) causes major difficulties when traditional patterns and attitudes remain entrenched, whether in primary, secondary or even tertiary sectors.

Nowadays, with 'catchment' areas used as 'key selling points' in estate agents' handbills and with industrial sponsorship sometimes highlighting instructional materials, some see this as a testimony to 'marketing'. For others, it demonstrates unnecessary 'unprofessional behaviour' damaging to a school's reputation. Clearly, such strategies have limited scope and may alienate potential 'customers'. It also remains dubious whether any level of expenditure would attract a potential education consumer with offspring at Eton to attend an 'estate' school in a socially deprived area. Regional or social differences affect not only the level of funding available to support maintained education, but also parental willingness to use private education alternatives.

ACTION

Which factors influence recruitment to your organization/area? How far do you have external relations policies which address recruitment issues, and what inhibiting factors are identifiable?

Although governing bodies report annually to parents and local communities in the spirit of more open dialogue between institutions and their 'clients', this aspect of the policy of greater openness and choice remains problematic. While schools at one end of the continuum publish 'quality policies', complaints and arbitration procedures and clear criteria for behaviour standards, homework and assessment, those at the other end often still display defensive attitudes to parents and students, where complaints sink without trace and 'customer services' are seen as irrelevant, objectionable or simply managerialist imposition. Naybour (1989) notes that parents frequently feel inadequate *vis-à-vis* home–school relationships and stresses that the emphasis on accountability and 'market responsiveness' has influenced relationship patterns, leading to changes like:

- more organized parents' evenings, with consultation by appointment, supported by pastoral staff;
- greater parental involvement in reporting processes through focused subject profile statements;
- greater parental involvement through PTA fund-raising, parental advisory committees, parents as ancillaries;
- more open home–school partnerships, especially *vis-à-vis* special needs.

These aspects reveal how external relations policies increasingly reflect schools' consciousness of the need to market themselves effectively, albeit at a low level. For some it simply becomes a question of 'all publicity must be good publicity', while others adapt commercial concepts to enhance their responsiveness and demonstrate accountability. Bagley *et al.* (1996), for example, explain how some schools audit community perceptions, often described as 'scanning the market'.

Since auditing may be systematic and planned (e.g. formal discussions, negotiation, recording telephone calls and complaints) or unplanned (e.g. *ad hoc* conversations), the implied subjectivity of perspective and data needs to be taken into account when judgements are made. Foskett (1998) articulates a tighter system based on responses to identified criteria and an index of staff 'culture', which helps to support strategic evaluation, an approach commonly seen in SWOT analyses (a strengths, weaknesses, opportunities and threats matrix). This has been extended by Weindling (1997) to incorporate the external environment, including potential political, educational, social and technological changes. As the cameo on page 234 illustrates, this is not necessarily an easy process.

Devlin and Knight (1990) suggest that any attempt to manage 'market' relationships with stakeholders involves:

- *Identifying your target audience*: who do you want to tell about your institution?
- *Identifying communications priorities*: how will your institution reach its audience?
- *Building up your media networks*: who can be trusted with e.g. unfavourable 'news'?
- *Building reactive systems*: who helps with immediate action and sensitive handling so that potentially difficult situations can be defused effectively?

Both Gray (1991) and James and Phillips (1995) apply the concept of a commercial 'marketing mix' to educational contexts. In their examination of how far decisions about ethos, course opportunities and community relationships can be seen as 'marketable' organizational features, they identify the five 'Ps' of marketing:

Cameo   Survival tactics?

Bushmere Primary School is one of four schools, each of which is notionally one form of entry at age four plus, for pupils in the southern suburban belt of a large city area. Jane Wilson, the head for five years, has stabilized the school's staffing and encouraged the idea of 'fairness for all while developing individual potential'.

Over the past two years total numbers on roll have declined in the catchment area of the four schools. Pressures to encourage Bushmere to change are being orchestrated by a group of parents living in a newly developed private housing estate built on the site of a former goods yard. While they are geographically nearest to Bushmere, parents criticize the school because there is no insistence on uniform, it lacks competitive team games and staff are unwilling to provide additional help for pupils seeking admission to a minor independent day school in the city.

Three families who favour the 'more traditional' approach of Wellsbourne, the smallest of the four schools, have recently left Bushmere. Tim Wells, the newly elected chairman of Bushmere's governors, comes from the private estate, but has met parents from two housing association redevelopment areas who are opposed to changing what they see as 'a thoroughly good school'. Recently, the LEA notified all four governing bodies that one school must close within five years, although it will resource a special needs unit to serve all schools on one site.

Jane and Tim agree to assess the school's strategic position by SWOT analysis. What would be the outcome?

- *Price*: a combination of both direct costs (e.g. fees) and indirect costs (e.g. travel).
- *Place*: the 'value' of the environment (e.g. attractiveness).
- *Product*: the subjects, courses, and extra-mural activities on offer.
- *Promotion*: how the institution 'packages' itself – publicity (e.g. prospectus), responsiveness (e.g. phone manner/reception), image (e.g. uniform).
- *People*: the nature of the relationships the institution has with its community(ies).

It is important, however, to remember that each aspect of external relations needs to be managed through an understanding of the 'client base'. Hirschman's (1970) work (admittedly focused on an American business context) has, nevertheless, been highly influential in reviewing 'customer' behaviour in education through its assessment of parental behaviour. When 'consumers' are dissatisfied with a product or service they tend to adopt one of three strategies: exit, voice or loyalty.

- *Exit*: where customers refuse to purchase the 'product'.
- *Voice*: where customers give producers an opportunity to improve.
- *Loyalty*: where customers are retained.

In an educational context, Westoby (1989) suggests that exit can weaken the voice of those remaining, who, in turn, may be overtaken by the 'loyalty' group. Whether all parents are willing to use their 'voice' or express their loyalty may be questionable, and while many would like to use exit as a response to a given policy or perceived culture, there is often no obvious alternative school, limiting options. Although it is difficult to compare industry with services like education and health directly, the impact of exit and voice on educational policy development cannot be denied, with governors being important as a bridge to the local community, particularly when stability is threatened by endemic change.

Stakeholders in the wider community

The impact of increased governor power and parental choice, alongside decreased local government influence, has pressured schools and colleges into more focused community relationships – as a source of support, broader experiences and sometimes finance. Open enrolment and the inception of educational markets have widened the perceived community which schools and colleges serve. For example, Glatter *et al.* (1992) have found that the development of an 'education market' has widened an individual school's sphere of influence, explicitly threatening traditional school–neighbourhood relationships. If this holds true in general, educational communities are likely to become both diffuse and diminished in future, with the concept of community education becoming undermined – an issue which has major implications for the future structures and relationships of education.

Critics of postwar education policy have long argued that schooling neither fully 'educates' the young for life nor 'trains' them for work. This is a claim supported in certain respects by the Dearing Report into higher education, which argued that too many people leave full-time education – even at university level – without possessing the 'core' skills necessary for employment or a commitment to 'lifelong learning' (Dearing 1997). In developing community initiatives, some educational institutions have endeavoured to meet this agenda through building up commercial and business links, which also enhances student numbers, 'adds value' and improves prospects for better local understanding and institutional loyalty.

The 'New Managerialist' climate in education has undoubtedly encouraged closer education–industry links at local, regional and even national community levels, frequently facilitated through agencies like Training and Enterprise Councils (TECs), many of which have a legal duty to collaborate with education and to commission training at all levels to support the 'knowledge revolution' and the 'Learning Age' (DfEE 1998e). There has been a plethora of curriculum strategies focused on enhancing these links, e.g. through work experience and shadowing, industry days, Young Enterprise, Compacts and Teachers into Industry initiatives. Even so, secondary schools often find managing industry–education relationships difficult for several reasons:

- employers expectations are difficult to match, and schools are sometimes seen as producing 'the wrong kind' of recruit;
- students have heightened expectations of work and 'work experience' and are alienated by 'menial' tasks;
- the school curriculum seems inappropriate for employer needs, e.g. 'the imperial versus metric' and 'basic skills' arguments.

Mitchell (1989) has argued that student learning is most effectively managed and fostered by the involvement of a full range of stakeholders. In relation to this, Glover (1993) outlines a three-stage evolution in the process of community stakeholder awareness:

1 *Information*: where details of the institution's activities are published to increase local awareness and develop reputation.
2 *Knowledge*: where community involvement develops through closer interactions with community users and parents by direct experience of the institution.
3 *Involvement*: where individuals develop loyalty through full involvement in the total programme.

There is evidence that the stronger the third stage of development, the greater the commitment to the local institution and the greater the understanding and defence of its policies.

REFLECTION

How far and in what ways does your organization have a 'community focus'?
How could it be further developed?

Seckington (1989) argues for both flexibility in professional approach and a willingness to enter into partnerships with community agencies, so that the teacher's role beyond school or college is seen as a 'community enabler' – contrasting with the perspective that teachers are now becoming little more than 'technicians' and 'social agents' who are progressively being 'proletarianized' (Ozga 1988). The validity of this latter perspective remains unconvincing and unproven in our view – not least because, as Hoyle and John (1995: 12) have commented, this notion of proletarianization 'implies that de-skilling, or de-professionalisation, is leading teachers to identify themselves as working class'.

Core 'stakeholder' partnerships (with, for example, governors, parents, LEAs and higher education) are frequently complemented by an ever widening range of evolving community relationships, some of which may be predominantly *developmental* (responsive, spontaneous and informal), while others are more *implementational* (formal, imposed and specific), with yet others being more *strategic* (focused on problem solving, networking, policy-oriented, resources) (Biott 1991). This developing complexity of partnerships and relationships is, however, accompanied by the 'chaos' of social, political and economic development (Stacey 1992) and an information explosion facilitated through global Internet-based relationships, which means that concepts of 'community' and 'stakeholders' are metamorphosing and becoming redefined.

As Senge *et al.* (1996) have argued, we now need to recognize that the 'habitat–community interface is permeable': as classrooms move into museums, businesses and homes; as teachers undertake what we would describe as 'professional work experience' in businesses and agencies; and as those in the wider community return to renew their own learning. In this way, Senge *et al.* argue, 'the community evolves its own sense of collective intelligence, greater than the sum of its parts' (p. 8). We now move on to examine how far this 'collective intelligence' can be supported through professional development. Managing CPD must be a central and underpinning concern for those focused on sustaining and reinvigorating a core community of staff and students and for those keen to maintain the long-term vigour of partnerships and relationships in the wider local, national and global communities.

Suggestions for further reading

Audit Commission (1989) *Losing an Empire, Finding a Role: the LEA of the Future.* London: The Audit Commission.

Exworthy, M. and Halford, S. (eds) (1998) *Professionals and the New Managerialism in the Public Sector.* Buckingham: Open University Press.

Fidler, B., Russell, S. and Simkins, T. (eds) (1997) *Choices for Self-managing Schools: Autonomy and Accountability.* London: Paul Chapman Publishing/BEMAS.

Glatter, R., Woods, P. A. and Bagley, C. (eds) (1997) *Choice and Diversity in Schooling: Perspectives and Prospects.* London: Routledge.

Riley, K. (1998) *Whose School Is It Anyway?* London: Falmer Press.

14 Leading and managing for professional development

> Probably nothing in a school has more impact on students in terms of skills development, self-confidence, or classroom behaviour than the personal and professional growth of their teachers.
>
> (Barth 1990: 49)

The policy framework

A decade ago, Blackburn and Moisan (1987: 3) described in-service education and training as 'an essential area with an unstable structure' and, in doing so, articulated the challenge facing those responsible for its management and organization. Until relatively recently, continuing professional development (CPD) had remained the 'Cinderella' of teacher education (Williams 1991), left on the sidelines of policy debates which centred on schooling and initial teacher training reform. It is now increasingly central to government policy initiatives for school improvement (Sammons *et al.* 1995; DfEE 1997a) and a key element in the management of effective educational achievement.

Given that it remained subject to 'recommendation and pragmatic action' for much of the past half-century (Burgess 1993), in-service education and training (INSET) had generally progressed on the basis of piecemeal ad-hocery – despite the James Report's strong commitment to teacher development during the early 1970s, which would, it asserted, 'help to enhance the status and independence of the teaching profession and of the institution in which many teachers are educated and trained' (DES 1972).

Because CPD was frequently driven by the vagaries of government funding changes rather than by focused policy making, it remained largely unplanned and reliant on personal, rather than organizational, commitment, often funded differentially by LEAs, some of whom exploited the government's funding 'pool', while others virtually ignored it (ACSET 1984; Dobbins 1992). However, as Gillian Shepherd, Secretary of State for Education, confessed at the point when the Major government began to grasp the CPD policy nettle: 'it is an area about which we know relatively little. We cannot afford that ignorance . . . INSET funding amounts to a huge investment nationally' (DfEE 1995c: 1).

Following the inception of school-based management in the early 1990s, and its challenge to what an earlier Conservative Education Secretary had deemed the 'producer capture' of teacher training (Baker 1993), the Conservative government turned its attention to the potential 'privatization of INSET' (Harland *et al*. 1993) and 'marketizing of relationships' in CPD (Law 1997b). The Major government's White Paper *Choice and Diversity* had declared that 'The government expects that increasingly the private sector will step in to provide these services' (DfE 1992: 32), a perspective reinforced by the 1992 Education Act, in which LEA roles in relation to inspection, advice and support were changed fundamentally. The rise of Ofsted and changed funding base for local authority inspection services required them to cast aside some of the more paternalistic elements in their relationships with schools and to embrace a quasi-market approach (Le Grand and Bartlett 1993). During the late 1980s the School Management Task Force (SMTF) had already challenged longstanding CPD assumptions and practices. Its report argued for:

- school-based in-service training;
- in-house collaborative approaches to teacher development;
- linking professional development with school improvement;
- planned approaches to professional development for all staff (DES 1990).

ACTION

How far do your own recent CPD experiences reflect SMTF recommendations? What benefits or disadvantages have accrued for you?

The 'new education management' climate has required senior managers in schools and colleges to adopt more focused negotiating roles *vis-à-vis* external providers (LEAs, HEIs and private consultancies) and more focused personnel roles *vis-à-vis* their own staff, with governing bodies being pressed to monitor and more actively account for CPD activities and funding. As the burgeoning agenda for school improvement has demanded a more overt 'payback' from the investments in staffing made by schools (emphasizing that staff costs may approach 90 per cent of a school's entire budget), teachers' development needs in supporting pupil achievement have become a high-profile issue. This focus is especially apparent in both DfEE's and TTA's heavy emphasis on the headteacher training and the perceived potential of 'leaders' to influence school and pupil success (Millett 1998; Morris 1998).

Thus, over the past decade, teacher development has been framed by three major influences:

- *Legislation*: stemming from the 1988 and 1992 Education Acts and incorporating a more prescriptive National Curriculum framework, focused on assessment, results and pupil-related funding to support school improvement, plus redesigned inspection and advisory structures.

- *Privatization*: reflected in the paradigm shift from an education 'service' to an education 'market' and from 'off-site' training to 'in-school' development supported by external agencies (Harland *et al.* 1993).
- *Self-management*: focused on both individualized and some mutual teacher support, with teachers taking greater personal and financial responsibility for their own learning alongside collaborative approaches via team teaching, paired work, observation and reflection.

Despite the apparently longstanding adhocracy surrounding policy making *vis-à-vis* teacher development, many schools have often undertaken a rough amalgam of both planned and unplanned activities, which have served a range of needs. As Bolam (1982, 1993) notes, CPD comprises an overall portfolio of activities which ideally adds to professional knowledge, improves professional skills, clarifies professional values and enables students to be educated more effectively. These elements are, he argues, provided through a combination of

- *Professional education*: longer courses, secondments, focused on theory and research-based knowledge.
- *Professional training*: shorter courses, conferences, workshops, emphasizing practice and skills.
- *Professional support*: job-embedded arrangements, e.g. mentoring.

While policy initiatives use a rhetoric which emphasizes professional *support* (and to a lesser degree professional *education*), it is clear that the language of CPD over recent decades is reflective of a policy thrust which stresses professional *training*. The TTA's endeavour to introduce a more coherent national policy framework has emphasized the need for more targeted professional development strategies which support primarily institutional needs and, where feasible, personal development needs. In doing so, it reflects four major themes which have, over the past decade, been woven into the environment for professional development planning:

- *Bureaucratization*: via school-based planning and delivery responsibilities located with senior managers.
- *Accountability*: through delegated CPD funding and associated governor accountability.
- *Coherence*: with links (and, ideally, an integration) between school development planning, professional development policies and practices, and personal development needs.
- *Diversification*: through an emphasis on marketization and privatization which encourages various providers to develop their own 'niches' in the education 'market'.

In terms of 'diversification', four kinds of provision are now apparent: LEA services (formerly centrally funded and now reliant on income from inspection and service level agreements with 'client' schools); LEA agencies (income-generating units competing in the open 'market'); higher education (focused on accrediting and pursuing a spectrum of teacher development); often integrated with research and private consultancies (initially perceived as 'quick fix' in approach, but now often highly professional 'grey power' LEA and HMI retirees).

REFLECTION

How far have these elements influenced CPD policy and planning in your own organization?

Changing teacher development

When teachers stop growing, so do their students.

(Barth 1990: 50)

The increased emphasis on cyclical processes for teacher development based around reviewing, planning, implementing and evaluating all teaching and learning objectives is articulated in the DfEE's and TTA's emphasis on the need to develop a well qualified and up-to-date teaching force across both initial training and in-service stages (DfEE 1998b, c; TTA 1998c). This focus has facilitated the drive towards more rational, formal and prescriptive curricula not only for those in initial teacher training, but also for those at senior management levels, e.g. in the TTA's portfolio of leadership training programmes, like HEADLAMP, NPQH and LPSH (see Table 14.1). While not intended to incorporate the entirety of management training and development needs for senior school staff, the TTA structure nevertheless represents a fundamental shift in perspective away from the concept of 'voluntarism' towards greater professional obligation and a more tightly prescribed training programme, which could be mandatory (although below-target registrations and critical comments from prospective heads regarding the NPQH curriculum and structure indicates an initial reluctance to commit to so tightly prescribed a framework for professional development).

Although it has proved contentious in some respects, the TTA's portfolio of management training initiatives has been generally well received, largely because it represents an *active* commitment to the centrality of CPD and particularly when there is consultation with providers and potential recipients, which is then actively fed into the development process. Marland (1998), for

Table 14.1 The TTA framework for senior management development in schools

NPQH	HEADLAMP	LPSH
National Professional Qualification for Headteachers For aspiring headteachers Intended to be mandatory	Headteacher Leadership and Management Programme For newly appointed headteachers Not mandatory, but with an accountability focus	Leadership Programme for Serving Headteachers For (long) serving headteachers Not mandatory, but with an accountability focus

example, suggests that the National Standards for Subject Leadership 'could be a major step forward'. However, the possible rigidity implicit in the focus on mandatory NPQH training has been challenged not only by senior managers and providers, but also by the House of Commons' Select Committee on Education and Employment scrutiny of 'the role of headteachers' (House of Commons 1998). By contrast, the Select Committee positively valued the flexibility offered by the TTA's earliest headteacher development initiative, HEADLAMP, which is geared specifically to meeting the induction needs of new headteachers in personalized, 'bespoke' ways (TTA 1995).

Rational approaches to CPD generally (and to headteacher development in particular) require that institutions try to identify:

- what their *aims* are in pursuing strategic objectives;
- which *specific activities/programmes* meet these aims;
- how *resources* (staff, finance and accommodation) will be deployed in pursuing aims;
- how *implementation* will take place;
- who will take *responsibility* and be *accountable*;
- which *criteria* will be used to monitor and evaluate plans.

While each point has professional development implications and influences its processes and content, recent research indicates that rational planning is potentially problematic. For example, Hargreaves (1995) suggests that 'too much planning' can inhibit development, while Mintzberg (1994) has argued that it can be too constraining and inhibiting of organizational flexibility and dynamism. Glover *et al.* (1996) also assert that too much planning inhibits effective management: a particularly important concern when tensions exist between individual, group and whole-school needs. Louis and Miles's (1992: 193) investigation of school improvement in five American high schools argues for *evolutionary* rather than *rational* planning approaches, suggesting that 'plenty of early action (small scale wins) creates energy and supports learning'. Plans that are evolutionary and flexible rather than rigidly rational and linear are more productive because 'planning is the first point where empowerment takes hold'.

ACTION

Briefly sketch the planning process within your own school or college. Highlight the link between the planning process and professional development.

There is, however, another side to this coin: there can also be too little planning. An emerging feature of CPD is that *ad hoc*, pragmatic and 'hit-and-miss' programmes are becoming less favoured within schools and colleges than more *integrated* practices – even if this presents them with organizational complexities and difficulties. For example, financial autonomy (albeit constrained by government funding systems and priorities) has encouraged schools to articulate more fully their value-for-money concerns and plan accordingly; the introduction of appraisal also encouraged a clearer articulation of personal and group needs. There is a wider acknowledgement that staff contributions can enhance and support school development planning (Hargreaves and Hopkins 1991). Despite these developments, however, McMahon's (1996) research with 66 schools indicates that understanding about good CPD practice remains limited because:

- only one-third of schools allocated time for professional development coordination, despite the fact that 65 out of 66 schools had a deputy head or senior teacher undertaking the role;
- fewer than 50 per cent of the schools used a professional development group/committee to plan their programme;
- only 50 per cent of teachers had copies of written professional development policies;
- only 40 per cent of schools used all five non-contact days for professional development.

REFLECTION

Where does your school or college stand in relation to these criteria? Why?

Consequently, schools nowadays often find that they have responsibility for planning and delivery but are without the back-up of internal structures, systems and support. School-based teacher development therefore presents a number of difficulties for those in organizational leadership positions.

Managing school-based professional development

The 1990s surge of government commitment to CPD is an overt encouragement to schools and colleges to grasp development opportunities while they can (Law 1995). However, school-based responsibilities for all kinds of development planning and organization have also brought major increases in senior management responsibilities, encouraging the use of rational and strategic planning to emphasize whole-staff participation and shared values systems. However, while decision making is increasingly a corporate activity in many schools and colleges, deputies or senior teachers also face considerable pressures in taking on professional development coordinator (PDC) roles, which require a combination of both administration and counselling/facilitation skills.

While CPD policy groups or committees may increasingly take decisions in many schools, PDCs are usually delegated to arbitrate and negotiate internally with staff and externally with providers in support of the institution's development planning process. In addition, the intersection and effort to integrate professional development, in-service education, initial teacher education and appraisal has created considerable administrative demands, with the danger that increased bureaucracy will actually obscure CPD purposes (Jones 1995).

REFLECTION

How does CPD support decisions taken within your institution? Does this reflect general management approaches or are there differences?

Because the privatization and repositioning of CPD as a core element in the national strategy for educational improvement delegates responsibility to schools and colleges, this realignment has produced its own tensions: where efforts are made to integrate CPD administrative and development roles, the demands on individuals can become overwhelming. Even though some basic PDC training is often offered via LEAs, there is little coordinated support for personnel-related CPD issues.

Despite the commonality of PDC responsibilities, it is clear that senior managers in schools and colleges often work very differently to support similar CPD aims: tasks are divided or delegated differently and the complex demands and personalities involved influence both perceptions and practices. PDC stress has emanated from growing institutional pressures to meet growing demands with diminishing resources. For example, our research indicates that up to 70 per cent of INSET expenditure in 1995 funded supply cover, emphasizing the fact that staff time (regardless of provider) comprises the single most expensive CPD element (Glover and Law 1996).

Adey and Jones (1997) point out that effective CPD coordination is inhibited by lack of role clarity, lack of time and lack of supporting information – each of which requires specific training. In an investigation of the changing role of PDCs, Lewes (1994) argues that lack of time becomes a necessary cost of enhancing staff development and commends the need for critical friend support, especially during the training and development period. This, of course, may reflect a universal feeling that senior managers are constantly short of time, a concern identified by research even before the 1988 Education Reform Act (Earley and Fletcher-Campbell 1989).

Broadhead *et al.* (1996) have shown how criteria based upon school development planning can liberate primary school PDCs from heavy administrative responsibilities by moving decision making to subject coordinators, although heads of small schools still find that administrative loads remain heavy. In addition, PD coordination has developed more slowing in primary schools because LEA-to-school budget delegation was not required until 1992. Responsibilities are, however, delegated to senior staff – a deputy or senior curriculum coordinator – as in secondary schools. In relation to the overall management of CPD, Glover and Law (1996) found that five key areas of focus and responsibility were crucial for the effective management of CPD in schools: first, effective information management (that which is externally generated as well as internally driven); second, integrated, timed and targeted planning which incorporates consultation and review; third, imaginative and open resource deployment enabling limited funds to be used in creative ways; fourth, clear and flexible evaluation processes where experience is logged and fully reflected upon as part of future plan making; fifth, and increasingly important, active networking at all levels in the organization and beyond. As Lieberman and McLaughlin (1992: 674–5) have noted, 'Networks offer a way for teachers to experience growth in their careers through deepened and expanded classroom expertise and new leadership roles . . . [They] provide teachers with the motivation to challenge existing practices and to grow professionally.'

ACTION

How are CPD activities at whole school, departmental and individual levels evaluated in your institution? In what ways do they support evaluation of teaching and learning?

Although many schools use their own staff as 'in-house providers', tensions between this strategy's cost effectiveness and the pressures it places on individuals are also becoming apparent. For example, O'Sullivan *et al.* (1997) suggest that schools are capable of providing highly supportive in-house development environments, e.g. through peer observation, mentoring, team teaching, work shadowing, curriculum development with 'expert teachers', group discussions and 'critical friend' consultants who act as catalysts for change. However, in spite of its cost-effectiveness, several management questions are pertinent for schools and colleges:

- *Quality*: how do we ensure 'in-house' CPD is of an appropriate quality to meet needs and support targets?
- *Administration*: how do we ensure that in-house CPD is genuinely developmental for staff rather than just administratively and organizationally convenient?
- *Integration*: how do we establish appropriate balances between meeting institutional, departmental *and* individual needs?

ACTION

Classify your INSET experiences according to an external/internal division and consider how far each has met personal, departmental and/or institutional needs.

Assessing and meeting needs

Although appraisal has encouraged staff to identify specific development and training needs and targets, a major problem remains insufficient funding, time and professional advice. High supply costs and concerns over what might be called 'supply fatigue' affecting pupils' lesson continuity make it especially important that middle and senior managers recognize the danger of *ad hoc* developments, of raising false CPD expectations and of creating false promises. While 'site-based' or 'in-house' INSET has been considered a resolution to

Table 14.2 Five 'doors' to organizational and personal development

'Doors'	'Opened by'
Collegiality	Creating a culture through professional relationships
Research	Familiarizing staff with research as a prompt to in-house development
Site-specific information	Providing student, course and outcomes-related data
Curriculum initiatives	Collaborative efforts to introduce curriculum change
Instructional initiatives	Enhancing teachers' skills and strategies

Source: after Joyce (1991).

these concerns, schools frequently become torn by the need to address related but different internal agendas. A major challenge remains the desire to meet and match the perceived CPD needs of individuals, groups *and* the whole school, as well as to 'cope with' the national agenda: with all of this overlaid by the need to determine the most appropriate kinds of provision. Needs prioritization is often linked to managerial role because senior staff tend to focus on whole-school objectives which are generally more cost-effective in terms of funds utilization (e.g. the avoidance of supply costs).

Bolam (1993) has identified five types of CPD need – staff group performance, individual job performance, career development, professional knowledge and personal education – while Joyce (1991) argues that there are five 'doors' which underpin organizational development and demonstrate the diversity of needs (see Table 14.2).

In the light of such diversity, it is vital that PDCs establish differentiated needs analysis strategies, as the following cameo indicates.

Cameo Meeting needs

School A. All members of staff complete a form detailing their needs for the coming year and related to self, year/subject and whole school roles. This is then entered on the CPD database, enabling needs to be matched against departmental and school development planning priorities where possible.

School B. An annual review of appraisal targets is undertaken by the PDC and deputy (planning), with all members of staff suggesting how their needs might be supported (at minimum cost). Although this takes up much of the summer term, staff actively contribute to planning and the process effectively raises fewer false training/development hopes.

School C. Personal, departmental and whole-school profiles of required knowledge and skills are developed with all teachers, middle and senior managers completing these documents annually and then using identified highest priority needs to plan the coming year's programme.

REFLECTION

What do you see as the shortcomings of the above schemes in terms of meeting the institution's strategic priorities and in ensuring flexibility?

Because it has such a potential impact on the level of staff expectations, it is essential that needs analysis is:

- open (enabling everyone to contribute to needs assessment and prioritization);
- flexible (enabling needs to be met even if resources diminish);
- responsive (enabling both immediate staff and strategic stakeholder needs to be recognized).

It has often been assumed that while teachers may occasionally benefit from 'development' opportunities they do not really need further 'training' after their initial teacher training (ITT). Some suggest that assumptions went even further than this, since 'Expectations were that once you had learnt to teach, you certainly should not need to keep *learning*, unless there was something wrong with you' (MacGilchrist *et al.* 1997: 113, italics added). Policy initiatives focused on new curricula and assessment strategies over recent decades have, however, been driven by a learning-by-training emphasis, with a number of highly specific, content-driven and targeted training programmes geared to knowledge acquisition and information-giving. We argue, however, that a range of issues are best supported through more interactive, experiential and process-driven development opportunities – emphasizing the need for balance within CPD between training and development. Jayne's (1996) review of the ways 'on-the-job' management training facilitates and enhances experience cites curriculum leadership, headteacher deputizing, task team management, resource management, liaison with agencies, INSET management and managing governor links as productive training opportunities.

Unfortunately, however, experience may reflect the difficulties identified by Rosenholtz (1989): that schools differ and development experiences vary widely, especially when school-based experiential learning masks what is effectively downward delegation without effective support. Moreover, even poor quality development opportunities can have a significant impact and, as Taylor and Bishop (1994) point out, 'unlearning is extremely difficult'. It is essential that CPD is balanced: structured, planned but related to individual learning processes (Oldroyd and Hall 1991). If they are to be successful, CPD activities must be rewarding for both participants and funders. Our research indicates that personal achievement and success occurs when:

- the work and development environment is propitious for alleviating stress;
- individuals feel a sense of ownership of their professional development;
- professional development activities are valued and relevant within the organization;
- a shared value system exists within the organization.

If viewed from an organizational perspective, we might add the following success criteria, where activities:

- offer value for money;
- offer quality content and delivery;
- impact at all levels – individuals, groups and institution;
- maintain motivation and boost morale.

Teacher development requires an integrated approach which links professional responsibilities with personal concerns at all levels. Although Shaw's (1994: 37) comment that, 'if learning is to be facilitated in the most effective way, good pastoral care is essential', emphasizes that effective teachers acknowledge their students' pastoral needs alongside the academic focus, and is a dictum equally appropriate in relation to staff development.

> **ACTION**
>
> Check one internal and one external professional development activity you have been involved in against the above criteria and identify those factors which, in your view, inhibited effectiveness.

Adult learning

Although significant levels of funding are invested annually in professional development and staff training across both business and educational organizations, it is only relatively recently that the particularities of 'andragogy' or adult learning have gained a higher profile, supported by the rhetoric of commitment to experiential and 'lifelong learning', an acknowledgement of the importance of personal approaches to learning (e.g. Honey and Mumford 1988) and an understanding of the need for an integration of organizational and individual development strategies. Levine's (1989) American research, for example, argues that the most effective school principals actively 'promote adult growth' in their colleagues by treating teacher development as a lifelong process.

Knowles (1983, 1984) has suggested that significant differences exist between the learning patterns of children and adults. Although this view is treated with some caution (Dennison and Kirk 1990), it has considerable potential implications for the way we deal with learners at different stages and ages. The issue becomes even more important when the diversification of provision and market context of education is taken into account: adult learning is also now more closely scrutinized because research indicates that 'effective' educational institutions have effective teacher development strategies and positive community roles, often facilitated through adult education and an acknowledgement that teaching must better service diverse learning needs (Sammons *et al.* 1995). Knowles sees a clear distinction between the 'pedagogy' appropriate for children's learning and the 'andragogy' appropriate for adults. Adult learners, it is argued, have particular characteristics:

- Their earlier learning is substantial, implicit, assumed and needs to be built upon through new learning experiences;
- They accept 'the need to learn' by recognizing its personal value;
- They are generally self-directed, but also require a climate of trust, collaboration and openness;
- They are biased towards learning through problem solving;
- They generally internalize their learning only if motivated by intrinsic factors;
- They need to see high practical relevance if their learning is to be committed (Knowles 1984).

In accepting the concept of andragogy we imply an acceptance of the importance of more focused and individualized learning strategies, rather than simply treating everyone homogeneously as a group with common needs and experiences. Inevitably, while this idea does not mean an end to collective learning experiences which can offer valuable opportunities for shared reflection, it has considerable implications for the nature of learning activities and teaching styles we employ.

Reflection and reflexivity

So-called 'new learning' approaches emphasize the value of reflection and review – an essential aspect of continuing professional development. However, the ease with which we tend to use the terms 'reflection', 'review' and 'reflexivity', along with the notion of 'lifelong learning', sometimes inhibits rather than enhances our own understanding of their nature and the processes involved. Schön (1983) has suggested that, in effect, our emphasis on 'reflection' stems from crises of confidence regarding our professional knowledge, while for Duignan (1989) reflection involves acquiring 'a vocabulary of practice' which facilitates thinking about earlier actions, helping us to evaluate responses and plan future actions. Implicit within both views is the need for opportunities to identify patterns of action, time for development and the scope to adopt a professional stance rather than just show basic 'competence'.

In adopting a working distinction between 'reflection' (e.g. reviewing and analysing situations or issues) and 'reflexive action' (e.g. developing an action plan based upon reflection), it is possible to see that creating opportunities for shared reflection has the potential to support observed and shared teaching. More importantly, however, it enables alternatives to be evaluated and future plans to be made through collaborative review and joint reflexive action.

Hutchinson (1995) also notes how one school has developed an 'integrated reflection' approach in its school development process, so that reflexivity helps to set the pace and content of organizational change: using the notion that 'if you write it down, it really does make you think your way through', it hints at both the simplicity of approach and its perceived evaluative merits. Another school researched by Glover and Law (1996) offers its staff a day for 'structured reflection' once a year, when 'personal investigations' are pursued by individuals or groups of staff who focus on linking corporate and personal expectations. Staff endeavour to analyse the current professional

Table 14.3   A five-level model of reflective practice

Reflection-in-action	Rapid reaction (instinctive and immediate)
	Repair (habitual, pausing for thought, on the spot)
Reflection-in-action	Review (time to reassess: over hours or days)
	Research (systematic, sharply focused: over weeks or months)
Reflection-about-action	Retheorize and reformulate (abstract, vigorous, clearly formulated: over months or years)

Source: after Day *et al*. (1993).

context within which they work and to 'second-guess' the future scenario and the actions needed to be successful, thus beginning to develop, refine and absorb an integrated vocabulary of change which incorporates a focus on reflection. This leads us to see that reflection is, in itself, a learning process and that reflection-on-action actively helps us to prepare for future similar circumstances (Duignan 1989).

It may be helpful to see reflection as part of an overarching process of lifelong learning. For example, Day *et al*. (1993) have identified a five-stage model of reflective practice (see Table 14.3), which is built around both Schön's (1987) and Griffiths and Tann's (1992) work. It outlines a possible learning route from reflection-in-action through reflection-on-action to reflection-about-action.

● Professionals and professionalism

No definition of a profession – whether through the promulgation of a code of conduct or by other means – is likely to be internalised in that profession's own consciousness of itself, unless it corresponds to the profession's own deepest intuitions of the service it has to offer and the values which are consonant with that service.

(Rodger 1995: 84)

In making a case for a General Teaching Council (GTC), Tomlinson (1995: 63) argues that 'teaching feels like a profession'. This is, however, no longer enough – even if it ever was. During the last quarter of the twentieth century those working in caring and state-service sectors like education, health, social work and the civil service have experienced a developing critique by successive governments against their 'professionalism' and autonomy. During the past few decades, these occupational groups have frequently been labelled as unproductive, as not contributing sufficiently to either the maintenance of 'professional standards' or national economic prosperity. Some have even been deemed 'parasitic' upon private-sector wealth creation (Perkin 1989).

While the New Labour government's rhetoric stresses support for a 'new professionalism' in teaching (DfEE 1998c), educationists remain sceptical about what this might mean in reality, given the emphasis also placed on issues like performance-related pay, line management, inspection and so on. The extent to which the new managerialist policy thrust actually supports or undermines teacher professionalism remains a key and unresolved issue. So what does it mean to be a professional?

Hoyle and John (1995) have argued that the term *profession* itself is 'an essentially contested concept'. Indeed, they suggest there is considerable evidence that 'professions are more easily instanced than defined'. However, the term itself retains a particular resonance among educationists, especially in a policy context where the establishment of a long-awaited GTC has long been anticipated with some impatience and is only new becoming a reality – seen as offering teachers a hoped-for parity with the General Medical Council (GMC). Hoyle and John (1995: 159) remind us, however, that in reality the term 'professional' hides a multiplicity of perspectives:

> the unitary notion of a 'professional community' masks a vast array of competing positions which characterise a service profession such as teaching (Liston and Zeichner 1990). In this sense, the role of teacher education is never static but is constantly changing according to the particular educational traditions that predominate at any particular historical juncture.

Nevertheless, despite its inherently problematic nature, the term 'profession' continues to be valued by educationists as both a concept-in-use and a theoretical underpinning. In Chapter 1 we acknowledged the difficulties faced by senior education managers in maintaining 'leading professional' roles alongside 'chief executive' roles: this leads us to consider what being a professional involves and, indeed, what the term 'profession' means. According to Hoyle (1980: 45), a profession:

- performs a crucial social function;
- demands considerable skills for use in routine and especially non-routine situations;
- requires its members to draw on a body of systematic knowledge;
- requires members to undertake a lengthy period of study which inculcates professional values;
- focuses on clients' interests and has a code of ethics;
- enables professionals to make their own judgements *vis-à-vis* appropriate practice;
- rewards training, responsibility and client-centredness, with high prestige and high levels of remuneration.

Linked with this, Garrett and Bowles (1997) focus on three aspects of being a professional in education:

- a professional will have undergone a lengthy period of professional training in a body of abstract knowledge (Goode 1960; Hughes 1985; Coulson 1986) and will have experience in the field;
- a professional is controlled by a code of ethics and professional values (Barber 1963, 1978; Hughes 1985; Coulson 1986);
- a professional is committed to the core business of the organization, i.e. the quality of student learning (Coulson 1986).

Despite the above framework for professionalism, at a practical level there is clearly considerable continuing disagreement between those who see the ongoing restructuring of education as *enhancing* the prospects for teacher professionalism (D. Hargreaves 1994) and those who see the post-1988 scenario as *diminishing* them, indicating a 'disrespect and disregard . . . for teachers themselves' (A. Hargreaves 1994: 6). While professional models of teacher accountability are premised on assumptions about the fundamentals of teacher autonomy, A. Hargreaves's critique of managerial models argues that managerialism strips away teacher professionalism and teachers' opportunities to use professional judgement, leaving them with little more than 'technician' status.

The opposing view is, however, that the current education project is constructed around what Millett (the outgoing Chief Executive of the TTA) has described as the 'reprofessionalization' of teaching and what the Green Paper on the 'new three Rs' – recruitment, retention and reward – calls 'a new professionalism' (DfEE 1998c: 13), implicitly registering a view that teaching's current status is no better than what has been described as a 'semi-profession' (Hoyle and John 1995). Clearly, issues of 'professionalism' remain fundamental to educational leaders' – and teachers' – self-image and perceptions of role and responsibilities. They are also reminiscent of the tensions outlined in Hughes's (1988) identification of the 'leading professional' and 'chief executive' strands. As Whitty *et al.* (1998) have noted, it remains unclear whether the current 'managerial project' is aimed at 'professionalizing' or 'deprofessionalizing' education: as they acknowledge, we are witnessing 'a struggle among different stakeholders over the definition of teacher professionalism and professionality for the twenty-first century' (Whitty *et al.* 1998: 65).

REFLECTION

How far do you consider that teaching has been deprofessionalized during the past decade? What evidence do you have to support your conclusion?

Eraut (1993) argues that, as adult learners, being aware of our own and others' perceptions is vital if we are to develop fully as professionals. In order to establish our 'professional expertise' as teachers, we need to acquire an appropriate balance of knowledge (e.g. subject base), skills (e.g. class management and differentiation) and attitudes (e.g. flexibility according to context). For him, professionalism and quality in teaching derives from a mixture of ingredients, including observation, stakeholder responses, feedback and outcomes or results. For Eraut, the quality of skilled professional behaviour can be improved through:

- gaining feedback from independent observers;
- recording and reviewing our classroom behaviour;
- developing awareness of the impact of our actions;
- observing others in action;
- expanding our repertoire of routines;
- using the information we have gathered to optimize our performance.

If these aspects are to have long-term significance, however, Eraut recommends that we must:

- read about, experience and discuss deliberative processes;
- possess interpersonal skills to manage deliberative activities;
- have a personal and group repertoire of concepts, practice and skills;
- have a recognition that thinking skills of a high order are needed to tackle practical problems.

Essentially, Eraut argues that self-development derives from both self-knowledge *and* self-management. There is the danger, however, that we may find this notion somewhat problematic to comprehend because the concepts themselves are effectively open to wide interpretation.

 ## Life and career cycles

If a key objective of professional development is to sustain teachers as professionals, it is important to recognize that individuals' personal and professional needs differ (sometimes widely), depending on age, career stage and aspirations. Undoubtedly, professional growth and development is influenced by the various life stages through which we pass. Erikson (1977) has argued that each phase offers both challenges and opportunities for development (see Table 14.4), thus facilitating greater psychological resilience and social competence. Support for personal growth may be highly variable and even discontinuous, often leaving us with difficult issues to resolve as we move into new stages.

To be fully effective, those responsible for managing professional development may find it helpful to take into account colleagues' individual perceptions and stages of development: the embittered or resigned (and often relatively senior) members of staff who feel they have not achieved their true potential can be (admittedly somewhat stereotypical) cases in point. Bolam (1990) has identified five stages relevant to teachers both in individual posts and across their professional careers:

- preparatory (applying for a new post);
- appointment (selection or rejection);

Table 14.4 Life cycle stages in human development

Age	Stage	Characteristics
0–2	Infancy	Trust v. mistrust
2–4	Early childhood	Autonomy v. shame and doubt
5–7	Play age	Initiative v. guilt
6–12	School age	Industry v. inferiority
13–19	Adolescence	Identity v. role confusion
20–30	Young adulthood	Intimacy v. isolation
30–60	Maturity	Generativity v. stagnation
Over 60	Old age	Integrity v. despair

- induction (the first two years in post);
- in-service (3–5, 6–10 or 11+ years in post);
- transitional (promotion, redeployment, moving towards retirement).

Within any educational organization, staff are likely to be at a variety of career stages, and this will create the demand for considerable diversity of focus and response to changing professional needs and demands based on individual career perceptions. Griffin (1987) has argued that we need to recognize that professional development begins when the appointment is made, since an individual's capacity to interact with others is, for example, a ready identifier of development needs – even at interview. Moreover, Leithwood (1992b) articulates the need for professional and career-planning development from the earliest moment, arguing that the planning process needs to take into account key career stages:

- *Teachers as trainees*: developing the ability to teach and manage classrooms.
- *Teachers in initial career stages*: developing classroom confidence and flexibility.
- *Teachers as administrators*: developing greater subject leadership and responsibility.
- *Teacher as policy makers*: developing management skills across the institution.

Although those endeavouring to climb promotional ladders may have readily identifiable and clearly defined development needs, those without clearly defined 'ambition profiles' or a promotional focus often have at least as great (and sometimes greater) professional needs. While the TTA's development of national standards for different career stages (initial training, induction, SEN, subject leadership, aspiring headteacher, newly inducted headteacher and serving headteacher) may be interpreted as being supportive of the concept of a 'professional portfolio' and 'professional development continuum', the danger is that it may, by implication, come to ignore those whose needs are potentially even more demanding, e.g. those who are less readily pigeonholed in professional development terms or those who are professionally 'discouraged' or even 'disenchanted'. Even in such situations, Day (1996: 124) argues that personal development profiles are valuable because they 'foster the development of teachers as whole persons throughout their careers . . . recognising that teachers are not technicians, but that teaching is bound up with their lives, their histories, the kind of persons they have been and have become.'

ACTION

Briefly review your career over the past five years and evaluate how far (a) planned and (b) unplanned professional development has supported your particular career stage(s). Who had operational responsibility for these opportunities?

As Whitaker (1993a: 47–8) has noted, those managing professional development need to take individual life and career cycles into account because they are:

essential cultural issues that need to be acknowledged and responded to. The links between the personal and the professional will be blurred and they are not easily separated. Only by making our needs and aspirations clear and explicit can we create the pool of information from which sensible and appropriate decisions can be made and in order for managers and leaders to build a sensitive awareness of developmental needs and differences.

Skills, competence and capability

Despite its increasingly high profile in management development, there is no clear agreement among educationists (or indeed among those in commerce) about what constitutes 'competence' or 'competency'. Despite this, 'competences', or 'capabilities' as clusters of competences are sometimes described (see for example Eraut 1994; Bennett 1997), are now a central feature of government education policy initiatives, even though some educationists argue that 'what we have is not a *crisis of competence* as alleged of our schools and teachers, but rather a deep-seated *crisis of confidence* going to the very heart of the system of Western capitalism' (Smyth 1991: xii, original italics). However, while acknowledging the increasing emphasis placed on skills and behaviour over self-confidence and knowledge, others (e.g. Everard 1990) have argued that professional development strategies would benefit from improved ways of identifying and developing competences for specific roles.

Competence frameworks initially developed in Britain have been driven largely by a business management development focus (see, for example, reports by Handy 1987; Constable and McCormick 1987) and were established through, among others, the Management Charter Initiative (MCI 1995). These developments stress the identification of *satisfactory* performance, while American competence (or, more precisely, 'competency') frameworks (e.g. McBer's) have focused on determining *superior* performance levels (see, for example, Boyatzis 1982).

Despite these distinctions, Bennett (1997) suggests that the concepts of skill, competence and capability 'are nested within each other', with clusters of skills comprising competence and clusters of competence comprising capability. Even so, much confusion and debate remains around the meaning of 'competence'. Pollard and Tann (1994: 64) offer what might be seen as a generic definition, describing it as a 'combination of knowledge, understanding and skill as well as the ability to apply them in particular situations. This includes motives, traits, attitudes and aspects of a teacher's self-image and role.' This definition does, however, mask some of the differences found between the two major approaches currently in favour.

While acknowledging the difficulties in reaching agreed definitions, we explore some of the working definitions currently in use, giving a flavour of the differences between the various approaches. We consider, first, some 'working assumptions' behind *competence-based* and *competency-based* approaches. According to Trotter and Ellison (1997: 40), *competence* 'is about what you have to be able to do in a job to satisfy specified standards', while *competency* is 'the predisposition to behave in ways shown to be associated with the achievement of successful outcomes' (Esp 1993: 61). Citing Hay

Table 14.5 Competence and competency approaches

Competence approaches (e.g. MCI)	Competency approaches (e.g. McBer, NEAC)
Emphasis on *competences*	Emphasis on *competencies*
Focused on *outputs* (achieving tasks) to specified minimum standards, resulting in a *satisfactory* performance	Focused on *inputs* (personal qualities) which individuals bring to a job, resulting in *superior* performance
Need to be demonstrated at a certain level for satisfactory performance	Need to be demonstrated at a 'threshold' level for superior performance
Are either possessed or not: competence cannot be 'partially' possessed	Can be possessed at several levels; can inform behaviour consciously or unconsciously, or as skills
Are related to a job's characteristics	Are related to the person doing the job
Are related to the roles which make up the job	Are related to the clusters of actions which make up the job
Each level of competence includes and extends competences shown at earlier levels of seniority	Does not automatically incorporate the competencies needed for superior performance at an earlier level

Group/McBer's definition, Trotter and Ellison (1997: 40) describe *competencies* (i.e. those derived through *competency* approaches) as 'the underlying characteristics which enable someone to perform a job better in more situations, more often, with better results. Competencies are those factors that distinguish the best from the rest in a given role. They are not the tasks of the job, they are what enable people to do the tasks.' Table 14.5 identifies some of the likely differences in approach between competence and competency approaches.

Reflecting the growing stress on performance and measurable success, both TTA and Ofsted have emphasized that demonstrable 'competence' is fundamental for quality leadership at various organizational levels (TTA 1996b; Ofsted 1997a). For example, the TTA's early consultation documents on its proposed national standards indicated that headteachers would be expected to 'successfully build and manage effective teams which plan and set targets to raise expectations, improve pupil achievement, increase teacher effectiveness and add value to previous school improvement' (TTA 1996c: 8), while subject leaders (e.g. heads of department) would need to 'express and instill clear educational values; motivate and inspire pupils, staff, parents, governors and the wider community; anticipate problems, collect and weigh evidence, make judgment and take decisions' (TTA 1996d: 11). The nearer the classroom, the more specific and limited in scope competences are likely to be.

Although TTA's national standards for headteacher leadership and subject leadership are indicative of the growth of a competence-based training focus, the Agency's keenness to avoid accusations of simplistic and mechanistic approaches can be seen in its endeavour to cluster competences together (as capabilities), reflecting, for example, the McBer/competency approach – a strategy already adapted relatively successfully to an English context via the National Educational Assessment Centre (see Jones and O'Sullivan 1997, for example), where the identification of effective school leadership has been based on an analysis of performance through twelve competencies in four areas (see Table 14.6).

Table 14.6 National Educational Assessment Centre competencies for successful school leaders

Administrative (areas 1–4)	Problem analysis; judgement; organizational ability; decisiveness
Interpersonal (areas 5–7)	Leadership; sensitivity; stress tolerance
Communicative (areas 8–9)	Oral communication; written communication
Personal breadth (areas 10–12)	Range of interest; personal motivation; educational values

Despite the growth in their use, both competence- and competency-based approaches have been subject to criticism (see, for example, Riches 1997b; Trotter and Ellison 1997). While both kinds of approach are attacked for their apparent undervaluing of the strengths deriving from collegiality and the collective action of groups and teams, each approach is also individually subject to criticism. For example, the competence-based approach is censured for:

- assuming that jobs are static and unchanging and only aiming at minimum (i.e. threshold) standards;
- adopting a reductionist approach, 'analysing competence to bits' (Tuxford 1989: 17);
- emphasizing the job rather than the person doing it (Spencer and Spencer 1993: 103);
- tending to make tasks too detailed to be practical;
- not differentiating between routine and really significant tasks;
- requiring too much assessment and making the collection of evidence time-consuming, onerous and not developmental;
- fragmenting competences, thus making 'objective' measurements unreliable and often impossible;
- being inflexible and overly prescriptive in use, especially at more senior management levels;
- being costly to implement and slow to progress.

Although subject to some of the same criticisms as the competence-based approaches, the competency-based approach is most often criticized for:

- failing to provide a ready fit between competencies and management work (Burgoyne 1989);
- being insufficiently flexible to cope with the 'shifting boundaries' of managerial work;
- failing to encourage thoughtful approaches but, instead, stimulating 'clone-like' and imitative behaviour (i.e. too behaviourist in approach);
- allowing the focus on individual competencies to undervalue collective efforts and the development of organizational competency.

Despite their successes in business – and in some areas of education – competence frameworks remain criticized for their heavy reliance on 'can do/can't do' approaches, even if the accreditation structures are based on role responsibilities which, at least in theory, facilitate more consistency and accuracy of assessment. It remains clear that the concepts of 'professionalism' (teacher autonomy) and 'competences' (teacher accountability) sit uneasily together.

While debate continues regarding the flaws surrounding the various competence approaches, there is also a growing acceptance of the need for demonstrable and 'evidence-based' approaches to professional development, in which practitioners are given opportunities to show what they can do as well as what they say they can do. This emphasis is evident in the stress now placed on skills-based and competence-led approaches throughout education. As we have seen, it has a high profile in: the use of educational assessment centres (a focus reinforced by the New Labour government's announcement of a national college for educational leadership); the construction of a competence-led National Curriculum for Initial Teacher Training (TTA 1998c, DfEE 1998b); the use of 'teaching' test situations as part of interview procedures for teaching posts; the use of observation as part of appraisal; the grading of teachers in Ofsted inspections; and the demand that candidates for leadership posts demonstrate their practical leadership skills (via presentations, decision-making exercises and round-table discussions/meetings).

Despite the difficulties inherent in what are frequently 'one-off' situations, the *demonstration* of what you can do is now a central element of success, whether you are a beginning teacher or a practised institutional leader. This does not necessarily mean, however, that a competence focus needs to supersede or replace other aspects of judgement, even if this is a danger. Opportunities remain to integrate competences with other less rigid approaches. For example, in training teachers, Whitty *et al*. (1998: 331) report that 'official competences' are effectively contextualized by practitioners, thus leaving 'little objection to the idea of competences among course leaders, because they felt that reflective competences could be added to the official list in order to sustain a broader definition of professionality.' This attitude appears to remain a feature within other professional scenarios, where judging 'raw' competences *adds to* the range of information rather than *replaces* no less valuable but more subtle, nuanced and less readily quantifiable processes. Such a balance is, nevertheless, potentially precarious and difficult to sustain.

Evaluation issues

The evaluation of staff development is complex precisely because it is about people.

(Middlewood 1997b: 196)

Even though it is generally acknowledged as important, the process of evaluation is too often a weak link in effecting change – whether in relation to individual professional development, to organizational development, to classroom practice or to other wider aspects of professional educational practice. The reconfiguration of educational structures and relationships in recent times has, however, brought with it a new emphasis on the nature and role of evaluation in the broadest terms.

Neave (1988) has argued that we are witnessing the rise of the 'evaluative state': policies once considered to be short-termist responses to mid-1970s oil crises and 1980s financial crises have, he argues, now taken on a much longer-term strategic importance in the context of endemic and chaotic development (e.g. Peters 1987). Although Neave suggests that the 'evaluative state' is not necessarily linked to any particular ideological perspective, he asserts that evaluatory practice of some kind has always been a feature – whether at government, institutional and individual levels. Educational policy realignment has given evaluation a greater currency, linking it with the strong emphasis on *outputs* and judgements based on performance outcomes and value-for-money concerns. Even so, Neave asserts that it is vital to distinguish between evaluation for *system maintenance* and evaluation for *strategic change*.

While much evaluation undertaken by managers – whether in education or elsewhere – is used for system maintenance (and tends to be justificatory of past practices), it is evaluation focused on strategic change which is both more important and more difficult to achieve. Evaluation for its own sake is of limited value: it needs to be less of a 'bolt-on' activity and more part of continuous institutional and individual improvement if it is to be fully effective (Russell and Reid 1997). While it may frequently become a concern in relation to professional development, its role as part of organizational and individual change within the context of national change is fundamental.

The strategic establishment of more formalized CPD structures and accountabilities (TTA 1998d) emphasizes the importance of an evaluative record of staff experiences and databases of provision and identifies:

- the personnel used, their competence, knowledge etc.;
- the working relationships, among and between clients and providers;
- value-for-money concerns, shown through a cost–benefit equation;
- the degree to which providers offer relevant, challenging opportunities, supportive of overall and ongoing school improvement concerns.

The evaluation of CPD has traditionally focused on off-site or single events and generally comprises only brief, subjective comments. When done well, evaluation incorporates more structured records of content, delivery and value, which then inform both termly and annual quality assurance data which can act as a stimulus to further development and professional learning; although, in CPD, evaluation is too often unsystematic, partial and limited in scope, being undertaken only in somewhat *ad hoc* circumstances (Law and Glover 1995). However, if handled well, it can become an essential management tool and component of organizational and personal renewal processes. Even though evaluation is increasingly recognized as a key link in the development chain, Baxter and Chambers (1998: 31–2) argue that:

> It is all too easy for the school's systems and culture to hinder rather than help the translation of staff learning into pupil achievement. The purpose of evaluation is to seek out the strengths and weaknesses of this intricate process in order to ensure that the development of staff has a positive impact on the school and its pupils . . . using evaluation as part of the developmental process, rather than divorced from it, has been liberating for many schools, enabling them to tackle evaluation with greater confidence.

Middlewood (1996) suggests that an evaluative hierarchy of learning can result from CPD activities, with each element contributing to a continuum of professional practice:

- reaction (to the learning event);
- learning (of those involved);
- changes (in professional practice);
- impact (of the changes on the individual and his or her immediate environment, e.g. classroom);
- impact (of the change on the organization).

Stake *et al.* (1987) argue that it is vital, at the earliest planning stage, that those managing professional development should develop the capacity to ask 'foreshadowing questions' relating to the evaluation process. For example, it is important to ask:

- Is what needs to be retained (as well as what needs to be changed) being given sufficient attention in this development activity?
- Is our staff development activity focused on those who most need it or on those who are already committed and 'expert'?
- How far do we agree about what needs to be changed and developed?
- How far are we building practitioner reflection into our staff and professional development opportunities?

We also need to adopt realistic perspectives on what is achievable, while keeping an eye on longer-term goals. Although it is valuable for evaluation processes to be congruent with more 'global' organizational development processes (e.g. institutional development planning), there is a danger that this can become 'a counsel of perfection', which assumes that a coherent and rational approach to development is in place that allows for regular, staged reviews and planning points. The reality is often very different, with evaluation becoming a problem-solving activity. As Fullan (1993: 26) notes,

> we cannot develop effective responses to complex situations unless we actively seek and confront the real problems which are in fact difficult to solve. Problems are our friends because it is only through immersing ourselves in problems that we can come up with creative solutions. Problems are the route to deeper change and deeper satisfaction. In this sense, effective organizations 'embrace problems' rather than avoid them.

While experience may demonstrate the difficulties involved in integrating planning and evaluation cycles, the *endeavour* to create some degree of consonance may provide valuable opportunities for learning as well as some synergy of outcomes.

Towards a culture of professional development

[It] is the ongoing, informal personal relations among staff which provide the cement.
(Maden and Hillman 1996: 346)

The importance of establishing a productive 'culture' and 'climate' for effective management and leadership cannot be underestimated. This is particularly
the case in terms of managing and supporting professional development – a
core issue for all organizations, whether educational or not. Even the most
efficient and well organized professional development programme is likely to
be ineffective if it is not *rooted* within a professional climate that can nurture,
sustain and enhance it. According to Drucker (1988b), the full benefits of
professional development become possible only when a collaborative culture
exists which demonstrates:

- explicit and clearly articulated organizational values;
- a holistic development focus;
- a development focus where the integration of theory and practice informs
  future actions;
- a focus on the continuous improvement of both processes and outcomes,
  for both individuals and the organization itself.

Drucker's emphasis on collaboration reflects Hoyle's (1974) articulation of
the importance of developing 'extended professionality' in teaching over a
more narrowly defined 'restricted professionality' (see Table 14.7).

While educational restructuring has articulated an ethos of centralized
control and delegated responsibility alongside a more prescriptive agenda

Table 14.7 Restricted and extended professionality

Restricted professionality	*Extended professionality*
Skills derived from experience	Skills derived by mediating experience with theory
Limited perspectives based on the immediate time and place of work	Broader perspectives based in wider social and educational context
Focus is on isolated classroom events	Focus on classroom events in relation to institutional policies and goals
Unidimensional and introspective about teaching methods	Comparative approach to teaching methods – shares with others
Personal autonomy valued	Professional collaboration valued
Limited involvement in non-teaching professional activities	Strong involvement in non-teaching professional activities
Limited engagement with professional literature	Regular engagement with professional literature
In-service focus largely confined to 'practical' courses	In-service focus broadly based, including engagement with 'theoretical' concerns
Teaching viewed as largely 'intuitive' activity	Teaching viewed as largely 'rational' activity

Source: based on Hoyle (1986).

determining teachers' work (Ball 1990, 1994; A. Hargreaves 1994; Gewirtz *et al.* 1995), there is also a growing acknowledgement that teacher development is now being taken more seriously by policy makers – as evidenced by recent DfEE and TTA policy drives (DfEE 1997a, 1998c; TTA 1998d). As Hoyle and John (1995: 123) have noted, 'over the past twenty years the professionality of most teachers has been extended. A culture of professional development has begun to emerge in teaching', supported by:

- an increased funding commitment to in-service training (even if it remains precarious);
- a growing emphasis on school-focused activities which entails greater professional collaboration;
- the increasing importance of professional development as a factor in promotion.

Nias *et al.* (1989) have also found that a well-founded collaborative culture provides a strong and highly effective platform for promoting genuine debate and for dealing productively with change issues – even where disagreements existed over specific development plans. However, despite the growing support for a collectivity of approach, it is clear that a delicate *balance* needs to be struck between individual and collective needs – an issue which, once again, demands effective leadership skills. In building a culture of professional development and encouraging collaborative professional approaches, it remains vital that individuality of approach and emphasis is not sacrificed but that there is *complementarity* of approach. As A. Hargreaves (1994: 183) has asserted, 'Vibrant teacher cultures should be able to avoid the professional limitations of teacher individualism, while embracing the creative potential of teacher individuality.'

● Suggestions for further reading

Bolam, R. (1997) Management development for headteachers: retrospect and prospect, *Educational Management and Administration*, 25(3), 265–84.

Glover, D. and Law, S. (1996) *Managing Professional Development in Education*. London: Kogan Page.

Harland, J., Kinder, K. and Keys, W. (1993) *Restructuring INSET: Privatization and Its Alternatives*. Slough: NFER.

Kydd, L., Crawford, M. and Riches, C. (1997) *Professional Development for Educational Management*. Buckingham: Open University Press.

Thompson, M. (1997) *Professional Ethics and the Teacher: towards a General Teaching Council*. Stoke on Trent: Trentham Books.

Tomlinson, H. (ed.) (1997) *Managing Continuing Professional Development in Schools*. London: Paul Chapman Publishing/BEMAS.

Postscript

As educationists face continuous and endemic pressures for both personal and system change, it is clear that the need *and* the demand for supportive leadership and effective management skills in schools and colleges will become ever stronger – particularly if pupil achievement and teacher motivation are to be maintained and enhanced. Whatever the rhetoric surrounding the concept of the 'self-managing' institution, the reality is that those responsible for supporting the education of others will, in future, have exceptionally high expectations placed upon their professional resources and skills.

In a context where the 'New' Labour government has committed itself to supporting 'education, education, education' – with an emphasis on 'standards not structures' – the demands created by a rapidly changing technological and professional environment merely serve to reiterate the need for teachers to be effective learners themselves, as well as capable managers. Teachers and educational leaders are expected to help others make sense of a complex world in which there is less predictability and more uncertainty – a major challenge which requires high-level skills, knowledge and understanding. The creation of so multifaceted a role can only be built on a strong platform of professional respect, where the emphasis is on ongoing *teacher renewal* rather than continuous *system reform* (Hargreaves and Evans 1997).

While educational leaders and teachers cannot necessarily explain a dramatically changing world, they can – with due personal recognition and professional support – become effective role models for others. Headteachers and principals have a particular responsibility in this respect, since, as Oldroyd (1996: 19) argues:

> Leading by example is a powerful process of modelling positive attitudes and a commitment to and belief in success . . . To become a model of positive, success-oriented thinking is then a key role of the leader of an organization striving for success and high performance from the rest of its members, from the least talented student to the caretaker.

In this respect, then, educational leaders can become 'head learners' (Barth

1990) and begin to share questions, offer ideas and support colleagues, pupils and students as they explore issues and endeavour to make sense of a dynamic world. This brings us back to where we started and our argument that headteachers and principals are capable of integrating 'leading professional' and 'chief executive' roles to create a synergy of leadership purpose, and that, within the context of a more scrutinized and market-focused educational climate, such an integration is essential.

Management skills are necessary, but not sufficient, for leadership success. Educational leaders in the twenty-first century need a fundamental underpinning of professionalism and pedagogy, overlaid by effective leadership and management skills and knowledge, capability and understanding, if they are to gain commitment and initiate success: 'It is because they understand the pedagogy, because they understand the intricacies of how a school works, that they can use their management most effectively' (Mortimore 1998, para. 42).

Some three decades ago, in a prescient comment, Alvin Toffler (1970: 108) highlighted the challenges which educational leaders must anticipate today and face tomorrow:

> Knowledge will grow increasingly perishable. Today's fact becomes tomorrow's misinformation. This is no argument against learning facts or data – far from it. But a society in which the individual constantly changes his job, place of residence, his social ties and so forth places an enormous premium on learning efficiency. Tomorrow's schools must therefore teach not merely data, but ways to manipulate it. Students must learn how to discard old ideas, how and when to replace them. They must, in short, learn how to learn.

Bibliography

Abbott, J. (1994) *Learning Makes Sense: Re-creating Education for a Changing Future.* Letchworth: Education 2001.

Acker, S. (1994) *Gendered Education: Sociological Reflections on Women, Teaching and Feminism.* Buckingham: Open University Press.

ACSET (1984) *The In-Service Education, Training and Professional Development of School Teachers.* Report of the Advisory Committee on the Supply and Education of Teachers. London: DES.

Adair, J. (1983) *Effective Leadership.* London: Pan.

Adair, J. (1986) *Effective Teambuilding.* London: Pan.

Adair, J. (1988a) *Effective Time Management.* London: Pan.

Adair, J. (1988b) *The Effective Communicator.* London: The Industrial Society.

Adams, J. S. (1965) Inequality in social exchange. In L. Berkowitz (ed.) *Advances in Experimental Social Psychology.* New York: Academic Press.

Adelman, C. (1984) *The Politics and Ethics of Evaluation.* London: Croom Helm.

Adey, K. and Jones, J. (1997) The professional development co-ordinator: obstacles to effective role performance, *Educational Management and Administration*, 25(2), 133–44.

Adler, M., Petch, A. and Tweedie, J. (1989) *Parental Choice and Educational Policy.* Edinburgh: Edinburgh University Press.

Al Khalifa, E. (1992) Management by halves; women teachers and school management. In N. Bennett, M. Crawford and C. Riches (eds) *Managing Change in Education: Individual and Organizational Perspectives.* London: Paul Chapman Publishing.

Aldrich, H. and Mindlin, S. (1978) Uncertainty and dependence: two perspectives on environment. In L. Karplk (ed.) *Organization and Environment: Theory, Issues and Reality.* Beverly Hills, CA: Sage.

Anthony, P. (1994) *Managing Culture.* Buckingham: Open University Press.

Argyris, C. (1957) *Personality and Organizations.* London: Harper and Row.

Argyris, C. (1964) *Integrating the Individual and the Organization.* New York: Wiley.

Argyris, C. (1991) Teaching smart people how to learn, *Harvard Business Review*, May/June, 99–109.

Argyris, C. and Schön, D. (1981) *Organizational Learning: A Theory of Action Perspective.* London: Addison-Wesley.

Armstrong, M. (1988) *A Handbook of Human Resource Management.* London: Kogan Page.

Armstrong, M. (1993) *A Handbook of Personnel Management Practice*, 4th edn. London: Kogan Page.

Armstrong, M. (1994) *How to Be an Even Better Manager*. London: Kogan Page.

Arnold, J. and Hope, T. (1983) *Accounting for Management Decisions*. Hemel Hempstead: Prentice Hall.

Asch, S. (1951) Effects of group pressure upon the modification and distortion of judgements. In H. Geutzknow (ed.) *Groups, Leadership and Men*. New York: Carnegie.

Aspinwall, K. and Pedlar, M. (1997) Schools as learning organisations. In B. Fidler, S. Russell and T. Simkins (eds) *Choices for Self-Managing Schools: Autonomy and Accountability*. London: Paul Chapman Publishing.

Astuto, T. and Clark, D. (1980) Achieving effective schools. In E. Hoyle and J. Megarry (eds) *The Professional Development of Teachers: World Yearbook of Education*. London: Kogan Page.

Audit Commission (1984) *Code of Local Government Audit Practice for England and Wales*. London: HMSO.

Audit Commission (1985) *Audit Commission Handbook: A Guide to Economy, Efficiency and Effectiveness*. London: Audit Commission.

Audit Commission (1989a) *Assessing Quality in Education*. London: The Audit Commission.

Audit Commission (1989b) *Losing an Empire, Finding a Role: The LEA of the Future*. London: The Audit Commission/HMSO.

Audit Commission (1991) *The Management of Primary Schools*. London: HMSO.

Babington Smith, B. and Farrell, B. (1979) *Training in Small Groups*. Oxford: Pergamon.

Bagley, C., Woods, P. and Glatter, R. (1996) Scanning the market: school strategies for discovering parental perspectives, *Educational Management and Administration*, 24(2), 125–38.

Baker, K. (1993) *The Turbulent Years: My Life in Politics*. London: Faber.

Ball, S. J. (1987) *The Micropolitics of the School*. London: Routledge.

Ball, S. J. (1990) *Politics and Policy Making in Education: Explorations in Policy Sociology*. London: Routledge.

Ball, S. J. (1994) *Education Reform: A Critical and Post-structural Approach*. Buckingham: Open University Press.

Barber, B. (1963) Some problems in the sociology of the professions, *Daedalus*, 92, 669–88.

Barber, B. (1978) Control and responsibility in the powerful professions, *Political Science Quarterly*, 93, 599–615.

Barber, M. (1994) *Young People and their Attitudes to School: an Interim Report of a Research Project in the Centre for Successful Schools*. Keele: Keele University.

Barber, M. (1997) *A Reading Revolution: How Can We Teach Every Child to Read Well?* Preliminary report of the Literacy Task Force. London: DfEE.

Barber, M., Evans, A. and Johnson, M. (1995) *An Evaluation of the National Scheme of School Teacher Appraisal*. London: HMSO.

Barker, D. (1980) *Transactional Analysis and Training*. Aldershot: Gower Publishing.

Baron, R. A. and Greenberg, J. (1990) *Behaviour in Organizations*, 3rd edn. London: Allyn and Bacon.

Barth, R. (1990) *Improving School from Within: Teachers, Parents and Principals Can Make the Difference*. San Francisco: Jossey-Bass.

Bartlett, L. (1991) Rationality and the management of curriculum change, *Educational Management and Administration*, 19(1), 20–9.

Bass, B. and Vaughan, M. (1966) *Training in Industry: The Management of Learning*. London: Tavistock.

Baxter, G. and Chambers, M. (1998) Evaluating staff development, *Professional Development Today*, 2(1), 31–8.

Beare, H., Caldwell, B. and Millikan, R. (1989) *Creating an Excellent School: Some New Management Techniques*. London: Routledge.

Beare, H. and Lowe Boyd, W. (eds) (1993) *Restructuring Schools: An International Perspective on the Movement to Transform the Control and Performance of Schools*. London: Falmer Press.

Beare, H. and Slaughter, R. (1993) *Education for the Twenty-first Century*. London: Routledge.

BECTA (British Educational Communications and Technology Agency) (1998) *Connecting Schools Networking People*. Coventry: BECTA.

Belbin, R. M. (1981) *Management Teams: Why They Succeed or Fail*. Oxford: Heinemann.

Belbin, R. M. (1993) *Team Roles at Work*. Oxford: Butterworth Heinemann.

Belbin, R. M. (1996) *The Coming Shape of the Organization*. Cambridge: Belbin Associates.

Bell, J. and Harrison, B. T. (eds) (1995) *Vision and Values in Managing Education: Successful Leadership Principles and Practice*. London: David Fulton.

Bell, L. (1992) *Managing Teams in Secondary Schools*. London: HMSO.

Bell, L. and Maher, P. (1986) *Leading a Pastoral Team*. Oxford: Blackwell.

Bell, L. and Rhodes, C. (1995) *The Skills of Primary School Management*. London: Routledge.

Benne, K. and Sheats, P. (1948) Functional roles of group members, *Journal of Social Issues*, 4, 41–9.

Bennett, N. (1976) *Teaching Style and Pupil Progress*. London: Open Books.

Bennett, N. (1995) *Managing Professional Teachers: Middle Management in Primary and Secondary Schools*. London: Paul Chapman Publishing.

Bennett, N. (1997) Analysing management for personal development: theory and practice. In L. Kydd, M. Crawford and C. Riches (eds) *Professional Development for Educational Management*. Buckingham: Open University Press.

Bennett, N., Crawford, M. and Riches, C. (1992) Introduction: managing educational change; the centrality of values and meanings. In *Managing Change in Education: Individual and Organizational Perspectives*. London: Paul Chapman Publishing.

Bennis, W. (1969) *Organization Development: Its Nature, Origin and Prospects*. Reading, MA: Addison-Wesley.

Bennis, W. (1989) *On Becoming a Leader*. London: Hutchinson.

Bennis, W. and Nanus, B. (1985) *Leaders*. New York: Harper and Row.

Berne, E. (1964) *Games People Play*. London: Andre Deutsch.

Bernstein, B. (1977) *Class, Codes and Control. Volume 3: Towards a Theory of Educational Transmissions*. London, Routledge and Kegan Paul.

Best, R., Jarvis, C. and Ribbins, P. (1989) *Perspectives on Pastoral Care*. London: Heinemann.

Bhindi, N. and Duignan, P. (1997) Leadership for a new century: authenticity, intentionality, spirituality and sensibility, *Educational Management and Administration*, 25(2), 117–32.

Bines, H. and Welton, J. (eds) (1995) *Managing Partnerships in Teacher Training and Development*. London: Routledge.

Biott, C. (1991) *Semi-detached Teachers: Building Support and Advisory Relationships in the Classroom*. London: Falmer.

Blackburn, V. and Moisan, C. (1987) *The Inservice Training of Teachers in the European Community*. Maastricht: Presses Interuniversitaires Européenes.

Blackmore, J. (1996) Breaking the silence: feminist contributions to educational administration and policy. In K. Leithwood, D. Chapman, P. Corson, F. Hallinger and A. Hart (eds) *International Handbook of Educational Leadership and Administration*. Dordrect: Kluwer Academic Publishers.

Blake, R. and Mouton, J. (1978) *The New Managerial Grid*. Houston, TX: Gulf.

Blanchard, K. and Zigarmi, D. (1991) *Leadership and the One Minute Manager*. London: Willow Books.

Bloom, B. (1956) *Taxonomy of Educational Objectives*. London: Longman.

Bohm, D. (1980) *Wholeness and the Implicate Order*. London: Routledge and Kegan Paul.

Bolam, R. (1982) *In-service Education and Training of Teachers: A Condition for Educational Change*. Paris: OECD.

Bolam, R. (1990) Recent developments in England and Wales. In B. M. Joyce (ed.) *Changing School Culture through Staff Development – 1990 Yearbook of the Association for Supervision and Curriculum Development*. Alexandria, Victoria: ASCD.

Bolam, R. (1993) Recent developments and emerging issues. In *The Continuing Professional Development of Teachers*. London: General Teaching Council for England and Wales.

Bolam, R. (1997) Management development for headteachers: retrospect and prospect, *Educational Management and Administration*, 25(3), 265–84.

Bolam, R., McMahon, A., Pocklington, D. and Weindling, D. (1993) *Effective Managment in Schools*. London: HMSO.

Bolman, L. and Deal, T. (1984) *Modern Approaches to Understanding and Managing Organizations*. San Francisco: Jossey-Bass.

Bottery, M. (1992) *The Ethics of Educational Management*. London: Cassell.

Bottery, M. (1994) *Lessons for Schools? A Comparison of Business and Educational Management*. London: Cassell.

Boud, D. (1995) Meeting the challenges. In A. Brew (ed.) *Directions in Staff Development*. Buckingham: Society for Research into Higher Education and Open University Press.

Bowe, R., Ball, S. J. and Gold, A. (1992) *Reforming Education and Changing Schools*. London: Routledge.

Bowring-Carr, C. and West-Burnham, J. (1994) *Managing Quality in Schools: Workbook*. Harlow: Longman.

Boyatzis, R. E. (1982) *The Competent Manager: A Model for Effective Performance*. New York: Wiley.

Bradley, D. (1996) Who dares wins: intended and unintended consequences of the Further Education Funding Council funding methodology, *Educational Management and Administration*, 24(4), 379–88.

Bridges, D. (1987) It's the ones who never turn up that you really want to see. The problem of the 'non-attending' parent. In J. Bastiani (ed.) *Parents and Teachers 1*. Slough: NFER-Nelson.

Bridges, D. (1994) Parents: customers or partners? In D. Bridges and T. McLaughlin (eds) *Education and the Market Place*. London: Falmer.

Bridges, D. and McLaughlin, T. (eds) (1994) *Education and the Market Place*. London: Falmer.

Bridges, E. M. (1992) *The Incompetent Teacher: Managerial Responses*. Lewes: Falmer Press.

Brighouse, T. (1986) *Effective Schools*. Oxford: Oxford LEA.

Brighouse, T. (1991) *What Makes a Good School?* Stafford: Network Education Press.

Brighouse, T. (1998) *The Role of the Headteacher: Report of House of Commons Select Committee on Education and Employment*. Evidence to the Committee, para. 60.

Brighouse, T. and Tomlinson, J. (1991) *Towards the Effective School: A Policy Paper*. London: IPPR.

Brighouse, T. and Woods, D. (1999) *How to Improve Your School*. London: Routledge.

Broadhead, P., Cuckle, P., Hodgson, J. and Dunford, J. (1996) Improving primary schools through school development planning, *Educational Management and Administration*, 24(3), 277–90.

Brookfield, D. (1987) *Developing Critical Thinkers*. Milton Keynes: Open University Press.

Brookover, W., Beady, C., Flood, P., Schweitzer, J. and Wisenbaker, J. (1979) *School Social Systems and Student Achievement: Schools Make a Difference*. New York: Macmillan.

Broudy, H. S., Smith, C. and Burnett, J. R. (1964) *Democracy and Excellence in American Secondary Education*. Chicago: Rand McNally.

Brown, M. (1993) Cutting down on stress, *Management in Education*, 7(2), 22–3.

Brown, M. and Rutherford, D. (1998) Changing roles and raising standards, *School Leadership and Management*, 18(1), 75–88.

Brown, M. and Taylor, J. (1996) Achieving school improvement through 'Investors in People', *Educational Management and Administration*, 24(4), 371–7.

Browne, S. (1979) The accountability of HM Inspectorate. In J. Lello (ed.) *Accountability*. London: Ward Lock.

Bruner, J. S. (1960) *The Process of Education*. Cambridge, MA: Harvard University Press.

Bryman, A. (1986) *Leadership and Organizations*. London: Routledge and Kegan Paul.

Buchanan, D. and McCalman, J. (1989) *High Performance Work Design: The Digital Experience*. London: Routledge.

Buckley, J. and Styan D. (1988) *Managing for Learning*. London: Macmillan.

Burgess, R. G. (1993) The context of in-service education and training. In R. Burgess *et al.* (eds) *Implementing In-Service Education and Training*. London: Falmer Press.

Burgess, R. G., Newton, M., Connor, J., Galloway, S. and Morrison, M. (eds) (1993) *Implementing In-Service Education and Training*. London: Falmer Press.

Burgoyne, J. (1989) Opinion. *Transition*, February.

Burrows, R. and Loader, B. (1994) *Towards a Post-Fordist Welfare State*. London: Routledge.

Bush, T. (ed.) (1989) *Managing Education: Theory and Practice*. Milton Keynes: Open University Press.

Bush, T. (1995) *Theories of Educational Management*, 2nd edn. London: Paul Chapman Publishing.

Bush, T., Coleman, M. and Glover, D. (1993) *Managing Autonomous Schools: The Grant Maintained Experience*. London: Paul Chapman Publishing.

Bush, T. and Middlewood, D. (eds) (1997) *Managing People in Education*. London: Paul Chapman Publishing.

Bush, T. and West-Burnham, J. (eds) (1994) *The Principles of Educational Management*. Harlow: Longman.

Busher, H. (1990) Managing compulsory INSET under teachers' new conditions of service, *Educational Management and Administration*, 18(3), 39–45.

Busher, H. and Saran, R. (1994) Towards a model of school leadership, *Educational Management and Administration*, 22(1), 5–13.

Busher, H. and Saran, R. (eds) (1996) *Managing Teachers as Professionals in Schools*. London: Kogan Page.

Buzan, T. (1982) *Use Your Head*. London: BBC Books.

Caldwell, B. and Spinks, J. (1988) *The Self-managing School*. London: Falmer.

Caldwell, B. and Spinks, J. (1992) *Leading the Self-managing School*. London: Falmer.

Caldwell, B. and Spinks, J. (1998) *Beyond the Self-managing School*. London: Falmer.

Carroll, S. and Walford, G. (1997) The child's voice in school choice, *Educational Management and Administration*, 25(2), 169–80.

Chadwick, E. (1988) Manpower planning. In D. Lock and N. Farrow (eds) *The Gower Handbook of Management*. Aldershot: Gower.

Chaudhry-Lawton, R., Lawton, R., Murphy, K. and Terry, A. (1992) *Quality: Change through Teamwork*. London: Century Business.

Cheng, Y. C. and Cheung, W. M. (1997) Multi-models of educational quality and models of self-management in schools, *Educational Management and Administration*, 25(4), 451–61.

Child, J. (1984) *Organization: A Guide to Problems and Practice*. London: Harper and Row.

Chin, R. and Benne, K. (1974) General strategies for effecting change in human systems. In W. Bennis, K. Benne and R. Chin (eds) *Planning of Change*. London: Holt, Rhinehart and Winston.

Clark, D. (1996) *Schools as Learning Communities*. London: Cassell.

Clemmer, J. and McNeil, A. (1989) *Leadership Skills for Every Manager*. London: Piatkus.

Codd, J. A. (1996) Professionalism versus managerialism in New Zealand schools: educational leadership and the politics of teachers' work. Paper presented at the British Educational Research Association Annual Conference, University of Lancaster, 12–15 September.

Cohen, M. D. and March, J. G. (1989) Leadership and ambiguity: the American college president. In T. Bush (ed.) *Managing Education: Theory and Practice*. Milton Keynes: Open University Press.

Coleman, M. (1994) Women in educational management. In T. Bush and J. West-Burnham (eds) *The Principles of Educational Management*. Harlow: Longman.

Coleman, M. (1996) The management style of female headteachers, *Educational Management and Administration*, 24(2), 163–74.

Coleman, M. (1997) Managing for equal opportunities: the gender issue. In T. Bush and D. Middlewood (eds) *Managing People in Education*. London: Paul Chapman Publishing.

Collinson, D. L., Knights, D. and Collinson, M. (1990) *Managing to Discriminate*. London: Routledge.

Connor, D. (1998) Becoming a professional development coordinator, *Professional Development Today*, 1(1), 47–52.

Constable, J. and McCormick, R. (1987) *The Making of British Managers*. Corby: British Institute of Managers.

Cook, R. (1992) *The Prevention and Management of Stress*. Harlow: Longman.

Cooper, M. (1998) Loosening the paternal grip of authorities, *Times Educational Supplement: School Management Update*, 13 November, 4.

Cooper, P. and McIntyre, D. (1996) *Effective Teaching and Learning*. Buckingham: Open University Press.

Coulson, A. (1986) *The Managerial Work of Primary Headteachers*. Sheffield Papers in Education Management No. 48. Sheffield: Sheffield Hallam University.

Cram, T. (1995) *The Power of Relationship Marketing*. London: FT/Pitman.

Cranwell-Ward, J. (1987) *Managing Stress*. London: Pan Business.

Crawford, K. and Riches, C. (eds) (1997) *Professional Development for Educational Management*. Buckingham: Open University Press.

Crawford, M., Glover, D., Bennett, N., Levačić, R. and Earley, P. (1998) *School effectiveness and efficient resource management: case studies of English urban primary schools*. Conference paper, Manchester, ICSEI.

Crawford, M., Kydd, L. and Riches, C. (eds) (1997) *Leadership and Teams in Educational Management*. Buckingham: Open University Press.

Critchley, B. and Casey, D. (1986) Team building. In A. Mumford (ed.) *Handbook of Management Development*. Aldershot: Gower.

Cropley, A. J. (1992) *More than One Way of Fostering Creativity*. Norwood, NJ: Ablex.

Crosby, P. B. (1979) *Quality Is Free*. New York: Mentor Books.

Crosby, P. B. (1986) *Running Things*. New York: McGraw-Hill.

Cuckle, P., Dunford, J., Hodgson, J. and Broadhead, P. (1998) Governor involvement in development planning: from tea parties to working parties, *School Organization*, 18(1), 19–34.

Darling-Hammond, L. (1989) Evaluation in the teaching profession. In A. Evans and J. Tomlinson (eds) *Teacher Appraisal: A Nationwide Approach*. London: Jessica Kingsley.

Darling-Hammond, L. (1995) Policy for restructuring. In A. Lieberman (ed.) *The Work of Restructuring Schools*. New York: Teachers College Press.

Dart, L. and Drake, P. (1994) Mentoring in a well established school based scheme. In D. McIntyre and H. Hagger (eds) *Mentoring in Initial Teacher Education*. London: Paul Hamlyn.

Davidson, M. (1992) *Shattering the Glass Ceiling: The Woman Manager*. London: Paul Chapman Publishing.

Davidson, M. J. (ed.) (1997) *The Black and Ethnic Minority Woman Manager: Cracking the Concrete Ceiling*. London: Paul Chapman.

Davies, B., Ellison, L., Osborne, A. and West-Burnham, J. (eds) (1990) *Education Management for the 1990s*. Harlow: Longman.

Davies, H. (1992) *Fighting Leviathan: Building Social Markets that Work*. London: Social Market Foundation.

Davies, J. and Morgan, A. (1989) Management and higher education institutions. In T. Bush (ed.) *Managing Education: Theory and Practice*. Milton Keynes: Open University Press.

Davies, L. (1990) *Equity and Efficiency? School Management in an International Context*. Lewes: Falmer.

Davis, I. (1976) *Objectives in Curriculum Design*. New York: McGraw-Hill.

Day, C. (1996) Leadership and professional development: developing reflective practice. In H. Busher and R. Saran (eds) *Managing Teachers as Professionals in Schools*. London: Kogan Page.

Day, C., Hall, C., Gammage, P. and Coles, M. (1993) *Leadership and Curriculum in the Primary School*. London: Paul Chapman Publishing.

Day, C., Hall, C. and Whitaker, P. (1998) *Developing Leadership in Primary Schools.* London: Paul Chapman Publishing.

Day, C., Johnston, D. and Whitaker, P. (1990) *Managing Primary Schools in the 1990s: A Professional Development Approach.* London: Paul Chapman Publishing.

Deal, T. (1985) The symbolism of effective schools, *Elementary School Journal,* 85(5), 601–20.

Deal, T. E. and Kennedy, A. (1982) *Corporate Cultures: The Rites and Rituals of Corporate Life.* Reading, MA: Addison-Wesley.

Deal, T. E. and Kennedy, A. (1983) Culture and school performance, *Educational Leadership,* 40(5), 140–1.

Dean, C. (1998) £110 million 'diverted' away from schools, *Times Educational Supplement,* 6 November, 2.

Dean, C. and Rafferty, F. (1998) Pupils pay price in Labour 'lottery'; and All's not fair in the bidding war, *Times Educational Supplement,* 13 November, 1, 6.

Dean, J. (1995) *Managing the Primary School,* 2nd edn. London: Routledge.

Dearing, Sir Ron (1997) *Higher Education in the Learning Society.* Report of the National Committee of Inquiry into Higher Education (NCIHE), July. London: HMSO.

de Bono, E. (1967) *The Uses of Lateral Thinking.* London: Penguin.

Deem, R. (1990) The reform of school governing bodies: the power of the consumer over the producer? In M. Flude and M. Hammer (eds) *The Education Reform Act 1988: Its Origins and Implications.* London: Falmer Press.

Deem, R. (1993) Educational reform and school governing bodies in England 1986–92: old dogs, new tricks or new dogs, new tricks? In M. Preedy (ed.) *Managing the Effective School.* London: Paul Chapman Publishing.

Deming, W. E. (1982) *Quality, Productivity and Competitive Position.* Cambridge, MA: Centre for Advanced Engineering Study.

Dennison, B. and Kirk, R. (1990) *Do, Review, Learn, Apply: A Simple Guide to Experiential Learning.* Oxford: Basil Blackwell.

DES (1967) *Children and Their Primary Schools.* A Report to the Central Advisory Council for Education (The Plowden Report). London: DES/HMSO.

DES (1972) *Teacher Education and Training* (The James Report). London: HMSO.

DES (1985) *Better Schools.* London: HMSO.

DES (1989) *School Teacher Appraisal: A National Framework.* Report of the National Steering Group. London: HMSO.

DES (1990) *Developing School Management: the Way Forward.* Report of the School Management Task Force. London: HMSO.

DES (1991) *Statistics of Education: Schools 1991.* London: DES.

Deutsch, M. and Gerrard, H. (1955) A study of normative and informational social influences upon individual judgements. *Journal of Abnormal and Social Psychology,* 51.

Devlin, L. (1995) The mentor. In D. Glover and G. Mardle (eds) *The Management of Mentoring: Policy Issues.* London: Kogan Page.

Devlin, T. and Knight, B. (1990) *Public Relations and Marketing for Schools.* Harlow: Longman.

DfE (1992) *Choice and Diversity.* London: HMSO.

DfEE (1995a) *Benchmarking School Budgets: Sharing Good Practice.* London: DfEE.

DfEE (1995b) *Statistics of Education: Teachers England and Wales 1993.* London: HMSO.

DfEE (1995c) Shepherd approves action on teacher quality, *DfEE News,* 251/95, 31 October.

DfEE (1996) *Setting Targets to Raise Standards: A Survey of Good Practice.* London: DfEE/Ofsted.

DfEE (1997a) *Excellence in Schools,* Cm 3681. London: DfEE.

DfEE (1997b) *From Targets to Action: Guidance to Support Effective Target-setting in Schools.* London: DfEE/Standards and Effectiveness Unit.

DfEE (1998a) *Education Development Plans: Local Education Authorities' Plans to Promote Improved Standards of Pupil Performance.* London: DfEE.

DfEE (1998b) *Teaching: High Status, High Standards.* Circular 4/98. London: HMSO.

DfEE (1998c) *Teachers: Meeting the Challenge of Change.* Green Paper, November. London: HMSO.

DfEE (1998d) *National Grid for Learning: Open for Learning, Open for Business.* London: DfEE.

DfEE (1998e) *The Learning Age: A Renaissance for a New Britain.* Green Paper, February. London: HMSO.

DfEE (1998f) *Effective Appraisal in Schools: A Discussion Document.* London: DfEE.

DfEE (1998g) *Fair Funding: Improving Delegation to Schools.* Consultation Document. London: DfEE.

Dimmock, E. (1993) *School Based Management and School Effectiveness.* London: Routledge.

Dobbins, D. A. (1992) The effect of the Training Grant Scheme on INSET in special education in Wales, *British Journal of In-service Education,* 18(1), 42–9.

Draper, J. and McMichael, P. (1998) Preparing a profile: likely applicants for primary school headship, *Educational Management and Administration,* 26(2), 161–72.

Drucker, P. (1967) *The Effective Executive.* London: Pan.

Drucker, P. (1988a) The coming of the new organization, *Harvard Business Review,* January/February, 45–53.

Drucker, P. (1988b) *Management.* London: Pan Books.

Drucker, P. (1989a) What business can learn from non-profits, *Harvard Business Review,* July/August, 89–93.

Drucker, P. (1989b) The spirit of performance. In C. Riches and C. Morgan (eds) *Human Resource Management in Education.* Milton Keynes: Open University Press.

Drucker, P. (1990a) *The New Realities.* London: Mandarin.

Drucker, P. (1990b) *Managing the Non-profit Organization.* London: Butterworth Heinemann.

Duignan, P. (1989) Reflective management: the key to quality leadership. In C. Riches and C. Morgan (eds) *Human Resource Management in Education.* Milton Keynes: Open University Press.

Duignan, P. A. and Macpherson, R. J. S. (1992) *A Practical Theory for New Administrators and Managers.* Lewes: Falmer Press.

Dunham, J. (1994) *Developing Effective School Management.* London: Routledge.

Dunlap, D. and Schmuck, P. (eds) (1995) *Women Leading in Education.* Albany, NY: SUNY Press.

Dunleavy, P. and Hood, C. (1994) From old public administration to new public management, *Public Money and Management,* July–September, 9–16.

Dunning, G. (1993) Managing the small primary school: the problem role of the teaching head, *Educational Management and Administration,* 21(2), 79–89.

Earley, P. (ed.) (1998) *School Improvement after Inspection? School and LEA Responses.* London: Paul Chapman Publishing.

Earley, P. and Fletcher-Campbell, F. (1989) *The Time to Manage: Faculty and Departmental Heads at Work.* Windsor: NFER-Nelson.

Echols, F., MacPherson, A. and Willms, J. D. (1990) Parental choice in Scotland, *Journal of Education Policy,* 6(2), 169–78.

Edwards, T. (1995) The politics of partnership. In H. Bines and J. Welton (eds) *Managing Partnerships in Teacher Training and Development.* London: Routledge.

Elliot Kemp, E. (1983) *The Management of Stress.* Sheffield: GEMS.

Elliot, J. (1990) Educational theory and the professional learning of teachers, *Cambridge Journal of Education,* 19(1), 81–103.

Elliott, J. (1996) School effectiveness research and its critics: alternative visions of schooling, *Cambridge Journal of Education,* 26(2), 199–224.

Emery, F. and Trist, E. (1965) The causal texture of organization environments, *Human Relations,* 18, 21–32.

Entwistle, N. J. and Entwistle, A. C. (1991) Forms of understanding for degree examinations: the pupil experience and its implications, *Higher Education,* 22, 205–27.

Eraut, M. (1993) The characterisation and development of professional expertise in school management and teaching, *Educational Management and Administration*, 21(4), 222–32.

Eraut, M. (1994) *Developing Professional Knowledge and Competence*. Lewes: Falmer.

Erikson, E. (1977) *Childhood and Society*. London: Triad/Granada.

Esp, D. (1993) *Competences for School Managers*. London: Kogan Page.

Evans, A. and Tomlinson, J. (eds) (1989) *Teacher Appraisal: A Nationwide Approach*. London: Jessica Kingsley.

Everard, B. (1990) The competency approach to management development, *Management in Education*, 4(2), 8–10.

Everard, K. B. and Morris, G. (1996) *Effective School Management*, 3rd edn. London: Paul Chapman Publishing.

Evetts, J. (1990) *Women in Primary Teaching: Career Contexts and Strategies*. London: Unwin Hyman.

Evetts, J. (1994) *Becoming a Secondary Headteacher*. London: Cassell.

Exworthy, M. and Halford, S. (eds) (1998) *Professionals and the New Managerialism in the Public Sector*. Buckingham: Open University Press.

Farber, B. (1991) *Crisis in Education*. San Francisco: Jossey-Bass.

Fayol, H. (1916) *General and Industrial Administration*, trans. C. Storrs, 1949. London: Pitman.

Ferguson, M. (1982) *The Aquarian Conspiracy*. London: Granada.

Ferris, R., Mifsud, J. and McEwen, A. (1993) Too much too quickly: primary curriculum reform, *Management in Education*, 7(1).

Fidler, B. (1989) Staff appraisal: theory, concepts and experience in other organizations and problems of adaptation to education. In C. Riches and C. Morgan (eds) *Human Resource Management in Education*. Milton Keynes: Open University Press.

Fidler, B. (1992) Job descriptions and organizational structure. In B. Fidler and R. Cooper (eds) *Staff Appraisal and Staff Management in Schools and Colleges: A Guide to Implementation*. London: Harlow.

Fidler, B. (1997) The school as a whole: school improvement and planned change. In B. Fidler, S. Russell and T. Simkins (eds) *Choices for Self-managing Schools: Autonomy and Accountability*. London: Paul Chapman Publishing.

Fidler, B. and Morris, R. (1996) The LEA contribution to school improvement. Paper presented to BEMAS Annual Conference, Coventry, September.

Fidler, B., Russell, S. and Simkins, T. (eds) (1997) *Choices for Self-managing Schools: Autonomy and Accountability*. London: Paul Chapman Publishing/BEMAS.

Fiedler, F. (1978) Situational control and a dynamic theory of leadership. In D. Pugh (ed.) *Organization Theory: Selected Readings*. Harmondsworth: Penguin Business.

Finch, J. (1986) *Research and Policy: The Uses of Qualitative Methods in Social and Educational Research*. Lewes: Falmer Press.

Finegold, D., McFarland, L. and Richardson, W. (1993) *Something Borrowed, Something Blue? A Study of the Thatcher Government's Appropriation of American Education and Training Policy*. Oxford: Triangle Books.

Fisher, R. and Ury, W. (1981) *Getting to Yes*. London: Arrow.

FitzGibbon, C. T. (1996a) *Monitoring Education: Indicators, Quality and Effectiveness*. London: Cassell.

FitzGibbon, C. T. (1996b) Judgments must be credible and fair, *Times Educational Supplement*, 29 March, 21.

Flude, M. and Hammer, M (eds) (1990) *The Education Reform Act 1988: Its Origins and Implications*. London: Falmer Press.

Foreman, K. (1997) Managing individual performance. In T. Bush and D. Middlewood (eds) *Managing People in Education*. London: Paul Chapman Publishing.

Foskett, D. (1998) Schools and marketisation: cultural challenges and responses, *Educational Management and Administration*, 26(2), 211–19.

Francis, D. and Young, D. (1979) *Improving Work Groups*. London: University Associates.

Freire, P. (1972) *Pedagogy of the Oppressed*. London: Penguin.

French, J. R. and Raven, B. (1959) The bases of social power. In D. Cartwright (ed.) *Studies of Social Power*. Ann Arbor: University of Michigan.

French, J. R. P. and Caplan, R. D. (1970) Psychosocial factors in coronary heart disease, *Industrial Medicine*, 39, 383–97.

French, J. R. P., Tipper, C. J. and Mueller, E. J. (1965) Workload of university professors. Unpublished research report, University of Michigan.

Friedman, M. and Rosenman, R. (1974) *Type A Behaviour and Your Heart*. London: Wildwood House.

Frogatt, H. and Stamp, P. (1991) *Managing Pressure at Work*. London: BBC Books.

Fryer, M. (1996) *Creative Teaching and Learning*. London: Paul Chapman Publishing.

Fullan, M. (1991) *The New Meaning of Educational Change*. New York: Teachers College Press.

Fullan, M. (1992) *What's Worth Fighting for in Headship*. Buckingham: Open University Press.

Fullan, M. (1993) *Change Forces: Probing the Depths of Educational Reform*. London: Falmer Press.

Fullan, M. (1999) *Change Forces: The Sequel*. London: Falmer Press.

Fullan, M. and Hargreaves, A. (1991) *Working Together for Your School*. Ontario: Public School Teachers Federation.

Fullan, M. and Hargreaves, A. (1992) *What's Worth Fighting for in Your School?* Buckingham: Open University Press.

Galbraith, J. K. (1992) *The Culture of Contentment*. New York: Houghton Mifflin.

Ganderton, P. (1991) Subversion and the organization: some theoretical considerations, *Educational Management and Administration*, 19(1), 30–7.

Gardner, H. (1983) *Frames of Mind: The Theory of Multiple Intelligences*. New York: Basic Books.

Gardner, H. (1993) *The Unschooled Mind*. London: Fontana Press.

Garrett, B. (1987) *The Learning Organization*. London: Fontana.

Garrett, V. and Bowles, C. (1997) Teaching as a profession: the role of professional development. In H. Tomlinson (ed.) *Managing Continuing Professional Development in Schools*. London: Paul Chapman Publishing.

Gewirtz, S., Ball, S. J. and Bowe, R. (1995) *Markets, Choice and Equity in Education*. Buckingham: Open University Press.

Glatter, R. (1982) The micropolitics of education: issues for training, *Educational Management and Administration*, 10(2), 160–5.

Glatter, R. (ed.) (1989) *Educational Institutions and Their Environments: Managing the Boundaries*. Milton Keynes: Open University Press.

Glatter, R., Johnson, D. and Woods, P. (1992) *Marketing Choice and Responses*. London: BEMAS.

Glatter, R., Preedy M., Riches, C. and Masterton, M. (eds) (1988) *Understanding School Management*. Milton Keynes: Open University Press.

Glatter, R., Woods, P. A. and Bagley, C. (eds) (1997) *Choice and Diversity in Schooling: Perspectives and Prospects*. London: Routledge.

Glichman, C. (1991) *Supervision of Instruction: A Developmental Approach*. Boston: Allyn and Bacon.

Glover, D. (1992) An investigation of criterion used by parents and community in the judgement of school quality, *Educational Research*, 34(1), 35–44.

Glover, D. (1993) Community perceptions of schools. Unpublished PhD thesis, Open University.

Glover, D., Gleeson, D., Gough, G. and Johnson, M. (1998) The meaning of management: the development needs of middle managers in secondary schools, *Educational Management and Administration*, 26(3), 279–92.

Glover, D. and Law, S. (1996) *Managing Professional Development in Education*. London: Kogan Page.

Glover, D., Levačić, R., Bennett, N. and Crawford, M. (1996) Leadership in very effective schools, *School Organization*, June, 135–48; September, 247–61.

Glover, D. and Mardle, G. (1995) *The Management of Mentoring: Policy Issues*. London: Kogan Page.

Goddard, D. and Leask, M. (1992) *The Search for Quality*. London: Paul Chapman Publishing.

Golby, M. (1993) Parents as school governors. In P. Munn (ed.) *Parents and Schools*. London: Routledge.

Goldsmith, W. and Clutterbuck, D. (1984) *The Winning Streak: Britain's Top Companies Reveal Their Formulas for Success*. London: Weidenfeld and Nicholson.

Goldstein, H. and Myers, K. (1997) *Freedom of Information: Towards a Code of Ethics for Performance Indicators*. London: University of London Institute of Education.

Goldstein, H. and Thomas, S. (1995) School effectiveness and 'value added' analysis, *Forum*, 37(2), 36–8.

Goleman, D. (1996) *Emotional Intelligence: Why It Matters More than IQ*. London: Bloomsbury Paperbacks.

Goode, W. (1960) Encroachment, charlatanism and the emerging professions: psychology, sociology and medicine, *American Sociological Review*, 25, 902–13.

Grace, G. (1995) *School Leadership: Beyond Education Management. An Essay in Policy Scholarship*. London: Falmer Press

Gray, H. and Freeman, A. (1987) *Teaching without Stress*. London: Paul Chapman Publishing.

Gray, H. L. (1993) Gender issues in management training. In J. Ozga (ed.) *Women in Educational Management*. Buckingham: Open University Press.

Gray, J. (1990) The quality of schooling: frameworks for judgements, *British Journal of Educational Studies*, 38(3), 204–23.

Gray, J., Reynolds, D., FitzGibbon, C. and Jesson, D. (1996) *Merging Traditions: The Future of Research on School Effectiveness and School Improvement*. London: Cassell.

Gray, J. and Wilcox, B. (1995) *Good School, Bad School: Evaluating Performance and Encouraging Improvement*. Milton Keynes: Open University Press.

Gray, L. (1991) *Marketing Education*. Buckingham: Open University Press.

Green, A. (1991) *Education Limited*. London: Unwin.

Greener, T. (1990) *The Secrets of Successful Public Relations and Image-making*. Oxford: Heinemann-Butterworth.

Greenfield, T. B. (1973) Organizations as social inventions: rethinking assumptions about change, *Journal of Applied Behavioral Science*, 9(5), 552–74.

Gregorc, A. F. (1982) *Gregorc Style Delineator: Development Technical and Administrative Manual*. Columbia, CT: Gregorc Associates.

GRIDS (1988) *Guidelines for the Review and Internal Development of Schools*. Harlow: Longman for Schools Council.

Griffin, G. (1987) The school in society: implications for staff development. In M. Wideen and I. Andrews (eds) *Staff Development for School Improvement*. Lewes: Falmer Press.

Griffiths, M. and Tann, S. (1992) Using reflective practice to link personal and public theories, *Journal of Education for Teaching*, 18(1), 69–84.

Gronn, P. (1996) From transactions to transformations, *Educational Management and Administration*, 24(1), 7–30.

Grundy, T. (1993) *Implementing Strategic Change*. London: Kogan Page.

Guest, D. (1984) What's new in motivation, *Personnel Management*, May, 21–3.

Habermas, J. (1972) *Knowledge and Human Interests*. London: Heinemann.

Haladyna, T. M., Nolen, S. B. and Haas, N. S. (1991) Raising standardized achievement test scores and the origins of test score pollution, *Educational Researcher*, 20(5), 7.

Hall, V. (1996) *Dancing on the Ceiling: A Study of Women Managers in Education*. London: Paul Chapman Publishing.

Hall, V. (1997) *Choices for Self-managing Schools: Autonomy and Accountability*. London: Paul Chapman Publishing.

Halpin, D. (1990) Review symposium, *British Journal of Sociology of Education*, 11(4), 473–6.

Halpin, D., Fitz, J. and Power, S. (1991) LEAs and grant-maintained schools policy, *Education Management and Administration*, 19(4), 233–42.

Halpin, D., Power, S. and Fitz, J. (1997) Opting into the past? Grant maintained schools and the reinvention of tradition. In R. Glatter, P. A. Woods and C. Bagley (eds) *Choice and Diversity in Schooling: Perspectives and Prospects*. London: Routledge.

Hamlyn Report (1994) *Mentoring in Initial Teacher Education*. Oxford: University of Oxford Department of Educational Studies.

Hammer, M. and Champy, J. (1993) *Re-engineering the Corporation*. New York: Harper-Collins.

Hammond, T. and Dennison, B. (1995) School choice in less populated areas, *Educational Management and Administration*, 23(2), 104–13.

Handy, C. (1987) *The Making of Managers*. London: NEDC.

Handy, C. (1989) *The Age of Unreason*. London: Pan Books.

Handy, C. (1990) *Inside Organizations*. London: BBC.

Handy, C. (1993) *Understanding Organizations*, 4th edn. Harmondsworth: Penguin.

Handy, C. (1994) *The Empty Raincoat: Making Sense of the Future*. London: Random House.

Handy, C. (1996) *Beyond Certainty: The Changing Worlds of Organizations*. London: Hutchinson.

Handy, C. (1997) Schools for life and work. In P. Mortimore and V. Little (eds) *Living Education: Essays in Honour of John Tomlinson*. London: Paul Chapman Publishing.

Handy, C. and Aitken, R. (1986) *Understanding Schools as Organizations*. Harmondsworth: Penguin.

Hannagan, T. (1995) *Management Concepts and Practices*. London: Pitman.

Hannah, M. T. and Freeman, J. (1984) Structural inertia and organizational change, *American Sociological Review*, 49, 149–64.

Hanushek, E. (1988) The economics of schooling: production and efficiency in public schools, *Journal of Economic Literature*, 24, 1141–77.

Hanushek, E. (1989) The impact of differential expenditures on school performance, *Educational Researcher*, 18(4), 45–65.

Hargie, C., Toursin, D. and Hargie, O. (1994) Managers communicating: an investigation of core situations and difficulties with educational organizations, *International Journal of Educational Management*, 8(6), 23–8.

Hargreaves, A. (1994) *Changing Teachers, Changing Times: Teachers' Work and Culture in the Post Modern Age*. London: Cassell.

Hargreaves, A. (1997) From reform to renewal: a new deal for a new age. In A. Hargreaves and R. Evans (eds) *Beyond Educational Reform: Bringing Teachers Back In*. Buckingham: Open University Press.

Hargreaves, A. and Evans, R. (eds) (1997) *Beyond Educational Reform: Bringing Teachers Back In*. Buckingham: Open University Press.

Hargreaves, D. H. (1982) *The Challenge for the Comprehensive School*. London: Routledge and Kegan Paul.

Hargreaves, D. H. (1994) *The Mosaic of Learning: Schools and Teachers for the Next Century*. London: Demos.

Hargreaves, D. H. (1995) School culture, school effectiveness and school improvement, *School Effectiveness and School Improvement*, 6(1), 23–46.

Hargreaves, D. H. and Hopkins, D. (1991) *The Empowered School*. London: Cassell.

Hargreaves, D. H. and Hopkins, D. (eds) (1994) *Development Planning for School Improvement*. London: Cassell.

Hargreaves, D. H., Hopkins, D., Leask, M., Connolly, J. and Robinson, P. (1989) *Planning for School Development: Advice to Governors, Headteachers and Staff*. London: DES/HMSO.

Harland, J., Kinder, K. and Keys, W. (1993) *Restructuring INSET: Privatization and Its Alternatives*. Slough: NFER.

Harris, A., Bennett, N. and Preedy, M. (eds) (1997) *Organizational Effectiveness and Improvement in Education*. Buckingham: Open University Press.

Harris, A., Jamieson, I. and Russ, J. (1995) A study of effective departments. *School Organization*, 15(3), 283–99.

Harrison, C. (1995) Strategies for improving examination results, *Management in Education*, 9(3), 30.

Hartley, H. (1979) Zero-based budgeting for secondary schools, *NASSP* Bulletin, 63, 22–8.

Harvey-Jones, J. (1988) *Making It Happen*. London: Collins.

Havelock, R. (1971) The utilization of educational research and development, *British Journal of Educational Technology*, 2(2), 84–97.

Hayes, D. (1996) Introduction of collaborative decision-making in a primary school, *Educational Management and Administration*, 24(3), 291–9.

Heller, R. (1994) Customer focus means commitment to constant change, *Management Today*, January, 42–6.

Heppell, S. (1998) Clarifying the role of ICT, *Professional Development Today*, 2(1), 39–44.

Heron, J. (1986) *Six Category Invention Analysis*. Guildford: Surrey University.

Hersey, P. and Blanchard, K. H. (1977) *Management of Organizational Behavior: Utilizing Human Resources*. London: Prentice Hall International.

Herzberg, F. (1966) The motivation–hygiene theory. In D. Pugh (ed.) *Organization Theory: Selected Readings*. Harmondsworth: Penguin.

Hilditch, B. (1993) Managing the curriculum. In H. Green (ed.) *The School Management Handbook*. London: Kogan Page.

Hirschman, A. (1970) *Exit, Voice and Loyalty: Response to Decline in Firms, Organizations and Stakes*. Cambridge, MA: Harvard University Press.

Hodgkinson, C. (1993) Foreword. In T. B. Greenfield and P. Ribbins (eds) *Greenfield on Educational Administration*. London: Routledge.

Hodgson, P. (1987) Managers can be taught, but leaders have to learn, *ICT*, November/December.

Holbeche, L. (1995) *Flattening Organizational Structures*. Horsham: Roffey Park Management Institute.

Hollander, E. (1964) *Leaders, Groups and Influence*. Oxford: Oxford University Press.

Honey, P. (1991) The learning organization simplified, *Training and Development*, July, 30–3.

Honey, R. and Mumford, A. (1988) *Manual of Learning Styles*. Maidenhead: Peter Honey.

Hopkins, D. (1994) School improvement in an era of change. In P. Ribbins and E. Burridge (eds) *Improving Education*. London: Cassell.

Hopkins D., Ainscow, M. and West, M. (1994) *School Improvement in an Era of Change*. London: Cassell.

Hopson, B. and Hough, P. (1985) *Exercises in Personal and Career Development*. London: Hobsons Press.

House of Commons (1998) *The Role of the Headteacher*. Report of the House of Commons Select Committee on Education and Employment. London: House of Commons.

Howarth, S. and Jelley, S. (1995) Middle management as leaders, *Management in Education*, 9(2), 6.

Howson, J. (1998) Is the glass ceiling beginning to crack? *Times Education Supplement: School Management Briefing*, 30 October, 24.

Hoyle, E. (1972) *The Curriculum: Conflict Design and Development. Facing the Difficulties*. Milton Keynes: Open University Press.

Hoyle, E. (1974) Professionality, professionalism and control in teaching, *London Educational Review*, 3(2).

Hoyle, E. (1980) Professionalization and deprofessionalization in education. In E. Hoyle and J. Megarry (eds) *The Professional Development of Teachers: World Yearbook of Education*. London: Kogan Page.

Hoyle, E. (1986) *The Politics of School Management*. Sevenoaks: Hodder and Stoughton.

Hoyle, E. (1989) Teacher appraisal and collaborative professionalism. In A. Evans and J. Tomlinson (eds) *Teacher Appraisal: A Nationwide Approach*. London: Jessica Kingsley.

Hoyle, E. and John, P. D. (1995) *Professional Knowledge and Professional Practice*. London: Cassell.

Hoyle, E. and Megarry, J. (eds) (1980) *The Professional Development of Teachers: World Yearbook of Education*. London: Kogan Page.

Huberman, M. (with Grounauer, M. M.) (1993) *The Lives of Teachers*. London: Cassell.

Huczynski, A. and Buchanan, D. (1991) *Organizational Behavior*. London: Prentice Hall.

Huddleston, P. and Unwin, I. (1997) *Teaching and Learning in Further Education: Diversity and Change*. London: Routledge.

Hughes, M. G. (1972) The role of the secondary school head. PhD thesis, University of Wales College, Cardiff.

Hughes, M. G. (ed.) (1975) *Administering Education: International Challenge*. London: Athlone Press.

Hughes, M. G. (1985) Leadership in professionally staffed organizations. In M. Hughes, P. Ribbins and H. Thomas (eds) *Managing Education: The System and the Institution*. Eastbourne: Holt, Rinehart and Winston.

Hughes, M. G. (1988) Leadership in professionally staffed organizations. In R. Glatter *et al.* (eds) *Understanding School Management*. Milton Keynes: Open University Press.

Hume, C. (1990) *Grievance and Discipline in Schools*. Harlow: Longman/AGIT.

Hunningher, E. (1992) *The Manager's Handbook*. London: Ernst and Young.

Hunt, J. (1979) *Managing People*. London: Pan Books.

Hutchinson, B. (1995) Appraising appraisal: some tensions and some possibilities, *Higher Education*, 29, 19–35.

Irvine, V. B. (1975) Budgeting: functional analysis and behavioural implications. In A. Rappaport (ed.) *Information for Decision-making: Qualitative and Behavioural Dimensions*, 2nd edn. Hemel Hempstead: Prentice Hall.

Isaac, J. (1995) Self management and development. In J. Bell and B. J. Harrison (eds) *Vision and Values in Managing Education: Successful Leadership Principles and Practice*. London: David Fulton.

James, C. and Phillips, P. (1995) The practice of educational marketing in schools, *Educational Management and Administration*, 23(2), 75–8.

Jayne, E. (1996) Developing more effective primary deputy heads, *Educational Management and Administration*, 24(3), 317–26.

Johnson, D. (1991) *Parental Choice in Education*. London: Unwin Hyman.

Johnson, M. (1998) *Report on the Implementation of Change Related to the Social Regeneration Budget in Lancashire Schools*. Keele: University Department of Education.

Johnson, P. E. and Short, P. M. (1998) Principal's leader power, teacher empowerment, teacher compliance and conflict, *Educational Management and Administration*, 26(2), 147–60.

Johnston, J. and Pickersgill, S. (1992) Personal and interpersonal aspects of effective team-oriented headship in primary schools, *Educational Management and Administration*, 20(4), 239–48.

Joiner, D. A. (1989) Assessment centres in the public sector: a practical approach. In C. Riches and C. Morgan (eds) *Human Resource Management in Education*. Milton Keynes: Open University Press.

Jones, D. (1986) *Accountability and Budgets in Colleges*. Bristol: Further Education Staff College.

Jones, G. (1995) School management: how much local autonomy should there be? *Educational Management and Administration*, 23(3), 162–7.

Jones, J. and O'Sullivan, F. (1997) Energising Middle Management. In H. Tomlinson (ed.) *Managing Continuing Professional Development in Schools*. London: Paul Chapman Publishing.

Joyce, B. (1991) The doors to school improvement. *Educational Leadership*, 48(8), 59–62.

Juran, J. (1980) *Quality Planning and Analysis*. New York: McGraw-Hill.

Kakabadse, A., Ludlow, R. and Vinnicombe, S. (1988) *Working in Organizations*. Harmondsworth: Penguin.

Kanter, R. M. (1979) Power failure in management circuits, *Harvard Business Review*, July/August, 65–75.

Kanter, R. M. (1983) *The Change Masters*. London: Unwin Hyman.

Kelly, M. J. (1988) *The Manchester Survey of Occupational Stress in Headteachers and Principals in the UK*. Manchester: Manchester Polytechnic.

Kelly, A. V. (1989) *The Curriculum: Theory and Practice*, 3rd edn. London: Paul Chapman Publishing.

Kennedy, G. (1989) *Everything Is Negotiable*. London: Arrow.

Knight, B. (1989) *Managing School Time*. Harlow: Longman.

Knight, B. (1993) *Financial Management for Schools*. London: Heinemann.

Knowles, M. (1983) Andragogy: an emerging technology for adult learning. In M. Tight (ed.) *Adult Learning and Education*. London: Croom Helm.

Knowles, M. (1984) *Andragogy in Action*. London: McGraw-Hill.

Kogan, M. (1978) *The Politics of Educational Change*. London: Fontana.

Kogan, M. (1986) *Education Accountability: An Analytic Overview*. London: Hutchinson.

Kolb, D. (1984) *Experiential Learning: Experience as a Source of Learning and Development*. Englewood Cliffs, NJ: Prentice Hall.

Kolb, D., Rubin, I. and McIntyre, J. (1971) *Organizational Psychology: An Experiential Approach*. Hemel Hempstead: Prentice Hall.

Kotler, P. and Armstrong, G. (1991) *Principles of Marketing*. Hemel Hempstead: Prentice Hall.

Kotter, J. (1989) What leaders really do, *Harvard Business Review*, 67(3), 103–11.

Kydd, L., Crawford, K. and Riches, C. (eds) (1997) *Professional Development for Educational Management*. Buckingham: Open University Press.

Lakein, H. (1984) *How to Get Control of Your Time and Your Life*. Aldershot: Gower.

Lancaster, D. (1993) Aspects of management information systems. In M. Preedy (ed.) *Managing the Effective School*. Buckingham: Open University Press.

Laswell, H. (1948) *The structure and function of communication in society*. In L. Bryson (ed.) *The Communication of Ideas*. New York: Harper and Row.

Law, S. A. (1995) Move to improve, *Education*, July, 181–92.

Law, S. A. (1997a) Learning lessons: why choose distance learning in education management? *International Journal of Educational Management*, 11(1), 14–25.

Law, S. A. (1997b) Privatising policies and marketising relationships: continuing professional development in schools, LEAs and higher education. In H. Tomlinson (ed.) *Managing Continuing Professional Development in Schools*. London: Paul Chapman Publishing.

Law, S. A. (1999) Leadership for learning: the changing culture of professional development in schools, *Journal of Educational Administration*, 37(1), 66–80.

Law, S. A. and Glover, D. G. (1995) The professional development business: school evaluations of LEA and higher education INSET provision, *British Journal of In-Service Education*, 21(2), 181–92.

Law, S. A. and Glover, D. G. (forthcoming) Teaching and learning in secondary schools: using the Ofsted criteria as a stimulus for staff discussion and debate.

Lawn, M. and Ozga, J. (1988) The educational worker? A reassessment of teachers. In J. Ozga (ed.) *Schoolwork: Approaches to the Labour Process of Teaching*. Milton Keynes: Open University Press.

Lawton, D. (1983) *Curriculum Studies and Educational Planning*. London: Hodder and Stoughton.

Lawton, D. (1990) *Education, Culture and the National Curriculum*. Lewes: Falmer Press.

Leask, M. and Terrell, I. (1997) *Development Planning and School Improvement for Middle Managers*. London: Kogan Page.

Leavitt, H. T. (1951) Some effects of certain communicative patterns on group performance, *Journal of Abnormal Psychology*, 36, 38–50.

Leavitt, H. T. (1978) *Managerial Psychology*, 4th edn. Chicago: University of Chicago Press.

Leavitt, H. T. and Pugh, D. (1964) *Readings in Managerial Psychology*. Chicago: University of Chicago Press.

Le Grand, J. and Bartlett, W. (eds) (1993) *Quasi-markets and Social Policy*. London: Macmillan.

Leithwood, K. (1990) The principal's role in teacher development: recent developments in England and Wales. In B. M. Joyce (ed.) *Changing School Culture through Staff Development: 1990 Yearbook of the Association for Supervision and Curriculum Development*. Alexandria, Victoria: ASCD.

Leithwood, K. (1992a) The move toward transformational leadership, *Educational Leadership*, 49(5), 8–12.

Leithwood, K. (1992b) *Teacher Development and Educational Change*. Lewes: Falmer Press.

Leithwood, K., Jantzi, D. and Steinbach, R. (1998) *Changing Leadership for Changing Times*. Buckingham: Open University Press.

Leonard, M. (1988) *The 1988 Education Act*. Oxford: Blackwell.

Levačić, R. (ed.) (1993) *Financial Management in Education*. Buckingham: Open University Press.

Levačić, R. (1995) *Local Management of Schools: Analysis and Practice*. Buckingham: Open University Press.

Levačić, R. and Glover, D. (1995) Estimated efficiency, *Managing Schools Today*, 4(4), 28–30.

Levine, S. L. (1989) *Promoting Adult Growth in Schools: The Promise of Professional Development*. Boston: Allyn and Bacon.

Lewes, M. (1994) The changing role of the professional development co-ordinator in schools. Unpublished MA dissertation.

Lewin, K. (1947) Frontiers in group dynamics, *Human Relations*, 1(1), 16–40.

Lewis, P. (1975) *Organizational Communications*, 2nd edn. Columbus, OH: GRID.

Lieberman, A. and McLaughlin, M. (1992) Networks for educational change: powerful and problematic, *Phi Delta Kappan*, 73(9), 673–7.

Lightfoot, S. (1983) *The Good High School: Portraits of Character and Culture*. New York: Coleman Basic Books.

Likert, R. (1967) *The Human Organization: Its Management and Value*. New York: McGraw-Hill.

Liston, D. P. and Zeichner, K. M. (1990) Reflective teaching and action research in pre-service teacher relations, *Journal of Education for Teaching*, 16(3), 235–54.

Lock, D. and Farrow, N. (eds) (1991) *The Gower Handbook of Management*. Aldershot: Gower Publishing.

Locke, E. A. and Latham, G. P. (1990) Work motivation: the high performance cycle. In U. Kleinbeck, H.-H. Quast and H. Hacker (eds) *Work Motivation*. Brighton: Erlbaum.

Lofthouse, M. (1994a) Managing learning. In T. Bush and J. West-Burnham (eds) *The Principles of Educational Management*. Harlow: Longman.

Lofthouse, M. (1994b) Managing the curriculum. In T. Bush and J. West-Burnham (eds) *The Principles of Educational Management*. Harlow: Longman.

Loucke-Horsley, S. and Hergert, L. (1985) *An Action Guide to School Improvement*. Andover, MA: Association for Supervision and Curriculum Development.

Louis, K. S. and Miles, M. B. (1992) *Improving the Urban High School: What Works and Why*. London: Cassell.

Lowe, R. (ed.) (1989) *The Changing Secondary School*. London: Falmer Press.

Lowe, T. J. and Pollard, I. W. (1989) Negotiation skills. In C. Riches and C. Morgan (eds) *Human Resource Management in Education*. Milton Keynes: Open University Press.

Lyons, G. and Stenning, R. (1986) *Managing Staff in Schools*. London: Hutchinson.

McBeath, J., Thomson, B., Arrowsmith, J. and Forbes, D. (1992) *Using Ethos Indicators in Secondary School Self-evaluation: Taking Account of the Views of Pupils, Parents and Teachers*. Edinburgh: HM Inspectors of Schools, The Scottish Office Education Department.

McClelland, D. C. (1961) *The Achieving Society*. Princeton, NJ: Van Nostrand.

McDougle, L. G. (1982) Orientation of new employees: implications for the supervisor, *Supervision*, 44(4), 3–5.

McElwee, G. (1992) How useful are performance indicators in the polytechnic sector? *Educational Management and Administration*, 20(3), 189–92.

MacGilchrist, B., Mortimore, P., Savage, J. and Beresford, C. (1995) *Planning Matters: The Impact of Developmental Planning in Primary Schools*. London: Paul Chapman Publishing.

MacGilchrist, B., Myers, K. and Reed, J. (1997) *The Intelligent School*. London: Paul Chapman Publishing.

McGregor Burns, J. (1978) *Leadership*. London: Harper and Row.

McGregor, D. (1960) *The Human Side of Enterprise*. New York: McGraw-Hill.

McIntyre, D. and Hagger, H. (1996) *Mentors in Schools: Developing the Profession of Teaching*. London: David Fulton.

McMahon, A. (1996) Continuing professional development: report from the field, *Management in Education*, 10(4), 5–6.

McMaster, M. (1995) *The Intelligent Advantage: Organising for Complexity*. London: Knowledge Based Development Co. Ltd.

McPherson, A. (1992) Measuring added value in schools. *National Commission on Education Briefing No. 1*, February.

Maden, M. (1990) Quality, accountability and the LEA, *Educational Management and Administration*, 18(2), 21–6.

Maden, M. and Hillman, J. (1996) Lessons in success. In National Commission on Education, *Learning to Succeed*. London: Heinemann.

Mager, R. F. and Pipe, P. (1989) Analysing performance problems. In C. Riches and C. Morgan (eds) *Human Resource Management in Education*. Milton Keynes: Open University Press.

Mahoney, M. J. (1991) *Human Change Processes*. New York: Basic Books.

Major, J. (1994) Interview, *Daily Express*, 17 February.

Management Charter Initiative (1995) *Senior Management Standards*. Sheffield: MCI.

Mann, J. (1989) Institutions and their local education authority. In R. Glatter (ed.) *Educational Institutions and their Environments: Managing the Boundaries*. Milton Keynes: Open University Press.

Margerison, C. and McCann, D. J. (1990) *Team Management: Practical New Approaches*. London: Mercury.

Markee, N. (1997) *Managing Curricular Innovation*. Cambridge: Cambridge University Press.

Marland, M. (1998) Moving from teaching to middle management, *Professional Development Today*, 2(1), 7–16.

Maslow, A. (1943) A theory of human motivation, *Psychological Review*, 1, 370–96.

Maslow, A. (1970) *Motivation and Personality*. New York: Harper and Row.

Mayo, A. (1991) *Managing Careers: Structures for Organizations*. London: Institute of Personnel Management.

Mayo, E. (1933) *The Human Problems of Industrial Civilization*. New York: Macmillan.

Mayo, E. (1949) Hawthorne and Western Electric Company. In D. Pugh (ed., 1990) *Organization Theory: Selected Readings*. Harmondsworth: Penguin Business.

Mescon, M., Albert, M. and Khedouri, F. (1985) *Management: Individual and Organizational Effectiveness*. New York: Harper and Row.

Middlewood, D. (1996) *Hierarchy of Learning*. Supplement to INSET Evaluation (1). Northampton: Leicester University/Northampton County Council.

Middlewood, D. (1997a) Managing recruitment and selection. In T. Bush and D. Middlewood (eds) *Managing People in Education*. London: Paul Chapman Publishing.

Middlewood, D. (1997b) Managing staff development. In T. Bush and D. Middlewood (eds) *Managing People in Education*. London: Paul Chapman Publishing.

Middlewood, D. and Lumby, J. (eds) (1998) *Strategic Management in Schools and Colleges*. London: Paul Chapman Publishing.

Miles, M. (1986) *Research Findings on the Stages of School Improvement*. New York: Centre for Policy Research.

Miles, M. B. and Ekholm, M. (1985) What is school improvement? In W. G. Van Velzen, M. B. Miles, M. Ekholm, U. Hameyer and D. Robin (eds) *Making School Improvement Work: A Conceptual Guide to Practice*. Leuven, Belgium: ACCO.

Millett, A. (1998) Address by TTA Chief Executive, Corporate Plan Conference, 19 May, London.

Mintzberg, H. (1990) The design school: reconsidering the basic processes of strategic management, *Strategic Management Journal*, 11(3), 171–95.

Mintzberg, H. (1994) *The Rise and Fall of Strategic Planning*. London: Prentice Hall.

Mitchell, D. E. and Tucker, S. (1992) Leadership as a way of thinking, *Educational Leadership*, 49(5), 30–5.

Mitchell, G. (1989) Community education and school: a commentary. In R. Glatter (ed.) *Educational Institutions and Their Environments: Managing the Boundaries*. Milton Keynes: Open University Press.

Mitchell, T. R. (1982) Motivation: New Directions for Theory, Research and Practice, *Academy of Management Review*, 7(1), 80–8.

Morgan, C. (1997) Selection: predicting effective performance. In L. Kydd, M. Crawford and C. Riches (eds) *Professional Development for Educational Management*. Buckingham: Open University Press.

Morgan, C., Hall, V. and Mackay, H. (1983) *The Selection of Secondary Headteachers*. Milton Keynes: Open University Press.

Morgan, G. (1989) *Creative Organization Theory*. Newbury Park, CA: Sage.

Morris, E. (1998) Speech at the Launch of the TTA Corporate Plan, 19 May, London.

Mortimore, P. (1991) The nature and findings of research on school effectiveness in the primary sector. In S. Riddell and S. Brown (eds) *School Effectiveness Research: Its Messages for School Improvement*, Edinburgh: HMSO.

Mortimore, P. (1998) *The Role of the Headteacher: Report of House of Commons Select Committee on Education and Employment*. Evidence to the Committee, para. 42. London: House of Commons.

Mortimore, P. and Mortimore, J. (eds) (1991) *The Primary Head: Roles, Responsibilities and Reflections*. London: Paul Chapman Publishing.

Mortimore, P., Mortimore, J. and Thomas, H. (1994) *Managing Associate Staff: Innovation in Primary and Secondary Schools*. London: Paul Chapman Publishing.

Mortimore, P., Sammons, P., Stoll, L., Lewis, D. and Ecob, R. (1988) *School Matters: The Junior Years*. Wells: Open Books.

Mulholland, G. (1991) *The Language of Negotiation: A Handbook of Practical Strategies*. London: Cassell.

Mullins, L. (1993) *Management and Organizational Behaviour*. London: Pitman.

Mumford, A. (ed.) (1986) *Handbook of Management Development*. Aldershot: Gower.

Mumford, P. (1991) Redundancy. In D. Lock and N. Farrow (eds) *The Gower Handbook of Management*. Aldershot: Gower.

Murgatroyd, S. and Gray, H. (1984) *Leadership and the Effective School*. London: Harling.

Murgatroyd, S. and Morgan, C. (1992) *Total Quality Management and the School*. Buckingham: Open University Press.

Murgatroyd, S. and Reynolds, D. (1984) The creative consultant: the potential use of consultancy as a method of teacher education, *School Organization*, 4(4), 321–35.

Myers, K. (ed.) (1995) *School Improvement in Practice: The Schools Make a Difference Project*. London: Institute of Education.

Naisbett, J. (1984) *Megatrends: Ten Directions Transforming Our Lives*. London: Macdonald.

National Commission on Education (1993) *Learning to Succeed*. London: Heinemann.

Naybour, S. (1989) Parents, partners or customers? In J. Sayer and V. Williams (eds) *Schools and External Relations: Managing the New Partnership*. London: Cassell.

Neave, G. (1988) On the cultivation of quality, efficiency and enterprise: an overview of recent trends in higher education in Western Europe, 1968–1988, *European Journal of Education*, 23(1/2), 7–23.

Nelson-Jones, R. (1996) *Relating Skills*. London: Cassell.

Nias, J. (1981) Teacher satisfaction and dissatisfaction: Herzberg's two-factor hypothesis revisited, *British Journal of Sociology of Education*, 2(3), 235–46.

Nias, J., Southworth, G. and Yeomans, R. (1989) *Staff Relationships in the Primary School*. London: Cassell.

Nisbet, J. and Shucksmith, J. (1986) *Learning Strategies*. London: Routledge.

Nixon, J., Martin, J., McKeown, P. and Ranson, S. (1996) *Encouraging Learning: Towards a Theory of the Learning School*. Buckingham: Open University Press.

Norris, K. (1993) Avoidable inequalities? *Management in Education*, 7(2), 27–30.

North, R. (1988) Restricted choice in the management of change, *Educational Management and Administration*, 16(3), 160–75.

Oakland, J. (1989) *Total Quality Management*. Oxford: Butterworth-Heinemann.

Ofsted (1995a) *The Ofsted Handbook: Guidance on the Inspection of Secondary Schools*. London: HMSO.

Ofsted (1995b) *Governing Bodies and Effective Schools*. London: Ofsted.

Ofsted (1995c) *The Annual Report of HM Chief Inspector of Schools, 1995: Standards and Quality in Education, 1994–5*. London: HMSO.

Ofsted (1996) *Initial Teacher Training (Secondary Phase)*. Circular 9/92. London: HMSO.

Ofsted (1997a) *Annual Report 1995–6*. London: Ofsted.

Ofsted (1997b) *Subject Management in Secondary Schools*. London: Ofsted.

Ofsted (1998a) *School Evaluation Matters*. London: Ofsted.

Ofsted (1998b) *Annual Report 1996/7*. London: Ofsted.

Ofsted (1998c) *Secondary Education 1993–7: A Review of Secondary Schools in England*. London: The Stationery Office.

Oldroyd, D. (1996) Developing self and school by positive affirmation. In V. Hall, N. Cromley-Hawke and D. Oldroyd (eds) *Management Self-development in Secondary Schools*. Bristol: University of Bristol, National Development Centre for Educational Management and Policy.

Oldroyd, D., Elsner, D. and Poster, C. (1996) *Education Management Today*. London: Paul Chapman Publishing.

Oldroyd, D. and Hall, V. (1991) *Managing Staff Development*. London: Paul Chapman Publishing.

Orton, J. and Weick, K. (1990) Loosely coupled systems – a reconceptualisation, *Academy of Management Review*, 15(2), 202–23.

Osborne, D. and Gaebler, T. (1992) *Reinventing Government: How the Entrepreneurial Spirit is Transforming the Public Sector*. Reading, MA: Addison-Wesley.

O'Sullivan, F. (1996) The high performing middle manager, *Management in Education*, 10(1), 5–6.

O'Sullivan, F., Jones, K. and Reid, K. J. (1997) The development of staff. In L. Kydd, K. Crawford and C. Riches (eds) *Professional Development for Educational Management*. Buckingham: Open University Press.

Ouchi, W. (1981) *Theory Z: How American Business Can Meet the Japanese Challenge*. Reading, MA: Addison-Wesley.

Ouston, J. (ed.) (1993) *Women in Education Management*. Harlow: Longman.

Ouston, J., Earley, P. and Fidler, B. (1996) *Ofsted Inspections: The Early Experience*. London: David Fulton.

Ouston, J., McMeeking, S. and Higgins, P. (1992) Schools and honeypot management, *Educational Management and Administration*, 20(3), 170–8.

Ozga, J. (1988) *Schoolwork: Approaches to the Labour Process of Teaching*. Milton Keynes: Open University Press.

Ozga, J. (ed.) (1993) *Women in Educational Management*. Buckingham: Open University Press.

Packwood, T. (1989) Return to the hierarchy, *Educational Management and Administration*, 17(1), 9–15.

Pascal, C. (1987) Democratised: primary school government conflicts and dichotomies, *Educational Management and Administration*, 15(3), 193–202.

Pascale, P. (1990) *Managing on the Edge*. New York: Touchstone.

Pease, A. (1990) *Body Language: How to Read Others' Thoughts by Their Gestures*. London: Sheldon Press.

Pedler, M., Burgoyne, J. and Boydell, T. (1986) *A Manager's Guide to Self-development*, 2nd edn. Maidenhead: McGraw-Hill.

Pedler, M., Burgoyne, J. and Boydell, T. (1996) *The Learning Company: A Strategy for Sustainable Development*, 2nd edn. Maidenhead: McGraw-Hill.

Perkin, H. (1989) *The Rise of Professional Society: England since 1880*. London: Routledge.

Perrott, E. (1982) *Effective Teaching*. London: Longman.

Peter, L. (1972) *The Peter Principle*. London: Allen and Unwin.

Peters, T. (1987) *Thriving on Chaos: A Handbook for a Managerial Revolution*. London: Macmillan.

Peters, T. and Waterman, R. (1982) *In Search of Excellence*. Glasgow: HarperCollins.

Pheysey, D. (1993) *Organizational Cultures*. London: Routledge.

Pocklington, K. and Weindling, D. (1996) Promoting reflection on headship through the mentoring mirror, *Educational Management and Administration*, 24(2), 175–92.

Pollard, A. and Tann, S. (1988) *Reflective Teaching in the Primary School*. London: Cassell.

Pollard, A. and Tann, S. (1994) *Reflective Teaching in the Primary School*. London: Cassell.

Pollitt, C. (1993) *Managerialism and the Public Services*, 2nd edn. Oxford: Basil Blackwell.

Poster, C. and Poster, D. (1993) *Teacher Appraisal: Training and Implementation*. London: Routledge.

Poster, C. and Poster, D. (1997) The nature of appraisal. In L. Kydd, M. Crawford and C. Riches (eds) *Professional Development for Educational Management*. Buckingham: Open University Press.

Postman, N. and Weingartner, C. (1971) *Teaching as a Subversive Activity*. London: Penguin.

Preedy, M. (1989) *Managing Schools: Managing Curricular and Pastoral Processes*. Milton Keynes: Open University Press.

Preedy, M. (ed.) (1993) *Managing the Effective School*. London: Paul Chapman Publishing.

Preedy, M., Glatter, R. and Levačić, R. (eds) (1997) *Educational Management: Strategy, Quality and Resources*. Buckingham: Open University Press.

Prosser, I. (1991) School ethos – 5 questions. Paper presented to the School Effectiveness Congress, Cardiff, January.

Ranson, S. (1991) Education citizenship and democracy. In M. Flude and M. Hammer (eds) *The Education Reform Act 1988*. Basingstoke: Falmer Press.

Ranson, S. (1994) *Towards the Learning Society*. London: Cassell.

Raspberry, R. W. and Lemoine, L. F. (1986) *Effective Managerial Communication*. Boston: Kent Publishing.

Rea, J. and Weiner, G. (1998) Cultures of blame and redemption – when empowerment becomes control: practitioners' views of the effective schools movement. In R. Slee and G. Weiner with S. Tomlinson (eds) *School Effectiveness for Whom? Challenges to the School Effectiveness and School Improvement Movements*. London: Falmer Press.

Reddin, W. (1971) *Managerial Effectiveness*. New York: McGraw-Hill.

Reid, K., Hopkins, D. and Holly, P. (1987) *Towards the Effective School*. Oxford: Blackwell.

Reimer, E. (1971) *School Is Dead*. Harmondsworth: Penguin.

Revans, R. W. (1982) *The Origins and Growth of Action Learning*. Bromley: Chartwell Bratt.

Reynolds, D. (1992) School effectiveness and school improvement: an updated review of the British literature. In D. Reynolds and P. Cuttance (eds) *School Effectiveness: Research Policy and Practice*. London: Cassell.

Reynolds, D. (1998) Teacher effectiveness: better teachers, better schools' presentation. *TTA Corporate Plan Launch 1998–2001*. London: Teacher Training Agency.

Reynolds, D. and Cuttance, P. (eds) (1992) *School Effectiveness Research, Policy and Practice*. London: Cassell.

Ribbins, P. (1989) Managing secondary schools after the act: participation and partnership? In R. Lowe (ed.) *The Changing Secondary School*. London: Falmer Press.

Ribbins, P. (1995) Understanding contemporary leaders and leadership in education: values and visions. In J. Bell and B. T. Harrison (eds) *Vision and Values in Managing Education: Successful Leadership Principles and Practice*. London: David Fulton.

Ribbins, P. and Sherratt, B. (1992) Managing the secondary school in the 1990s: a new view of headship, *Educational Management and Administration*, 20(3), 151–60.

Richards, C. and Taylor, P. (eds) (1998) *How Shall We School Our Children? The Future of Primary Education*. Lewes: Falmer Press.

Riches, C. (1994) Communication. In T. Bush and J. West-Burnham (eds) *The Principles of Educational Management*. Harlow: Longman.

Riches, C. (1997a) Communication in educational management. In M. Crawford *et al.* (eds) *Leadership and Teams in Educational Management*. Buckingham: Open University Press.

Riches, C. (1997b) Managing for people and performance. In T. Bush and D. Middlewood (eds) *Managing People in Education*. London: Cassell.

Riches, C. and Morgan, C. (eds) (1989) *Human Resource Management in Education*. Milton Keynes: Open University Press.

Richmond, K. (1971) *The School Curriculum*. London: Methuen.

Riddell, S. and Brown, S. (eds) (1991) *School Effectiveness Research: Its Messages for School Improvement*. Edinburgh: HMSO.

Riffel, J. A. and Levin, B. (1997) Schools coping with the impact of information technology, *Educational Management and Administration*, 25(1), 51–64.

Riley, K. (1998) *Whose School Is It Anyway?* London: Falmer Press.

Riley, K. A., Johnson, H. and Rowles, D. (1995) *Managing for Quality in an Uncertain Climate: Report II*. Luton: Local Government Management Board.

Riley, K. and Rowles, D. (1997) Managing with governors. In B. Fidler *et al.* (eds) *Choices for Self-managing Schools*. London: Paul Chapman Publishing.

Roberts, B. and Ritchie, H. (1990) Management structures in secondary schools, *Educational Management and Administration*, 18(3), 17–21.

Robertson, I., Smith, J. and Cooper, M. (1992) *Motivation: Strategies, Theory and Practice*. London: Institute of Personnel Management.

Rodger, A. R. (1995) Code of professional conduct for teachers: an introduction, *Scottish Educational Review*, 27(1), 78–86.

Rogers, C. (1980) *A Way of Being*. Boston: Houghton Mifflin.

Rogers, C. R. and Roethlisberger, F. J. (1952) Barriers and gateways to communication, *Harvard Business Review*, July/August, 44–9.

Rosenholtz, S. (1989) *Teachers' Workplace: the Social Organization of Schools*. New York: Longman.

Rossman, G. B., Corbett, H. D. and Firestone, W. A. (1988) *Change and Effectiveness in Schools: a Cultural Perspective*. Albany, NY: SUNY Press.

Rudduck, J., Chaplain, R. and Wallace, G. (1995) *School Improvement: What Can Pupils Tell Us?* London: David Fulton.

Russell, S. and Reid, S. (1997) Managing evaluation. In B. Fidler, S. Russell and T. Simkins (eds) *Choices for Self-managing Schools: Autonomy and Accountability*. London: Paul Chapman Publishing.

Rutter, M., Maughan, B., Mortimore, P. and Ouston, J. (1979) *Fifteen Thousand Hours: Secondary Schools and Their Effects on Children*. London: Open Books.

Sallis, J. (1989) Working with governors. In J. Sayer and V. Williams (eds) *Schools and External Relations*. London: Cassell.

Sammons, P., Hillman, J. and Mortimore, P. (1995) *Key Characteristics of Effective Schools: A Review of School Effectiveness Research* (a report commissioned by the Office for Standards in Education). London: Ofsted.

Savage, W. W. (1987) Communication: process and problems. In C. Riches and C. Morgan (eds) *Human Resource Management in Education*. Milton Keynes: Open University Press.

Schachter, S. (1951) Deviation, rejection and communication. In D. Cartwright and A. Zander (eds, 1968) *Group Dynamics*, 3rd edn. London: Tavistock.

Scheerens, J. (1992) *Effective Schooling*. London: Cassell.

Schein, E. H. (1969) *Process Consultation: Its Role in Organization Development*. Reading, MA: Addison-Wesley.

Schein, E. H. (1983) *Organizational Psychology*. Hemel Hempstead: Prentice Hall.

Schein, E. H. (1985) *Organizational Culture and Leadership*. San Francisco: Jossey-Bass.

Schmuck, P. A. (1986) School management and administration: an analysis by gender. In E. Hoyle and A. McMahon (eds) *The Management of Schools: World Yearbook of Education, 1986*. London: Kogan Page.

Schön, D. (1971) *Beyond the Stable State*. London: Temple Smith.

Schön, D. (1983) *The Reflective Practitioner: How Professionals Think in Action*. London: Maurice Temple Smith.

Schön, D. (1987) *Educating the Reflective Practitioner*. San Francisco: Jossey-Bass.

Schrage, M. (1990) *Shared Minds*. New York: Random House.

Schutz, W. (1966) *The Interpersonal Underworld, Science and Behavior*. New York: McGraw-Hill.

Scott, P. (1989) Accountability, responsiveness and responsibility. In R. Glatter (ed.) *Educational Institutions and Their Environments: Managing the Boundaries*. Milton Keynes: Open University Press.

Scott, W. R. (1997) Organizational effectiveness. In A. Harris, N. Bennett and M. Preedy (eds) *Organizational Effectiveness and Improvement in Education*. Buckingham: Open University Press.

Seckington, R. (1989) Teachers' role outside school. In J. Sayer and V. Williams (eds) *Schools and External Relations*. London: Cassell.

Seifert, R. (1996a) *Human Resource Management in Schools*. London: Pitman.

Seifert, R. (1996b) *Industrial Relations in Education*. London: Pitman.

Seldon, A. (1990) *Capitalism*. Oxford: Basil Blackwell.

Selye, H. (1956) *The Stress of Life*. New York: McGraw-Hill.

Senge, P. M. (1992) *The Fifth Discipline: The Art and Practice of the Learning Organization*. London: Century Business.

Senge, P. M., Kleiner, A., Roberts, C., Ross, R. B. and Smith, B. J. (1996) *The Fifth Discipline Fieldbook*. London: Nicholas Brealey.

Sergiovanni, T. J. (1987) The theoretical basis for cultural leadership. In L. T. Shieve and M. B. Schoenheit (eds) *Yearbook of the Association for Supervision and Curriculum Development*. Alexandria, VA: ASCA.

Sergiovanni, T. J. (1995) *The Principalship: A Reflective Practice Perspective*. London: Allyn & Bacon.

Shakeshaft, C. (1987) *Women in Educational Administration*. Newbury Park, CA: Sage.

Shakeshaft, C. (1993) Women in educational management in the United States. In J. Ouston (ed.) *Women in Education Management*. Harlow: Longman.

Shaw, M. (1994) Current issues in pastoral management, *Pastoral Care in Education*, 12(4), 37–41.

Shearman, T. (1995) First know your image, *Management in Education*, 9(3), 12.

Shieve, L. T. and Schoenheit, M. B. (eds) (1987) *Yearbook of the Association for Supervision and Curriculum Development*. Alexandria, VA: ASCA.

Shipman, M. (1990) *In Search of Learning*. Oxford: Blackwell.

Silcock, P. (1993) Can we teach effective teaching? *Educational Review*, 45(1), 13–19.

Simkins, T. (1989) Budgeting as a political and organizational practice. In R. Levačić (eds) *Financial Management in Education*. Milton Keynes: Open University Press.

Simkins, T. (1994) Efficiency, effectiveness and the local management of schools, *Journal of Education Policy*, 9(1), 15–33.

Simkins, T. (1995) The equity consequences of educational reform, *Educational Management and Administration*, 23(4), 221–32.

Simkins, T. (1997) Managing resources. In B. Fidler *et al.* (eds) *Choices for Self-managing Schools: Autonomy and Accountability*. London: Paul Chapman Publishing.

Sisson, K. (ed.) (1994) *Personnel Management: a Comprehensive Guide to Theory and Practice in Britain*. Oxford: Blackwell.

Sisson, K. and Timperley, S. (1994) From manpower planning to strategic human resource management. In K. Sisson (ed.) *Personnel Management: A Comprehensive Guide to Theory and Practice in Britain*. Oxford: Blackwell.

Skillbeck, M. (1989) A changing social and educational context. In B. Moon (ed.) *Policies in the Curriculum*. Milton Keynes: Open University Press.

Slee, R. and Weiner, G. (1998) Introduction: School effectiveness for whom? In R. Slee and G. Weiner with S. Tomlinson (eds) *School Effectiveness for Whom? Challenges to the School Effectiveness and School Improvement Movements*. London: Falmer Press.

Slee, R. and Weiner, G. with Tomlinson, S (eds) (1998) *School Effectiveness for Whom? Challenges to the School Effectiveness and School Improvement Movements*. London: Falmer Press.

Smith, M., Beck, J., Cooper, C., Cox, C., Ottaway, D. and Talbot, R. (1990) *Introducing Organizational Behaviour*. London: Macmillan.

Smith, M. L. (1991) Put to the test: the effects of external testing on teachers, *Educational Researcher*, 20(5), 8–11.

Smith, R. (1995) Staff appraisal in higher education, *Higher Education*, 30, 69–77.

Smyth, J. (1991) *Teachers as Collaborative Learners*. Buckingham: Open University Press.

Smyth, J. (1993) *A Socially Critical View of the 'Self-managing School'*. London: Falmer Press.

Smyth, L. and van der Vegt, R. (1993) Innovation in schools: some dilemmas of implementation, *Educational Management and Administration*, 21(2).

Southworth, G. (1988) Primary headship and collegiality. In R. Glatter (ed.) *Understanding School Management*. Milton Keynes: Open University Press.

Southworth, G. (1993) School leadership and school development: reflections from research, *School Organization*, 13, 73–87.

Southworth, G. (1994) School leadership and school development: reflections from research. In G. Southworth (ed.) *Readings in Primary School Development*. London: Falmer Press.

Spencer, L. M. and Spencer, S. M. (1993) *Competence at Work: Models for Superior Performance*. New York: Wiley.

Spitz, R. (1945) Hospitalism: genesis of psychiatric conditions in early childhood, *Psychoanalytic Studies of the Child*, 1, 53–74.

Stacey, R. (1992) *Managing the Unknowable*. San Francisco: Jossey-Bass.

Stacey, R. (1993) *Strategic Management and Organisational Dynamics*. London: Pitman.

Stake, R., Shapson, S. and Russell, L. (1987) Evaluation of staff development programs. In M. Wideen and I. Andrews (eds) *Staff Development for School Improvement*. Lewes: Falmer Press.

Steiner, G. A. (1965) *The Creative Organization*. Chicago: University of Chicago Press.

Steward, I. and Joines, V. (1987) *TA Today: A New Introduction to Transactional Analysis*. Nottingham: Lifespace Publishing.

Steward, I. and Joines, V. (1997) *TA Today: A New Introduction to Transactional Analysis*. Dover: Smallwood Publishing.

Stillman, A. and Maychell, K. (1986) *Choosing Schools: Parents, LEAs and the 1980 Education Act*. Windsor: NFER.

Stoll, L. and Fink, D. (1996) *Changing Our Schools*. Buckingham: Open University Press.

Stoll, L. and Myers, K. (1997) *No Quick Fixes: Perspectives on Schools in Difficulty*. Basingstoke: Falmer.

Stott, K. and Walker, A. (1992) The nature and use of mission statements in Singaporean schools, *Educational Management and Administration*, 20(1)

Strain, M., Dennison, B., Ouston, J. and Hall, V. (eds) (1998) *Policy, Leadership and Professional Knowledge in Education*. London: Paul Chapman Publishing.

Strand, S. (1997) Key performance indicators for primary school improvement, *Educational Management and Administration*, 25(2), 145–54.

Swieringa, J. and Wierdsma, A. (1992) *Becoming a Learning Organization: Beyond the Learning Curve*. Cambridge: Addison-Wesley.

Tannenbaum, R. and Schmidt, W. (1973) How to choose a leadership pattern, *Harvard Business Review*, May/June, 162–80.

Taylor, D. and Bishop, S. (1994) *Ready Made Activities for Your Staff*. London: Pitman.

Taylor, F. (1947) *Scientific Management*. London: Harper and Row.

Teddlie, C. and Stringfield, S. (1993) *Schools Make a Difference: Lessons Learned from a 10 Year Study of School Effects*. New York: Teachers College Press.

Terrell, K., Clinton, B. and Sheraton, K. (1996) Quality middle management: a D-I-Y quiz on criteria, *Management in Education*, 10(1), 1.

TES (Times Educational Supplement) (1999) Ofsted fails to grasp subtle issues of poverty, 18 June.

Thomas, H. and Martin, J. (1996) *Managing Resources for School Improvement: Creating a Cost-effective School*. London: Routledge.

Thomas, P. (1997) Leadership and team learning in secondary schools – some implications for schools, a headteacher's response, *School Organization*, 17(3), 331–2.

Thompson, M. (1991) Finishing the management jigsaw, *Management in Education*, 5(3), 31–3.

Thompson, M. (1992) Appraisal and equal opportunities. In N. Bennett, M. Crawford and C. Riches (eds) *Managing Change in Education*. London: Paul Chapman Publishing.

Thompson, M. (1997) *Professional Ethics and the Teacher: Towards a General Teaching Council*. Stoke on Trent: Trentham Books.

Thompson, M. (1998) Modernising appraisal? *Professional Development Today*, 2(1), 23–30.

Timperley, H. and Robinson, V. M. (1997) The problem of policy implementation: the case of performance appraisal, *School Leadership and Organization*, 17(3), 333–46.

Toffler, A. (1970) *Future Shock*. London: Pan.

Toffler, A. (1981) *The Third Wave*. London: Pan.

Toffler, A. (1990) *Power Shift*. New York: Bantam Books.

Tofte, B. (1995) A theoretical model for implementation of total quality leadership in education, *Total Quality Management*, 6, 469–86.

Tomlinson, H. (ed.) (1997) *Managing Continuing Professional Development in Schools*. London: Paul Chapman Publishing/BEMAS.

Tomlinson, J. R. (1995) Professional development and control: the role of the General Teaching Council, *Journal of Education for Teaching*, 21(1), 59–68.

Tomlinson, S. (ed.) (1994) *Educational Reform and Its Consequences*. London: IPPR/Rivers Oram Press.

Torrington, D. and Weightman, J. (1989) *The Reality of School Management*. Oxford: Blackwell Education.

Travers, C. and Cooper, C. (1995) *Teachers under Pressure: Stress in the Teaching Profession*. London: Routledge.

Trethowan, D. (1987) *Appraisal and Target Setting*. London: Harper and Row.

Trotter, A. and Ellison, L. (1997) Understanding competence and competency. In B. Davies and L. Ellison (eds) *School Leadership for the 21st Century: A Competency and Knowledge Approach*. London: Routledge.

TTA (1995) *HEADLAMP: Leadership and Management Programme for New Headteachers*. London: TTA.

TTA (1996a) *Teaching as a Research-based Profession*. London: TTA.

TTA (1996b) *The National Professional Qualification for Headship: Key Principles and Draft National Standards for New Headteachers*. London: TTA.

TTA (1996c) *Consultation Paper: Standards and a National Professional Qualification for Headteachers*. London: TTA.

TTA (1996d) *Consultation Paper: Standards and a National Professional Qualification for Subject Leaders*. London: TTA.

TTA (1997) *Corporate Plan: 1997–2000*. London: TTA.

TTA (1998a) *National Standards for Headteachers*. London: TTA.

TTA (1998b) *National Standards for Subject Leaders*. London: TTA.

TTA (1998c) *National Standards for Qualified Teacher Status*. London: TTA.

TTA (1998d) *Corporate Plan: 1998–2001*. London: TTA.

TTA/Ofsted (1996) *Joint Review of Headteacher and Teacher Appraisal. Summary of Evidence*. London: TTA.

Tuckman, B. (1965) Development sequences in small groups, *Psychological Bulletin*, 63, 384–99.

Tuckman, B. and Jensen, N. (1977) Stages of small group development revisited, *Group and Organizational Studies*, 2, 419–27.

Turner, C. K. (1996) The roles and tasks of a subject head of department in secondary schools in England and Wales: a neglected area of research, *School Organization*, 16(20), 203–18.

Turner, G., Mountford, B. and Morris, B. (1991) School governor training in Hampshire: an evaluation, *Educational Management and Administration*, 19(3).

Tuxford, E. (1989) Competence-based education and training, background and origins. In W. J. Burke (ed.) *Competency-based Education and Training*. Lewes: Falmer.

Tyler, R. (1949) *Basic Principles of Curriculum and Instruction*. Chicago: University of Chicago Press.

Van Velzen, W. G., Miles, M. B., Ekholm, M., Hameyer, U. and Robin, D. (eds) (1985) *Making School Improvement Work: A Conceptual Guide to Practice*. Leuven, Belgium: ACCO.

Vroom, V. (1964) *Work and Motivation*. New York: John Wiley.

Vroom, V. (1974) A new look at managerial decision-making, *Organizational Behaviour*, 5, 66–8.

Vroom, V. and Jago, A. (1988) *The New Leadership: Managing Participation in Organizations*. Englewood Cliffs, NJ: Prentice Hall.

Walford, G. (1990) *Privatisation and Privilege in Education*. London: Routledge.

Wallace, M. and Hall, V. (1994) *Inside the SMT: Teamwork in Secondary Schools Management*. London: Paul Chapman Publishing.

Waterman, R. (1987) *The Renewal Factor*. London: Transworld.

Watts, M. and Cooper, S. (1992) *Relax: Dealing with Stress*. London: BBC Publications.

Webb, R. and Vulliamy, G. (1996) A deluge of directives: conflict between collegiality and managerialism in the post-ERA primary school, *British Educational Research Journal*, 22(4), 301–15.

Weber, M. (1924) Legitimate authority and bureaucracy. In D. Pugh (ed., 1990) *Organization Theory: Selected Readings*. Harmondsworth: Penguin Business.

Weber, M. (1947) *The Theory of Social and Economic Organization*. New York: Free Press.

Weick, K. (1989) Educational organizations as loosely coupled systems. In T. Bush (ed.) *Managing Education: Theory and Practice*. Milton Keynes: Open University Press.

Weindling, D. (1997) Strategic planning in schools: some practical techniques. In M. Preedy, R. Glatter and R. Levačić (eds) *Educational Management: Strategy, Quality and Resources*. Buckingham: Open University Press.

Weindling, D. and Earley, P. (1986) How heads manage change, *School Organization*, 6(3), 327–38.

West, N. (1990) Monitoring the curriculum in action: a question of quality, *Educational Management and Administration*, 18(2), 35–7.

West-Burnham, J. (1990) The management of change. In B. Davies, L. Ellison, A. Osborne and J. West-Burnham (eds) *Education Management for the 1990s*. Harlow: Longman.

West-Burnham, J. (1992) *Managing Quality in Schools*. Harlow: Longman.

West-Burnham, J. (1994) Inspection, evaluation and quality assurance. In T. Bush and J. West-Burnham (eds) *The Principles of Educational Management*. Harlow: Longman.

Westoby, A. (1989) Parental choice and voice under the 1988 Education Reform Act. In R. Glatter (ed.) *Educational Institutions and Their Environments: Managing the Boundaries*. Milton Keynes: Open University Press.

Wheatley, M. J. (1992) *Leadership and the New Science: Learning about Organizations from an Orderly Universe*. San Francisco: Berrett-Koehler.

Wheeler, D. (1967) *Curriculum Process*. London: University of London Press.

Whitaker, P. (1993a) *Managing Change in Schools*. Buckingham: Open University Press.

Whitaker, P. (1993b) *Practical Communication in Schools*. Harlow: Longman.

Whitaker, P. (1995) *Managing to Learn*. London: Cassell.

Whitty, G. (1989) The new right and the national curriculum: state control and market forces, *Journal of Education Policy*, 4(4), 329–42.

Whitty, G., Power, S. and Halpin, D. (1998) *Devolution and Choice in Education: The School, the State and the Market*. Buckingham: Open University Press.

Wideen, M. and Andrews, I. (eds) (1987) *Staff Development for School Improvement*. Lewes: Falmer Press.

Wikeley, F. (1998) Dissemination of research as a tool for school improvement, *School Organization*, 18(1), 59–74.

Wild, P., Scivier, J. and Richardson, S. (1992) Evaluating information technology supported local management of schools; the user acceptability audit, *Educational Management and Administration*, 20(1), 40–8.

Wildavsky, A. (1994) *The Politics of the Budgetary Process*, 2nd edn. Boston: Little Brown and Co.

Wilkin, M. and Sankey, D. (1994) *Mentoring in Schools*. London: Kogan Page.

Williams, M. (1991) *In-service Education and Training*. London: Cassell.

Williams, R. P. and Mullen, T. (1990) The awareness of and attitudes towards teacher appraisal of secondary school teachers, *Educational Management and Administration*, 18(4), 3–10.

Willms, J. (1992) *Monitoring School Performance*. London: Falmer Press.

Wilson, B. and Corcoran, T. (1988) *Successful Secondary Schools*. London: Falmer Press.

Winstanley, D., Sorabji, D. and Dawson, S. (1995) When the pieces don't fit: a stakeholder power matrix to analyse public sector management restructuring, *Public Money and Management*, 15(2), 19–26.

Wirt, F. (1981) Professionalism and political conflict, *Journal of Public Policy*, 1(1), 61–93.

Woodcock, M. (1979) *Team Development Manual*. Aldershot: Gower.

Wortman, B. and Matlin, M. (1995) *Leadership in Whole Language*. London: Paul Chapman Publishing.

Wragg, E. C. (1996) *Teacher Appraisal Observed*. London: Routledge.

Wright, M. (ed.) (1980) *Public Spending Decisions: Growth and Restraints in the 1970s*. London: Allen and Unwin.

Zaleznik, A. (1977) Managers and leaders: are they different? *Harvard Business Review*, May/June, 67–78.

Name index

Subject index